RUFFIANS, YAKUZA, NATIONALISTS

RUFFIANS, YAKUZA, NATIONALISTS

The Violent Politics of Modern Japan, 1860–1960

Eiko Maruko Siniawer

CORNELL UNIVERSITY PRESS   ITHACA AND LONDON

First published 2008 by Cornell University Press

Printed in the United States of America

Library of Congress Cataloging-in-Publication Data

Siniawer, Eiko Maruko.
  Ruffians, yakuza, nationalists : the violent politics of modern Japan, 1860–1960 /
Eiko Maruko Siniawer.
      p.   cm.
  Includes bibliographical references and index.
  ISBN 978-0-8014-4720-4 (cloth : alk. paper)
  1. Political violence—Japan—History. 2. Democracy—Japan—History. 3. Japan—Politics and government—1868– I. Title.

  HN730.Z9V55   2008
  306.20952'09034—dc22

                                          2008023735

Cornell University Press strives to use environmentally responsible suppliers and materials to the fullest extent possible in the publishing of its books. Such materials include vegetable-based, low-VOC inks and acid-free papers that are recycled, totally chlorine-free, or partly composed of nonwood fibers. For further information, visit our website at www.cornellpress.cornell.edu.

Cloth printing   10 9 8 7 6 5 4 3 2 1

To my parents, and in memory of obāchan,
and to Pete

Contents

Acknowledgments

The writing of this book was, in many ways, a collaborative endeavor. From its inception to its publication, this project was shaped and improved by colleagues and friends who have taught, challenged, and supported me over a number of years. In those moments when research and writing felt solitary, someone would remind me of how much this work is a dialogue with others. So I am grateful for this opportunity to remember, acknowledge, and express my appreciation to all those who helped make this book better than it otherwise would have been.

I owe an intellectual debt to Andrew Gordon, whose approach to Japanese history has greatly influenced my own. Only recently have I come to realize just how much this book reflects his concerns, from democracy to transwar history. Always fully engaged with my work, even when juggling many responsibilities, he has been a model of both scholarship and academic citizenship. I am also indebted to Daniel Botsman, whose expertise in the history of crime and extensive knowledge of Japanese historical scholarship added depth to several chapters. His thoughtful provocations and high expectations were welcome intellectual challenges. Finally, I would not be a historian of Japan were it not for Peter Frost, who introduced me to the subject and continues to be a true mentor. His incisive questions helped shore up the weaker parts of the manuscript, but it is his generosity of spirit above all that I have long appreciated. All three former advisers have had a direct impact on this book, having read and critiqued its many iterations.

Others were kind enough to share their ideas about all or part of the manuscript. John Dower's eye for the big picture and commitment to comparative history have, I hope, left an imprint here. Fujino Yūko has been an extraordinary sparring partner. Her enthusiasm and insights about this topic, willingness to put me in touch with scholars in Japan, and desire to tackle difficult questions have been incredibly heartening. Amy Stanley brought her expertise in Tokugawa history to bear on the first chapter, pointing me toward important reading and interesting ideas. David Ambaras and Sabine Frühstück were also very giving with their suggestions and time. And Thomas Havens commented on an earlier version of this work.

While conducting research, I was aided by many who opened new lines of inquiry. Hiraishi Naoaki sponsored several stays at the University of Tokyo and gave useful advice at key stages. Thought-provoking conversations about violence were had with Anzai Kunio, Nakajima Hisato, and Suda Tsutomu. Hoshino Kanehiro, Nemoto Yoshio, and Iwai Hiroaki all shared their considerable experience with studying the yakuza. The faculty at the Ōhara Institute for Social Research at Hōsei University was very welcoming. And others (such as Mitani Hiroshi, Nakamura Masanori, Narita Ryūichi, Obinata Sumio, and Tamai Kiyoshi) kindly met with me when I was still groping my way through the dark. At a later stage, Helena Harnik endured a demanding summer as my undergraduate research assistant, making sense of a pile of sources on the 1960s that have since made their way into the last chapter.

The staffs at various libraries and archives were also indispensable. This was particularly true at the Ōhara Institute, Freedom and People's Rights Movement Archive in Machida City, National Archives of Japan, and Harvard-Yenching Library. I was also glad to explore the collections at the Ministry of Foreign Affairs, National Diet Library, Tokyo Metropolitan Library, Ōya Sōichi Library, National Theater, Fukuoka Prefectural Library, U.S. National Archives in Maryland, and the various libraries of the University of Tokyo.

I have been fortunate to enjoy several institutional homes. Williams College is an exceptionally supportive place to work and has been generous with both leave time and funding. My colleagues in the history and Asian studies departments have been especially helpful with this project—I am very appreciative of their engagement and encouragement. The Institute of Social Science at the University of Tokyo hosted me on several occasions, and the Reischauer Institute of Japanese Studies at Harvard University invited me into its community as a visiting scholar. Through various experiences at Harvard I was touched by the intellectual camaraderie of Cemil Aydin, Jeff Bayliss, Jamie Berger, Marjan Boogert, Michael Burtscher, Rusty Gates, Hiromi Maeda, Noriko Murai, Izumi Nakayama, Emer O'Dwyer, Hiraku Shimoda, Jun Uchida, and Laura Wong. And Yoichi Nakano worked through the themes of the book with me, with great perspective and honesty.

I must thank Roger Haydon at Cornell University Press, who took interest in this project when it was still embarrassingly rough and who guided the book through the publication process with ease and good humor. Two anonymous reviewers also provided very constructive feedback on the manuscript.

As much help as I have received, the voice and decisions in this book are mine. Many of those mentioned above take issue with certain approaches and arguments presented here. And as always, the responsibility for all flaws and weaknesses rests on my shoulders alone.

Finally, the book could not have been researched and written without generous funding from the Japan Foundation, Social Science Research Council, Reischauer Institute, and National Endowment for the Humanities.

To my parents, for their sacrifices and belief in my abilities—I am most grateful. Extended family warmly took me in when I was in Japan. And I hope that *obāchan*'s strength, spirit, and love of history have found their way into this book. I am sorry she did not live to see its publication.

To my husband Pete, I cannot adequately express how much his confidence in my work, patience, and unwavering support in all things have sustained me these many years. My hope is that he knows how truly appreciative I am.

EIKO MARUKO SINIAWER

Williamstown, Massachusetts

RUFFIANS, YAKUZA, NATIONALISTS

Introduction

Violence has been an enduring force in the history of modern Japanese politics. The very birth of the modern Japanese state was violent. In the 1850s, the early modern Tokugawa regime (1600–1868) faltered when threatened by ominous foreign gunboats that appeared off its shores, and in the 1860s was forced to its knees by rebel assassins and armies of defiant domains. The fall of the Tokugawa shogunate in 1868 has been described by many historians as peaceful, with the new Meiji emperor declaring the abolition of the old order in January and the last Tokugawa shogun surrendering the capital in April. Although the Meiji Restoration of 1868 was relatively bloodless when compared to the extraordinary carnage of the French Revolution in particular, it should not be forgotten that the civil war between Tokugawa holdouts and Meiji loyalists continued well into late June of 1869, claiming the lives of thousands of men. In this sense, the founding of the new Meiji government was a moment of violent rupture.

The emergence of a modern Japan did not translate into an era of peaceful and gentlemanly politics; quite to the contrary, it spawned a certain political roughness that persisted in various forms over the next hundred years. Protesters turned to violence in political movements, the earliest being the Freedom and People's Rights Movement of the 1870s and 1880s in which activists put pressure on the Meiji oligarchs to write a constitution, establish a parliament, and widen political participation. Then, in the years between the signing of the Treaty of Portsmouth in 1905 and the so-called "rice riots" of 1918, tens of thousands of people voiced their discontent with specific government policies by physically attacking symbols of the state. Violence was also a volatile component in ideological battles, especially in the decades after the Russian Revolution, as leftists of various stripes, from anarchists to labor unionists, clashed with nationalist organizations and a nervous state. Assassinations littered this period from the

1860s to the 1920s, but perhaps best known are those that were part of the at-tempted coups d'état of the 1930s through which young officers in the military, though failing to seize the reins of government themselves, facilitated the military's ascent to political power.

Interwoven with these violent politics were the central figures of this book—ruffians, yakuza, and their kin. They were, in short, those who were practiced in the use of physical force and known for their main purpose: to be violent. These violence specialists, as I call them, were not just bound up with the popular protests, assassinations, and coups d'état familiar to students of Japanese history. They also wielded a kind of violence, much less known, that transcended these eruptive moments. Their ruffianism—brawls and fistfights that often went to-gether with vandalism, threats, and intimidation—was embedded in the practice of politics, demonstrating that violence was not an episodic phenomenon, but a systemic and deeply rooted element of modern Japanese political life.

The questions of how and why violence specialists became so entwined with politics drive this exploration of a rough political world. At issue too are the meanings and ramifications of violence for politics in Japan, from the last years of the early modern regime in the 1860s through the post–World War II re-birth of democracy in the 1950s. This is also a story of how violence specialists and their violence were legitimized, and how there formed a culture of political violence in which the use of physical force was viewed by many political actors as a viable and at least tacitly acceptable strategy. This culture of political vio-lence, however dynamic and changing, helped perpetuate a brand of politics that was consistently and often unapologetically violent.

Political Violence in Historiographical Perspective

By placing violence at the center of a story about Japanese political history, this book attempts to demonstrate that politics was often dangerous and far more violent than has been previously understood. The general subject of political violence in Japan was understudied for many years; when it was dealt with, vio-lence was mainly considered in the context of social or political movements and treated only as evidence of other political phenomena, be it the emergence of a democratic consciousness or right-wing extremism. Violence was rarely exam-ined as a phenomenon in and of itself.

In the United States, violence was initially neglected by historians in the sev-eral decades after World War II. American historians of the 1950s and 1960s were working against wartime stereotypes that lingered into the postwar years, one of which was the popular image of "the Japanese" as an aggressive and savage people. Accordingly, historians emphasized what they appreciated as the positive aspects (or in the words of historian Marius Jansen, the "brighter side") of Japan's past.[1] Scholars of the so-called modernization school attempted to divert attention from the idea of a repressive and feudalistic Japanese political system by framing Japan as an extraordinary success story, highlighting what they viewed as the country's rapid progress in the Meiji period (1868–1912).[2] The misstep of war acknowledged but largely set aside, Japan was held up as a model for modernization and a bulwark against communism.[3]

This is not to say that modernization scholars avoided the topic of violence altogether, but they seldom grappled with the implications and meanings of violent action. Jansen, for example, did innovative research on rebels and adventurers who were not shy about using physical force. Yet even he occasionally slipped into presenting these violent types as patriots and reformers, inadvertently legitimizing their own self-perception, and seemed more interested in ideologies (liberalism, nationalism, pan-Asianism) than the violence wielded in their name.[4] In one essay, Jansen did consider violence in relation to modernization, focusing on three assassination attempts (or actual assassinations, in the last two cases)—of statesman Katsu Kaishū in 1862, Prime Minister Inukai Tsuyoshi in 1932, and socialist politician Asanuma Inejirō in 1960. Jansen selected these particular incidents to illustrate how Japan had grown more politically and socially complex over these hundred years. The political and social contexts of these examples were unquestionably different, but to frame such violence in terms of progress is not only questionable but also reveals the extent to which Jansen's concern with modernization tempered his treatment of violence.[5]

Other historians countered the stereotype of Japanese aggression more directly than the modernization scholars, implying or even claiming a supposed Japanese cultural affinity for harmony. Unfounded generalizations about a Japanese desire to avoid conflict crept into the fundamental assumptions of works that made misleading arguments about the strong sense of community in early modern villages, the lack of strife in postwar labor relations, and a weak Japanese legal consciousness.[6]

Finally, the political historians of this generation tended to leave violent conflict unexamined, focusing instead on institutions, thought, and elite figures.[7] This was important work, but it did tend to paint the political world as consisting mainly of dignified oligarchs, calculating politicians, lofty intellectuals, and respectable bureaucrats.

In Japan during these same decades, there was an initial postwar flurry of writing about the violence of the recent past, especially in newspapers and journals. And some historians, such as Shinobu Seizaburō, began to tackle the history of protests including the "rice riots" of 1918.[8] Considered mainly in the context of protest, violence was framed as a form of political expression and a challenge to the government.

Outside this subfield, most Japanese historians of the 1950s, heavily influenced by Marxism, were primarily concerned with economic structures as a precipitating factor in social change and revolution.[9] Even those who wrote books on the fascism of the country's recent past rarely dealt with violence; there were notable exceptions, but most authors honed in on the ideological or institutional causes of what had transpired in the 1930s and early 1940s.[10] In his classic essays on the topic, historian Maruyama Masao grappled with the structures, functions, ideologies, and social bases of Japanese fascism but rarely confronted the issue of violence.[11] The nationalist thought of specific organizations and figures generally garnered more attention than their violence, save the obligatory descriptions of the attempted coups d'état in the 1930s. Also, as in the United States, political histories tended to be rather narrowly conceived, as studies of structures and ideas.[12]

This changed in the 1960s and 1970s as the topics of interest to historians such as Shinobu were embraced by a group of scholars who began to place "the people" at the forefront of their research. Inspired in part by the mass demonstrations against renewal of the U.S.-Japan Security Treaty in 1960, those who wrote people's history (*minshūshi*) divorced themselves from their Marxist heritage and took issue with modernists and modernization theory, choosing instead a grassroots approach that highlighted the role of the nonelite as a driving force in history.[13] Kano Masanao and Yasumaru Yoshio thought about politics writ large, publishing books on "Taisho democracy" and social movements. Violence also became more of a concern, with Irokawa Daikichi in particular writing about the popular uprisings of the Freedom and People's Rights Movement. This work of the people's historians, especially Irokawa and Yasumaru, has left its mark here, through both its conceptual move away from a singular concern with political elites and its rich body of research on which I have drawn.[14]

Like the *minshūshi* scholars, American historians of Japan in the late 1970s and 1980s began to incorporate violence into their work, mainly through research on popular protest. Roger Bowen wrote a compelling book on the place of "commoners" in the Freedom and People's Rights Movement, Michael Lewis penned an important monograph on the "rice riots" of 1918, and Andrew Gordon reconceptualized Japanese democracy, bringing attention to the "era of popular protest" that extended from 1905 to 1918.[15] Tropes about Japanese harmony slowly began to lose their appeal as they were exposed as an invented tradition, and more attention was given to the place of conflict in Japan's modern history.[16]

All of this scholarship was groundbreaking, but was fairly unconcerned with problematizing the violence of conflict and social movements. Violence was considered significant primarily as evidence of the political consciousness and vigor of the masses, speaking to arguments about popular participation in politics and the grassroots elements of Japanese democracy. There was little treatment of the possible ramifications of political violence. Nor was there much discussion of how popular violence might have connected to other forms of violent politics.[17]

Violence, Violence Specialists, and Politics

This book treats violence itself as a significant historical phenomenon, defining the kind of violence discussed here and throughout as physical coercion of the physical body. It will be noticed that I periodically use "physical force" as a synonym for "violence," to mean and refer to this specific type of physical force that coerces the body.[18] This is not to slight other forms of violence, such as psychological violence, that can have the same coercive power and cause the same mental devastation as physical violence. But there is a qualitative difference when violence is physical, when harm and pain are inflicted on the body as well as on the mind.[19] Accordingly, many political theorists treat violence as an act that violates the physical body.[20]

A focus on violence specialists in particular highlights the instrumental nature of violence, the ways in which violence was wielded as a political tool. The term "violence specialist" has most often been used by political theorists, such as Charles Tilly, to refer to those who concentrate on the infliction of physical damage, such as soldiers, police, armed guards, thugs, gangs, terrorists, bandits, and paramilitary forces.[21] The spirit of this definition has been adopted here as it illustrates how violence is interwoven into the functioning of states and politics. But my focus is on those outside the violent arms of the state and how they can blur conceptions of legitimate and illegitimate violence.[22] I thus use "violence specialists" to mean those nonstate actors who made careers out of wielding physical force in the political sphere, or who received compensation for performing acts of political violence.

Given the messiness of defining both violence and violence specialists, a quick aside on the self-conscious use of language is in order. To the greatest extent possible, when speaking of violence specialists I have usually attempted to choose words that are neutral, that evoke the fewest connotations be they positive or negative. This is particularly true when it comes to the yakuza. I have decided to use this term rather than the English "gangster," which may evoke romantic images of Prohibition-era bosses for a movie-watching American audience. "Gangster" is also too inclusive, referring to members of any form of organized crime from street gangs to sophisticated syndicates. Where appropriate, the yakuza have been equated specifically to a mafia, a clearly defined subset of organized crime.[23] Also, I have avoided the Japanese "kyōkaku" (men of chivalry), a euphemism often employed by the yakuza themselves. This is not to say that the term "yakuza" does not have its own conceptual and linguistic baggage, but the constructed image is less uniform than "kyōkaku," subject as yakuza are to romanticization and demonization alike. And, at the very least, the Japanese term may have fewer connotations for an American readership than does "gangster." In generally choosing as neutral a word as possible, I am not suggesting that violence or the violent should not be judged, that there are not important moral meanings and implications to the use of physical force. But violence, in my mind, is so varied in kind and intent that it cannot be uniformly lauded or condemned. Violence used in the context of a grassroots movement for democracy, for example, is not the same as the assassination of an elected political leader or imperialist war. Charged language, then, can not only distort but also does not adequately capture this complexity. At certain points in the book I obviously do offer my own judgments of political action, and here I use terms that indicate my views, choosing "activist" or "protester" over "rioter," for example. Care has also been taken throughout to explicitly address contemporary constructions of violence and violence specialists.

An examination of the history of violence specialists in Japan illustrates that violence was not just a form of political expression, it was also a tool—to gain and exert influence, to attempt to control, to amass power, to disorder so as to reorder in one's vision.[24] The antagonistic nature of politics (and, arguably, democratic politics in particular) tends to cultivate the need for such an instrument, and Japan was no different as its politics were rife with contention and confrontation.[25] Violence was appealing not just for its utility but also because of a political culture that, within limits, tolerated and sometimes even encouraged the wielding of physical force. Both structural and cultural factors thus made violence a seductive political tool. As such, the use of violence was attractive to activists, protesters, politicians, and statesmen alike. Violence was not just seen in occasional outbursts or political movements, though these contexts are treated here, but was also a part of the routine practice of politics.

Violence and Democracy

The book begins by asking what happened to the violence of the late Tokugawa period in the transition from early modern to modern rule, and what implications the violent birth of the Japanese nation-state had for the modern politics that followed. Central here is an examination of how the forerunners of modern violence specialists—*shishi* ("men of spirit") and *bakuto* (gamblers)—navigated the pivotal years from the 1860s through the mid-1880s. *Shishi* were typically lower-ranking samurai who attempted to topple the early modern regime in the 1860s through a campaign of assassinations that targeted foreigners and allegedly traitorous Japanese officials. Although *shishi* as a political force did not survive into the Meiji period, they did leave behind a malleable precedent for patriotic and rebellious violence on which their various modern successors could selectively draw to inform and justify their own political violence. *Bakuto,* gamblers and a kind of yakuza, did not just leave an ideological legacy for the modern period but also became themselves violence specialists in a modern political context. Some *bakuto* were recruited by domains to fight in the Boshin Civil War of 1868–1869 because they were more battle tested than the samurai who had been languishing in relative inaction for some time. And in the 1880s, they were participants and even leaders in the most violent phase of the Freedom and People's Rights Movement, becoming violence specialists conscious of and acting in an unquestionably political realm.

The Freedom and People's Rights Movement is also a jumping off point for one of the main concerns of the book: exploration of the interplay between violence and democracy in modern Japanese politics. Compared to the discussion of violence above, democracy is defined rather simply, as a participatory form of government with a representative body and a constitution. This conceptualization is intentionally rudimentary to underscore an approach concerned not with lofty notions about ideal democracies but with democracy as it was actually practiced. Democracy is to be understood as an ongoing experiment, and one that is not necessarily evolutionary; I do not use the word "democratization," so as to emphasize the point that democracy itself is a process and not a point of arrival. It is fairly easy to argue that violence has no place in a perfect democracy, but such a political system has never existed in reality.[26] The more difficult questions are what violence reflected about Japanese democracy and what consequences it had for the country's political life.

In speaking of Japanese democracy, I purposely avoid the phrase "Taisho democracy," a description most often evoked by historians in Japan who have characterized the politics of the Taisho era (1912–1926) by its broadened grassroots political activity and popular embrace of ideas from democracy to nationalism.[27] As much as "Taisho democracy" captures the various currents of this time, it is chronologically rigid and narrow, and makes difficult the drawing of connections both backward and forward in time.[28] The popular politics of the Meiji period (1868–1912) are sidelined by the focus on the Taisho years; indeed, historian Banno Junji has taken to using "Meiji democracy" to counterbalance this tendency.[29] The term also slights the links from the nationalism and imperialism of the 1910s and 1920s to the total war and militarism of the early Showa era (1926–1989). By talking of democracy without a chronological qualifier, I hope to underscore important continuities across periods and significant moments of change that did not necessarily fall on era markers.

The book asks, then, to what extent we can speak of Japan from the 1880s through the early 1960s as, to use Daniel Ross's term, a "violent democracy." Ross is primarily concerned with how the violence of democracy's foundational moment reverberates through what follows. I am interested in this question as well, but focus more on how violence and democracy coexisted in Japan—on how violence could promote democracy but also threaten it, on how democracy could both give birth to violence and contain it, on how a culture of political violence and a democracy could operate at one and the same time.

Of the 1880s and 1890s, I explore what it meant that violence was present at the very birth of parliamentary and constitutional government in Japan. Prevalent in these decades were *sōshi,* young activists of the Freedom and People's Rights Movement who, over the course of the 1880s, became more like political ruffians. As politics became more popular and visible, with public meetings and debates and election campaigns, so too did their brand of violence: ruffianism. It became increasingly common for *sōshi* to storm and disturb political gatherings, physically intimidate political opponents, and protect political allies from the violence of antagonistic *sōshi,* becoming fixtures in the early decades of Japan's democracy. The issue is not only why and how *sōshi* violence became a part of democratic practice, but also why it persisted. Of interest too is whether *sōshi* should be understood as a product and reflection of the shortcomings of Japanese democracy, and what consequences *sōshi* violence had for politics in these years.

Around the turn of the twentieth century, *sōshi* became even more embedded in politics, institutionalized into the very structure of political parties as violent wings of their *ingaidan* (pressure groups). In the 1910s and 1920s, *ingaidan* of the major political parties supported the protection and harassment work of ruffians and also served as organizers and agitators in some of the great political contests of the era. It seems strange that *ingaidan sōshi* would flourish during a time also known for its vibrant democracy, but perhaps this relationship was not as contradictory as it might initially seem. The larger questions here are whether and how *sōshi,* and the culture of political violence they helped feed, can be reconciled with our understandings of democracy in these decades.

Delving into the relationship between violence and democracy also encourages thinking about the violence of fascist movements, and what ramifications violent democracy might have had for the political ascent of the military in the 1930s. In the 1920s and 1930s, violence specialists—namely yakuza—shaped the ideological landscape as active participants in, and leaders of, nationalist organizations such as the Dai Nihon Kokusuikai (Greater Japan National Essence Association) and Dai Nihon Seigidan (Greater Japan Justice Group), squaring off against labor unions, strikers, socialists, and others of a leftist orientation. For a time, the political world was inhabited by both the violence of these nationalist groups and that of *ingaidan*. Explored are the connections between these two forms of ruffianism and what they meant for contemporary views of political violence, the future of the political parties, and the fate of violent democracy.

Finally, the theme of democracy's relationship with violence is revisited for the post–World War II years in which some violence specialists reemerged and others faded from the political scene. Yakuza continued to take a nationalistic and anticommunist stance, but *sōshi* and violent *ingaidan* ceased to be a phenomenon, and political fixers who brokered relationships between politicians and violence specialists were forced into the political background. Especially after the early 1960s, even yakuza violence in politics became less visible as money outpaced physical force as the political tool of choice. These transformations raise questions about why Japan's early postwar democracy allowed for violence specialists in certain forms and roles, and whether it makes sense to speak of Japan in the 1950s as a violent democracy.

This inquiry into the history of violence specialists is thus intended to serve as a lens through which to examine broad issues about the place and meaning of violence in various forms of politics—from the formation of the Meiji state to Japan's experiment with democracy and encounter with fascism.

Approaches to Comparative History

Violence specialists were interwoven into much of the violent politics in the hundred years after 1860, but the book does not pretend to be a comprehensive history of political violence in Japan. One volume simply could not do justice to the many manifestations of physical force over this century. In addition, the book's focus on violence should not be taken to mean that violence was the most significant characteristic of Japan's modern politics.

I also do not want to suggest that Japan was unique in its political violence or to encourage the reemergence of wartime stereotypes of Japan and "the Japanese" as exceptionally violent. To underscore this point, comparative asides sprinkled throughout the book draw parallels with cases beyond Japan's borders. In some places, these are intentionally kept to mere mentions to simply illustrate the universality of political violence.

In other places, the comparative analysis is more sustained, treating not just similarities but also particularities and speaking directly to a central contention of the chapter. A word should be said, then, about the selection of cases. Perhaps the most meaningful comparisons are those between Japan and Italy, for the two countries have faced similar historical challenges and continue to share political characteristics. As political scientist Richard Samuels has commented, both countries have played the game of "catch up" since the 1860s and continue to seek "normality" even as they have become wealthy democracies that enjoy the rule of law and healthy civil societies.[30] Even more pertinent to our concerns, Japan and Italy both had encounters with fascism, and have witnessed significant intrusions of mafiosi into their political lives.

I also discuss political violence in the United States and Great Britain, two countries often held up as model democracies. To demonstrate that they, too, have struggled with violence is to reiterate the point that no democracy has ever been immune from violent politics and that Japan was not singularly or uncommonly violent.

Taken as a whole, this is a history of political characters who have largely escaped the attention of historians.[31] By bringing violence specialists out of the historiographical shadows, the book reveals that violence was systemic and deeply embedded in the practice of politics for much of Japan's modern history. And we discover a political world that could be both ordered and rough, exciting and frightening, dignified and cruel.

1

Patriots and Gamblers

Violence and the Formation of the Meiji State

Standing before an overflowing crowd on the grounds of a local shrine, Tashiro Eisuke announced himself president and commander of the assembled and christened them the Konmingun (Poor People's Army).[1] This fighting force of farmers and other members of rural society wore headbands, had their sleeves rolled up, and stood ready with bamboo spears, swords, and rifles.[2] On this first day of November in 1884, they converged in the Chichibu District of Saitama Prefecture and then launched a rebellion against those they deemed responsible for their poverty and powerlessness: rapacious lenders and the Meiji state. As its members murdered usurers, attacked sites of state authority, and battled govern- ment forces in the days that followed, the Konmingun was held together by Tashiro Eisuke and his second in command, Katō Orihei. Tashiro and Katō are especially remarkable because they were *bakuto* (gamblers)—technically outlaws, and a kind of yakuza. Before the mid-1800s, it would have been almost unheard of for such men to be at the helm of a peasant protest or political rebellion. And yet, in the second decade of the Meiji period, some *bakuto* assumed roles that thrust them onto the national political stage.

Tashiro and Katō will be considered here as part of a larger examination of how forerunners of modern violence specialists—*shishi* ("men of spirit") as well as *bakuto*—navigated the tumultuous transition from early modern to modern rule which spanned the 1860s to 1880s. *Shishi* and *bakuto* were not remnants of a feudal past that staggered on beyond their time, but were refashioned through the tremendous upheaval of the Tokugawa shogunate's fall and the turbulent early decades of the Meiji period. The end of samurai rule, the emergence of the nation-state, and the burgeoning of various kinds of democratic politics remade the early modern violence of *shishi* and *bakuto* into their modern incarnations. Yet *shishi* and *bakuto* negotiated these transformative decades quite differently.

Shishi were typically lower-ranking samurai, and as warriors of the Tokugawa period they were officially the violent arm of the early modern state. Given the paucity of opportunities for samurai to actually serve as the realm's defenders, however, they were fighters more in name than in practice. What eventually compelled them to take up arms—against the political order they were supposed to protect—was their profound dissatisfaction with how the shogunate handled the arrival of the West in Japan in the 1850s. Frustration with their status as lower-ranking samurai coupled with ideologies of "direct action" and disdain for the government gave birth to *shishi* who, in the late 1850s and early 1860s, used violence (mainly in the form of assassination) to try to topple the Tokugawa shogunate. *Shishi* were not violence specialists in the most technical sense, for they were rebels who used force in an attempt to realize their own political goals and were not acting violently for others. Nor did they survive the Meiji Restoration as a political force. Nonetheless, *shishi* provided a model of violent rebellion against a seemingly delinquent state that would be adopted in the early Meiji period. And although they were variously constructed as patriotic activists and xenophobic terrorists in their own time, it was their patriotism that was remembered and resurrected by modern violence specialists in the Meiji period and beyond.

Bakuto of the Tokugawa period were gamblers who had honed their physical skills to protect their enterprises and territories. Precisely because of the violence of the *bakuto,* the Tokugawa shogunate made the somewhat ironic move of asking them to help police the realm, and certain domains recruited them to fight in the civil war of the Meiji Restoration. In the context of the Freedom and People's Rights Movement of the 1880s, the ability to wield violence helped propel some *bakuto,* like Tashiro Eisuke and Katō Orihei, into prominent leadership roles. *Bakuto* did not just leave an ideological legacy, as *shishi* did, but also became themselves violence specialists in a modern political context.

Both *shishi* and *bakuto* speak to questions about what happened to the violence of the Tokugawa period in the process of nation-state formation, about how and why violence persisted in certain forms, about how violence was remade to become distinctly modern. The violence of the Tokugawa to Meiji transition did not disappear with the emergence of Japan as a modern nation-state but endured, however transformed, to have implications for political life and practice for decades to come.

Shishi: Assassins, Rebels, Patriots

The arrival of American gunboats off the coast of the capital in 1853 sparked a contentious and divisive debate about foreign policy in a country that had been secluded from official contact with much of the West for some two centuries. While opinions ranged from appeasement to expulsion, key government officials decided they had no choice but to cooperate with the militarily superior Americans. The perceived impotence of the Tokugawa shogunate in the face of the West crystallized concerns about its ability to protect and defend the country and encouraged in some a turn toward violent reform. Particularly offensive to those who saw Japan prostrating itself before the outside world were the signing in 1858 of the so-called "unequal treaties" that established diplomatic and trade relations with a handful of Western countries, and the subsequent two-year purge of opponents by the chief shogunate official, Great Elder (*tairō*) Ii Naosuke. Fanned by the country's forced opening by the West, an incipient form of patriotism encouraged the use of violence to express deep dissatisfaction with the early modern state. What resulted was one of the few acts of violent samurai rebellion in over 200 years.

This anti-Tokugawa group has variously been called loyalist or *shishi*, a term that had connotations of self-sacrifice for realm or country. Confucius had defined a *shishi* as one who denied his body for the sake of virtue and benevolence; in the context of late Tokugawa Japan, *shishi* leader Yoshida Shōin characterized his kin as exercising their will for the country (*kokka*) in times of battle.[3] In these years, the slogan that encapsulated their ideological stand was "revere the emperor, expel the barbarian" (*sonnō jōi*). The intellectual pedigree of these ideas was long and complex, but they were honed in the early 1800s by scholars from Mito Domain and then taken up by key *shishi* figures in the 1850s and early 1860s.[4] Prominent among them was Yoshida Shōin from the domain of Chōshū, who especially after 1858 was vociferous in his entreaties for *shishi* as "humble heroes" to act—the Tokugawa regime was to be challenged by those outside it, and foreigners were to be attacked to force the shogunate into action against the "barbarians." Yoshida also called for a restoration of the emperor led by self-sacrificing and loyal "unattached patriots" (*sōmō no shishi*). He was not just a man of words. In 1858, he was arrested for planning the assassination of Ii Naosuke's emissary to Kyoto and was executed the following year. His teachings lived on in his pupils, at least 15 of whom would become *shishi* who engaged in violent action and a handful of whom—like Itō Hirobumi and Yamagata Aritomo—would play important roles in the Meiji Restoration and the politics that followed. Like Yoshida, fencing teacher Takechi Zuizan of Tosa Domain had a core following of *shishi* students, including notables Sakamoto Ryōma and Nakaoka Shintarō, and advocated the use of force to undermine the authority of the Tokugawa shogunate and to restore power to the imperial court.[5]

Assassination was a common violent tactic of the *shishi*, wielded against foreigners and those fellow countrymen viewed as kowtowing to the demands and presence of Westerners on Japanese soil. Historians have often described these assassinations as acts of terrorism. Indeed, they were symbolic acts intended to elicit fear—calculated to punish allegedly traitorous Japanese, bring about the expulsion of foreigners, and endanger the objectionable treaty settlement.[6]

A number of assassinations were carried out in the capital of Edo, a central site of official relations between the shogunate and foreign diplomats. Here, *shishi* were recognizable by their long hair, unshaven faces and unwashed bodies, light and casual clothing, and bare feet in wooden clogs. The opening shot that ushered in several years of *shishi* violence sounded outside an Edo castle gate, where Ii Naosuke was assassinated in March 1860. Eighteen *shishi,* one from Satsuma Domain and the rest from Mito, punished Ii with death for concluding the "unequal treaties."[7] Also on the list of *shishi* victims was Kobayashi Denkichi, a translator in the employ of the British legation. He was known to frequent establishments that catered to the amorous needs of foreign residents and served as a guide for members of the legation, but what allegedly caught the attention of his attackers was the disrespect that he and some of his British coworkers showed to the headstones of the famed 47 loyal *rōnin* (masterless samurai). Whether this was the true motivation for the assassination is unclear, as it sounds more like myth than reality, but Kobayashi was killed by angered *shishi* in early 1860.[8] Also in Edo, a small group of *shishi* from Satsuma targeted Dutchman Henry Heusken, secretary and interpreter for the American legation who had used his linguistic skills in negotiations of the "unequal treaties." On the evening of January 15, 1861, the masked *shishi,* dressed in black, ambushed Heusken and his retinue at a checkpoint and managed to inflict fatal sword wounds. The assassins were later found to be part of a *shishi* group known as Kobi no Kai (Association of the Tiger's Tail) that was organized by Kiyokawa Hachirō, who ran a school where one could study Chinese classics, practice swordsmanship, and discuss politics. The Kobi no Kai consisted only of Kiyokawa's most trusted associates who embraced the "revere the emperor, expel the barbarian" ideology.[9] A number of months later, in July 1861, *shishi* attacked the British legation at Tōzenji. Fourteen or 15 *shishi* managed to breach the supposedly well-guarded defensive perimeter and stormed the compound, which resulted in the death or injury of several dozen people.[10] During these years, other *shishi* attacks were aimed at a Russian naval officer, a Dutch merchant captain, and a Chinese in French employ.[11]

Although *shishi* considered their assassinations heroic, many foreigners naturally did not agree. Illustrating the idea that violence can be understood differently depending on where one stands, foreigners viewed *shishi* violence as terrorism and a reaffirmation of Japanese incivility. The first British minister to Japan, Consul General Rutherford Alcock, did acknowledge the determination and self-devotion of *shishi* when discussing the assassination of Ii Naosuke.[12] On the whole,

however, Alcock was understandably critical of the threat of violence that he felt
so keenly. In a protest against the poor treatment of foreigners that he submitted to
the Japanese government (presumably the shogunate) on August 9, 1859, Alcock
explained to the host country the perils of everyday life in Edo:

> No officer of the Missions of either country, Great Britain or the United
> States, can walk out of their official residence without risk of rudeness,
> offense, and latterly—more especially latterly—violence of the most
> wanton and determined character. Stones are thrown, blows are struck,
> swords are drawn on gentlemen passing along the great thoroughfares
> inoffensively and peaceably, offering neither offense nor provocation to
> any one.[13]

Alcock spoke almost two years later, just before the attack at Tōzenji, of how the
constant danger was so "intolerable" that it made those around him "grow hard-
ened and indifferent."[14] In his mind, the assassinations spoke to Japanese and
Oriental treachery, cruelty, and vindictiveness. They also revealed the flaws of
the shogunate for not controlling such unruly behavior, especially in the capital;
this kind of "mob violence," as he often called it, was reminiscent of bygone feudal Europe, and in the Europe of the present day, claimed Alcock, the equivalent
of *shishi* violence would not be permitted by the government.[15] Violent attacks on
foreigners thus confirmed for the British minister his conceptions of the inability
of Japanese people and politics to measure up to European civility, rationality,
and advancement.

　　Shishi assassinations peaked in the early 1860s, with 70 carried out in a two-year
period starting in mid-1862.[16] Among them was the May 1862 attack on Tosa
Domain's chief minister. Orchestrated by Takechi Zuizan, the assassination was
considered retribution for domain reform proposals viewed as pro-shogunate.[17]
Then, in September, British merchant Charles Richardson and three of his com-
panions were attacked by *shishi* from Satsuma in what became known as the
Namamugi Incident. A member of the British consular service, Ernest Satow,
commented on the resultant panic: "This [the assassination] had a most powerful effect on the minds of Europeans, who came to look on every two-sworded
man as a probable assassin, and if they met one in the street thanked God
as soon as they had passed him and found themselves in safety."[18] British subjects were targeted again in early 1864, when two soldiers were murdered in
Kamakura.[19]

　　Violence was especially visible in Kyoto, the site of the imperial court, as *shishi*
from Tosa, Satsuma, and Chōshū gathered around antiforeign and antishogunate court figures and created a highly charged atmosphere. These *shishi* justified
their violence as acts of "heavenly punishment" (*tenchū*) and threatened—through

signs, handbills, and other forms of public display—to bring it to bear on those who crossed them. One of the first victims of "heavenly punishment" was Shimada Sakon, a steward of imperial regents for the shogunate who in the late 1850s had been paid to spy and inform on loyalists who spoke ill of the Tokugawa regime. Shimada was enjoying an evening bath some years later when he was killed by *shishi* from Tosa, Satsuma, and Higo. In a style that evoked official punishment by the shogunate, his head was put on display under a sign that included the explanation, "He is a great traitor, unfit for heaven or earth. Therefore we have punished him."[20] A couple of months later, 24 *shishi* descended upon four men who had been responsible for carrying out Ii Naosuke's purge. The four were in travel lodgings on their way from Kyoto to Tokyo when they were attacked; three died immediately and the one who escaped expired shortly thereafter. The political significance of *shishi* targets was made especially clear in the second month of 1863 when this time, the victims at the end of their swords were not living men but statues of the Ashikaga shoguns. Vilified by the *shishi* for having turned their backs on Emperor Go-Daigo in the fourteenth century, three Ashikaga shoguns (or rather, their likenesses) were beheaded. As with Shimada's head, the Ashikagas' wooden ones were put on display with an explicit message for those who might have missed the symbolic one: "we are imposing Heaven's Revenge on the disgraceful images of these traitors."[21]

Although this *shishi* violence was effective in creating an atmosphere of terror, it soon became clear that assassinations alone would not lead to either expelling the barbarian or overthrowing the shogunate. In 1863, the attempt to use violence on a larger scale revealed the limits of *shishi* power, as they were defeated by shogunate forces. By the end of 1864, some *shishi* had been punished, many were killed in conflicts, and most of the rest acknowledged the futility of expelling the militarily superior Western powers from Japan. The most violent or visible of the *shishi* had been rounded up; several hundred were arrested or thrown out of Kyoto. Domain militaries had handed defeats to *shishi,* as had corps of *rōnin* like the Shinsengumi that had been formed to support the shogunate by fighting fire with fire. Punishment and containment also came at the hands of foreigners, who demonstrated the impossibility of expelling the barbarian. In August 1863, British warships fired on Kagoshima in Satsuma to force a settlement regarding the assassination of the merchant Richardson. And a little over a year later, the navies of Britain, France, the Netherlands, and the United States bombarded Shimonoseki in Chōshū as retaliation for the domain's attacks on Western vessels, a move that had been encouraged by *shishi.* All of these developments spelled the end of the politics of assassination and the fading of "revere the emperor, expel the barbarian" ideology, for the remaining *shishi* either retreated from political life or joined armies to topple the Tokugawa shogunate.[22]

Shishi Legacies in the Early Meiji Period

Although the *shishi*'s crucial phase in the antishogunate movement waned before 1868, they provided a precedent for violent rebellion against the state that would inform the actions of discontents in the modern period. And they created a rich ideological past that would be resurrected and refashioned by their successors to justify their own political violence.[23] This legacy was attractive because it was so malleable—depending on one's political orientation, the *shishi* could be eulogized for their spirited opposition to the state, loyalty to the emperor, or dedication to protecting the country. All of these possibilities, though sometimes taken up by those of fundamentally different political stances, fed a romanticization of *shishi*. Casting *shishi* as courageous, brave, and heroic young men made their violence and the violence of their modern incarnations palatable, even admirable.

Adopting and reinterpreting ideologies from foundational moments to justify violence was also seen in the United States after the American Revolution, when the language and concept of "sovereignty of the people" was invoked as an explanation for vigilantism, lynching, and tarring and feathering of those deemed "enemies of the public good." In the mid-1840s, antirent protesters in upstate New York labeled their enemies "Tories" and dressed as "Mohawks" to fashion themselves after the "Indians" of the Boston Tea Party. And the minutemen have been resurrected multiple times, as by the paramilitary, anticommunist minutemen of the 1960s who were involved in a bank robbery and various assaults.[24]

In early Meiji Japan, *shizoku* (or former samurai) were inspired by *shishi* and their ideas to violently challenge the new government.[25] These *shizoku* rebellions, informed by the *shishi* past, brought the idea of heroic action into the modern era. Loss of privileges in the late 1860s and 1870s angered the *shizoku,* as the modernizing Meiji government did away with their military role by enacting conscription (January 1873), robbed them of their symbols of status by prohibiting the wearing of swords (March 1876), and threw them into economic insecurity by decreeing that their hereditary stipends would be converted into government bonds (August 1876). Disgruntled former samurai wanted to regain samurai privileges, much like *shishi* wanted to regain a country free of "barbarian" intrusion; both were upset with a government they saw as blocking their conservative agenda. Between 1874 and 1877, this antipathy toward the Meiji government along with other political concerns motivated a turn to violence in the form of six rebellions.

The decision to rebel was shaped by a direct legacy from the early 1860s—ex-*shishi* themselves. All six rebellions were led by early adherents of the antishogunate movement in the Bakumatsu period (the last decade and a half of the

Tokugawa regime). One author has convincingly suggested that these rebels firmly believed in using force to settle political matters because they were products of the Restoration.[26] More specifically, the leader of the Hagi Rebellion had been a *shishi* from the former domain of Chōshū. Maebara Issei was a student of *shishi* leader Yoshida Shōin in the late 1850s, and lessons in "direct action" may have had a lasting impact on the young Maebara. In October 1876, he planned to head a group of rebels from Chōshū (now Yamaguchi Prefecture) in an attack on the prefectural office at Hagi; the rebels were, however, captured by government troops.[27]

In the Shinpūren Rebellion, *shishi* influence was ideological. The political orientation and cosmology of the rebels were rooted in the teachings of Hayashi Ōen, a Shintō priest and scholar who had expressed virulently xenophobic views in the Bakumatsu era. He had argued that the "foreign barbarians" should be resisted and could be expelled by the force of the Divine Wind and by the united effort of samurai. Hayashi established a school in 1837 known as the Gendōkan, which survived the Restoration. In 1872, two years after Hayashi died, the more xenophobic of his pupils—those who bitterly opposed the Westernizing reforms of the Meiji government—founded the Keishintō, or Shinpūren: the League of the Divine Wind. On October 24, 1876, two days before the Hagi Rebellion that it helped inspire, 181 members of the Keishintō dressed in samurai gear and attacked the Kumamoto garrison in what would become known as the Shinpūren Rebellion. By the time the siege was put down the next day, 28 of them were dead and 85 had committed suicide.[28]

The last and most dramatic rebellion—the Southwestern War (Seinan Sensō), more commonly known in English as the more diminutive "Satsuma Rebellion"— had only loose connections with ex-*shishi* and their ideologies, but in being an act of violent action it would become entwined with *shishi* in memory and imagination. Fodder for romanticization of the Southwestern War was provided by its leader, Saigō Takamori, a former samurai from Satsuma Domain who had gained the respect of some Satsuma *shishi* in the Bakumatsu years and fought to unseat the Tokugawa regime. He assumed important roles in the early Meiji government as imperial councillor, army general, and commander of the imperial guard, but after a falling out with fellow statesmen over relations with Korea, he famously resigned in 1873. Back in Kagoshima (previously Satsuma), he remained aloof from political affairs save for the Shigakkō, a network of private schools that he founded in 1874 that specialized in military training (infantry and artillery) as well as some academic subjects. Over the next several years, the impingement of the central government on the former domains, the retraction of samurai privilege, and government surveillance of activities in Kagoshima upset the Shigakkō students who, at the end of January 1877, launched a rebellion against the Meiji government led by Saigō. After eight months of sporadic fighting, the rebel army was thoroughly defeated—18,000 of their men had been killed or injured, and Saigō committed suicide.[29]

All of these *shizoku* rebellions resonated with the violence and ideology of their *shishi* predecessors, and so their own legacy for the modern period was often interwoven with that of the *shishi*. Some rebels became legendary figures, spawning myths beyond state control. Saigō Takamori, though labeled by the government as a traitor at the time, became popular as newspapers reported that he had ascended to the heavens as a comet and, later, that he had become the planet Mars; Buddhist prints depicted him as an enlightened being. Among those who embraced Saigō were activists of the Freedom and People's Rights Movement, who adopted him as a symbol of "freedom and resistance" because of his opposition to the Meiji regime.[30] The Shinpūren rebels too were glorified by some, most notably Mishima Yukio, the postwar writer who on November 25, 1970, took over the Tokyo headquarters of the Self-Defense Forces, called for a coup d'état and imperial restoration, and committed suicide.[31]

Not only rebels but also the Meiji state itself attempted to appropriate the *shishi* past by making symbolic gestures intended to commend *shishi* loyalty to the emperor. Nine of the leaders of an attempted *shishi* rebellion in 1863, for example, were granted posthumous imperial court ranks. Similarly, seven members of the *shishi* organization Kobi no Kai were given that honor. Two of those who received this award had participated in the assassination of Henry Heusken.[32]

Shishi also inspired men who would go on to become fervent, and powerful, nationalists. As one example, members of the political organization founded in 1881 as the Gen'yōsha (Dark Ocean Society) fancied themselves Meiji-era incarnations of the Bakumatsu *shishi*. Especially as the group took on a clearly nationalist hue, materials produced by the Gen'yōsha and its sympathizers referred to its followers as "shishi" and emphasized similarities in their concerns about the country, particularly when it came to forwarding an aggressive foreign policy.[33]

This appropriation of *shishi* identity was direct, as some future Gen'yōsha leaders had participated in *shizoku* rebellions of the 1870s. For the Hagi Rebellion, heavyweights Hakoda Rokusuke, Shindō Kiheita, and Tōyama Mitsuru had helped recruit the rebel army. They were subsequently put under close surveillance by the Fukuoka police who, upon searching Tōyama's home, found papers relating not just to the rebellion but also to a planned assassination of Home Minister Ōkubo Toshimichi, the man who had raised the ire of some *shizoku* in 1873 for his stand against invading Korea at that time. Tōyama, Hakoda, Shindō, and others were arrested and kept in prison; Hakoda served his time of imprisonment with hard labor; Tōyama and the others were held until September 1877 when they were found not guilty by reason of insufficient evidence.[34] In another episode, which unfolded in March 1877, members of two Gen'yōsha parent groups, the Kyōninsha (Perseverance Society) and Kyōshisha (Society to Train the Will), recruited about 800 rebels from Fukuoka to stage an attack on Akizuki Castle in sympathetic support of the Southwestern War. They took the castle but were forced out by imperial troops and arrested as they attempted to flee to the site of the Southwestern War.[35] After the defeat of Saigō in September, these Meiji-era "shishi" realized they had to abandon hopes of resurrecting samurai privilege and subsequently developed a somewhat more progressive vision, but they retained their antagonism toward the Meiji state as well as their patriotism. It is not surprising, then, that Gen'yōsha bigwigs Tōyama Mitsuru and Uchida Ryōhei viewed Saigō Takamori as a hero—constructing him as a rebel against the Meiji government, a patriot, and an advocate of a hawkish foreign policy. Uchida, in fact, edited a six-volume history of Saigō and the Southwestern War, published in 1908.[36] At the helm of the Gen'yōsha and its political spin-offs, men like Tōyama Mitsuru and Uchida Ryōhei influenced decades of Japanese domestic politics and foreign policy all the way through the 1930s. Although their stances on specific issues were obviously not static over six decades, their ideology and tactics would be informed and often justified by their experience, understanding, and remaking of what they saw as their *shishi* predecessors.

Shishi violence, so wrapped up with various triumphant narratives about the birth of the Meiji state, did not remain something of the early modern past but was refashioned to become a part of modern political life.

Bakuto: Outlaws, Robin Hoods, Local Leaders

Both *shishi* and *bakuto* became involved in political life during the Bakumatsu years, when the Tokugawa shogunate was weak. Unlike the *shishi*, however, *bakuto* were propelled into political matters not out of concern for the nation or fear of Western encroachment, but because they were local notables known for their violence.

The ability to wield physical force was part and parcel of the very emergence of *bakuto* in the Tokugawa period. Although gambling seems to have been a popular pastime as early as the seventh century, spaces designated for gambling began to appear during the mid-Tokugawa period in substantial numbers across the country, an alternative to more informal games in places such as people's homes.[37] These gambling dens were run by *bakuto* groups that in their early forms were composed mainly of labor contractors, laborers, and firefighters.[38] As these groups became more organized, they formed *ikka*, or "families" of fictive kinship ties based on the relationship between boss (*oyabun*) and henchmen (*kobun*).[39] These *ikka* increasingly consisted of those who thought of being a *bakuto* as their main or even sole occupation, so it was not unusual for a *bakuto* to be an "unregistered" (*mushuku*), that is, someone who had neither an official residence nor a place in the Tokugawa status system.[40] With the formation of numerous *bakuto ikka,* which depended on revenues from their gambling dens, the ability to defend and expand one's territory in the face of competing groups became central in maintaining the lifeline of a "family." And so brute physical strength became a significant asset for aspiring *bakuto* and a prerequisite for successful bosses.

Powerful *bakuto* bosses emerged in the 1800s, extending and exerting their influence in part by cutting down enemies through fights and murders. Among the big *bakuto* bosses (*ō oyabun*) of the Bakumatsu period was a man named Kunisada Chūji, who became famous during his lifetime for his swashbuck- ling ways.[41] Born in 1810 to a farming family in central Japan, he was schooled not only in reading and writing but also in the art of fencing. At the age of 17, Kunisada murdered his opponent in a fight and then severed ties with his village and family, who removed him from the census register, making him a *mushuku.* Several *bakuto* bosses took him under their wings as he circulated around what is now Gunma Prefecture, and not long thereafter he established the Kunisada *ikka* in the village of Tamegai. During his career as a *bakuto* boss, Kunisada fought for territory, killed a number of men, and sent out groups of several dozen hench- men armed with spears and even guns to engage in bloody brawls. It speaks to his power that the Kantō Regulatory Patrol (Kantō Torishimari Shutsu Yaku) felt it necessary to round up 600 people to help pursue this one boss. When he was eventually crucified by the Tokugawa government in 1850 before a crowd of over 1,000 spectators, signs publicized his seven crimes, including the serious of- fenses of evading a checkpoint (while armed with spears and guns) and murders (including that of a Kantō Regulatory Patrol guide). All of these actions have led historian Abe Akira to describe Kunisada's *ikka* as a "violent group of rogues" (*burai no bōryoku shūdan*).[42]

The violence of *bakuto ikka* complicated their relationship with the local soci- eties in which they lived and operated, as well as with the Tokugawa authorities. On the one hand, the kind of violence wielded by men like Kunisada Chūji did provoke, in this case, hundreds of people to come together to capture him. And it should not be forgotten that *bakuto ikka* engaged in the predatory activities of extortion, blackmail, and burglary that likely did not go unpunished by the villages in which they occurred.[43] On the other hand, some *bakuto* seem to have been viewed as legitimate and even important figures in some communities. At the very least, certain *bakuto* behavior drawn from wider social practice suggests that the line between outlaw and "nonoutlaw" could be blurry. Tattooing, for example, was used from the early 1700s by the shogunate to mark the bodies of criminals, but it eventually became a popular practice among groups of laborers and artisans including firefighters, carpenters, palanquin bearers, construction workers, and day laborers. In their hands, the shogunate's preferred tattoos of lines on the arm to denote the crime committed (e.g., two lines on the forearm for a person's second theft offense) were transformed into colorful and decorative designs that were a self-created sign of identity.[44] It could be speculated that tattoos then became a symbol not just of reclaiming one's body, but also of the physical strength it took to endure the lengthy and painful process of being tattooed. *Bakuto* too displayed these elaborate markings, fashioning a culture that resonated with the common practice of certain groups of people that often served as fodder for *bakuto* groups and did not seem to shun *bakuto* as outlaws. In this cultural practice drawn from the (nonoutlaw) society in which they were embedded, *bakuto* skirted the line between illegitimate outlaws and legitimate laborers and artisans.[45]

More important, in a number of ways, *bakuto* were integrated in and welcomed by the villages in which they ran their gambling dens. The wide popularity of gambling meant they were providing a desired service, and dens became spaces in which community members of varying status converged. In the early Tokugawa period, some *bakuto* might have been considered town soldiers or servants (*machi yakko*) who protected local communities, especially from the aggression of *rōnin*.[46] *Bakuto* also allegedly tried to endear themselves to the less fortunate in the village. One *bakuto* boss named Seiriki, for example, was known to give money (one or two *ryō*) to the poor in his village and to provide peasants with spears so they could protect themselves. Other bosses made it a point to contribute to village life. Kunisada Chūji was trusted with the task of cleaning out the village well(s), and in return the village headman not only permitted him to run gambling dens but also warned him when the shogunate authorities would be making their rounds. These relationships within the village allowed *bakuto* to transcend their status as unregistereds or as outlaws and made them, in the words of historian Yasumaru Yoshio, a kind of "men of influence" (*yūryokusha*) in local communities.[47] As such, it was not unusual for bosses to mediate various disputes within the village, and we know of incidents from the late Tokugawa period when they even became leaders in rural uprisings. In the mid-1800s, a man named Bansuke, arrested half a dozen times for gambling and other offenses, was sentenced to life in prison for leading poor farmers, tenants, and smallholders in various protests in the province of Shinano.[48] In terms of their embeddedness in rural society, *bakuto* were similar to the bandits that historian Eric Hobsbawm discusses in the context of Italian social movements—though *bakuto* were not robbers by profession, they were a kind of "social bandit" who were technically outlaws but had the respect of at least some members of peasant society.[49]

The shogunate also tried to maintain a delicate balance in its relationship with *bakuto,* attempting to control behavior viewed as disorderly or threatening to its authority while condoning less offensive behavior that served its interests. On the one hand, the shogunate issued a plethora of regulations throughout the period to control gambling and gamblers.[50] Though the sheer number of regulations suggests they were not heeded, the shogunate did punish flagrant violations, as when *bakuto* like Kunisada Chūji jeopardized the shogunate's authority. *Bakuto* could also be made into scapegoats for economic insecurity and alleged moral decline, as with the shogunate's Bunsei Reforms of 1827 that included instructions for village officials to report troublesome bandits and *bakuto.*[51] On the other hand, the shogunate turned a blind eye to some of the illegal *bakuto* activity and sought their cooperation in maintaining order.

In the earlier part of the Tokugawa period, the flexible treatment of *bakuto* could be explained by a conscious and thoughtful approach to law enforcement. This was the case with the Tokugawa officials' use of informants (*meakashi*), or criminals—including *bakuto*—who agreed to help capture wanted lawbreakers in exchange for release from jail and a small fee. Because they were criminals themselves and often continued their illegal pursuits even when they served as *meakashi,* they had the knowledge, network, and connections to bring in wanted offenders. They were particularly attractive to domainal lords (*daimyō*) because they were not constrained by official boundaries; a *meakashi* could go after someone who crossed over into another jurisdiction without making any kind of formal appeal, in a way that a warrior retainer could not. Such strategic use of *meakashi* mitigated the confusion caused by overlapping and fragmented official jurisdictions and reflected the shogunate's focus on apprehending serious offenders rather than petty criminals. As historian Daniel Botsman has argued, the maintenance of *meakashi* networks was rooted in a system that valued selective, visible punishment ("the occasional body-as-sign") over punishing all crimes.[52]

In the latter half of the Tokugawa period, and especially during the Bakumatsu decades, the shogunate's willingness to cooperate with *bakuto* stemmed less from a conscious and thoughtful strategy than sheer weakness.[53] The shogunate had already struggled to deal with famines and resulting peasant protests in the 1830s, and was then faced with the daunting challenge of handling the forceful and painful "opening" of the country in the 1850s. Financially strapped, the shogunate decided to cut back on the number of officials at magistrates' offices (*daikansho*) and on lands administered by direct retainers (*hatamoto*) of the shogunate in areas under its direct control. In these regions, influential *bakuto* thrived, and *bakuto ikka* would battle publicly in the light of day without fearing or facing repercussions. The shogunate had difficulty maintaining order where jurisdictions were many and ambiguous. Such was the case in Mikawa Province (present-day

Nagano Prefecture), which bred significant numbers of *bakuto*. Known for its poor policing, Mikawa also became a safe haven for *bakuto* bosses who committed crimes in other provinces and wanted to dodge the law.[54] When the shogunate attempted to crack down on the excesses of certain *bakuto*, it found itself needing to rely on the help of the less offensive of the very element it was seeking to contain. In 1805, when the shogunate established the Kantō Regulatory Patrol mentioned above, it had to depend on *bakuto* bosses to act as guides (*michi annai*) in its efforts to track down wanted criminals. This was not always an effective strategy. In an August 1844 case, the Kantō Regulatory Patrol garnered the assistance of boss Iioka Sukegorō as a guide to apprehend one of his *bakuto* rivals, Sasakawa no Shigezō. Sasakawa's side got wind of Iioka's approach, however, and was able to counterattack, assailing Iioka's house in retaliation before running away and evading capture.[55] In this incident, it seems that the shogunate's cooperation with a *bakuto* boss was not only unfruitful, but also encouraged violence between *ikka*.

Accepting and even working with *bakuto* also had the unintended consequence of tacitly authorizing their violence. In enlisting them as informants and later as guides, the shogunate signaled to the *bakuto* that force would be condoned so long as it did not challenge the state. Local communities may have tolerated *bakuto* violence if they contributed positively to village life. Moreover, those bosses like Seiriki who looked out for poor farmers would provide fodder for later ideas that *bakuto* "protected the weak and crushed the strong." Those who embraced this Robin Hood–like image would refer to *bakuto* not as mere gamblers but as *kyōkaku*, or "men of chivalry." Very much like the Sicilian mafia's "men of honor," *kyōkaku* would be popularized first in folklore, then in fiction and film through the glorification of *bakuto* such as Kunisada Chūji.[56] In Itō Daisuke's 1927 silent film *Chūji tabi nikki* (Chūji's Travel Diary), Kunisada was romanticized as a heroic *bakuto* boss who had to become a fugitive after killing a villainous magistrate who levied high taxes on destitute farmers. Through a number of similar stories and films, Kunisada became legendary as the quintessential chivalrous *bakuto*, a man whose existence outside the law was valorized because of his honorable code of ethics.[57] More to the point, the idea that *bakuto* "protected the weak and crushed the strong" would be marshaled and distorted in the modern period to justify acts of violence that were anything but chivalrous.

In the late Tokugawa period, *bakuto* mainly used violence among themselves but were starting to be seen as providers of force for the shogunate and perhaps in some local communities as well. Yet even when they served as shogunate informants or as guides for the Kantō Regulatory Patrol, *bakuto* could not be described as overtly or explicitly political—they did not seek or achieve a political goal, nor were they implicated in any sort of political ideology. It is worth mentioning too, as a side note, that *bakuto* are conventionally viewed as precursors to the Japanese mafia.[58] They did, in this period, begin to develop as "families" that provided protection on occasion, but *bakuto ikka* did not yet seek a monopoly on protection—one of the defining characteristics of a mafia.[59]

Bakuto and the Meiji Restoration

In the Tokugawa to Meiji transition, *bakuto* would become providers of violence in an unquestionably political realm. During the Meiji Restoration, specific *bakuto* bosses and their henchmen with a demonstrated history of wielding violence were recruited by domains to fight in the Boshin Civil War, a series of battles between Tokugawa holdouts and Meiji loyalists that took the lives of thousands of men before the last pro-Tokugawa resisters were subdued in late June 1869.

Historian Hasegawa Noboru has pieced together sources that illustrate how prominent *bakuto* bosses in Owari Domain were handpicked by domainal authorities to lead commoner (nonsamurai) troops consisting mainly of *bakuto,* precisely because of their reputation for being violent. Two of the *bakuto* bosses approached were Kondō Jitsuzaemon and Kumokaze no Kamekichi. Kondō, a well-known *bakuto* boss and swordsman, had started out as a sumo wrestler and in his twenties was taken in by a neighborhood *bakuto* boss who had heard of his reputation for fighting and recklessness. Kondō eventually established his own territory and became the head of the Kitaguma *ikka,* the most powerful of Owari Domain's *bakuto* groups. Kumokaze was the boss of the Hirai *ikka,* the foremost *bakuto* group in the relatively lawless Mikawa Province. He had a reputation for fighting often, out of malice and spite, and had proved his skills in battles against the *bakuto* great, Shimizu no Jirōchō.[60] Both Kondō and Kumokaze seem to have worked with the authorities before, but it is probably fair to say that their service in the Boshin Civil War was unprecedented. In mid-January 1868, Owari Domain authorities made overtures to both bosses to recruit and lead units to subdue pro-Tokugawa holdouts in the northeastern part of the country. Kumokaze amassed a unit of 86 *bakuto* henchmen, Kondō managed to gather 50; in March, these two groups officially became the backbones for the First and Second Battalions of what was called the Shūgitai (Justice Corps). Both battalions consisted of civilian volunteers, not domain soldiers, and tapped *bakuto* beyond those who belonged to Kumokaze's and Kondō's *ikka.* In May, the Shūgitai left Nagoya and fought in a series of battles over the next seven months before returning in triumph at the end of December.[61]

In calling for the formation of Kumokaze's and Kondō's battalions, even the relatively large domain of Owari made a calculated decision to reinforce its regular troops of unproven samurai with *bakuto* who had regularly demonstrated their fighting skills in battle. Kumokaze and Kondō were singled out specifically because of their physical prowess, and the domain was willing to overlook the fact that they were outlaws.[62] By agreeing to spearhead the Shūgitai, Kumokaze and Kondō were launched onto a political stage that extended beyond their domain. They certainly did not have larger political aspirations or goals, but they unwittingly helped put a nail in the coffin of the old order and consolidate the power of a new regime.

With the inauguration of the Meiji era, these *bakuto* fell out of favor for a time with the Westernizing government that was trying to bolster its own capacity for violence through a modern military and police force, not through alliances with outlaws. When *bakuto* were politically active, it was in opposition to the Meiji state. And the state, in response, would attempt to criminalize *bakuto* even though some, like Kumokaze and Kondō, had fought on its side in the civil war of the late 1860s.

Bakuto as Political Violence Specialists: The Freedom and People's Rights Movement

The context in which *bakuto* prominently reentered politics was the Freedom and People's Rights Movement. As the Meiji government began to take shape in the 1870s, many Japanese asked what the role of the people should be in the burgeoning political system. Those who advocated expanded popular participation in politics through the writing of a constitution and the establishment of a national assembly constituted the Freedom and People's Rights Movement. While the call for parliamentary and constitutional government was the uniting element of this movement, it embraced a spectrum of ideologies, motivations, and backgrounds. Some key leaders were former Meiji oligarchs who, like Saigō Takamori, had left the government because of the debate over Korea in 1873 but took a very different path. Itagaki Taisuke is a prime example of a popular rights activist in this mold. He was supported mainly by former samurai and even left the movement to rejoin the Meiji government on multiple occasions. Other strands were less elitist than that of men like Itagaki. Truly grassroots, farmers formed study groups and local political associations to discuss ideas and even write their own constitutions.[63]

The Chichibu Incident, with which this chapter opened, was part of the popular and revolutionary phase of the movement in the 1880s that consisted of numerous violent incidents (*gekka jiken*). This stage of the Freedom and People's

Rights Movement was fueled by grassroots frustration with the policies of the new Meiji state. Impoverished farmers protested their economic condition by turning to force, as peasants had done in the late Tokugawa period. But now their poverty was exacerbated by the national fiscal policy of Matsukata deflation, the expression of their grievances was shaped by the language and ideas of the Freedom and People's Rights Movement, and their targets included symbols of the Meiji state. As leaders of and participants in this violence, *bakuto* became a part of politics that were in many ways modern.[64] The transformation of *bakuto* was particularly evident in three protests I deal with here: the Gunma, Nagoya, and Chichibu Incidents.

Bakuto involvement in the Gunma Incident stemmed from the embeddedness of both gambling and gamblers in the local community. During the early Meiji period in Gunma Prefecture, it was said that the only people who did not gamble were enshrined buddhas (*honzon*) and stone statues of the bodhisattva Jizō. In this largely mountainous area in central Japan, farmers would gamble while visiting the shrines and Buddhist temples around the town of Takasaki, which was a goldmine for those who ran the gambling houses. Gambling had thrived here since the Tokugawa period because of complicated jurisdictions and, by the mid-nineteenth century, because of the flow of cash from sericulture through the hands of farmers.[65] There was also a large number of *bakuto* in this area, with at least ten *bakuto* groups in western Gunma alone.[66]

As part of this local community, *bakuto* experienced financial hardship alongside the farmers. And in the early 1880s, usurious lenders and the Meiji government were the ones doing the financial squeezing. At the local level, a kind of financial institution called *seisan gaisha* managed to issue loans at high interest rates despite an 1878 law (Risoku Seigen Hō) intended to prevent usurious lending.[67] The pressure to pay back loans that could triple in one year was heightened by policies at the national level. Finance Minister Matsukata Masayoshi's deflationary measures were driving down the value of silk, from ¥7.459 for one *kin* of raw silk in 1881 to ¥5.844 in 1884.[68] This made it difficult for farmers to repay the loans they had taken out during prosperous times, and sericulturists were also forced to incur high-interest debts to survive the drop in prices. *Bakuto* too felt this financial hardship, not just because of a presumed decline in gambling revenue but because *bakuto* were also farmers and raised silkworms.[69]

Bakuto likely felt the grip of the Meiji state even more tightly after the January 1884 proclamation of a national antigambling law (Tobaku Han Shobun Kisoku), which stipulated broad parameters for punishing gamblers and members of gambling groups.[70] The law left the specifics of enactment and punishment to the local level, and in March, Gunma Prefecture announced detailed regulations regarding issues such as the length of prison terms, amount of fines, and commutation of sentences.[71] In 1884 alone, 1,297 people in Gunma were punished under the antigambling law.[72]

As *bakuto* and farmers experienced financial difficulty and felt the reach of the Meiji state, they began to establish connections with the Jiyūtō (Liberal Party), the country's first national political party and a product of the earlier stages of the Freedom and People's Rights Movement. A nexus formed between *bakuto,* a people's rights group called the Yūshinsha (Society of Sincerity), and the Jiyūtō's radical wing known as the *kesshiha* (death faction).[73]

One *bakuto* who formed close ties with the uprising's leaders was Yamada Jōnosuke, originally Yamada Heijurō, who would become the most significant *bakuto* in the Gunma Incident. Yamada was a *bakuto* boss from the Usui District who, from the Bakumatsu era, had henchmen in Jōshū and Shinshū (Meiji-era Gunma and Nagano Prefectures).[74] A member of the well-known Arai *ikka* from the Tokugawa period, Yamada had been taken in by its founder Onoyama Nobugorō when he was a youth learning to fence and frequenting gambling dens. Eventually a boss of the Arai *ikka*, Yamada was known for his energy as he traveled between gambling houses in his large territory.[75] Along with other members of the Arai *ikka,* Yamada developed a network in the region with the other key figures in the Gunma Incident.

Frustrations began to take an organized form in the spring of 1883, when farmers appealed to the prefecture regarding their plight and to financial institutions for a postponement on the payment of their loans. Starting in March 1884, the Yūshinsha held political meetings encouraging farmers to join the Jiyūtō. The local leaders of the movement—activist Yuasa Rihei, prefectural assembly member Shimizu Eizaburō, schoolteacher Miura Momonosuke, and former samurai Hibi Yuzuru—advocated force to achieve people's rights and freedom; recruited hundreds of farmers, *bakuto,* hunters, and sumo wrestlers; and gave them military training in the local mountains.[76]

At one political meeting on April 14, some of these trained recruits fought with local police. Those gathered at the Yūshinsha event waved bamboo spears and matted flags in the air and sang a revolutionary song:

> If you think about the past, it was also the matted flag that freed America. If it doesn't rain blood here, then the foundation for freedom will not be firm.[77]

As skirmishes between the police and the crowd developed into an outright clash, *bakuto* boss Yamada Jōnosuke arrived on the scene, storming into the melee with 100 of his armed henchmen, forcing the police to retreat and bringing an end to the meeting without any arrests. That night, a banquet was held in appreciation for Yamada's efforts.[78]

Unlike *bakuto* in the Meiji Restoration, at least some bosses in this incident were not simply hired guns—Yamada was not just valued for his ability to wield force, he also played a role as an organizer. It was at his home that the leaders gathered to map out the protest. May 1 was to be the fateful day: the emperor would be attending an opening ceremony in Takasaki to celebrate the completion of a section of the Nakasendō railroad that would connect Tokyo and Kyoto. The plan was for approximately 3,000 farmers to take captive the high-ranking officials traveling with the emperor, not at the ceremony site in Takasaki itself, as that would be disrespectful to the emperor, but at the Honjō station where the train would take a short break. In the meantime, Yamada would lead a force of 2,500 *bakuto* in an attack on the Takasaki garrison, and then, at Numata Castle, justice would be declared to the world.[79] Yamada was to be aided in this task by fellow Arai *ikka* member and henchman, Seki Tsunakichi. Seki had been in prison on a gambling conviction but escaped while on work detail in time to join forces with Yamada.[80]

The incident was, in many ways, a failure. As the Jiyūtō members began to gather near Honjō in groups of 20 to 30, the police became suspicious of such a large-scale mobilization and so come May 1, there was no opening ceremony. From what the leaders of the incident could gather, the ceremony had been postponed until May 5, so they went to Takasaki to consult with Yamada regarding plans for the new date and headed back to Honjō. On their return trip, they attacked the home of a village headman who was a known hater of the Jiyūtō but did not manage to kill him as planned. May 5 arrived, but again there was no ceremony. It was finally agreed that something had to be done—it would be a waste and a perceived deception to have gathered so many participants to no end, and they might therefore have difficulty recruiting in the future.[81] Thus late in the night of May 15, thousands of farmers carrying big torches gathered in Jinbagahara at the base of the Myōgi mountains and set fire to the home of the head of a lending institution, robbed several wealthy farmers, and, according to some sources, charged the Matsuida police station.[82] They then attempted to strike the garrison in Takasaki, but morale was low and the number of deserters was high, so they failed and were arrested in great numbers by the police.[83] The Takasaki attack was made difficult too because the forces from Chichibu under Miura did not arrive, nor did the *bakuto* army under Yamada.

Police arrested participants through May, tracking down a total of 52 people, and continued to search for leaders as late as December.[84] On July 29, 1887, the Maebashi Court of Grave Offenses handed down a number of sentences, the most severe of which were 12 to 13 years of penal servitude (*tokei*); Miura was punished with seven years of imprisonment with hard labor (*keichōeki*).[85] Yamada Jōnosuke evaded punishment, and it has been said that he helped protect Hibi and Shimizu from capture.[86]

The leadership of *bakuto* Yamada Jōnosuke and Seki Tsunakichi in the planned May 1 attack on the Takasaki garrison and recruitment of their henchmen to form the backbone of this fighting corps suggest that *bakuto* were seen as central providers of force in this incident. It is difficult to argue the counterfactual, that the attempted storming of the Takasaki garrison on May 15 would have been successful with *bakuto* participation, but it is notable that it was such an utter failure without them.[87] This lends some weight to Charles Tilly's argument that the "presence or absence [of violence specialists] often makes all the difference between violent and nonviolent outcomes."[88] And *bakuto* were not just strongmen, they were planners and organizers of this political protest aimed at high-ranking Meiji government officials and a garrison which were symbols of the Meiji state.[89] *Bakuto* leadership of and participation in the Gunma Incident suggest that they adapted fairly quickly to a society in the throes of becoming modern and that they themselves, through their consciousness of a greater political context, were assuming a modern form.[90]

Because the *bakuto* were a part of the Freedom and People's Rights Movement, the Meiji government sought to control them and their violence. The national antigambling law of 1884 mentioned above was a case in point, likely aimed more at politically active *bakuto* than gambling. Contrary to the government's expectations, however, the law may have encouraged *bakuto* violence. This was particularly evident in the Nagoya Incident, which was less a discrete event than a series of robberies to fill the popular rights activists' war chest, topped off by the brutal murders of two policemen, which caused the movement to unravel. As with the earlier incident in Gunma, this one intertwined economic hardship with a political aim: overthrowing the government and catapulting people's rights advocates into power. All of this was compounded by the recent history of *bakuto*-state antagonism. The *bakuto*'s frustration with the Meiji regime developed soon after the Boshin Civil War ended, when in January 1872 all members of the Shūgitai volunteer civilian corps were deemed commoners (*heimin*) and not former samurai (*shizoku*), a status that at least some of them had previously been granted for their service. Thus began a lengthy process of demanding reinstatement as former samurai, which did not end in success until July 1878.[91] Moreover, the national antigambling law hit Aichi Prefecture, home of Nagoya, particularly hard. As it was interpreted and enforced in Aichi, mere participation in a *bakuto* group could be punished—*bakuto* bosses could be disciplined for "corralling" (*kaiketsu*) *bakuto* and "infesting" (*ōkō*) neighboring areas, and henchmen had to answer for being one of the assembled. This provision, like the U.S. Racketeer Influenced and Corrupt Organizations Act of 1970, was much harsher than the previous practice of arresting only those caught in the act of gambling, and the punishments were also more severe, with longer prison times and stiffer fines.[92] It seems too that the law was not simply on the books but was enforced, with arrests of *bakuto* peaking from February to May 1884. Historian Hasegawa Noboru has noted that the state likely targeted *bakuto* groups known for displaying their power through bloody battles over territory. Of the approximately 40 *bakuto* groups in Aichi Prefecture, only seven or eight were pursued, two of which—the Hirai and Kitaguma *ikka*—had formed the core of the Shūgitai during the Boshin Civil War. Given that they had more weapons and fighting experience than other *bakuto* groups, these *ikka* that had been assets in the Boshin Civil War came to be seen as threats to the Meiji regime's attempt to establish order.

The national antigambling law dealt a severe blow to targeted *ikka*—as gambling became an increasingly dangerous activity, it was discontinued, shutting off a source of *bakuto* income, and groups collapsed. Because it was these financially insecure *bakuto* who joined forces with the people's rights activists, Hasegawa suggests that *bakuto* were motivated to organize the violent incidents less because they were farmers upset with Matsukata deflation and more because they were *bakuto* pressed by the antigambling law. Such was the case with the *bakuto* at the center of the Nagoya Incident: Ōshima Nagisa. Ōshima was a member of the Kitaguma *ikka* and had fought in the Shūgitai's Second Battalion. His active involvement with the incident began after the unrelenting arrests of fellow Kitaguma *ikka* members; he rallied former Shūgitai colleagues as well as those *bakuto* who had not fought in the Boshin Civil War to take action.

Ōshima brought this group of *bakuto* together with the other two main (non-*bakuto*) contingents in the incident: the Aikoku Kōshinsha (Patriotic Friendship Society) and the Aichi Jiyūtō. The Aikoku Kōshinsha was composed largely of members of the urban underclass and advocated national strength and the establishment of a parliament. This group's participants in the Nagoya Incident were led by a man named Yamauchi Tokusaburō, who had met Ōshima through a common interest in fencing. The Aichi Jiyūtō was represented by its young members who believed in action (*kōdōha*). They were essentially ruffians, as became evident in a March 1883 incident at a high-class restaurant in Nagoya. Here, the youths disturbed the inaugural meeting of their rival political party; they heckled the honored guest Ozaki Yukio, cheered for the Jiyūtō, and generally caused the meeting to fall into confusion. Later that night, 30 of these youths led by Naitō Roichi armed themselves with a barrel full of excrement and pursued rival party members, using a night soil dipper to fling feces at their political enemies and all over the restaurant's main hall.[93]

These three groups first acted together in late December 1883, when Ōshima and Yamauchi persuaded Jiyūtō member Kuno Kōtarō to join them in a robbery.

Ōshima's group had already been involved in four thefts, Yamauchi's in three. They typically targeted wealthy merchants and farmers and likely used their spoils to maintain a lifestyle that had declined due to Matsukata deflation or the antigambling law, or a combination of both. For Ōshima, Yamauchi, and their men, the robberies were mainly about securing money on which to live and, to a certain extent, protesting against usurious lending. For Kuno, the primary motivation may have been somewhat different. Known as one of the more intellectual Jiyūtō members, Kuno decided that stealing was an acceptable means to raise money for the ultimate goal of overthrowing the government; he would go on to participate in 11 robberies. Regardless of the given justifications and levels of political commitment, illegality and violence were acceptable means to an end for all involved.

Over a dozen robberies later, several of Kuno's Jiyūtō colleagues were among a 12-person group implicated in the murder of two policemen. On a mid-August evening in 1884, a planned theft was foiled by difficulties with a door lock and so the men headed home, reaching the area by the Hirata Bridge around 2:00 A.M. Walking in three separate units, one of them came across two policemen, Nakamura and Katō, who began asking questions. Suddenly, Ōshima fired his pistol and called out to the others, prompting everyone to unsheathe their swords and attack the policemen. They pursued Nakamura and Katō, and some of the men held back the people from the neighborhood who were stirred from their homes by the commotion. Nakamura sustained 19 injuries, seven of which were to his head, and died on the spot. Katō suffered 15 injuries, eight of which were to his head, and died in a nearby rice field.[94]

About a dozen robberies later, police began to discover who was involved in these thefts and to tie them to the murders of Nakamura and Katō. On December 14, 1884, a group robbed the town hall in Nagakusa Village, Chita District, of the tax money stored there, and in the process hurt three and tightly bound five employees. As they were trying to escape, one participant was caught and arrested, revealing and disentangling the whole enterprise that was the Nagoya Incident. Although some thefts were committed in August 1886, most of the main players seem to have been arrested in the aftermath of this robbery.[95]

The Nagoya Incident trial began on February 4, 1887, under the jurisdiction of the Nagoya Court of Grave Offenses. Two weeks later, when the decisions were handed down, 26 of the 29 tried were found guilty of some crime. The most serious of these was manslaughter (*kōsatsu*) to evade a crime committed, for which three men including Ōshima were sentenced to death. Kuno was punished with 15 years of penal servitude for armed robbery with two or more people.[96]

As in the Gunma Incident, the motivations of the *bakuto* leaders and participants were not purely political for they robbed and looted at least in part for their own financial gain. Yet in joining forces with the Aikoku Kōshinsha and the Aichi Jiyūtō, they consciously framed their actions politically even when they need not have had political reasons for their theft. What drew them to their partners in crime were a shared sense of antipathy toward the Meiji state and the willingness and ability to wield violence.

Finally, we return to the Chichibu Incident, with which this chapter opened. Compared to what transpired in Gunma and Nagoya, the movement in Chichibu was a fairly sustained, full-scale rebellion that pitted several thousand rebels against the forces of the Meiji government. The initial group of approximately 1,000 that gathered at the local shrine on November 1 swelled to roughly 3,000 at the height of the uprising and spilled over from Saitama into neighboring Gunma and Nagano Prefectures before it was defeated by citizens' self-defense groups (*jieidan*), police, and government troops.[97]

As in Gunma and Nagoya, the Chichibu Incident was sparked by a confluence of factors—rural poverty worsened by Matsukata deflation and aggravated by usurious lenders, the ideology and organization of the Jiyūtō, and the willingness to use force—all of which were embodied in its leader, *bakuto* Tashiro Eisuke. It was not unprecedented for *bakuto* to be involved in rural, grassroots movements such as the Chichibu Incident. In the 1860s, *bakuto* had participated in what were known as "world renewal rebellions" (*yonaoshi ikki*), or peasant protests in which impoverished farmers, tenants, and agricultural day laborers attacked the more wealthy in the village, as well as usurers, pawnbrokers, and merchants.[98] The Chichibu Incident was, in many ways, a continuation of this story of dislocation in the face of economic change and the desire for "world renewal."[99] But the Chichibu Incident is notable for the political context of the Freedom and People's Rights Movement as well as the prominence of *bakuto* in key roles and the Meiji government's attempt to delegitimize the rebellion through careful construction of *bakuto* and their violence.

Tashiro Eisuke was grounded in the rural community from early in his life. He was born into a family of local leaders in the district of Ōmiya; his father was a village headman and his eldest brother would later fill that post. Although Tashiro would never assume that role, he seems to have taken care of some of the less fortunate in his village. A household register indicates that, in 1880, Tashiro kept two houses with a total of 23 residents, suggesting that he not only supported his immediate family of nine people, which included his wife, Kuni, four sons, a daughter, an adopted son and his wife, but also took in a number of other people as well—likely those who were too poor to support themselves. Tashiro also built ties with the local community through his work as a mediator in disputes, presumably as an unlicensed lawyer (*sanbyaku daigennin*).[100]

As a sericulturist, Tashiro experienced firsthand the hardships born of Matsukata deflation and usurious lending. Tashiro collected wild silkworm cocoons and was affected by the steep downturn in the silk market in the early 1880s, a financial hit for sericulturists that was exacerbated by a poor crop in the spring of 1884. A dire financial situation led Tashiro, like many farmers in the region, to turn to a moneylender, from whom he had borrowed a total of ¥153 by 1883.[101]

Widespread financial distress was the primary motivation behind the formation of the Konmintō (Poor People's Party), which began to take shape in July 1884 to protest against high-interest loans after a petition campaign to freeze outstanding debts had failed.[102] The Konmintō's political stance—demanding a national assembly, tax reduction, and overthrow of the Meiji government—was also heavily influenced by its close relationship to the Jiyūtō, with which it shared many members.[103]

In early September, this emerging Konmintō asked Tashiro Eisuke to serve as its president. Tashiro was approached not just because he was a member of the local community who likely understood financial struggle, but because he already had a reputation for physical prowess. Indeed, Tashiro was recommended for the presidency by Katō Orihei, *bakuto* boss and future vice president of the organization, who stressed Tashiro's willingness to use violence against usurious lenders.[104] Katō himself was a student of judo and a man described in police records as round-faced with a tall and thick stature who allegedly had 30 to 40 henchmen.[105] When Katō had stood before the group at a meeting that summer, he spoke of how Tashiro had killed a usurious lender in Shimo Kagemori Village by breaking the man's neck, and reminded the members gathered that though they might be ashamed of violent death, it was their duty to die for justice. This idea of justice had also been evoked in Katō's use of the phrase "we *kyōkaku*" when he addressed the group, calling upon the *bakuto* language of protecting the weak and crushing the strong.[106] Regardless of whether Tashiro did commit the murder, Katō supported him both for his alignment with the group's views and for his ability to act. And the members who recruited Tashiro were aware of the skills he would bring to leading a possible uprising.[107]

It should be mentioned here that there is debate among historians about whether Tashiro was a *bakuto*. Admittedly, it does not seem that he was a full-time *bakuto* or proprietor of a gambling house. Nonetheless, Tashiro was deeply embedded in this world and presented himself as a *bakuto* boss. In a police interrogation, Tashiro testified that he "like[s] to help the weak and crush the strong" and that he had over 200 henchmen. And a court would later note that he was known in his rural circle as a *kyōkaku*. It is certainly possible that coercion was involved in Tashiro's testimony and that the courts were invested in labeling him as unsavory (although this would have been more effective had they used the term "bakuto" instead of "kyōkaku"). Yet Tashiro used this language of Robin Hood-like justice in Konmintō meetings, and those in the community seem to have known him as "Ōmiya's *kyōkaku.*" He had served 60 days of imprisonment with hard labor (*chōeki*) in early 1884 for an unidentified crime (which the *Yomiuri shinbun* argued was a gambling conviction), and known *bakuto* were allegedly among Tashiro's henchmen.[108] Regardless of the extent to which Tashiro was a *bakuto,* it is clear that he acted like, and was perceived as, such—particularly when it came to his ability and willingness to wield violence.

Tashiro Eisuke assumed the presidency of the Konmintō at its official birth on September 7 when the four demands of the organization were clearly articulated: "(1) Due to usurious lending, fortunes are declining and many people are having difficulty making a living, so we urge creditors to implement a 10-year freeze on, and a 40-year amortization of, debts; (2) to reduce school fees, we urge the prefectural office to close schools for three years; (3) we petition the Home Ministry for a reduction of miscellaneous taxes; and (4) we urge village officials to reduce village expenses."[109] Although these four principles dealt with financial matters, Tashiro also expressed a political dimension to the group's concerns that was a direct challenge to state authority from the local to the national level. Standing before those assembled, the new president allegedly declared, "This is a truly important matter [as outlined in the four principles]. We must oppose the country (*kuni*) and the prefecture and the village and police power."[110]

When Tashiro embarked on his presidential duties in earnest in mid-October, it was clear that his ability to wield force would be an asset to the Konmintō. By this time, the group had increased its membership; approximately 100 farmers had joined the group in September, and by the following month, 30 of the 84 towns and villages in Chichibu had selected Konmintō representatives. More significant, they had realized the limitations of legal action and resolved to carry out an armed uprising.[111] Tashiro began preparing for the rebellion the day after this decision was made, planning with Katō the procurement of funds and ammunition. On the night of October 14, in a theft not unlike those of the Nagoya Incident, Tashiro led an attack on the homes of two wealthy men in Yokoze Village—binding the people present and then threatening them with a sword while they were robbed. On the night of October 15, a group targeted a home in Nishiiri Village. Tashiro then turned his attention from funds to recruitment and he spent the following eight or nine days touring various villages to enlist rebels.[112] It is difficult to say how many of these rebels were *bakuto,* but gamblers do make sporadic appearances in materials on the rebellion. The official Jiyūtō history of the incident names *bakuto,* after farmers, as participants.[113]

The crowd before which Tashiro stood on November 1, true to its name of Konmingun, was organized as a military. The officers of the Konmintō took on

military titles—Commander Tashiro Eisuke and Vice Commander Katō Orihei—
and those assembled were broken into battalions and companies, each with com-
manding officers. Read aloud was a five-article document on military discipline,
which forbade looting money and goods for oneself, violating women, drinking excessively, committing arson and other violent acts out of personal revenge,
and disobeying the orders of a commander. Also pronounced was the five-article
statement of aims, essentially instructions for the army, which included permission to murder moneylenders if negotiations failed and a directive to free any
captured leaders by attacking the police station.[114]

After the ceremony ended, Tashiro took the helm of the army that was then
divided into two battalions that approached the town of Ogano from opposite
directions. On their way, Tashiro's Second Battalion burned and stole from the
home of a usurious lender in Shimo Ogano Village, and the First Battalion set
fire to the home of a usurer in Shimo Yoshida Village. When the two battalions
met in Ogano, they attacked police stations, local government offices, and the
homes of a handful of usurers while a dispatched guerrilla unit successfully hit
outlying targets. On the morning of November 2 around 6:00 A.M., the army
left Ogano and headed southeast toward Ōmiya. Reaching their destination by
around noon, the rebels burned the homes of usurers, rushed and occupied the
district office, robbed wealthy and elite families of approximately ¥3,000, forced
merchant families to provide them with food, and broke into police stations and
the courts. That night, the Konmingun officers held a meeting in the Ōmiya district office where they spoke of causing turbulence in the whole country and
establishing a new government (shinsei).[115]

The next day, however, the resolve and skills of the rebel army were tested by
the forces of the Meiji government, namely police troops and several military
police units.[116] With news of their impending arrival, the Konmingun divided
into three battalions. The First Battalion smashed its way through a number of
villages, procuring funds and dispatching a guerrilla troop to a nearby mountain.
The Second Battalion exchanged fire with police and military police forces around
3:00 or 4:00 P.M. and triumphed, but only because the military police had brought
the wrong bullets for their guns. The Third Battalion, under Tashiro, eventually
met up with the first and established its headquarters at an inn in Minano.

At this point, the situation seemed dire for the Konmingun. Leaders were
missing or injured, a citizens' self-defense group was in pursuit, and government
troops were encircling the area. In the afternoon of November 4, the Konmingun
officers at Minano dissolved the command of the army and scattered. Tashiro
successfully evaded capture until November 15, when he was arrested in Kuroya
Village around 3:30 in the morning, gagged, and put into a bamboo cage used for
transporting criminals (tōmarukago).[117]

Although November 4 marked the dissolution of the original Konmingun command and the end of Tashiro's leadership, other *bakuto* emerged to become key figures in the second, guerrilla phase of the Chichibu Incident. On November 5, over 100 rebels regrouped into one unit and for the next five days fought from Saitama to Gunma and Nagano Prefectures against approximately 80 police and 120 garrison troops that had been dispatched from Tokyo.[118] This guerrilla group was commanded by newly installed leaders: Kikuchi Kanbei as president, Sakamoto Sōsaku as vice president, Inano Bunjirō as chief of staff, as well as Arai Torakichi, Yokota Shūsaku, and Kobayashi Yūzō. Almost all of this second generation of leaders were either *bakuto* or had prior gambling convictions.[119]

On November 6, replete with new recruits, this Konmingun guerrilla unit faced off against a self-defense group on the Nakagawa riverbank for approximately 50 minutes until the rebels were forced to flee. On November 7 and 8, the Konmingun unit continued its recruitment efforts, killed a policeman it had captured, and continued smashings in village after village while various subunits attacked loan offices and usurious lenders. By this point, the guerrilla group included a swordsman squad and a smashing corps (*uchikowashi-gumi*) which called itself the "freedom unit." In the end, however, the guerrilla tactics did not win out over the sheer strength of government forces. On November 9, the rebels were overwhelmed by Nagano Prefecture police and the Takasaki garrison; 36 people were killed, 200 were arrested, and approximately 200 fled. Those who escaped were defeated the following afternoon.[120]

After it had marshaled force to put down the Chichibu rebels, the Meiji state then relied on its legal arm to punish those who had challenged it so blatantly. Courts in Saitama Prefecture alone punished 296 people for grave offenses, 448 people for minor offenses, and 2,642 people with fines. On February 19, 1885, Tashiro Eisuke was sentenced to death by the Urawa Court of Grave Offenses; he was one of seven who received the death penalty.[121]

While the state labeled the Chichibu rebels as criminals, newspapers sympathetic with the Meiji government had attempted to delegitimize their actions throughout the rebellion by portraying them as undesirable elements. One way these newspapers exaggerated the insidious nature of the incident was to highlight the fact that Tashiro and others were *bakuto* in the hope that this label would carry a negative connotation and that all of the rebels would be criminalized by association.[122] Some publications were explicit in their criticism of *bakuto*. The *Tōkyō nichinichi shinbun*, for example, depicted the *bakuto* as base, at home in low society. By calling them "villainous gamblers and radical wanderers," the newspaper conjured up images of Tokugawa-era *rōnin* and *mushuku*, implying that the *bakuto* rebels were throwbacks to feudal times.[123] *Bakuto* were also castigated by some who seemed to have little connection to the government.

Tanaka Sen'ya, a priest at a temple in Shimo Yoshida Village, denigrated them as an uneducated lot who did not understand morality and did not respect imperial government.[124]

Bakuto leadership and participation in the Chichibu Incident were also condemned by the *Yūbin hōchi shinbun,* a newspaper that, though friendly to the Freedom and People's Rights Movement, was a mouthpiece for the Jiyūtō's rival, the Rikken Kaishintō (Constitutional Reform Party). The editors were scathing in their coverage of the rebellion: "If the disturbance was really conducted by men in alliance with gamblers, their actions might be regarded as those of a gang of robbers who must...be sooner or later brought to trial and punished."[125] Another article from the same newspaper suggested that the deeds in loan offices were burned "for the purpose of evading their [the rebels'] liability," and that the protesters simply "sought the opportunity of creating a disturbance in the hope of promoting their personal interest."[126] Although it is true that the rebels did not wish to repay their loans and were forwarding their own agenda, the choice of words such as "evade" and "personal interest" in conjunction with the characterization of the protesters as "unprincipled gamblers" conveyed a decidedly negative view of the Chichibu participants and the incident as a whole. As would be expected, this kind of portrayal did not appear in publications that were more sympathetic to the Jiyūtō. The *Kaishin shinbun,* for example, fervently disagreed with those who claimed the rebels were simply swept along by radicals and violent *bakuto.*[127]

This kind of effort to criminalize the unruly was not uncommon in emerging modern nation-states. In Italy, for example, the government's attempt to consolidate power after unification in 1861 met considerable resistance, especially in Sicily, from those who were upset by higher taxes, unemployment, and conscription. The Italian government, rather than deal with the underlying causes of unrest, focused more on criminalizing resistant Sicilians as immoral participants in a widespread and conspiratorial organization, or "the Mafia." The first official reference to something called a "mafia" appeared in an April 1865 letter to the minister of the interior from a Count Filippo Gualterio, the prefect of Palermo who was overwhelmed by the political disorder in the province and was likely searching for a scapegoat. Most commentators at the time insisted that there was likely no "Mafia" in the sense of a vast criminal society or network.[128]

Not all newspapers singled out *bakuto* for criticism. Some were just as critical of the Meiji government's part in instigating the rebellion, namely for its handling of *bakuto* prior to 1884. The *Chōya shinbun* did not pull punches in characterizing *bakuto* as a poison and gambling as socially disruptive, but also implied the incident would not have happened if the government had tried to control *bakuto* earlier.[129] A number of newspapers placed blame on what they saw as an unreasonable crackdown on *bakuto* under the 1884 national antigambling law, which created a population of impoverished and unemployed *bakuto* who subsequently instigated the uprising. The *Meiji nippō,* for example, argued that the new gambling law had, counter to its intent, pushed the *bakuto* toward committing atrocious crimes.[130]

It is unclear how the journalistic discourse around *bakuto* and the Chichibu Incident was read. The audience for these newspapers may very well have agreed that *bakuto,* a societal ill, had caused unnecessary political grief for the new Meiji government. Yet it could not be argued that there was a widespread criminalization of *bakuto,* for they had been embraced by many grassroots members of the rural community as well as the political leadership of the Jiyūtō and many participants of the Freedom and People's Rights Movement. The Meiji state certainly could not claim to have established an orthodox view of the *bakuto* as troublemaking lowlifes. Indeed, the ambiguous status and varied perceptions of *bakuto* would help them and their political violence endure.

By the mid-1880s, violence intended to overthrow the government and the existing political order—be it through a series of assassinations or full-scale rebellions—had shown itself to be virtually futile in the face of a modernizing state that was consolidating its power. In many ways, the new Meiji regime was adept at quelling violent threats to its rule. Rebellious ex-samurai, with their connections to pre-Restoration *shishi,* were put down rather handily, as were the violent incidents of the Freedom and People's Rights Movement of which *bakuto* were a part.

Yet *shishi* and *bakuto,* each in their own way, would manage to survive beyond the early Meiji years. The alleged patriotism of the *shishi* would continue to be evoked as justification for rebellious and antistate violence, some of which were emulations of *shishi* tactics, if on a different scale. This *shishi* model of intertwining patriotism and violence would have profound consequences for the direction of Japanese politics in the early decades of the twentieth century. *Bakuto* of the 1880s were transitioning with the times, and some were playing the role of violence specialists in politics that were a hybrid of early modern and modern strategies and aims. The violent incidents of the 1880s that were transformative for *bakuto* were part protest in the early modern mold and part modern, democratic movement. As *bakuto* did not desperately cling to the Tokugawa past and began to refashion themselves, they helped ensure that they would remain relevant in politics. The open question in this second decade of the Meiji period was whether they would continue to be grassroots, antistate violence specialists.

The resilience of *shishi* in political imaginations and the emergence of *bakuto* as political actors reveal a Meiji state that was capable of combating the most immediate and violent challenges to its rule through a combination of military, legal, and cultural means, but that did not exercise pervasive control over violent elements. Indeed, the strength of the early Meiji state should not be exaggerated. Especially in its first two decades, the Meiji government was in a tenuous position as it attempted to preside over the unprecedented and unpredictable experience of modern state formation. This process may have been unrelenting, but it was not certain, especially from the perspective of a regime that had taken power by force and now had to delegitimize the very kind of violent rebellion in which it had just engaged.[131] The inability of the Meiji state to discipline all who were violent should not, however, be seen as a failing—stifling all violence would require a militaristic state; most achieve a balance somewhere between absolutist repression and chaotic disorder. I interpret Max Weber's well-known theory about the state's monopoly on the use of force not as total control but as a baseline, however ambiguous, at which the state can manage to quell the most fundamental challenges to its rule.[132] The Meiji state did exercise this monopoly, but because it did not and could not prevent all violent political acts, the violence of the modern state's foundational moment necessarily became a part of that which followed.

In the newly unified Italy, the state struggled much more than its Meiji counterpart to uproot opposition, violent or otherwise, to its attempts at centralization. Historians have argued about why this was so, especially when it came to incorporating the South, variously citing as explanations the failure of leaders to embrace the subaltern, government coercion, and the lack of support from local elites. The shortcomings, some would even say failure, of state formation and nation building motivated, and was simultaneously exacerbated by, a turn to severe military repression; such measures did not address underlying social and economic challenges and did not bolster the foundations for state control in local communities. This would have the consequence, among others, of encouraging those in the South, and Sicily in particular, to turn increasingly to powerful non-state actors (mafias) for protection and security.[133]

Unlike the Italian state, which hoped that liberal government would somehow lift up southern Italy and was unperturbed about using physical force to establish and maintain power, the struggle in 1790s France was between liberty and security. When the directorial regime was created by the constitution of 1795, its focus was the construction of a liberal democratic republic. And in the face of political disorder (worsened by violence such as fighting between leftist Jacobin extremists and the royalist right, foreign war, and banditry), it lacked the institutions to establish order and implemented measures that privileged liberty over security. The resulting persistence of challenges to the regime over the next two years prompted the Second Directory to turn away from the rule of law and toward purges, summary justice, and the military. What took shape was a security state that arguably marked the end of the French Revolution and served as the foundation for Napoleon Bonaparte's dictatorship.[134]

Because the Meiji Restoration in Japan was not carried out in the name of liberty or democracy and there was no expectation that the new regime would be a liberal democracy, the Meiji government avoided—for a moment—France's challenge of establishing a liberal democratic republic in the face of violent opposition. Yet as the Freedom and People's Rights Movement gained momentum over the 1870s and the Meiji government committed itself to parliamentary and constitutional government, violence would become very much wrapped up with Japan's democratic experiment.

2

Violent Democracy

Ruffians and the Birth of Parliamentary Politics

On February 11, 1889, the Meiji Constitution was promulgated in a carefully orchestrated ceremony intended to exhibit Japan's emergence among the politically "civilized" nations of the late nineteenth-century world. In a historical moment intended to symbolize enlightened politics, the Emperor Meiji, outfitted in military uniform, stood in front of his European-style throne to pronounce the Constitution of the Empire of Japan before a small audience of foreign and Japanese dignitaries adorned in formal Western dress.[1] This scene, crafted to epitomize regal and gentlemanly politics, optimistically portended political stability and order in a new era of constitutional and parliamentary government.

Contrary to this idealized vision of politics, the reality of demanding wider political participation and implementing the constitution's more democratic provisions was a violent process that was often destabilizing and disorderly. As with all representative forms of government, actual practice was not as inclusive or egalitarian as it might have been. In Meiji Japan, the oligarchs' reluctance to share political influence with their citizens and a certain insecurity about their own power made them move toward constitutional and parliamentary government only with hesitation, and more out of a desire to be viewed as "a member of the family of Western constitutional states" than to welcome new voices into politics.[2] The drawn-out process of writing a constitution in the 1880s and severe restrictions on who could vote encouraged the use of violence by those who refused to be sidelined by the Meiji oligarchs' attempt to manipulate politics. And the oligarchs' decision to fight back with state violence only added fuel to the fire, exacerbating political volatility and helping violence become endemic in political life.

What took shape in the 1880s and 1890s was a political system and culture best characterized as a "violent democracy," in which violence and democracy coexisted in an uneasy and sometimes contradictory relationship. The term "violent democracy" has been popularized by political philosopher Daniel Ross, whose conviction that "the origin and heart of democracy is essentially violent" resonates with the case of Meiji Japan. Ross captures well the irony of violence giving birth to democracy; in his view, the establishment of democracy is always and necessarily violent, and this violent foundational moment then "haunts everything that follows it."[3] In Meiji Japan, the violent foundational moment was the Freedom and People's Rights Movement, and what came out of the 1880s was indeed a democracy. It is true that there were restrictions on political participation, a constitution bestowed on the people by the emperor, and limited notions of popular sovereignty. But scholars such as Irokawa Daikichi and Roger Bowen have demonstrated that grassroots activism was a progressive force in Meiji politics, and historian Banno Junji has used the phrase "Meiji democracy" to underscore the significance of popular energies that pushed for a constitution, political representation, and expanded political participation.[4] By the 1890s, Japan could boast a constitution, an elected parliamentary body in the House of Representatives, and general elections.

Politics of this time were also violent, with young people's rights activists of the 1880s willing to use physical force in the name of democracy and liberalism. These *sōshi*, as they came to be known, developed a reputation for roughness and ruffianism as they wielded violence as political protectors and agitators. When the Freedom and People's Rights Movement lost momentum around 1890, some *sōshi* exported their violence to Korea and China as *tairiku rōnin*, or continental adventurers. Others remained in the domestic political realm, undergoing their own transformation as they became less activist and more professional ruffian. The violence of *sōshi* and *tairiku rōnin*, present at the creation of parliamentary government and empire, became an inextricable part of the practice of modern politics. Why ruffianism did not abate, but in fact proliferated, with the inauguration of parliamentary democracy is of central concern here, as are questions of what this violence meant for Japan's early democratic experiment and how it "haunted" democratic politics in the decades that followed.

From Activist to Ruffian: *Sōshi* in the 1880s

The word "sōshi"—literally, manly warrior—became a part of the political lexicon in the early 1880s to describe the young, politically engaged men who took up the cause of expanding popular rights. This new and flattering appellation was embraced by those of the Freedom and People's Rights Movement and the Jiyūtō (Liberal Party), with at least two of their ranks claiming to have coined the term. Jiyūtō member Hoshi Tōru allegedly recommended the word in lieu of "shishi," the late Tokugawa-era "men of spirit" discussed in the previous chapter. And another politician, Ozaki Yukio, recounts how he suggested the term as a replacement for the stale "yūshika," or supporter.[5] Regardless of who originally conceived of the *sōshi* label, it was popularized by men like Hoshi and Ozaki and maintained a positive ring for a large part of the 1880s, at least in popular rights circles. One *sōshi*, writing his dying words in 1886, venerated his fellow political youth: "We *sōshi* have already cast away our fortunes for the sake of the nation (*kokka*), and even as soon as tomorrow too we will sacrifice our lives for freedom."[6] Books published around this time spoke highly of *sōshi*; one characterized them as the vitality (*genki*) of the country.[7]

It took time, however, before the use of "sōshi" as a replacement for "shishi" or "yūshika" became widespread. Through the mid-1880s, some newspapers continued to refer to political youth as "shishi," usually to highlight their position outside the government or to connect them to the noble patriotism of their late Tokugawa predecessors.[8] Sometimes the three terms were treated as interchangeable.[9] At least one newspaper, the liberal and antigovernment *Chōya shinbun*, merged the two words to create the neologism "shishi sōshi."[10] This mishmash of terminology may have stemmed from confusion about who exactly the *sōshi* were or, alternatively, from a realization of the relatively diverse backgrounds of these youth. It also reflected the hybridity of early *sōshi* who were much like their *shishi* predecessors in their political activism, skepticism of the government, and patriotism, and yet entirely unlike the late Tokugawa youth in their progressive championing of popular rights.

The first phase of *sōshi* activity, spanning the first half of the 1880s, was indeed characterized by a kind of hybridity. *Sōshi* were similar to their Bakumatsu counterparts in their turn to the symbolic act of assassination or small-scale revolts to destabilize the governing regime. Like *shishi*, they were not violence specialists in the sense that they were wielding physical force only for themselves, driven by their desire to change the political order.[11] Yet *sōshi* were new and different in their embrace of a more democratic vision. Like the *bakuto* (gamblers) discussed in the previous chapter, they participated in the violent incidents (*gekka jiken*) of the Freedom and People's Rights Movement.[12] In the Kabasan Incident of September 1884, for example, *sōshi* rebels (called "shishi" by some historians) planned to assassinate key Meiji officials with bombs to pave the way for the establishment of a more democratic form of government. This was considered retaliation against those leaders who had clamped down on the Fukushima Incident of 1882, in which *sōshi* had criticized the ruling clique for its abuse of state power and suppression of free speech. In the Osaka Incident of 1885, activists planned an invasion of Korea to install in power the Japan-friendly reformist

Kim Ok-kyun. *Sōshi* were responsible for helping to procure funds and make weapons for the effort; those put in charge of weaponry gathered at a house in the Bunkyō ward of Tokyo, disguised it as a blacksmith's workshop, and secretly made bombs.[13]

This phase of *sōshi* violence gradually came to an end in the second half of the 1880s, mainly due to the arrest and punishment of its participants. After the Kabasan Incident, over a dozen rebels were tried and seven were sentenced to death; with the Osaka Incident, over 100 were arrested and more than 30 participants convicted.[14] The state's crackdown on these *sōshi* helped deplete the popular rights movement of those willing to turn to violence, dissuade those who were considering such action, and demonstrate the futility of mass uprisings or revolts. Perhaps more important, symbolic assassination of a few key Meiji leaders became less meaningful as political participation broadened with the opening of prefectural assemblies, the rise of politicians who belonged to political parties, and the establishment of the Diet. With political power no longer concentrated in a handful of men, assassinating one leader would not be as effective in instigating change or reform. And the move toward a more participatory system of government rendered a democratic overthrow less pressing.

The second phase of *sōshi* activity was marked by a different form of violence that became more common in the late 1880s: ruffianism consisting of brawls, fistfights, destruction of property, threats, intimidation, and the like. The proliferation of this kind of violence, as opposed to the tactics of assassination, has numerous explanations. One has to do with intent. *Sōshi* of this time were seeking to influence political behavior, not fundamentally change the political order. An undecided elector might be coerced by the fist, but it would simply not serve the *sōshi*'s interests to kill him and eliminate a potential vote.

The expansion of political participation as well as the more public nature of politics also fed into the growth of ruffianism. As political power became more diffuse, extinguishing all of one's political opponents was inconceivable, but it was still effective and possible to try and influence political outcomes through ruffianism. Physical force was thus no longer reserved for prominent Meiji leaders or local figures but found targets in a larger body of candidates, aspiring politicians, party members, and prefectural and national parliamentarians. Also, as politics become more popular and more visible—with its speech meetings (*enzetsukai*), debates, and election campaigns—there were more opportunities to wield violence as a political tool. As public political events became more ordinary and everyday occurrences, so too did the violence that accompanied them. It became standard practice for *sōshi* to storm and disturb political gatherings, threaten and physically intimidate political opponents, and protect political allies from the violence of antagonistic *sōshi*.

Sōshi ruffianism was fostered by continuing constraints on political participation as well. Restrictions on who could run and vote in elections meant that the body of politicians, though larger than in the past, was still small enough that *sōshi* influence could be potentially meaningful. In a different vein, restraints created a pool of young men who wanted to participate in the nation's political life but were left out of the formal political process. Youth who had limited outlets for their political energies could be seduced into becoming *sōshi,* expressing through violence what they could not at the ballot box.

Ruffianism was not only encouraged by these systemic factors, but was also actively cultivated by popular rights leaders who fostered and organized *sōshi* violence. The Jiyūtō had trained *sōshi* from earlier in the decade, deciding at an 1883 meeting that party contributions would be used to found a school to teach fencing. This funding may have supported the establishment in 1884 of the Yūitsukan, a school for literary and military arts attached to the Jiyūtō headquarters in Tokyo. The Yūitsukan was the training ground for party *sōshi* and organized a number of political speech meetings to discuss freedom. Members included some who had participated in the Osaka Incident, and the school was headed by Naitō Roichi (mentioned in conjunction with the Nagoya Incident in the previous chapter). Other schools included those in the Santama region, just outside Tokyo, where movement leaders ostensibly covered both literary and military skills, but emphasized physical strengthening.[15] The Kantōkai (Kantō Association), for example, was an organization consisting mainly of Santama *sōshi.* In the late 1880s, various *sōshi* groups and associations proliferated. The Ōsaka Sōshi Kurabu (Osaka Sōshi Club) was founded in April 1888, and in the spring of 1889, the Tōkyō Sōshi Kurabu (Tokyo Sōshi Club) ran a newspaper advertisement to recruit *sōshi,* specifically targeting those who had criminal records. Other groups were formed farther outside the capital, including one large league of 350 *sōshi* in Aomori Prefecture.[16]

In general, the organization of *sōshi* was fairly loose and varied. Some were directly connected to a political party, as members of its *ingaidan* (pressure group). The Jiyūtō, for example, formed an *ingaidan* in the 1880s that seems to have coordinated *sōshi* ruffianism to serve party interests. Other groups, clubs, and associations were more informally associated with a political party, if at all. The documentary record on the recruitment of *sōshi* is frustratingly sparse, but it does seem as though there were key leaders, politicians or political bosses who rallied local youth to join these various organizations. At least in the case of the Jiyūtō *sōshi,* allegiances to a particular politician could be more defining than party affiliation.

Sōshi violence was fanned during the late 1880s by political contention in the form of the Movement for a United Front (Daidō Danketsu Undō), a sustained effort from 1886 to 1890 to shore up the power of the more progressive and liberal political parties such as the Jiyūtō and Shinpotō (Progressive Party) in preparation for the inauguration of the new national parliamentary system in 1890. Hand in hand with this endeavor was the Movement to Memorialize Three Important Items (Sandai Jiken Kenpaku Undō) of 1887, which proved to be pivotal in bringing sustained national attention to *sōshi*.[17] Provoked by the revelation that Foreign Minister Inoue Kaoru had suggested only minimal changes to the "unequal treaties" Japan had signed with a handful of Western powers in the 1850s, angry popular rights activists demanded more substantial treaty revision. Also on their list of "three important items" were reduction of the land tax and greater freedom of speech and assembly.

As part of these movements, *sōshi* organized and participated in frequent large-scale public gatherings in the latter half of 1887. These often took the form of *undōkai,* demonstration marches that incorporated sports contests, costume parades, and drinking parties. Typically, several hundred *sōshi* would come together by word of mouth or handbills or newspaper announcements, carry flags with slogans written on them, and take part in public displays that were both pleasurable and political. At an *undōkai* in Kyoto on November 25, for example, 150 to 160 *sōshi* marched while waving red and white banners and flags, shouting "banzai" to the imperial house and to freedom.[18] These *undōkai* tested the Meiji government with their political content and with their form, for the multifaceted nature of the gatherings was an attempt to circumvent the Public Assembly Ordinance (Shūkai Jōrei) issued in April 1880 to control the Freedom and People's Rights Movement by, among other things, prohibiting outdoor political meetings and political activity by students.[19] The *undōkai* also reflected the ways physicality was valued and cultivated in *sōshi,* with the extent to which sport, the exercise and training of the body, was a part of these events.[20]

The physical prowess of *sōshi* was also witnessed at various political events where they served as agitators and bodyguards, often for a particular politician who orchestrated their violence. Hoshi Tōru, part of a regrouping Jiyūtō and a leader of the Movement for a United Front, was one politician with his own retinue of ruffians. In an October 1887 incident, Hoshi let personal antagonism overwhelm his political goal of liberal unity when he unleashed his *sōshi* on Shinpotō politician and publisher of the *Tōkyō Yokohama mainichi shinbun,* Numa Morikazu. At a joint public meeting of the Jiyūtō and Shinpotō, Hoshi was allegedly goaded by a drunk Numa—when the better pedigreed Numa insulted Hoshi by calling him a peasant, a shouted verbal exchange ensued. The lights were then switched off and Hoshi called in his *sōshi,* who surrounded Numa and beat him with brass candlesticks until the police arrived to stop them. Numa died as a result of the injuries he sustained and, in protest, the Shinpotō did not send a representative to the next scheduled meeting of the two parties. Apart from this political fallout, Hoshi seems to have suffered little for this assault on Numa.[21] Such lack of legal consequence only encouraged the self-perpetuating phenomenon—as more politicians recruited *sōshi*, those who did not yet benefit from their services found themselves in need of private protection. The resulting prevalence of *sōshi* did not neutralize violence, but created a more highly charged atmosphere in which political divisions were punctuated by physical fights.

The movement gained so much momentum by the end of 1887 that it raised the eyebrows of the Meiji government. At a national meeting of supporters in November, speeches vociferously attacked the government. And in December, a public show of national support was planned after organizer Gotō Shōjirō's repeated attempts to submit a petition to the emperor were rebuffed. Activists intended to assemble 3,000 *sōshi* in Tokyo for a demonstration in front of the imperial palace to demand the cessation of talks regarding the "unequal treaties." *Sōshi* did trickle into the capital, though their numbers were only about 300 due in part to poor organization.[22] But the presence of several hundred *sōshi* in Tokyo was enough to worry a government already shaken by the resignation of Foreign Minister Inoue in August over the treaty issue and concerned about the strength and escalation of the progressive movement, especially as the curtain was rising on parliamentary government. Thus on December 25, 1887, the government issued and put into immediate effect the Peace Preservation Ordinance—seven articles restricting political assembly and expression. The idea of such constraints was not new, as the government had already enacted the Press Ordinance of 1875 and the Public Assembly Ordinance of 1880 in an attempt to contain the Freedom and People's Rights Movement. A desire to clamp down on armed *sōshi* in particular was a provision of article 5, which empowered individual districts to forbid the wearing, transportation, or trafficking of "small arms, pistols, gunpowder, swords or sword canes [canes with blades set in them]"—*sōshi* weapons of choice—without the permission of local authorities. More reflective of *sōshi* pressure on the government, and more pertinent to the movement's demonstrations in Tokyo, was article 4, which allowed the Metropolitan Police with the permission of the home minister to remove from a three-*ri* (approximately seven-mile) perimeter around the imperial palace anybody deemed to be "plotting sedition or breaching the public peace." Under article 4, more than 500 politicians and *sōshi* were thrown out of the capital, some escorted by local police out of the designated zone. Although the Peace Preservation Ordinance did manage to rid central Tokyo of antigovernment activists, it did not dampen their enthusiasm or energy. Some *sōshi* simply retreated to nearby Yokohama and Hachiōji.[23]

With the promulgation of the constitution on February 11, the Peace Preservation Ordinance was temporarily lifted, though not rescinded, and those who had been imprisoned for political crimes under it or the Publication or Press

Ordinances were granted amnesty and released.[24] In addition, Tokugawa-era *shishi* leader and teacher Yoshida Shōin as well as *shizoku* rebel Saigō Takamori were among those posthumously pardoned. Others, including *bakuto* participants in the violent incidents of the Freedom and People's Rights Movement, were given amnesty and were released or had their sentences reduced. In short, enemies of the Meiji state were pardoned, even venerated, at the moment constitutional law was born. It has been argued by historian Kimura Naoe that these amnesties were an act of generosity by the Meiji government rooted in confidence about its ability to triumph over these antagonistic, violent elements—the law and the state and its legitimacy, it was believed, would prevail.[25]

Yet *sōshi* ruffianism continued unabated. In Osaka that very month, after a celebration of the promulgation of the constitution (complete with much drinking), approximately 100 *sōshi* stormed a public works company and the office of the *Ōsaka mainichi shinbun*. Several months later in Okayama Prefecture, *sōshi* entered the prefectural assembly hall and shouted from the gallery.[26] *Sōshi* also added duels, or the threat of duels, to their arsenal of political weapons, delivering to their opponents letters requesting one-on-one combat. The prefectural governors of Tokushima and Okayama were both targets of challenges, and between March and April of 1889, recently inducted cabinet minister Gotō Shōjirō received 12 such letters. It is not clear whether any of these showdowns took place, but at least in Aomori Prefecture, *sōshi* so insistently dared prefectural assembly members to fight and pressured them to resign that by 1889, politicians would vacation in faraway places or shut themselves inside their homes.[27] Even months after the promulgation of the constitution, enforcement of the Peace Preservation Ordinance seemed uneven at best; in October 1889, *sōshi* from Tokyo and Yokohama were able to make rounds to the cabinet ministers to submit a petition regarding the treaty revision issue.[28]

By the late 1880s, *sōshi* had become such a presence in political life that it became possible to define a prototypical *sōshi* by what Kimura Naoe has called *pratique* (*jissen*, or practice) such as clothes, hairstyle, and manner of speech. As a *Mainichi shinbun* article from May 1889 explained, *sōshi* could be identified by their rough demeanor, complete with dirty and torn clothes, long hair, loud voices, and woolen hats that were so old and shapeless that they conveniently drooped over the wearer's face.[29] A *sōshi* would also bear weapons such as sword canes, swords, and pistols. And they carried themselves in a certain way; as one former member of a *sōshi* group, songwriter Soeda Azenbō, observed, they were "rough (*bankara*) and unrefined and walked around with their shoulders thrown back twirling a large club."[30] Historian Jason Karlin has suggested that this roughness was a "'masculinized' masculinity," or an "authentic masculinity," that served as a counterpoint to the more feminine masculinity of the Westernized Japanese gentleman.[31]

Variations on this prototype could indicate a *sōshi*'s regional and perhaps political affiliation as well. *Sōshi* from Kanazawa in central Japan were known as
hakama sōshi because they wore short, pleated, culotte-like trousers (*hakama*)
as well as extremely high wooden sandals. They wrapped their unusually wide
sashes low, carried especially fat sticks, and held their left shoulders high. The
Santama *sōshi,* a specific type of Kanazawa *sōshi,* were outfitted with headbands
made out of white cloth, wore sashes, and carried sword canes about two *shaku*
(approximately two feet) in length, as well as sticks, clubs, and pistols. *Sōshi*
from Shinano were known as *buranketto sōshi* (blanket *sōshi*) because they wore coarse
blankets when cold. Length of clothes could also indicate political affiliation.[32]

Sōshi not only had identifiable styles of dress and manner, they also promoted
their own culture—one that was both politically conscious and often violent.
They performed political plays (*sōshi shibai*) that were critical of the government
and wrote popular songs (*enka*) such as one from around 1887 that included the
lyrics, "Advance the nation's interest and the people's welfare, restore power to the
people! If not, then dynamite—bang!"[33]

This culture of roughness overlapped with, and was encouraged by, the masculine bravado of student ruffians (*kōha*). As historian David Ambaras has described them, these particular ruffians were "a type of student who concentrated
on physical activities like jūdō,
adopted a swaggering, aggressive
style, and rejected contact with
women out of fear of becoming weak and effeminate."[34] This
kind of deportment dated back
to the early Meiji years, when
certain students fashioned themselves after *shishi,* and was seen
among those who became activists in the Freedom and People's
Rights Movement. By the turn
of the century, student violence

2.1. Two types of Meiji-era *sōshi*
(May 1889). A typical Kanazawa
sōshi on the left, with characteristic tall wooden sandals, fat
stick, and high left shoulder. On
the right, a *sōshi* from Shinano,
also known as a "blanket *sōshi*"
(*buranketto sōshi*). From *Mainichi
shinbun,* May 28, 1889.

in Tokyo was public and commonplace: "Many [student ruffians] carried short swords, cane swords, or knives, and 'showdowns' among groups of students were, in one critic's words, 'virtually a fashion.'"[35]

Sōshi were unified by this culture that marked them as young and masculine. But aside from their age and gender, they were a varied lot with different backgrounds and motivations. It is a shame that a paucity of sources does not allow for a fuller understanding of the sociology of *sōshi*. Issues of class and educational background are too clouded to discuss with confidence, and other questions about the composition of *sōshi* can be dealt with only tentatively. *Sōshi* of the 1880s seem to have been a mix of former samurai, farmers, merchants, industrialists, *bakuto*, and the kind of students described above, as well as drifters and toughs with no fixed occupation.[36] And so it could be that many *sōshi* of this decade were part-time ruffians who split their energies between their political lives and their work or education. Those who had another occupation would not have had to depend on ruffianism for their livelihood because they had another source of income, be it agriculture, business, or gambling.

As the Freedom and People's Rights Movement lost its drive at the tail end of the 1880s, however, the character of *sōshi* began to shift. Now known more for their ruffianism than their commitment to popular rights, the ranks of *sōshi* may have swelled with an increasing number of young men who were simply interested in making some money by wielding violence, who were more attracted by the paycheck or even the excitement of violence than political reform. With the Santama *sōshi*, for example, the farmers and landowners who had been popular rights activists would gradually be eclipsed over the next several decades by a more "yakuza-like" type of ruffian, antisocial idlers who were the second and third sons of landlords.[37] To argue that this was a generalized trend that extended beyond the Santama *sōshi* would be speculative, but a supposedly new kind of *sōshi* did become an object of criticism in certain magazines and newspapers in the late 1880s. One intellectual opinion magazine, *Kokumin no tomo* (The Nation's Friend), ran a series in July and August 1887 on the youth and politics of the "new Japan" and dedicated the second installment to considering the place of *sōshi* in contemporary politics. The editorial acknowledged that *sōshi* had played an important role in the first decade of the Meiji period as youth motivated by their sense of justice and humanity to bring about political change. However, their essentially destructive behavior, though well suited to Bakumatsu Japan, was now considered utterly inappropriate in the constructive era of Meiji's second decade. With the dawn of the "new Japan," *sōshi* with their reckless plans and unfair methods were seen as unnecessary, and it was hoped that they would simply disappear from the political world. Condemning this violence was, as Kimura Naoe has argued, the newspaper's way of encouraging the development of a new political subject by constructing the *sōshi* as its negative other. Appropriately enough, the editorial ran under the newspaper's masthead that included a quote from John Milton: "Oh! Yet a nobler task awaits thy hand, (for what can war but endless war still breed?), till truth and right from violence be freed."[38]

Even publications that had been more supportive of the popular rights cause made similar assessments about the uncivil and anachronistic nature of *sōshi*. A *Chōya shinbun* editorial from September 1887 described a disjuncture between the civilized world of the present day and the world of force (*wanryoku*) to which *sōshi* belonged. *Sōshi* vulgarity, it claimed, sapped the nation of its energy, motivation, and life.[39] In March 1889, the newspaper accused *sōshi* of being hypocrites who cared only about their own freedom of speech and not that of others. Their disruptions of speech meetings were interpreted as a clear infringement on people's right to speak, and the editorial urged *sōshi* to respond to political opinions with words instead of force. The editorial's jabs were also aimed at the politicians whose personal rivalries and impetuousness were seen as encouraging roughness.[40] By late February 1890, the publication was calling *sōshi* "rioters" or "rowdies" (*bōto*) whose violence (*ranbō*) was antithetical to the freedom of speech and assembly at the heart of a constitutional system. The newspaper lamented that prefectural assembly elections had been marred by bribery, fear, force, and violence (*bōkō*).[41]

One of the Jiyūtō's own publications, the *Eiri jiyū shinbun*, also denounced violence as uncivilized but stopped short of a blanket condemnation of all *sōshi*. An editorial from October 1887 drew a line between the ideal of "civilized *sōshi*" (*bunmei sōshi*) and "barbarous *sōshi*" (*yaban sōshi*) so as not to smear the ideal of young popular activists from the party's recent past. But it did not hold any punches in demanding that barbarous *sōshi* relinquish their violent ways. Their lack of respect for their own bodies and those of others was considered antiquated, corrosive to liberalism, and lethal to notions of equality.[42] By the late 1880s, at the dawn of parliamentary and constitutional government, *sōshi* had come to be known more for their roughness and violence than political ideology.

Exporting Violence: Nationalist *Tairiku Rōnin* across Borders

As the Freedom and People's Rights Movement lost steam in the early 1890s with the promulgation of the constitution and the opening of the Diet, some *sōshi* shed their commitment to popular rights and threw all of their energies behind expanding Japan's influence in East Asia. Those who traveled abroad to forward this agenda were known as *tairiku rōnin* (continental adventurers). And their violence, though born of a democratic movement, was largely undemocratic in its consequences, driven as it was by the desire to steer Japanese foreign policy toward nationalist expansionism.

This wholehearted turn outward in the 1890s was not new or sudden, but was an outgrowth of popular rights ideology and violence from the previous decade. A common refrain of the Freedom and People's Rights Movement throughout the 1880s was the embrace of the nation—democracy was not an end in itself but was to contribute to the development of a better, stronger Japan. Some popular rights organizations, such as the Kōyōsha (Sun Facing Society) of Fukuoka Prefecture, placed more emphasis on nationalism than others. Founded in April 1879, the Kōyōsha was formed by young men—Hakoda Rokusuke, Tōyama Mitsuru, and Shindō Kiheita—who had served time in prison for participating in the *shizoku* rebellions of the mid-1870s, discussed in the previous chapter. The statement of purpose for the group's school, the Kōyō Gijuku, exhorted the use of education not only to "cultivate people's rights," but also to foster the growth of the country. The Kōyōsha as a whole embraced the slogan of "restoring national strength" (*kokken kaifuku*). When the Kōyōsha was renamed the Gen'yōsha (Dark Ocean Society) in February 1881, its new appellation suggested a somewhat greater engagement with foreign affairs, as it referred to the Genkai Sea that separates Fukuoka from the continent. Yet at this point, the organization was still as committed to popular rights as national strength, vowing in its three official principles to revere the emperor, love and value the nation, and defend the rights (*kenri*) of the people (*jinmin*).[43]

Most Gen'yōsha members were *sōshi*, as they were young activists who took up the violence of ruffianism to press the Meiji oligarchs for popular rights. Although they often referred to themselves as *shishi*, mainstream newspapers usually described them as "Gen'yōsha *sōshi.*" They were engaged in a domestic political battle for expanded political participation, but the Gen'yōsha's acute concern about national strength also began to propel their violence beyond the boundaries of Japan in the form of *tairiku rōnin*.

"Tairiku rōnin" is a broad term that has been used to describe intellectuals, leaders of nationalist organizations, businessmen, and even military men who traveled to the continent.[44] Historians have variously constructed them as idealistic pioneers or forerunners of Japanese imperialism.[45] I focus here on Gen'yōsha members as they epitomized a particular type of *tairiku rōnin*—young, nonstate actors who were motivated by profound apprehensions about the nation's future and a deep antipathy toward the new Meiji government to pursue the contradictory goals of spreading liberalism and promoting Japanese expansion in Korea and China. These Gen'yōsha *tairiku rōnin* were not violence specialists in the strictest definition: they were wielding violence in pursuit of their own vision and were likely not paid by others to do their bidding. In this sense, they differed from those *sōshi* of the same period who were mere hired guns, absent political conviction. Yet it would be a mistake to draw a stark distinction between *tairiku rōnin* as political visionaries and *sōshi* as mercenaries. Some *tairiku rōnin* were likely motivated by monetary considerations or the desire for adventure, and some *sōshi* likely had political convictions, however vague, about liberalism or party politics. It should also be remembered that political conviction and financial self-interest need not have been mutually exclusive. Moreover, *tairiku rōnin* and *sōshi* were both products of the 1880s and overlapped in the following decades. Not only could certain *sōshi* and *tairiku rōnin* be one and the same, but there was also a fluidity between violence at home and abroad—*sōshi* would go abroad and become *tairiku rōnin,* and *tairiku rōnin* would return home and become *sōshi.*

The Gen'yōsha began to cast its eyes toward the continent as early as the first half of the 1880s, but its violence during this time seems to have had little effect. When the Imo Mutiny broke out in Korea in 1882, the Gen'yōsha was frustrated by the Meiji government's "passive policy" to abstain from countering anti-Japanese violence or Chinese intervention on the peninsula. Taking matters into its own hands, the Gen'yōsha rallied recruits for a volunteer army to put pressure on government-level negotiations. The effort was spearheaded by Hiraoka Kōtarō and Nomura Oshisuke, prison mates from the Southwestern War, and was kicked off by an advance team that hijacked a steamship and forced its captain to take the group to Pusan. By the time they arrived, negotiations had ended. The main body of the army followed nonetheless to assassinate bureaucrat Inoue Kowashi, but this effort too was unsuccessful. In 1884, the Gen'yōsha hoped to raise an army to support a reformist, pro-Japanese coup d'état in Korea but aborted its plans when Ōi Kentarō's similarly intentioned Osaka Incident failed, resulting in greater police surveillance of Gen'yōsha members.[46]

In 1889, however, an assassination attempt by a Gen'yōsha member had some ripple effects on high-level politics. The very visible and symbolic target of the Gen'yōsha's dissatisfaction with the Meiji government's foreign policy was Foreign Minister Ōkuma Shigenobu, widely viewed as kowtowing to the West in his attempt to renegotiate the "unequal treaties." Gen'yōsha member Kurushima Tsuneki resolved to assassinate the foreign minister and garnered the support of Tōyama Mitsuru, who took it upon himself to secure the necessary weaponry. The person that Tōyama approached for help was Ōi Kentarō, just released from prison, who followed a trail of contacts until he arrived at Murano Tsuneemon and Morikubo Sakuzō—two well-known *sōshi* leaders (and important characters in the following chapter) who had a bomb tucked away that they were willing to give to the cause. In the late afternoon of October 18, 1889, as Ōkuma was returning to the foreign ministry building, Kurushima threw the bomb at Ōkuma's carriage. Believing that he had successfully killed the foreign minister, Kurush-ima took his own life on the spot by slitting his neck. Ōkuma was not killed but sustained serious injuries for which he had to temporarily resign his position; ultimately, the treaty revision proposal was withdrawn and negotiations were broken off, mainly due to widespread popular discontent with Ōkuma's handling of the entire matter. About 40 Gen'yōsha members involved in the assassination attempt were investigated, but only one was imprisoned for attempted murder and most of the others were simply held until March of the following year.[47]

In the early 1890s, the Gen'yōsha divorced its former popular rights colleagues to pursue its aggressive foreign policy agenda and wielded violence that became more potent because it was overlooked or even bolstered by the state. When a religious group known as the Tonghaks launched a massive rebellion in Korea during the spring of 1894, the Gen'yōsha seized the opportunity to help rid the peninsula of Chinese dominance.[48] Members of the Gen'yōsha together with Japanese *tairiku rōnin* already in Korea (also known as *Chōsen rōnin,* or Korea *rōnin*) merged to form the Ten'yūkyō (Heavenly Grace and Chivalry).[49] There were five Gen'yōsha *tairiku rōnin* among the original Ten'yūkyō group of 14: Takeda Hanshi, Suzuki Tengan, Ōhara Yoshitake, Shiramizu Kenkichi, and 20-year-old Uchida Ryōhei. Seven of the others were Korea *rōnin,* men not affiliated with the government or the military who were connected by the Ōsaki Law Office (Ōsaki Hōritsu Jimusho) in Pusan; the other two were military men.[50] Much of the Ten'yūkyō's energy was spent attempting to procure arms and ammunition. Even before leaving Japan for Pusan, Uchida and Ōhara tried to carry out dyna-mite from a coal mine managed by Gen'yōsha notable Hiraoka Kōtarō. Once in Pusan, the group was foiled in its attempt to steal the Japanese consulate's store-house of ammunition, but finally managed to get its hands on dynamite by rob-bing a gold mine run by a Japanese expatriate.[51] For this they were pursued by the Japanese legation with an arrest order for the crime of robbery with violence (*gōtōzai*), but the Japanese military's commissariat eventually arrested only one Ten'yūkyō member for his involvement in the incident—and, when a connection at the consulate was able to finagle testimony favorable to the defendant, he was found not guilty.[52]

Given their status as foreigners in Korea and their friendships with some key people at the Japanese consulate, Ten'yūkyō members were able to act violently with few repercussions. As they traveled around southern Korea, their rough-ness toward Korean villagers dismayed local government authorities who could do little more than urge the Japanese legation and the consulate in Pusan to act, though it seems that such demands fell on deaf ears. It was clear that some branches of the military were willing to cooperate with Ten'yūkyō members, sharing their suspicion of the Chinese. And when the Sino-Japanese War broke out in August 1894, many Ten'yūkyō members ended up working with the Japanese military to gather information and do reconnaissance work on the Chinese enemy. This service to the military convinced the government not to punish any of the other Ten'yūkyō members who were involved in the robbery of the mine.[53] With the Sino-Japanese War, the Gen'yōsha *tairiku rōnin* lost any remnants of antipathy toward the Meiji government as they converged on the idea of using violence to protect Japan's interests abroad.

In one of the most well-known and pivotal acts of Japanese violence in Korea during this decade, two Ten'yūkyō *tairiku rōnin* (along with former Jiyūtō *sōshi*) were among those who assassinated Queen Min in October 1895 at the behest of the Japanese state. The assassination was orchestrated by the Japanese minister to Korea, Miura Gorō, who worried that the anti-Japanese faction led by the queen would jeopardize reform efforts and Japanese influence. Miura brought together Japanese settlers of various sorts to attack the palace and murder the queen and her retinue. Included among the plotters were the Ten'yūkyō *tairiku rōnin* Takeda and Ōsaki, and two Gen'yōsha members—one who had participated in the Freedom and People's Rights Movement and then worked as a fencing and judo instructor, and another who came from a family of Gen'yōsha devotees and was employed as a secretary for Tōyama. This assassination in which they participated is widely seen as a precipitating factor in the Japanese colonization of Korea and was punished by a mere slap on the wrist by the Meiji government back in the metropole. The 48 people involved in the coup were arrested and imprisoned in Hiroshima, but were released several months later on the grounds of insufficient evidence. Miura continued his career in politics and was even named to the Privy Council in 1910.[54]

The story of expansionist *tairiku rōnin* gathering intelligence and joining forces to fight an enemy would play itself out again in the years leading up to the Russo-Japanese War, with Manchuria as the setting and Russia as the new threat to Japanese power. This time it was Gen'yōsha member Uchida Ryōhei who conducted reconnaissance in Siberia and Vladivostok, where he established a martial arts school that would become a hub for *tairiku rōnin*. Uchida ultimately organized, in 1901, the Kokuryūkai (Amur River Society), named after the aqueous border between China and Russia below which Russian influence was not to extend. The Kokuryūkai brought together hawkish *tairiku rōnin* and politicians alike, including Hiraoka and Tōyama from the Gen'yōsha, Ōi Kentarō from the Jiyūtō, military men, journalists, and members of other political parties. By 1903, the Kokuryūkai was providing the military with information gathered by *tairiku rōnin* in Siberia and had secured the permission of the army chief of staff to mobilize Manchurian bandits to sever Russian communication lines.[55] In May 1904, after the outbreak of the Russo-Japanese War, the army accepted a

Gen'yōsha proposal to incorporate members into the military as a special duty corps (*tokubetsu inmutai*) known as the Manshū Gigun (Manchurian Righteous Army). The original group of 16 consisted of military men and nine Gen'yōsha personnel; their numbers would swell to a total of 55 people who were armed with rifles and trained.[56] Once on the front in Manchuria, the Manshū Gigun actively recruited civilian soldiers and Manchurian bandits (allegedly by the thousands) who served as violence specialists. These men waged guerrilla warfare, did reconnaissance work, and acquired provisions; they experienced several dozen battles before the war ended in September 1905.[57]

By the turn of the century, these *tairiku rōnin*—younger cousins of the *sōshi* of the 1880s—were wielding violence that was undemocratic in intention and consequence. The *tairiku rōnin* of the Gen'yōsha were consciously using tactics of assassination to change the course of Japanese foreign policy, an inherently unequal means of leveraging political influence. Other types of *tairiku rōnin* would follow in their footsteps, and they make appearances in later discussions of prewar nationalist groups and postwar political fixers. As for the Gen'yōsha *tairiku rōnin,* their initial hostility toward the Meiji government gradually thawed as they became part of a burgeoning nexus of expansionists, and their violence merged with state violence in the name of war and empire.

Parliamentary Politics and the Professionalization of *Sōshi*

The convergence of the Gen'yōsha and the Meiji government on an aggressive foreign policy had ramifications at home as the Gen'yōsha's ruffians came to stand behind the oligarchs. Gen'yōsha *sōshi* were now squaring off against former political allies: those *sōshi* who continued to affiliate with the progressive political parties. This schism fell along the main political fault line of the early 1890s: the division between the conservative government parties (*ritō*), backed by the Meiji oligarchs, and the people's parties (*mintō*), outgrowths or descendants of the popular rights movement. Both sides rallied their own ruffians, which were now identified as either *ritō sōshi* or *mintō sōshi*. There were also internal conflicts within the parties, which too were punctuated by *sōshi* violence.

The question of how *sōshi* came to be present on all sides of political contests is only partially addressed by ideological differences. In the case of the Gen'yōsha, the organization's nationalist and expansionist platform did eventually push it toward supporting the government parties. And the *mintō sōshi* included those who had been dedicated popular rights activists in the previous decade. But others wielded violence for whatever side would have them or were simply swept along by the tide. Indeed, the term "pseudo *sōshi*" became popular around this time to refer to those who were nothing more than hired ruffians; one newspaper described them as a disease, comparing their infection of the nation to cholera's infection of the human body.[58] The extent to which *sōshi* were valued only for their violence could be seen in one *sōshi*'s statement to potential employers that outlined his motivations and qualifications for the job. He explained, "If I have some coadjutors, I can intimidate either farmers or merchants, or secretly assault a political opponent....My stick is somewhat thick and clumsy but I have no money to buy a sword cane. I am accustomed, however, to carry [sic] this stick."[59] As violence specialists, *sōshi* became indistinguishable from petty criminals in the eyes of the police. One police magazine ran an article in 1892 that put *sōshi* in the same lowly category and social world as the undesirable rickshaw puller and *bakuto*.[60] This characterization should not be swallowed whole, for the police were attempting to characterize the *sōshi* as unsavory, and not all *sōshi* were apolitical hired guns. The body of ruffians included full-time and part-time employees, those with political ambition and those who just needed money for a meal or a roof over their head, leaders who mobilized their fellow youth and followers who went where they were told. Yet in keeping with the trend from the late 1880s, *sōshi* of the early 1890s were becoming quintessential violence professionals—employed, organized, and valued because of their ability to wield physical force.

Not only were *sōshi* becoming consummate violence specialists, but their numbers were increasing as well. Ironically, it was a more participatory politics that continued to encourage the proliferation of ruffianism. With the advent of parliamentary government, there was an expansion in the body of people who needed and called upon the services of *sōshi*. Ruffians found themselves in demand by the first crop of elected Diet members (300 in the Diet's House of Representatives) as well as key party members.

At the same time, enduring restrictions on political participation also continued to fuel the demand for *sōshi*. The Meiji government may have established a parliament with a representative lower chamber, but the Law of Election, promulgated with the constitution, limited the electorate to men over the age of 25 who had been a permanent resident in a prefecture for at least one year and who had paid the substantial sum of at least ¥15 per year in direct national taxes for no less than a year, three years in the case of income tax. Under these provisions, just over one percent of the population was eligible to vote in the first general election in July 1890. The percentage of potential voters varied by region; because the law favored the land tax over the income tax, rural areas were disproportionately represented and only 0.38 percent of the population of Tokyo could cast ballots.[61] As historian Irokawa Daikichi has suggested, the limited electorate meant that every vote carried a great deal of weight, so *sōshi* coercion of electors could potentially be quite effective in influencing election outcomes.[62] It was the Meiji oligarchs' attempts to hoard political power in the face of parliamentary government that not only made ruffianism politically valuable, but also encouraged the very *sōshi* activity that challenged government control over the nation's political life.

When all of these elements coalesced—the ideological differences and the widening of political participation and the Meiji government's restrictions on the electorate—the presence of *sōshi* in politics became a self-perpetuating phenomenon. Each side in a political contest would find itself needing its own muscle when faced with the ruffians of the opposition. And the dynamism of political contention ensured the persistence of *sōshi* as protection and ammunition against opponents.

In the campaigns leading up to the first general election in 1890, *sōshi* were indeed prevalent and created a tense political atmosphere. Reports of *sōshi*-related incidents came from the prefectures and cities of Kumamoto, Kōchi, Ishikawa, Toyama, Niigata, Hyōgo, Saitama, Tochigi, Gunma, Aichi, Mie, Yokohama, Osaka, and Tokyo. For the most part, ruffians seem to have compromised the electoral process. Typically, *sōshi* disrupted public meetings, threatened opposition candidates and voters, and faced off against each other. They were thus partly canvassers of sorts, as in a race in Osaka where a candidate hired *bakuto* he knew to approach electors in groups of four or five to influence their vote. Or in Yokohama, where *sōshi* posted fliers at every intersection that threatened to kill anyone who voted for the opposition candidate. *Sōshi* were also providers of protection, and their role as defenders and advocates of a certain candidate or political party led them to clash with other *sōshi*, as in Kumamoto Prefecture where a fight broke out at the end of June between the *sōshi* of two different factions. In general, *sōshi* violence was organized and purposeful and strategic, sometimes even routinized or ritualized. Accounts of *sōshi* breaking up speech meetings read so much alike—the meeting begins, *sōshi* enter, storm the dais, attack the speaker and others, destroy some property, and exit—that *sōshi* come off as professionals performing a specific task.

It is unclear whether such coercion and intimidation swayed voters; the image of "the rowdies of one side encounter[ing] and glar[ing] at the bullies of the other side in front of the gate of every elector"[63] suggests that the hiring of *sōshi* by all sides might have neutralized their influence. The government, however, was clearly concerned about the violence leading up to election day. On May 29, it issued the Supplementary Penal Regulations for the House of Representatives Election Law that made individual intimidation of voters, as well as the kidnapping of electors and obstruction of their movement to the polls on election day, punishable offenses. These regulations were intended to shore up the Law of Election that had already outlawed mass intimidation of voters, riots at polling places and election meetings, and general acts of violence against voters. There was also a substantial police presence on the day of the election. In Tokyo, each polling station was assigned six police officers, and in Kagawa and Kanagawa Prefectures, hundreds of policemen were placed on duty. Election day itself was surprisingly calm, though *sōshi* did make their presence known in certain places.[64] Nonetheless, in the several months leading up to the election, *sōshi* had developed specific roles for themselves in the practice of parliamentary politics that set a precedent for years to come. And the triumph of the people's parties over the government's parties—171 seats to 129—only heightened the Meiji government's anxieties about losing its grip on political power.[65]

The violence of the 1890 election was not a flash in the pan, a moment of particularly rough politics that faded as the country became more practiced in national elections and parliamentary politics. Instead, it helped solidify the importance of *sōshi* in politics. With the election of the first Diet, a distinction came to be made between parliamentary and extraparliamentary actors. The election of certain party members to the House of Representatives created two categories within political parties, and the resurrected Rikken Jiyūtō (Constitutional Liberal Party, hereafter Jiyūtō) in particular: the group of party members who were elected representatives (*giindan*), and the group of party members who were not (*ingaidan*).[66] Both were valued by the party, and *sōshi,* already endemic in politics, would carve out a niche as important executors of *ingaidan* activities.

The extent to which *sōshi* ruffianism had already become part and parcel of parliamentary politics was evident at the very establishment of the Jiyūtō in September 1890. The ceremony marking the official birth of the party took place on September 15 at Yayoi Hall in Shiba Park, where over 300 party members and several hundred other attendees gathered to hear the founding documents read aloud. There were those, Endō Hidekage prime among them, who opposed the formation of the Jiyūtō. Endō was a parliamentarian who would eventually become a member of the more conservative and nationalist Kokumin Jiyūtō (National Liberal Party) which had a short life, formed in November and dissolved in 1891.[67] Endō and some of his colleagues disturbed the proceedings with *sōshi.* Tumult ensued, as the hall was stormed by armed *sōshi* from the Kantō region as well as those from Ishikawa, Fukuoka, Kumamoto, and Kōchi Prefectures. Jiyūtō *sōshi,* looking like egrets dressed as they were in white cotton kimono, had been stationed in groups of six or seven around the hall and engaged in a shouting match with the intruders. There were several hundred policemen standing guard inside and outside the hall, but it is unclear what their presence accomplished—*sōshi* were seen in the park and were certainly able to pour into the meeting. Given all of the commotion, the ceremony was ended and everyone was dismissed. For the next several days, *sōshi* persisted in their attempt to disrupt Jiyūtō affairs. On September 16, *sōshi* sat in the gallery of a party meeting but were restrained from causing a ruckus. On September 17, while Endō was engaged in a debate of his own, *sōshi* of various sides yelled back and forth at each other. And on September 18, tensions resulted in a physical fight. This gathering in the Kobiki area of Tokyo opened at 10:00 A.M. to elect officers and take care of other party business but came to a halt for about half an hour while *sōshi* clashed in the second-floor balcony. There, rival *sōshi* who had been seated on opposite sides of the gallery duked it out until policemen managed to subdue the ruffians, after which the *sōshi* of Endō and his colleagues left.[68]

These *sōshi* did not escape the attention of journalists. The *Chōya shinbun* continued to speak of the ruffians as "thugs" (*bōkan*) and specifically referred to Jiyūtō *sōshi* as "rioters" and "rowdies." The newspaper described the hearts of *sōshi* as feudal, accused them of dirtying the honor of Japanese boys, and called for greater police regulation. Similarly dismayed was the *Yomiuri shinbun*, which attributed the prevalence of *sōshi* as "the violent" or "assaulters" to those politicians who turned to physical force out of desperation.[69]

Despite these condemnations, *sōshi* violence persisted in large part because of the host of divisions that marked the political landscape. The overarching tension between the *mintō* and the government endured, especially regarding the issue of "transcendental cabinets." These cabinets were controlled by the Meiji oligarchs and excluded party politicians in order to "be above" partisan party politics. They were thus vigorously opposed by the *mintō*, particularly the Jiyūtō and the Rikken Kaishintō (Constitutional Reform Party, hereafter Kaishintō), who advocated party cabinets in order to weaken bureaucratic control over executive powers. There were also strains between the Jiyūtō and Kaishintō, and within the parties as well. All of this was evident in the heated debates over the government budget that erupted in early 1891. Members of the Jiyūtō and the Kaishintō opposed the cabinet's proposed expenditure of ¥83.32 million and supported a call from a committee of the House of Representatives for an ¥8.88 million reduction in the original figure. The budget issue was complicated by a split in the Jiyūtō between a "hard-line" faction that stood by the demand for a budget cut and a "soft" faction that was willing to reach a compromise with the cabinet.[70]

Sōshi violence perpetuated, and was perpetuated by, these divisions—the budget debates, like elections, were a form of political contest in which physical force was viewed as an asset, and this violence certainly did not facilitate discussions that could lead to compromise. On January 7, for example, *sōshi* disrupted a meeting of the Yayoi Club, a group of Diet members from the Jiyūtō. About 70 members of the club were in attendance, and just as the agenda was to turn to the budget, two or three dozen *sōshi* armed with sticks stormed past the receptionist and into the hall yelling things such as, "Jiyūtō members take bribes from the Kaishintō!" The *sōshi* split into groups, some surrounding the president's table while others approached Diet member Ueki Emori. When Ueki refused to talk with them, seven or eight *sōshi* beat him with sticks until he collapsed. Yasuda Yuitsu who was nearby also sustained severe blows from some *sōshi*. To fight them off, Diet member Hayashi Yūzō inspired people to use their chairs against the *sōshi*, who were then forced to retreat into the lobby where they were assaulted by the Diet members' rickshaw pullers and other assembled people. Two of the *sōshi* were arrested, Ueki suffered serious head injuries, Yasuda was also wounded, and the hall was left in complete disarray. The meeting continued with police on guard.[71]

In other cases, *sōshi* focused their attention on a single individual. The chairman of the Budget Committee, Ōe Taku, was a particularly attractive mark. *Sōshi* would visit his house regularly, and on at least one occasion, rumors circulated that he had been assassinated. As a defensive measure, Ōe maintained a cadre of almost 100 *sōshi*.[72] Others less prominent were also threatened. On the evening of January 10, *sōshi* seemingly of the hard faction targeted Toyoda Bunzaburō, who was attending a gathering of the soft faction at the Imperial Hotel. Toyoda was called out of the meeting by someone who had approached the front desk and requested to see him; when the conversation between these two men was winding down, 11 armed *sōshi* sought to intimidate him. No harm befell Toyoda due to intervention by the police, who accompanied him home.[73]

Diet members were thus constantly on guard. According to politician Inukai Tsuyoshi, everyone had their sword canes at the ready when in the halls of the Diet. And at the close of business for the day, each individual member's *sōshi* would take up their positions in front of the Diet building. When they saw their boss emerge from the gate of the House of Representatives, they would protect him immediately and escort him away.[74]

Government attempts to rid the capital of *sōshi* seemed even less successful now, in the early 1890s, than they had been in the late 1880s. On January 13, the chief of the Metropolitan Police invoked article 4 of the Peace Preservation Ordinance and did manage to expel 60 to 70 *sōshi* from Tokyo. Yet, as in 1887, many *sōshi* only retreated to nearby Yokohama, Kawasaki, and Kanagawa. According to the *Yūbin hōchi shinbun*, over 1,600 *sōshi* remained in the city.[75] This figure seems high, but even the more modest figures cited by the *Chōya shinbun* in late February suggest the limited scope of the eviction. According to this paper, there were 151 *sōshi* in the regular employ of the parties, several hundred attached to particular politicians, plus those *sōshi* who were hired on a temporary basis.[76]

What is more clear than the murky numbers is that *sōshi* activity remained vigorous despite the crackdown, even inside the halls of the Diet building. Inoue Kakugorō, a Diet member who opposed the budget reduction, was headed

2.2. *Sōshi* keeping an eye out for parliamentarians by the exit of the Diet building. From *Za gurafikku*, April 15, 1893.

toward the dining room during a House of Representatives midday recess on February 14 when he was hit on the right side of his face with an iron stick. He managed to pin the 30-year-old *sōshi* against the wall and held him there until the police arrived.[77] And parliamentarian Ozaki Yukio's laundry list of injured politicians spoke to the frequency of *sōshi* attacks:

> It was not unusual to see members arriving at the Diet all bandaged up. Inukai [Tsuyoshi] was wounded in the head. Shimada Saburō was attacked a couple of times and badly hurt. Takada Sanae was cut down with a sword from behind and the blade almost reached his lungs; he would have died on the spot had he not been obese. Kawashima Atsushi, Ueki Emori, and Inoue Kakugorō were all attacked at different times and came wearing bandages. Suematsu Kenchō was hit by horse manure thrown from the gallery. Members often even got into fist fights on the floor of the House, which became a rather rough place to be.[78]

In one of the incidents on the House floor, politician Nakamura Yaroku punched Inukai Tsuyoshi in the face for suggesting he had received bribes to sit out a vote.[79]

This prevalence of *sōshi* can be explained in a number of ways. There was the mindset that physical force was an effective tool for political suasion; indeed, violence could be influential given the relatively small number of participants (targets) in parliamentary government. This created a need for protection and the reality that eschewing *sōshi* would be dangerous and even disadvantageous once they had become a fixture in political contests. The culture of political violence that resulted, in which physical force was widely accepted as standard practice, was perpetuated by a systemic lack of accountability. With only one percent of the population eligible to voice their opinions at the polls, politicians did not have to explain their actions to the public at large. And even if the voter base had been larger, it is unclear how people might have used the vote to protest a kind of political behavior exhibited on all sides.

State Violence and the Second General Election

In 1892, the already violent atmosphere was ratcheted up even further by the unleashing of state violence in the second general election of Japan's history. Displeased with the people's parties' majority in the Diet and their opposition to the proposed budget, the Meiji government—more specifically, the cabinet of Prime Minister Matsukata Masayoshi—resolved to use all forms of violence at its disposal to prevent the election of people's parties candidates and win a majority for the government parties. The architect of this plan was Home Minister Shinagawa Yajirō, a native of Chōshū Domain and a former *shishi* who had studied at Yoshida Shōin's academy. After the Meiji Restoration, he spent six years in Europe, was appointed vice minister of agriculture and commerce in 1882, and established a transportation company before becoming home minister in 1891. The exact wording of the instructions he gave to local authorities is not known, but the directive to block the election of people's parties candidates took various forms in practice. Police put pressure on business owners under their jurisdiction to vote for government party candidates; visited voters individually, house by house, to sway their vote; fought against *mintō sōshi*; and, along with *ritō sōshi*, obstructed voters from going to polling places on the day of the election. There were other forms of "election interference" (*senkyo kanshō*), as it came to be known, that were coercive without involving physical force: the buying of votes, and the selective application of the law, especially as it pertained to newspaper publishing.[80] Government hiring of *sōshi* was not new, but the sheer numbers of *ritō sōshi* was greater in the 1892 election than in any political contest of the previous several years.[81] That, as well as the egregious overextension of police power to intimidate voters, resulted in an exceedingly violent and chaotic second general election—24 people would lose their lives and 388 would be injured before a new House of Representatives was elected.[82]

There were reports of *sōshi* activity in many prefectures—Tochigi, Ibaraki, Toyama, Aichi, Shiga, Mie, Nara, Hyōgo, Kagawa, Fukuoka, Kumamoto, Miyazaki, and Kagoshima among others—with the worst violence in and around Saga Prefecture in Kyūshū and Kōchi Prefecture in Shikoku.[83] Saga Prefecture suffered 92 injured, the highest in the country, and the second largest number of deaths at eight. Kōchi had the greatest number of deaths at ten, and the second largest number of wounded at 66.[84] These two prefectures suffered a high number of fatalities and injuries in part because they were the birthplaces of the two most significant people's parties—the Jiyūtō had originally been founded by Kōchi (Tosa Domain) native Itagaki Taisuke, and the Kaishintō by Ōkuma Shigenobu from Saga. They were therefore hotbeds of *sōshi* activity and, perhaps, special targets for the government's election interference.[85] Kaishintō politician Ozaki Yukio commented on how Saga's chief of police "personally instructed his own men and paid miscellaneous scoundrels and toughs off the street to threaten citizens. He gave them instructions to draw their swords without hesitation on people who did not vote for the official [government] party."[86] Violence was also exacerbated by the Gen'yōsha which originated in, and was particularly active around, this area. The organization made the decision in this election to turn against its former allies from the popular rights movement and side with the government. The Matsukata cabinet's promise to push for an increase in military expenditures against the wishes of the people's parties was welcomed by a Gen'yōsha that had become much more dedicated to an aggressive foreign policy than to liberalism at home. The group thus campaigned for the government parties, calling for *sōshi* reinforcements from neighboring areas, mobilizing miners and former samurai, and forming alliances with yakuza bosses.[87]

Especially in Saga and Kōchi, but also across the country, the scale of violence was much larger in this election than in 1890. While there were reports of *sōshi* canvassing in bands of four or five as had become standard practice by this time, it was not uncommon for them to operate in groups of 100 or more. In Kōchi, for example, over 100 *ritō sōshi* gathered in Sagawa Village on the morning of January 29 and provoked a fight with Jiyūtō *sōshi*. A newspaper article indicated that two captains and 40 police officers armed with sabers dissolved the battling crowd, but it is not clear whether the police subdued both sides with equal force or stepped in on the side of the *ritō sōshi*.[88] The numbers of *sōshi* active in the campaign swelled by the days surrounding the election on February 15. In one village in the Hata District of Kōchi, 1,300 *mintō sōshi* squared off against 1,000 *ritō sōshi* creating a "great disturbance"; and in another village, 800 *sōshi* were brought in as reinforcements for an ongoing fight to which 11 police officers and five military police were dispatched.[89] In another incident, 2,000 Jiyūtō *sōshi* threw rubble at the offices of the Kōchi Nipponsha newspaper company, then ran away from the 20 to 30 armed military police.[90] Military police and army units were dispatched in Kōchi ostensibly to maintain order, but liberal politician Ozaki Yukio claimed they were more coercive toward the people's parties.[91] Substantial numbers of sōshi were amassed outside Kōchi as well. In Miyazaki Prefecture, on the opposite coast of Kyūshū, 300 ritō sōshi threw rocks to disrupt a people's parties public meeting in Honjō Village.[92]

Violence was also more intense than in the 1890 election, extending beyond ruffianism to murder. Again in Kōchi, a Jiyūtō sōshi killed a ritō sōshi named Kikuchi Yoshisaburō in a village in Hata District on February 4.[93] One week later, ritō sōshi were responsible for the murder of Jiyūtō sōshi in Takaoka District in two separate incidents. In Kitahara Village, a ritō sōshi stabbed to death two Jiyūtō sōshi, and in Iwano Village, another ritō sōshi was arrested for killing a Jiyūtō sōshi.[94] In the same district of Takaoka, four government party supporters were murdered on the night of February 14. And in Agawa District, Jiyūtō sōshi were surrounded and attacked by 150 ritō sōshi; two Jiyūtō sōshi were killed and a prosecutor and a judge were sent to investigate.[95] One publication, Kokumin no tomo, commented on the scale of this violence, denouncing murders as barbaric and an embarrassment not only for the people, police, and prefectural governor of Kōchi, but also for the Japanese people in the eyes of the outside world.[96]

The attempt to threaten voters continued right up until election day itself, which was marred by sōshi blocking, and fighting at, polling places. In Ishikawa Prefecture, ritō sōshi were stationed at voting sites to prevent potential people's parties supporters from voting by attacking them, as they did in one incident, or by lighting a fire in front of the polling place, as they did in another. Voter intimidation was also acute in Tokyo where the military police were mobilized, likely adding to the tense atmosphere as much as contributing to a more secure voting environment. In the first voting district, several hundred military police guarded the polls located at the Kōjimachi ward office. Military police officers were stationed at the entrance, to the right and left of the ward office's main gate, and on both sides of the road that led from Hanzōmon to Kōjimachi. Voters began to line up around 6:00 A.M. in anticipation of the 9:00 A.M. commencement of voting, and it seems that the police officers were relatively successful in protecting them from physical assaults by the sōshi who campaigned outside the gate. There were, however, several incidents of attacks. Around 8:10 A.M., a voter getting out of a rickshaw in front of the ward office was beaten by a sōshi who was eventually caught by a patrolman. Around 10:00 A.M., a man originally of Okayama Prefecture assaulted supporters of a certain candidate Kusumoto with a blade normally used for cutting wood; he was arrested by the military police, taken to the military police office and then to Tokyo Regional Court for interrogation, and was detained. And around 10:30 A.M., a voter who had cast his ballot was leaving through the gate of the ward office when the rickshaw in which he was traveling was attacked by two *sōshi,* who were arrested by military police.[97] Overall, it seems that the military police, though fairly effective in maintaining order, were not able to ensure the security of the voters or the voting process.

The security of ballot boxes was also a concern on election day. Given the mutual distrust between the people's and government parties, it was unclear who could be and actually was entrusted with their protection. In one example, a certain Captain Satō and 14 military police were reported to have guarded a ballot box, but in two other villages in the same district, at least 3,000 Jiyūtō *sōshi* were said to have ensured the safe delivery of the boxes.[98] Politician Ozaki Yukio recalled the insecurity of the ballot boxes, noting that the voting process had to be repeated in the second voting district of Kōchi Prefecture after a mob absconded with the original votes.[99] And in Takaoka District, about 1,000 *ritō sōshi* tried to steal the voting box which provoked an altercation with the Jiyūtō.[100] In Tokyo too, at the Senjū polling place, a *sōshi* ran away with a ballot box.[101]

In Saga Prefecture, violence extended so far beyond polling places that voting had to be discontinued and postponed for several days.[102] In the particularly turbulent Mine District, armed *mintō sōshi* numbering around 1,000 traveled in divisions, battled with *ritō sōshi,* and attacked a police station. Shiroishi was also a hotbed of *sōshi* activity, due to an influx of 50 to 60 ruffians from Kagoshima. Military police, police forces from a number of areas within the prefecture, as well as those from nearby Kumamoto and Kagoshima Prefectures were dispatched to restore order to the various sites of conflict.[103]

Ultimately, election interference proved costly for the Meiji government and the Matsukata cabinet in particular. The audacity and extent of the government's coercive methods created a split within the cabinet between those who opposed the interference, such as Minister of Agriculture and Commerce Mutsu Munemitsu and Minister of Communications Gotō Shōjirō, and those who stood by the strategy. Home Minister Shinagawa himself was not the least bit apologetic, at least in the recollection of Ozaki Yukio, believing he had done what was in the best interest of the country:

> When the special election was called I, as home minister, did all in my power to support the election of loyal men at the expense of those elements who if re-elected would do great harm to the maintenance of national security. And if ever during my time in office a similar situation occurs again, I swear to heaven that I will do whatever is needed to defeat the forces of destruction.[104]

Mounting pressures from within the Matsukata government did eventually force the resignation of Shinagawa on March 11. What helped seal Shinagawa's fate was the embarrassing failure of election interference—the people's parties retained a majority in the House of Representatives, having won 163 seats to the government parties' 137. Once the new Diet convened in May, the people's parties sought revenge and justice for the government's wrongdoing.[105] The parties' efforts were supported by the House of Peers, which passed a resolution chastising the government for raising the ire of the people:

> The bureaucracy having intervened in the election has incurred the wrath of the people and as a result blood has been shed. This is now public knowledge and a source of public complaint. Throughout the country people are enraged at the bureaucracy's intervention in the election and regard it with hostility.[106]

The House of Representatives followed suit by passing a resolution in a vote of 154 to 111 urging that "cabinet ministers all undertake soul searching and in the light of their given mandate take appropriate actions."[107] The Matsukata cabinet managed to stagger along for another couple of months but, with the resignations of the army and navy ministers as the final straw, collapsed in August 1892.[108]

The police also found themselves the target of criticism for their close collaboration with the cabinet, and charges of corruption prompted discussions about reform of the police system to separate it from other organs of the state.[109] Police misconduct had included preferential treatment of *ritō sōshi*, who seem to have been particularly immune from punishment. The Gen'yōsha *sōshi*, for example, should have been punished for violating not only the Law of Election, but also the Criminal Code of 1880, under which all of the following were considered illegal: murder (article 294), inflicting bodily harm of varying degrees (articles 299 and 300), threatening murder or arson (article 326), and committing arson (article 402). Yet Gen'yōsha *sōshi* do not seem to have been arrested or punished for these breaches of the law due to the legitimacy granted their actions by the home minister and the cooperation of local officials and law enforcement.[110]

Election interference spoke not only to police malfeasance, but also to its weakness, in at least two possible ways. If the overarching goal of the police was to prevent victories of *mintō* candidates, then the election outcome itself suggests they fell short. There are numerous interpretations of and reasons for the triumph of the people's parties: it may have reflected disdain of government violence, support for more popular politics, or the ability of *mintō sōshi* to coerce voters. In any case, the police could not intimidate enough voters into casting their ballots for *ritō* candidates. If one of the aims of the police was to maintain order and contain *mintō sōshi*, they were not very effective on that count either. *Mintō sōshi* were rampant during the campaign and on the day of the election. While there do not seem to be precise figures on the number of *sōshi* arrested, most reports only mention an investigation or short-term detention when violence was egregious. There was no arrest, trial, or imprisonment of a mass number of *sōshi*.

Subsequent elections in the 1890s were not free of *sōshi* violence, though they did not reach the fevered pitch of the 1892 election. This was partly because of a new law, the Sōshi Regulatory Law (Sōshi Torishimari Hō) of late June 1892, that urged citizens to report threatening *sōshi* behavior to the police.[111] The more important factor was the government's decision to avoid any potential abuse of its power, at least for a time. The government's restraint can be explained by the criticism and internal tension engendered by past interference and by the personal convictions of the next home minister. Home Minister Inoue Kaoru had disapproved of election interference in 1892, and in the next general election two years later, he made a point of refraining from such behavior.[112] Nonetheless, in the weeks leading up to March 1, *sōshi* attacks and fights broke out in many regions around the country. These incidents involved anywhere from one or two *sōshi* to several dozen and occasionally up to 100, and seemed to become more frequent right before, and on, the day of the election. Among the many reports of *sōshi* violence were those of ruffians who: inflicted casualties in Ibaraki Prefecture; interrupted prefectural assembly elections and flaunted pistols in Saitama; injured political speakers in Gunma; threatened those who opposed the Jiyūtō in Chiba; assaulted campaigners in Nagano; wounded others in Tochigi and Nara and Nagoya; barged into a Kaishintō election office in Shizuoka; butted heads in Tokyo and Aichi; disturbed a speech meeting in Okayama; made appearances in Niigata and Mie; and roughed up voters in Kobe and Gifu.[113] Mentioned also were squabbles with *bakuto*, attempted bribery, and some *sōshi* arrests, although it is unclear whether they were prosecuted and punished for their violence. Ozaki Yukio described this continuity in the presence of *sōshi*: "They ['thugs'] were sent out from both camps to intimidate voters, chase them away from ballot boxes or use unloaded guns to frighten them, using tricky tactics as if they were combatants in little wars. An election in a particular constituency developed all too often into a contest between these bands, and [in Ozaki's opinion] the side that employed them most effectively usually won."[114]

Election violence did seem to wane, or garner less attention, for a short time after this third election in 1894, most likely because of the outbreak of the Sino-Japanese War. As the nation rallied around the war effort, the major tensions of the early general elections temporarily thawed for several years thereafter. Yet ruffianism still made appearances. In mid-December 1897, *sōshi* activity persisted over several days during a Jiyūtō congress in Tokyo. In one incident, a clash between detectives and *sōshi* at a Jiyūtō youth meeting prompted police to dispatch 100 officers to the scene who, after a quarrel, took in the gathering's organizers. Leaders of the Yūitsukan present at the event resisted the police, which led to several injuries.[115] And in the fifth general election of January 1898, a meeting in the fifth ward of Saitama Prefecture was disrupted by the discovery of an explosive planted at the assembly hall.[116]

Sōshi-like election violence was not unique to mid-Meiji Japan. In late eighteenth-century Britain, election fraud escalated to violence in an attempt to garner votes so that "[b]y 1776 the uses of violence seem to have become a recognized electoral maneuver and elections in the larger constituencies were characterized by hosts of hired ruffians and bludgeon-men."[117] Even decades later, in the early and mid-1800s, toughs or "professional bruisers" such as gypsies, boxers, and navvies were brought in to hassle opponents and cause disorder. In the 1830s in Coventry, these "bullies" were given all they could drink and five shillings a day for their work. And in Birmingham in an 1867 by-election, the town was said to be in "the possession of blacklegs, prize fighters and thieves."[118] Intimidation and violence were so widespread that voting was considered a danger. As historian and politician George Grote commented in 1838, "In numberless cases the franchise is felt and hated as a burden; and if any man doubts this, the bitter experience and the humiliating answers of a canvass will be quite sufficient to teach it to him."[119]

Election violence persisted because the public was much more tolerant of physical force than bribery during these years, according to historian Theodore Hoppen. This was the case with certain literary figures as well. Writer and statesman Benjamin Disraeli, for example, held his punches when describing these "hired gangs" in his 1844 political novel *Coningsby*: "[they] were the safety-valves for all the scamps of the borough, who, receiving a few shillings per head for their nominal services, and as much drink as they liked...were bribed and organized into peace and sobriety."[120] Disraeli almost seemed to suggest a positive societal role for these gangs that served as "safety-valves" and imposed order on ruffians.

Election violence was also not unheard of in the United States during the nineteenth century, especially in larger cities. The Sixth Ward of New York, which encompassed the infamous Five Points neighborhood, was well known for its rough politics as was the city as a whole. During the 1844 presidential race, for example, a certain Isaiah "Ike" Rynders organized the Empire Club to coerce voters into casting ballots for the Democrat James K. Polk over Whig opponent Henry Clay. The Empire Club was composed of prizefighters and "sporting men"—typically "muscular bruisers" who did not maintain steady employment and amused themselves with gambling, politics, boxing, and horse racing. On election day, Rynders and his men used physical force and intimidation to keep

Whigs from voting. From then on, Rynders and the Empire Club were fixtures in New York politics as they disrupted political gatherings and hijacked Tammany Hall meetings. These were not the first violent struggles at the polls; there had been a notorious election riot in the early 1830s, and fighting (often involving street gangs) was commonplace throughout the 1840s and into the 1850s.[121]

Violent tactics were also used outside New York City. In Baltimore, home to especially violent elections before the Civil War, political gangs sported nicknames such as the "Blood Tubs" and "Plug Uglies." The Blood Tubs were so dubbed after they doused voters in the First Ward "with blood taken from barrels or tubs."[122] And the Plug Uglies were named after the slang for the kind of "tough or rough-neck" seen in Baltimore, New York, and Philadelphia.[123] Members of such gangs stationed themselves in front of voting windows on election day, forcing voters to show them their ticket and then blocking or permitting their passage.[124] Physical intimidation was exacerbated by the free flow of liquor at the polls, which were often located in places such as saloons and livery stables. Whether a perquisite of voting or a bribe, liquor turned the area outside a voting window into "a kind of alcoholic festival in which many men were clearly and spectacularly drunk."[125]

Violence was often planned to prevent people from voting, with protection provided only to those who agreed to cast their ballots for a certain ticket.[126] In antebellum Philadelphia, gangs would block select voters and protect ballot boxes to avoid arrest and gain favors.[127] Police coercion was also not unheard of. In Chicago, police worked on behalf of the Democratic Party; in an 1894 election, they kidnapped 25 Republicans the day before the election and held them until after voting was closed.[128] Voter intimidation was so rampant that, in 1884, a Midwestern newspaper reported that "nearly everywhere in America, voting was an arduous task attended by personal danger. Every peaceable man and every household dreads the approach of election day."[129] Election violence had national consequences in the infamous Rutherford Hayes–Samuel Tilden presidential election of 1876, when violent intimidation cast a shadow over results in three of four states where the electoral college count was contested. The uncertainty of the election's outcome was exacerbated by the fact that Hayes was named the winner, even though he had fewer popular votes than Tilden.[130]

Such political violence was encouraged in all of these contexts—Japan, Britain, and the United States—by the phenomenon of elections itself. As political scientists David Rapoport and Leonard Weinberg have pointed out, the visibility of candidates and voters during a campaign makes them targets. Moreover, elections are by nature competitive and divisive moments of political succession.[131]

Ruffianism endured in these three countries for similar reasons, with reforms instituted piecemeal over many decades. The absence of impartial bodies to carry out elections invited abuses of various sorts, as with patrolmen in the

United States who exerted their authority according to their own political whims or with the Meiji state's mobilization of the police in the second general election.[132] Efforts to reform the urban police in the United States and separate them from local politics took dozens of years, as did the establishment of a professional police in Britain.[133] Creating a mechanism for punishment of election fraud also took time. In the United States in 1870, Congress gave federal officials jurisdiction over this matter and only when it pertained to voting for national office. The presence of federal election inspectors did help prevent repeat voting in places such as the Sixth Ward, though it seems to have encouraged the alternative tactic of "miscounting."[134] In Britain, judges and not election committees presided over investigations into corruption starting in 1868, and election disputes were moved from Parliament to the courts in 1883.[135] It also took time to make voting more secure. The advent of secret ballots during the late nineteenth century in both the United States and Britain was a substantial disincentive for both bribery and physical coercion of voters, as ruffians and those who hired them could not check to see if they got a return on their investment.[136] Most significant, the expansion of the franchise, which made it increasingly difficult to intimidate voters, was a gradual and contested process.

The persistence of political ruffianism was thus not unique to Japan, and the period in which violence plagued elections was not longer in Japan than elsewhere. Struggles with partiality in the conduct of elections, compromised police, and the influence of local boss politics transcended national boundaries. The Japanese case did differ in that sōshi were visible in politics well into the twentieth century, after parallel occurrences in Britain and the United States had dissipated. But this was largely an issue of timing: Japan had come more recently to constitutional government, party politics, and thus reform. Reformers may have had different motivations in various contexts; early efforts in Japan were driven by commercial and industrial interests as well as liberals, and were absent the nativist overtones of their U.S. counterparts.[137] Yet Japan too was in the process of instituting secret ballots (used after 1900) and extending the vote (with the enactment of universal manhood suffrage in 1925). Issues such as election campaign laws, punishment for offenses, and redistricting were also debated as the original Law of Election of 1889 was reformed in a series of new electoral laws in 1900, 1919, 1925, and 1934.[138]

This particular timeline of electoral violence, extending as it did well into the 1900s, influenced the path that ruffians and ruffianism took in Japan. Divergences from the British and U.S. cases can be largely explained by the intersection of sōshi and their violence with some of the most significant phenomena of the early twentieth century—aggressive imperialism, socialist movements, chauvinistic nationalism, and fascism.

Thinking of ruffianism in the long term brings us back to the question, obviously complicated, of whether *sōshi* violence "haunted," jeopardized, or destabilized Meiji democracy. The prevalence of *sōshi* in parliamentary politics reflected the heterogeneity of the domestic political landscape and suggests there were vigorous differences and debates in Meiji politics—the scope of the government's political influence prime among them—that are healthy in a democracy. Yet as *sōshi* became less political activist and more professional ruffian, they were not motivated by the kind of democratic impulse (the desire for popular and democratic revolution, the right to organize, or civil rights) that makes violence more palatable, at least to some theorists.[139] The *tairiku rōnin* of the 1890s certainly were not driven by a liberal or democratic agenda. Finally, violence likely had undemocratic consequences. This seems more clear in the case of *tairiku rōnin,* as their violence was bound up with the projects of war making and empire building. With the *sōshi,* we venture out into the uncertain territory of counterfactual history, but it is probably fair to say that *sōshi* narrowed political participation by intimidating voters and creating an atmosphere of fear during election campaigns and at speech meetings. Their violence at these sites of political expression may very well have shut down possibilities for debate and the exchange of ideas. And their very presence made the political battleground uneven, favoring those with enough money to hire more *sōshi.*

Above all, *sōshi* helped create a culture of political violence that had the potential to shake Japan's experience with democracy at its core. Political scientist Victor Le Vine has commented that "political violence does beget political violence... eventually to the point where a culture of political violence can come into being, and with it the very real possibility of democratic breakdown."[140] In Japan, the culture of political violence did not render the disintegration of democracy inevitable, but it did present a "possibility of democratic breakdown" that made for an uneasy relationship between violence and democracy. This tension is the subject of the next chapter, which focuses on the period from the first decade of the twentieth century through the 1920s—a time when both a culture of political violence and democracy existed, one intertwined with the other.

3

Institutionalized Ruffianism and a Culture of Political Violence

In mid-February 1922, the economic daily *Chūgai shōgyō shinpō* ran a three-part series to herald a "new era of brute courage and tenacity" in politics. Entitled "Biographies of Brave Diet Members," the articles stressed the importance of physical strength in political life and applauded those politicians who were skilled at fighting, be it in Diet-floor brawls or in martial arts such as judo. Spotlighted in two of the articles were Diet members known for their physical prowess, such as: Tsunoda Koreshige from Nara Prefecture who was rumored to make 10,000 enemy soldiers cower just by unsheathing his saber; Ayabe Sōbei who had crushed voting boxes in elections of the early 1910s; Nakano Torakichi who was nicknamed "the violent Bantora"; Iwamoto Heizō from Mie Prefecture who was known as King of the Asuras; and the tattooed Koizumi Matajirō (future communications minister and grandfather of early twenty-first-century prime minister Koizumi Jun'ichirō) who had tried to strike a fellow parliamentarian during a Diet session.[1] The third part of the series focused on cabinet ministers, noting those who were trained in martial arts and had connections to the Kōdōkan, a well-known judo school in Tokyo. Home Minister Tokonami Takejirō and Education Minister Nakahashi Tokugorō were mentioned for their support of the Kōdōkan, and Foreign Minister Uchida Kōsai also got a nod for his judo abilities.[2]

This celebration of physical strength in political life was a reflection, however overstated, of the extent to which ruffianism had become accepted and commonplace in parliamentary politics. Since their emergence in the 1880s, *sōshi* remained a political force all the way through the mid-1920s, continuing to use physical force to threaten, coerce, and intimidate in an attempt to elicit a desired political outcome. Over these decades, *sōshi* not only survived but also became more embedded in the political system—after the turn of the twentieth century, there was greater institutionalization of *sōshi* into the very structure of political parties as part of their *ingaidan,* or pressure groups. *Ingaidan* were not new to the early 1900s. The Jiyūtō (Liberal Party) of the mid-Meiji period had had an *ingaidan* starting in the 1880s, which fed into one created by the Rikken Seiyūkai (Friends of Constitutional Government Party, hereafter Seiyūkai) shortly after the party's founding in 1900. But the Seiyūkai *ingaidan* was more defined and complex in organization than its Jiyūtō predecessor. It came to secure a place in the party's operations and remained influential in politics as the Seiyūkai maintained its position over the next several decades as one of the country's dominant political parties.

The institutionalization of ruffianism into the political parties was driven by an extraordinarily powerful self-perpetuating logic and inertia, whereby any given side felt it necessary to organize *sōshi* to compete with its opponents. Much like politicians and parties of the 1890s felt compelled to hire their own *sōshi* to protect themselves and fight against rival *sōshi,* the major political parties of the early twentieth century felt compelled to establish *ingaidan* to remain politically competitive. To put it another way, once *sōshi* had become a part of various political contests, it became very difficult to extricate them from the practice of politics. Politicians had no incentive to divorce themselves from *sōshi,* and the state tolerated ruffianism so long as its authority was not challenged.

Ingaidan thus came to reflect, and contribute to, a certain culture of political violence, one in which the use of violence was considered a viable and at least tacitly acceptable strategy by many of those who engaged in parliamentary politics. Such an embrace of violence was not new, considering that various sides had turned to ruffianism in the political debates and elections of the early 1890s. But in the first several decades of the twentieth century, it proliferated in parliamentary politics as violence became a structurally entrenched weapon in political battles.

Ruffianism was institutionalized into party politics at precisely the same time that political parties reached the height of their power, during an era known by many historians for its flourishing democracy. In 1918, Hara Kei became the first prime minister drawn from a political party, not from the peerage or ruling clique (*hanbatsu*) that had been so dominant in the government of the Meiji period. Hara was also the first to lead a cabinet composed largely of party members. Between 1918 and 1932, with several exceptions, control of the cabinet would be in the hands of one of the two major political parties of the time: the Seiyūkai and the Kenseikai (Constitutional Association), later known as the Rikken Minseitō (Constitutional Democratic Party, hereafter Minseitō). This was also a period that witnessed great popular participation in politics, including grassroots calls for the protection of constitutional government and universal manhood suffrage.[3]

That institutionalized ruffianism and a widespread culture of political violence accompanied this vibrant democracy raises questions about the relationship between violence and democratic practice in the first three decades of the twentieth century. To what extent did violence hamper and undermine democracy, and to what extent could it promote more inclusive politics? Of concern too is whether the culture of political violence became so embedded that it became toxic, slowly but surely eroding the institutions and practices at the heart of Japan's democracy.

The Jiyūtō *Ingaidan* and Its Bosses

Although the Jiyūtō had a loosely organized *ingaidan* as early as the 1880s, the body assumed a more defined form after the first general election in 1890. With the inauguration of the Diet, a clear distinction was made within the Jiyūtō between party members who were parliamentarians (*giindan*) and those who were not (*ingaidan*). Yet the Jiyūtō *ingaidan* was not very cohesive, consisting largely of *sōshi* whose primary allegiance was to a particular politician rather than the party as a whole. The *ingaidan sōshi* did not constitute a pooled resource on which any Jiyūtō member could draw, but usually worked for a politician to whom they had some allegiance. *Ingaidan sōshi* could also become pawns in internal contests for power, as the downfall of one politician meant that others could attempt to win control over his *sōshi*. The Jiyūtō *ingaidan* was thus less a party organization than an amalgamation of groups of *sōshi* that worked for the party's most powerful politicians.

One such politician was Hoshi Tōru, mentioned in Chapter 2, who was nicknamed "Oshi Tōru" (Pushy Tōru) for his aggressive style. Hoshi was originally a lawyer, studied in England in the 1870s, and then worked for the Ministry of Justice. He joined the Jiyūtō at its founding in 1881 and was a defense lawyer in the trial of those involved in the Osaka Incident of 1885. In this trial, Hoshi represented Ōi Kentarō, the architect of the planned military invasion of Korea, even though he considered Ōi's liberal ideology too extreme for his taste.[4] This difference between the more moderate stance of Hoshi and the more radical liberalism of Ōi created tension between the two men in late 1890 and 1891, prompting Hoshi to try to undercut Ōi's influence in the party. One of Hoshi's strategies was to shake the base of Ōi's power: the Kantōkai, a group that had at its core Santama *sōshi* (*sōshi* from the Santama region). The Kantōkai was bolstered by the support of a Diet member named Ishizaka Masataka and provided the foundation for Ōi's Tōyō Kurabu (Eastern Club), which promoted freedom, self-government, independence, and national strength. Hoshi convinced Ishizaka to withdraw from the Kantōkai, which threw the Tōyō Kurabu into confusion.[5]

Hoshi also took aim at Ōi by working to limit the power of extraparliamentary party members (like Ōi) over the party's elected representatives. Hand in hand with Jiyūtō bigwig Itagaki Taisuke, Hoshi successfully spearheaded an effort to place more decision-making power in the hands of the party's Diet members by replacing the party committee (tōgiinkai) and council (hyōgiinkai) with a caucus (taikai) in which the elected representatives were predominant, and by strengthening the executives of the representatives' caucus (daigishikai). For Itagaki, this was partially a move to discourage sōshi violence, which he had expressly criticized in the past. For Hoshi, however, these reforms were more strategic. When Ōi was eventually pushed out of the party in 1892, a triumphant Hoshi exhibited no qualms about absorbing his rival's sōshi.[6]

These sōshi supplemented those Hoshi had recruited in the last several years. In October 1890, sōshi displayed their support for Hoshi—when he arrived in the port at Yokohama after a trip abroad, there among the crowd gathered to greet him were sōshi, sitting in a row.[7] By the time he made his successful bid for a Diet seat as a Jiyūtō candidate from Tochigi Prefecture in 1892, Hoshi clearly had a cadre of his own sōshi. In one election-related incident, two of his sōshi armed with sword canes seriously wounded voters.[8] And by the 1894 election, Hoshi had the power to recruit sōshi by the hundreds. In this campaign, around 400 sōshi from Kanagawa and Saitama Prefectures made their way to the first election ward in Tochigi to help get him elected.[9]

Hoshi himself was not a refined gentleman who stayed above the fray, as one might imagine a foreign-trained lawyer of this period to be. He was very much on the ground with his sōshi and projected an image as a rough leader of violent ruffians. One politician, Ozaki Yukio, was so struck by his initial impression of Hoshi that he described their initial encounter in his autobiography:

> Suddenly, he [Hoshi] turned brusquely to me, without even so much as a bow, and called out, "You there, you must be Ozaki. I'm Hoshi." For a moment I was quite startled. He looked more like a gangster (bakuchi no oyakata) [literally, gambling boss] than a politician.[10]

Ozaki was, admittedly, of a different political mind than Hoshi, and while this may explain some of his jabs—describing Hoshi as a man with "a stick in his right hand and money in his left"—it does not distract from his genuine surprise that Hoshi's demeanor was not that of the "gentleman scholar" he was reputed to be.[11]

Hoshi was able to gain the support of sōshi, and Santama sōshi in particular, because he forged relationships with their organizers. One of them, Murano Tsuneemon, was an important sōshi leader of the 1880s who would go on to play a key role in the further consolidation of ingaidan. Murano was a popular rights activist in the 1880s and had established a school in the Santama region named the Ryōsōkan (Overcoming Frost School) that educated village children; here, Murano studied John Stuart Mill's *Principles of Political Economy* and colleague Morikubo Sakuzō, discussed below, lectured on the thinker's work on the history of the French Revolution. The Ryōsōkan also hosted fencing practices and cultivated many of the participants in the Osaka Incident as well as those who were active in the years around the first Diet in the early 1890s. Murano himself was imprisoned in the mid-1880s for his involvement in the Osaka Incident; in jail, he bided his time reading Bentham, Spencer, and Mill. When he was released in September 1888, he decided to make a name for himself in politics and began to train and organize a corps of at least several hundred *sōshi* over the next ten years. He led these men in the infamous 1892 election, during which he directed *sōshi* to protect certain candidates and voters from opposition ruffians; Murano was eventually constrained in his home by several dozen prefectural police. In these early years of the Diet, Murano rose to become an influential figure in Ōi Kentarō's Kantōkai.[12] After Ōi failed to be elected to the House of Representatives in 1892 and left the Jiyūtō to form his own party, Murano and his *sōshi* allied themselves with Hoshi Tōru.

The final member of this triumvirate of *sōshi* leaders was Morikubo Sakuzō, a man colleague Murano described as a "Tokyo Tammany Hall boss." Morikubo's early political career paralleled that of Murano—he too was imprisoned for his role (testing bombs) in the Osaka Incident, dabbled in local politics as a member of the Kanagawa prefectural assembly later in the decade, was held captive in his home during the 1892 election, and became a known figure in the Kantōkai.[13] Morikubo too stood by Hoshi's political career, even after Hoshi was ousted from his position as speaker of the house on charges that he was accepting bribes.[14] As Hoshi turned his energies to expelling rival Rikken Kaishintō (Constitutional Reform Party, hereafter Kaishintō) influence from Tokyo, Morikubo designed and executed a plan to install about 3,000 Santama *sōshi* into various strategic positions in the capital as police officers, teachers, train conductors, and the like. He also established the Musashi Kurabu (Musashi Club), whose office in Yūrakuchō became the headquarters of the movement to expand Hoshi's power in Tokyo.[15]

Morikubo was significant not only as a *sōshi* organizer, but also as someone who helped influence the ideological bent of these youth, encouraging in them a sense of nationalism. A concern about national strength had been an undercurrent of the Freedom and People's Rights Movement, and for Morikubo as for many others, the Sino-Japanese War of the mid-1890s cultivated a deeper sense of commitment and responsibility to country. In this context, Morikubo wanted to contribute to the war effort; he proposed that a volunteer army be organized from a youth group in Kanagawa. When this suggestion was denied, he launched a movement in late November 1894 to form a *gunpudan,* a group that would be on fatigue duty for a military regiment. Morikubo's idea was taken up by Naitō Buhei of the Yūitsukan, the *sōshi* school at Jiyūtō headquarters in Tokyo, and on January 26, 1895, a *gunpudan* named the Tama-gumi was officially established. The group consisted of 432 people, the core of which was about 160 *sōshi* from the Santama region. Among the leaders were several drawn from the Yūitsukan. As Morikubo had wished, those in the Tama-gumi did get the opportunity to serve their country. The group was dispatched to Taiwan, where it faced difficult conditions and disease (mainly cholera)—101 of the group's men died of illness between March and June 1895.[16]

The Tama-gumi suffered this harrowing experience in support for its nation at the same time that many in the people's parties began to abandon their oppositional stance toward the Meiji government. These reformers realized they had enjoyed little success in toppling the Meiji oligarchy from the outside and considered leaving their days of grassroots protest behind. Their new strategy was to compromise with the *hanbatsu* in order to subvert its power from within. What they sought was party cabinets, or cabinets composed mainly of party politicians rather than oligarchs. In the words of popular rights activist Kōno Hironaka, "Instead of dividing the political world horizontally with the *hambatsu* and the parties fighting one another as previously, [the tactic should now be] to divide the political world vertically, draw the leaders of the *hambatsu* into the parties, and by tearing [the *hambatsu* leaders] from their roots, open the way for a situation in which two large political parties would oppose one another."[17] Morikubo was one politician who agreed with this strategy. After returning from Taiwan, he was elected to the Diet, and in 1897, he argued that the Jiyūtō should reconcile with the cabinet of oligarch Matsukata Masayoshi. Thirsting for a party that was more open to compromise, Morikubo left the Jiyūtō that year to help form a new party, the Shin Jiyūtō (New Liberal Party), that went on to work with Matsukata as well as big business, namely the Mitsubishi *zaibatsu*. When Morikubo split from the Jiyūtō, he took his *sōshi* with him. At the Shin Jiyūtō's official establishment, 2,000 Santama *sōshi*, complete with their big black hats, went to Tokyo to join the festivities.[18]

The kind of political compromise advocated by Morikubo helped pave the way for Japan's first, but short-lived, party cabinet. The cabinet ministers belonged to the Kenseitō (Constitutional Party), newly created in 1898 by a merger between the Jiyūtō and the Shinpotō (Progressive Party). Itagaki Taisuke, leader of the former Jiyūtō, was home minister; Ōkuma Shigenobu, leader of the former Shinpotō, served as both prime minister and foreign minister. All of this activity beckoned Hoshi Tōru back to the country from the United States, where he had been serving as Japan's ambassador since 1896. He need not have rushed, for the Kenseitō fell apart within the year, splintering back into the former Jiyūtō under Itagaki Taisuke (which retained the Kenseitō name) and the former Shinpotō under Ōkuma

Shigenobu (now known as the Kensei Hontō, or True Constitutional Party). By the late 1890s, Hoshi seems to have viewed other political parties, not the Meiji oligarchy, as his main political opponent. Originally a Jiyūtō man, Hoshi disliked Ōkuma Shigenobu and his succession of parties (first the Kaishintō, then the Shinpotō, and now the Kensei Hontō). At the same time, Hoshi did not hesitate to try to broker compromises with oligarch Yamagata Aritomo.[19] It was likely this mutual willingness to work with the *hanbatsu* and distaste for the various Ōkuma parties that kept the bond between Hoshi and Morikubo intact even as parties shifted under their feet.

In the late 1890s, all three men—Morikubo, Murano, and Hoshi—enjoyed political success. Murano had followed in Morikubo's footsteps and become a member of the House of Representatives, due at least in part to his training and organization of a force of over 1,000 *sōshi*. And Hoshi was elected to the Tokyo municipal assembly in the spring of 1899, a capstone to his efforts to establish a political power base in the capital.

This triumvirate of politicians played a crucial role in consolidating *sōshi*. As *sōshi* bosses, they had brought their own coterie of ruffians under the large umbrella of the Jiyūtō *ingaidan* in the early 1890s. Then, later in the decade, Hoshi agreed to help statesman Itō Hirobumi create a new party out of the old Jiyūtō and its direct descendant, the existing Kenseitō. When their efforts culminated in the founding of the Seiyūkai in 1900, Morikubo and Murano agreed to support Hoshi and joined the party. All three men brought their *sōshi* to this venture, transforming their ruffians into Seiyūkai *sōshi*.[20]

The Seiyūkai *Ingaidan* in Party Politics

The Seiyūkai embodied the spirit of compromise with the *hanbatsu* that had grown out of the 1890s because it brought the old Jiyūtō and now defunct Kenseitō together with some Meiji oligarchs, bureaucrats, and big business. The establishment of the Seiyūkai and its ascendance thus marked the end of a sharp dichotomy between *mintō* and *ritō* (people's parties and government's parties) that had characterized much of mid-Meiji politics. This distinction faded in part because of the cooperation between the *hanbatsu* and the party, but also because the Seiyūkai itself became less of a liberal, reformist party over the next several decades. Although an offspring of *mintō*, the Seiyūkai came to be known as a *kisei seitō*, or established party, especially in journalistic publications.[21] The violence of *ingaidan* must be considered in this context of the shifting place of political parties vis-à-vis the people they were supposed to represent.

Sōshi officially became incorporated into the party structure on December 1, 1903, with the establishment of the Seiyūkai *ingaidan.*[22] Both Morikubo Sakuzō and Murano Tsuneemon played important roles in the new party. Morikubo became a powerful boss of the political world in Tokyo and Murano the head of the Seiyūkai *ingaidan.*[23] Hoshi was not so lucky and did not live to see the official founding of the Seiyūkai *ingaidan.* After the establishment of the Seiyūkai, he only had a moment in the sun, serving as communications minister for a mere two months before he was entangled in a financial scandal. His next position, as head of the Tokyo municipal assembly, was cut short by Iba Sōtarō, a local notable and fencing instructor who assassinated Hoshi in June 1901. Iba was apparently angered by what he saw as Hoshi's corruption of Tokyo politics.[24] Although Hoshi did not have a long career in the Seiyūkai, he had been instrumental in laying the groundwork for the party's *ingaidan* by bringing together, and advancing the political careers of, both Murano and Morikubo.

The purposes of the Seiyūkai *ingaidan,* and those of other parties that would be established in subsequent decades, were not unlike those of the Jiyūtō *ingaidan:* to collect information, facilitate communication, serve as security for Diet members and as guards at public meetings, disrupt opposition parties' public meetings, campaign and canvass during elections, assist in overthrowing cabinets, and organize and participate in political movements.[25] But the Seiyūkai *ingaidan* was more defined in structure and function than its Jiyūtō counterpart had been. In 1910, a dedicated office for the *ingaidan* was set up inside Seiyūkai headquarters and employed its own clerks.[26] There was a governing committee and a nominal organizational distinction made between two bodies within the *ingaidan:* the intellectual group (*interidan*) and the violent group (*bōryokudan*). The intellectual group consisted of defeated candidates, former Diet members, recent graduates, and older *ingaidan* members who remained interested in politics. They were allegedly more concerned about substantive issues than the violent group; its young members, for example, were considered knowledgeable in current political theory. The violent group consisted of *sōshi* and was known to function much like a "street gang" (*machi no gyangu*), hanging about both outside and inside the Diet when it was in session. Such a fixture were these *ingaidan* members that a popular saying—"For every boss, there is a henchman"—emphasized how all Diet members had ties to *sōshi.*[27] Although the distinction between the intellectual and violent groups was blurred in practice, there was at least some sense of different subgroups of the *ingaidan* performing different functions.

As part of the institutionalization of *sōshi* into the party structure, financial rewards also became more clearly defined. *Ingaidan sōshi* could make money by charging admission to their own political meetings and received pay for disrupting those of others. When inflicting physical harm, they were paid according to whom they hit and where they hit them. Assaulting a more prominent politician meant more pay, and payment varied according to whether the blow landed on the face, the hands and feet, or the torso.[28] An understanding of the financial aspect of the job seemed to exist between *ingaidan sōshi*, for there was an unspoken code that if opposition *sōshi* attended one's public meeting, they were to be allowed to disrupt the gathering at least briefly before being hauled off so that they would receive their pay.[29] This emphasis on financial compensation suggests that these ruffians viewed themselves primarily as professionals carrying out a particular job and that any political convictions were secondary to their occupational identity as *sōshi*.

The *ingaidan* as an institution was somewhat like the political machines of urban U.S. politics in the late nineteenth and early twentieth centuries. Generally speaking, both the *ingaidan* and U.S. political machines served similar functions and used similar methods—forwarding the party's agenda and expanding its influence through graft and coercion. The violent wing of the *ingaidan*, in particular, was much like the groups on which U.S. political bosses relied for violence and protection. In New York City's Sixth Ward, fire company foreman Matthew Brennan was rewarded with favors for providing "a gang of forty or so tough young men" for primary meetings and elections.[30] Likewise, in antebellum Philadelphia, politicians would court the help of volunteer fire companies, street gangs, and other neighborhood groups. The street gangs, especially, were known to receive payment, patronage, and immunity from criminal prosecution in return for protecting ballot boxes and blocking polls.[31] The parallel between these groups and *ingaidan* breaks down, however, when considering that the *ingaidan sōshi* did not have an identity as part of an independent organization (such as a fire company or a gang) outside the *ingaidan*. The *ingaidan's* sole purpose was political, incorporated as it was into the structure of the political parties.

Because the *ingaidan* operated from within the political parties, it is not particularly helpful to compare them to the pressure groups of British politics, which attempted to influence political parties from without. British pressure groups were not the promoters of party interests, as *ingaidan* were, but special-interest lobbies that occupied a position outside political parties.[32]

It should also be noted that *ingaidan* were not as sophisticated as U.S. political machines. When Tammany Hall was at its height between the end of the Civil War and the beginning of the New Deal, it functioned as a Democratic political machine whose success "rested on its ability to dominate nominations and elections, as well as its virtual monopoly over appointive governmental positions."[33] No political party's *ingaidan*, or the political parties themselves, had this much power in Taisho Japan. And the sheer scope of the web of patronage around Tammany seems much greater than any Japanese counterpart, though this may be for lack of adequate research into corruption in prewar Japan.[34]

Perhaps the most illuminating parallel when considering the *ingaidan* as an organization is not to political machines or pressure groups in other countries, but to *bakuto* (gambler) groups in Japan itself. Both organizations were based on boss-henchmen (*oyabun-kobun*) relationships that were reinforced by a pay structure in which the boss determined the salary of the henchmen.[35] The two groups also used violence as a means of doing business. There are limits to this analogy, for *bakuto* viewed their colleagues and bosses as an adopted family bound together by fictive kinship ties, and the *bakuto* groups were more businesses than political organizations. Yet that both groups were labeled "bōryokudan" by those outside them suggests that their violence was visible enough to be considered their defining feature. Both *ingaidan* and *bakuto* did not eschew the use of physical force and cultivated a certain culture of violence within their organizations. It should not be surprising, then, that *ingaidan* would work together with some *bakuto* in nationalist organizations which, as will be discussed in the following chapter, also indirectly connected *ingaidan sōshi* to the military and the bureaucracy.

Although the *ingaidan* did wield violence, their overarching political aims were not necessarily undemocratic. The Seiyūkai *ingaidan*, for example, was intended to serve as a check on the influence of the *hanbatsu* and the military. Even as the Seiyūkai cooperated with certain oligarchs and bureaucrats, it sought to prevent the encroachment of either on its power. This defensive stand was seen in three specific resolutions made at the time of the *ingaidan*'s establishment. The *ingaidan* was to help denounce the government for mishandling negotiations with Russia; oppose the government's financial plans that ignored earlier promises; and inquire about possible unconstitutional disbursements from the reserves for expenditures rejected by the previous Diet.[36] Jockeying for power, the Seiyūkai *ingaidan* sometimes found itself in league with popular elements that also sought to contain overreaching by the *hanbatsu*, bureaucracy, and the military. In negotiating this political terrain, the *ingaidan*'s tactics melded with those of protesters who took to the streets, especially during what historian Miyachi Masato has called "the era of popular violence." Between the Hibiya "riot" in 1905 and the widespread "rice riots" of 1918, people called for policies true to the imperial and popular will.[37] The Seiyūkai may not have had such a popular vision, but its interests overlapped with those of the protesters and reinforced their shared anti-*hanbatsu* position.

Such was the case in the First Movement to Protect Constitutional Government (Kensei Yōgo Undō) of 1912–1913, in which the Seiyūkai became a part of a popular movement protesting the decision to install as the next prime minister Katsura Tarō, a so-called elder statesman and *hanbatsu* politician originally from Chōshū Domain. As part of this effort, the Seiyūkai worked together with the Rikken Kokumintō (Constitutional Nationalist Party, hereafter Kokumintō), founded in 1910 by Inukai Tsuyoshi, who led the faction of the party that refused any compromise with the oligarchs. The *ingaidan* of both the Seiyūkai and the Kokumintō did not necessarily act violently to forward this movement; on many occasions, they held rallies to whip up support for their anti-*hanbatsu* cause. One such gathering put on by the Seiyūkai *ingaidan* in the Nihonbashi area of Tokyo attracted about 1,000 participants. *Ingaidan* also organized smaller deliberative meetings to discuss strategies for the movement.[38] As the Seiyūkai and Kokumintō came together, so did their *ingaidan*, which held joint rallies and meetings in January and February 1913.[39] It was Murano Tsuneemon who officially created a Seiyūkai-Kokumintō *ingaidan*, which included 3,000 Seiyūkai *sōshi* who had been under Morikubo Sakuzō. At a speech meeting, Morikubo was allegedly praised as the parties' equal to Katsura Tarō.[40]

That the *ingaidan sōshi* inhabited the same political space as popular protesters could be seen in the early political career of Ōno Banboku, who transcended the fine boundary between popular and *ingaidan* violence with relative ease. During the First Movement to Protect Constitutional Government, Ōno was a law student at Meiji University in Tokyo and was on the way to a library to study for a law exam one day when he stumbled upon a public meeting where Inukai Tsuyoshi and Ozaki Yukio were advocating the preservation of constitutional government. Drawn by their political message, Ōno decided to join the movement, and in February 1913 he participated in a protest calling for a vote of no confidence in the Katsura Tarō cabinet. On the morning of February 10, Ōno and his colleagues surrounded the Diet building and yelled in support of the Seiyūkai and Kokumintō representatives as they arrived. These Diet members wore white roses to distinguish themselves, so the student groups and *ingaidan* would cheer for them by shouting, "White-rose group *banzai!*" By the afternoon, the crowd had swelled to tens of thousands of people, and when it learned the Diet had been prorogued, it flowed from the vicinity of the Diet building to Hibiya Park and toward Ginza, attacking newspaper companies such as the Kokumin Shinbun and the Yomiuri Shinbun along the way. The police marked the protesters in the crowd with chalk, and using this method they were able to identify Ōno as a participant and arrest him along with 250 others.[41] After this incident, Ōno realized that he, as a popular protester and not a formal party member, had helped forward the Seiyūkai's cause without monetary gain. To be rewarded for his efforts, he decided to go to Seiyūkai headquarters to request monetary compensation. Ōno eventually secured an appointment with Murano Tsuneemon, who by this time was the secretary-general of the Seiyūkai. Murano treated him to lunch with sake and beer, gave him money, and suggested that he begin spending time at party headquarters. Ōno followed his advice and became friendly with *ingaidan* executives who convinced him to join their group.[42]

Ōno became a member of the *ingaidan*'s youth division, known as the Tes-shinkai (Iron Spirit Association), which was born in a moment of elation over the success of the First Movement to Protect Constitutional Government in top-pling the Katsura Tarō cabinet. The Tesshinkai was originally composed of the many youth who had gathered in Tokyo for the movement, and through this division, the *ingaidan* was able to build ties with groups of college students in the capital as well. The Seiyūkai became known for recruiting Meiji University students like Ōno, many of whom were in the debate club. These students with a flair for public speaking were enlisted to appear at party speech meetings in and around Tokyo and to participate in election campaigns in return for an oc-casional free, nice meal. Ōno himself regularly gave such orations and was so vociferous in his criticism of the foreign policy of the Ōkuma Shigenobu cabinet (1914–1916) and proactive in his organization of these meetings that he was found guilty of violating the Public Order and Police Law.[43] Although the *in-gaidan* lawyer advised him to skip town and keep a low profile, Ōno went against this recommendation and served out his term in prison. When he was released, a crowd of fellow *ingaidan* members was there to greet him, holding a banner that read: "Hurrah to the patriotic *shishi* Ōno Banboku!" (*Yūkoku no shishi Ōno Banboku banzai!*).[44]

In addition to students, the Tesshinkai also recruited yakuza, both *bakuto* and *tekiya* (itinerant merchants). The Seiyūkai was not alone in its enlistment of yakuza; its main opposition party (the Kenseikai) also tapped *bakuto* for help. One of the leaders of the Tesshinkai, Ōno Shigeharu, made it a point to mo-bilize these violence specialists and was known himself for epitomizing physi-cal strength. One *ingaidan* member remembered Ōno as being tall with broad shoulders, and the kind of man who was very much like a yakuza.[45]

The wielding of physical force was not exclusive to the yakuza elements of the *ingaidan*—those who engaged in the more cerebral *ingaidan* activities, like giving speeches, were not above using violence. Ōno Banboku, for example, par-ticipated in Seiyūkai meetings and disrupted those of the opposition party. In one incident, Ōno went to a gathering of the Kenseikai, a party formed in 1916 through the mergers of various parties with the Rikken Dōshikai (Constitutional Association of Friends, hereafter Dōshikai, founded in 1913 by Katsura Tarō). The Kenseikai had its own *ingaidan* and formed ties with Waseda University, fos-tering a Seiyūkai–Meiji University versus Kenseikai–Waseda University rivalry.[46] Not surprisingly, the *ingaidan* of these two main party adversaries—the Seiyūkai and the Kenseikai—clashed on a number of occasions. In this particular case, Ōno and his colleagues heckled Kenseikai speakers from the second floor of a theater. When a speaker taunted them to come down to the stage, one did and was promptly attacked by the Kenseikai *ingaidan*. Ōno tried to help, shrugging off a policeman and jumping down from the second floor, but his efforts were too late as his friend had already been dragged off by the police.

The physicality of the work of *ingaidan sōshi*, along with the culture of drinking that seems to have accompanied it, put them in a world that overlapped with others in which violence was not considered aberrant. The recruitment of yakuza by *ingaidan* was a prime example of how violence created a fluidity between the political and, legally speaking, criminal realms. This blurring of boundaries was evident on the ground, sometimes in strange ways. On one occasion, Ōno Banboku apparently approached a well-known yakuza boss named Takebe Kosaku for money because he and his friends had spent ¥40 more on an evening than they had planned. Takebe had been a member of the Jiyūtō before he became a *bakuto* and then branched out into protection and extortion in the business world through the use of corporate racketeers (*sōkaiya*).[47] Although Takebe likely retained his political connections, it is unclear why Ōno thought the yakuza boss would feel compelled to give him money, and Takebe was apparently puzzled as well for, after a battle of words, he ordered his henchmen to surround Ōno and beat him. Ōno managed to fend off the henchmen and make his way toward the door, but Takebe called after him and expressed his respect for the way Ōno had talked to him, gave him money, and invited him to stay for sake and beer. The two apparently had a "man to man relationship" (*otoko dōshi no tsukiai*) after that encounter.[48] Although the specifics of this incident are somewhat dubious, it does seem that ideals of courage, masculinity, and physical strength were shared by political violence specialists whether they were *ingaidan sōshi* or yakuza.

The tone in which Ōno described his various *ingaidan* tussles and scuffles also suggests that he, and perhaps many others, enjoyed being a *sōshi* and was drawn to the *ingaidan* as much by the opportunity to drink and roughhouse as by his political commitment to protecting constitutional government or criticizing Ōkuma's foreign policy. Looking back on these days from the postwar period, Ōno described his *ingaidan* days as fun and was nostalgic about this time in his life when he could get a free lunch and pocket some money for his ruffianism.[49] This attitude resonates with the argument of British historian Carolyn Conley that violence can sometimes serve as a pastime, a form of recreation. Conley characterizes recreational violence by "clearly defined rules, willing participants, a sense of pleasure in the activity and an absence of any malicious intent."[50] Although the intent is questionable when it comes to *ingaidan sōshi*, they were certainly willing participants and at least some of them, like Ōno, seem to have experienced pleasure through their ruffianism. There were also rules, however unspoken, to *ingaidan* violence. There was the "code," mentioned above, whereby *ingaidan* allowed their opposition to create at least some disturbance at their meeting so that their fellow ruffians, though working for the other side, could be paid.

There was also an understanding between the *ingaidan sōshi* and the police that as long as ruffianism did not escalate to assassination or severe disruption of order, those who perpetrated *ingaidan* violence might be rounded up but would not be charged and processed through the legal system. It is difficult to speak about police treatment of *ingaidan sōshi* with specificity given the lack of statistics about ruffianism. But Ōno, at least, claims that ruffians who disrupted public meetings were often taken to prison where they were fed and then released as soon as the meeting ended.[51] On some occasions, *sōshi* and the Metropolitan Police worked together, as in early February 1914 when the police allowed several hundred ruffians under Morikubo Sakuzō to help guard the residences of the prime minister and the home minister.[52] *Sōshi* understood that their use of physical force should be kept at the level of brawls and fistfights, and that any escalation in violence or direct challenge to the government (as in the First Movement to Protect Constitutional Government) would be considered a departure from accepted practice and run them afoul of the police. From the perspective of the police, the *ingaidan sōshi,* unlike their Meiji-era predecessors, did not pose a significant or immediate threat to the government or the state. Though they may have made the practice of politics dangerous and even tumultuous, they generally did not provoke widespread upheaval or turmoil. The police thus had little to gain from the effort and expense of cracking down on ruffians. That *ingaidan sōshi* of the Ōno Banboku mold understood these rules and were willing, even eager, to wield physical force gives weight to the idea that there was a recreational element to their violence.

The unspoken limits on ruffianism also suggest that violence often served as a kind of performance, a ritualized demonstration of power and one's political stance. Even when physical force itself may not have affected outcomes, the show of *sōshi* violence was an important sign of political resources and seriousness of interest. Just because ruffianism could be performative did not mean the menace of violence was neutralized; however restricted, punches and kicks and destruction of property could still coerce and evoke fear. And the rules of violent engagement may have contributed to the sense that certain acts of physical force were acceptable, thereby perpetuating a culture of political violence.

In the mid-1910s, Ōno had stumbled on the Seiyūkai *ingaidan* during a resurgence of ruffianism. Politician Ozaki Yukio commented on this phenomenon: "In the past, gangsters (*sōshi*) had frequently been employed in politics, but much less had been seen of them lately. With the emergence of the Terauchi [Masatake] administration [1916–1918], however, the thugs (*bōto*) began to stalk again. They were at every public speech. I was attacked a number of times."[53] In a January 1917 incident, Ozaki was on stage giving a speech at a public meeting before a crowd, including an opposition mob, when he was assaulted by a "thug" who ran at him with a seven-inch knife.[54]

There are several possible explanations for this heightened *sōshi* violence in the mid-1910s. The March 1915 election campaign was marred by government interference (*senkyo kanshō*), the first on such a large scale since the notoriously violent second general election in 1892. At stake this time was an increase in military expenditures, opposed by the Seiyūkai the previous year and supported by the Dōshikai. In its zeal to defeat the Seiyūkai on this issue, the government employed a number of strategies. Home Minister Oura Kanetake, a Satsuma Domain native and former superintendent general of the police, bought votes to help secure the election of Dōshikai and other favorable candidates in national races. Oura pressured prefectural governors to deliver victories at the local level as well. Money, mainly from *zaibatsu,* was doled out to friendly candidates in increments of around ¥5,000, and votes were purchased at prices anywhere from three to several dozen yen. Police also visited the homes of electors to coerce them to vote for the Dōshikai and other amenable parties, while closely monitoring the Seiyūkai to prevent illegal vote-getting on that side. Election law abuses were rampant; figures are somewhat unreliable and vary depending on the source, but the Home Ministry reported 958 cases of election violations involving 10,554 people. These numbers were higher than in the previous general election when there were 551 cases involving 4,923 people.[55] The Seiyūkai did surrender its absolute majority in the House of Representatives with this election, losing 81 seats while the Dōshikai gained 51. This outcome was not due solely to the government's interference for Prime Minister Ōkuma Shigenobu enjoyed great popularity; his introduction of Harry Truman-esque whistle-stop campaigning was also successful.[56] Nonetheless, in this context where no holds were barred, it is not surprising that ruffianism, along with money, was widely used to gain political leverage. And in the years after 1915, physical force was perpetuated by the combative division between the two major political parties, the Seiyūkai and the Kenseikai (created out of a merger between the Dōshikai and several other parties) and, at times, between certain parties and the cabinet.

The rivalry between the Seiyūkai and the Kenseikai was reminiscent of the divide between *mintō* and *ritō* of the Meiji years and was especially acute during elections. This tension was exemplified in a local race in 1920 between the Seiyūkai's Murano Tsuneemon and Kenseikai candidate Yatsunami Takeji. As part of his campaign, Murano mobilized around 150 Tesshinkai *sōshi* to descend upon his opponent's election office in Hachiōji and left the place a mess.[57] In this city in southwestern Tokyo, *sōshi* walked about with sticks and clubs, and they concealed other weapons inside their breast pockets. Both sides not only called on youth but also hired longshoremen from nearby Yokohama and Shibaura and mobilized *bakuto* as well. Clashes between the ruffians of Murano and Yatsunami reached a climax in April when 200 of them fought, provoking the dispatch of armed police officers and resulting in the imprisonment of 68 people.[58]

The two parties also clashed over universal manhood suffrage, the most prominent political issue in these years and a lightning rod for both *sōshi* and popular violence. While the origins of the call for universal manhood suffrage dated back to the 1890s, the movement reached a peak in 1919 and 1920 with the support of the Kenseikai and less powerful Kokumintō. Demonstrators took to the streets, at first in modest rallies and then in huge crowds of tens of thousands of people. In one mass demonstration in February 1920, a core group of participants marched on Seiyūkai headquarters to protest the party's stand against universal manhood suffrage. The party's impenetrable front gate, protected by *sōshi* and police officers, then opened to let in four spokesmen from the assembled crowd. Over an hour later, one of the protesters was ejected, "his face streaming blood from a beating at the hands of the Seiyūkai *sōshi*."[59] The Kenseikai side did not refrain from using this kind of violence. When it formed an alliance with other pro-universal manhood suffrage parties in June 1923, a coalition youth group was established, led in part by a prominent Kenseikai *ingaidan* figure. This equivalent of the Seiyūkai's Tesshinkai also used *sōshi* methods.[60]

In 1924, the Kenseikai and a portion of the Seiyūkai came together on the question of universal manhood suffrage out of apprehension about the cabinet. Both parties feared a return to transcendental, nonparty cabinets, having enjoyed party cabinets since Hara Kei's in 1918. A faction of the Seiyūkai thus compromised with the Kenseikai, agreeing to support universal manhood suffrage so that the two parties could work together to topple the cabinet of bureaucrat-politician Kiyoura Keigo—a cabinet minister several times over, president of the Privy Council, and ally of elder statesman Yamagata Aritomo. As part of what became known as the Second Movement to Protect Constitutional Government, the Seiyūkai spearheaded *ingaidan* activities and organized rallies and meetings.[61] The Seiyūkai *ingaidan* also mobilized several hundred Santama *sōshi*. Yokoda Sennosuke, a parliamentarian and future minister of justice, helped form a special squad of 20 *sōshi* who beat people up and smashed property. The *ingaidan* also planned disturbances within and on the front steps of the Diet to try to rattle the Kiyoura cabinet.[62]

The issue of universal manhood suffrage united parts of the Seiyūkai and the Kenseikai, but it also created a fault line within the Seiyūkai and its *ingaidan*. The party's compromise with the Kenseikai drove a faction to split off and form the Seiyū Hontō (True Seiyū Party) which stood by the Kiyoura Keigo cabinet and opposed expanded suffrage. The Seiyū Hontō promptly established its own *ingaidan*, composed of several dozen youth from the cities of Hachiōji and Fuchū—the split in the party thus created a split between *ingaidan sōshi*.

Like the First Movement to Protect Constitutional Government, the second was ultimately successful in forcing the resignation of the cabinet. A coalition of the Kenseikai, Seiyūkai, and Kakushin Kurabu (Reform Club) won a majority in the House of Representatives in the 1924 election and formed a cabinet (*goken sanpa naikaku,* or cabinet of three groups protecting the constitution) under Kenseikai premier Katō Takaaki. This cabinet is best known for overseeing passage of two significant laws in 1925: the Universal Manhood Suffrage Law (Futsū Senkyo Hō), which extended the vote to males 25 years of age and older, but also the Peace Preservation Law (Chian Iji Hō), which greatly restricted freedom of speech and assembly in an attempt to control the political activity of communists and anarchists.[63]

The 1928 general election was the first under universal manhood suffrage, and this broadening of political participation significantly influenced the conduct of elections in both the short and long terms. In the short term, universal manhood suffrage exacerbated Seiyūkai fears about the party's loss of control in politics. The Seiyūkai was already being challenged by the Minseitō, a party formed in 1927 through a merger of the Kenseikai and Seiyū Hontō. Within weeks of its founding, the Minseitō had held an inauguration for its *ingaidan* at which 500 members were present, including former home minister and now *ingaidan* adviser Tokonami Takejirō.[64] Universal manhood suffrage added unpredictability to the mix, prompting the Seiyūkai to engage in election interference, the third major instance of such manipulation after 1892 and 1915. In this case, Seiyūkai Home Minister Suzuki Kisaburō abused his influence over the bureaucracy and legal arms of the state to disadvantage the rival Minseitō. Suzuki dispatched a dozen representatives from the Home Ministry as well as prefectural governors to follow Minseitō inspectors who were investigating campaign practices. And police disrupted opposition meetings. The home minister also prohibited "certain campaign speakers, pamphlets, and posters" and had his detectives arrest for election violations 1,701 Minseitō supporters and 3,001 backers of other parties, but just 164 Seiyūkai faithful.[65]

Universal manhood suffrage not only exacerbated Seiyūkai concerns about losing ground in the 1928 election but, more significant in the long term, it was also pivotal in tipping the scales away from ruffianism and toward other forms of influence in election campaigns. Simply put, the tremendous expansion of the electorate rendered violence an inefficient and costly method of shaping voter behavior. Since the last general election in 1924, the size of the electorate had almost quadrupled from just above three million people to over 12 million, or about 20 percent of the population.[66] This was too many people to try to intimidate or coerce by force, and it made better financial sense to bribe voters than to pay *ingaidan sōshi* to rough them up.

In addition, the new election law of 1925 that granted universal manhood suffrage also restricted opportunities for ruffianism and cracked down on violence. It banned door-to-door canvassing and placed limits on the number of employees that candidates could hire. The law also specified that those who used violence (*bōkō*) or force (*iryoku*) against electors, candidates, campaigners, or elected politicians would be subject to a maximum of three years of imprisonment (with or without hard labor) or a fine of no more than ¥2,000. The same punishment would be applied to those who obstructed communication, assembly, or speeches, or otherwise used deceptive or illegal methods to disturb the freedom of elections (article 115). Those found in possession of guns, swords, clubs, or other weapons sufficient to kill or wound someone would face a maximum of two years of imprisonment without hard labor or a fine of no more than ¥1,000 (article 121). This punishment was increased to a maximum of three years of imprisonment and a fine of no more than ¥2,000 for those found guilty of carrying such weapons at election halls, polls, or places where votes were being counted (article 122).[67] Historian Matsuo Takayoshi has convincingly suggested that these provisions of the law were intended to undercut the handful of burgeoning proletarian political parties at a time when more people would be heading to the polls.[68] The fear was that these parties, not as wealthy as the major ones such as the Seiyūkai and Minseitō, would resort to violence (using their own fists, not those of hired *sōshi*) as a means of exerting influence. The new election law should not be read, then, as a fundamental shift in the state's treatment of all *sōshi* or a blanket condemnation of ruffianism. Nevertheless, though aimed at the proletarian parties, the law may have dissuaded *sōshi* violence of the major political parties as well.

For all of these reasons, by the late 1920s, ruffianism seems to have been outpaced by bribery.[69] In the next general election held two years later, the number of people prosecuted for bribery doubled from 216 to 474. Those prosecuted for violence did triple, but the figures were so small (an increase from two to six) that the jump seems insignificant at best and unreliable at worst.[70] Although the statistics may be questionable, there were also far fewer mentions of election violence in journalistic outlets and by politicians themselves during these years, suggesting at least a slight waning of *ingaidan sōshi* ruffianism in the late 1920s.

Cultures of Violence: Yakuza Bosses in Diet Politics

The embrace of violence specialists by political institutions during the first several decades of the twentieth century was seen not just in the recruitment of *sōshi* and yakuza into *ingaidan*, but also in the election of yakuza bosses to the House of Representatives. One such Diet member was featured in the *Chūgai shōgyō shinpō* series with which this chapter opened. Yoshida Isokichi, a *bakuto* boss with a big territory in Kyūshū, was reported to possess unparalleled courage and was held up as an ideal for aspiring parliamentarians. Apparently known as the Banzuiin Chōbei of his generation, he was painted as the modern equivalent of the seventeenth-century *bakuto* boss and mythically brave "man of chivalry" (*kyōkaku*).[71] In Diet sessions, Yoshida was (misleadingly) described as sitting like a golden buddha, in dignified silence.[72] Yoshida was joined in the House of Representatives by at least one other yakuza boss turned politician: Hora Sennosuke. Considered together, these two men had political careers that spanned the Taisho and early Showa periods and personified the acceptance of yakuza in national politics at the highest levels.

One reason voters and fellow politicians did not look askance at Yoshida and Hora was because the culture of political violence was not contained within the *ingaidan,* but permeated parliamentary politics. *Sōshi* quite literally passed through the parliament's gates and were found wandering in the corridors and anterooms of the Diet building.[73] What is more, elected representatives themselves did not shun violence and were encouraged by party leaders to turn to force when speech was insufficient.[74] Many parliamentarians did not leave physical ruffianism to hired strongmen but flexed their own muscle when deemed necessary, even within the Diet chamber. As described by historian Peter Duus, brawling on the Diet floor was standard practice by the 1920s: "The seats of the two major parties were separated on the floor of the House of Representatives by an aisle down the middle of the chamber. It became customary for the largest and strongest members of each party to sit along the edge of this no-man's land in the event tempers flared. The nameplates of the Diet members, originally movable, were nailed to the desks, because they made handy and exceedingly damaging implements of offense."[75] Beneath the positive gloss of the *Chūgai shōgyō shinpō* series was the actuality that physical strength had indeed become an asset in political life, making Yoshida and Hora attractive politicians in this regard. The election of Yoshida and Hora also suggests something about the status of yakuza—that they, or at least certain yakuza bosses in certain regions, were not regarded as part of a shadowy "underworld" but were considered worthy representatives of particular interests in their local communities. And their presence in the Diet reflected, and perpetuated, a brand of politics in which violence laced political discourse even within the walls of the parliament itself.

Before launching into a discussion of the political careers of Yoshida and Hora, a note must be made about the difficulty of writing about two men whose lives were captured in materials that often embellish or seek to distort certain aspects of their careers. Yoshida in particular has become an almost legendary figure. Even today, his statue and a plaque commemorating his achievements stand in a large park in Kita Kyūshū City. More to the point, Yoshida has been the model for characters in works of fiction, such as Hino Ashihei's *Hana to ryū* (The Flowers and the Dragon).[76] He is also discussed in books and magazines generally complimentary of yakuza that lean toward hagiography, including Fujita Gorō's *Ninkyō hyakunenshi* (A Hundred-Year History of Chivalry) and an article in *Jitsuwa jidai* (True Story Times), a tabloid-esque publication about yakuza.[77] I have deliberately avoided using such materials for insights into his life as it was lived, but even the biography, newspaper articles, and people's recollections that have been combed are potentially misleading. Compared to Yoshida, Hora is a lesser-known figure who has not been the subject of apotheosis. Yet the dearth of writing about him means that great reliance is placed on his autobiography, a project of self-eulogy. Although these sources are problematic in some ways, it is precisely the bombastic misrepresentations in the materials on Yoshida and Hora that are the most telling about the nature of yakuza involvement in Diet politics. The decisions about what to exaggerate speak to how yakuza portrayed themselves in the political world, what functions they served, and why they were embraced by other politicians. For example, Yoshida's biography and Hora's autobiography characterize the two men as *kyōkaku*, not as yakuza. Hora in particular argued vehemently that he made a transition at one point in his life from being a yakuza to being a *kyōkaku*. The use of this euphemism underscores the fact that Yoshida and Hora presented themselves as *kyōkaku* to constituents and fellow politicians. The *kyōkaku* slogan of "helping the weak and crushing the strong" was likely attractive to certain members of their districts, and the patriotic overtones of being a *kyōkaku* resonated with various political supporters.

Sources have also exaggerated the fighting skills of both men, retelling confrontations with yakuza or politicians like samurai myth in which a desperately outnumbered protagonist miraculously prevails over his mightier foe. That there was no attempt to conceal, and in fact an effort to stress, the ability of Yoshida and Hora to use force suggests that violence was acceptable when interwoven with a political justification or ideology, even one as broad and ambiguous as acting like a patriotic *kyōkaku*. The willingness and ability of the two men to both wield and justify their violence, inside and outside the Diet, may have been one reason why "respectable" politicians sought their favor.

Yoshida Isokichi made his entrance into Diet politics as an anti-Seiyūkai candidate in the infamous March 1915 election that was tainted by government interference. Having defeated Noda Utarō of the Seiyūkai, he was selected to represent the Chikuhō region of northern Kyūshū.[78]

Yoshida's early life did not foretell a career in elite politics. His father, Tokuhira, was a tenth-generation samurai but was forced to leave his domain after a dispute and became a wanderer. Tokuhira traveled from domain to domain, suffered the death of his wife Nobu along the way, and eventually settled in a town called

Ashiya, in present-day Fukuoka Prefecture, with his second wife, Saku. Tokuhira and Saku led a relatively poor life, as Tokuhira's employment opportunities were limited by the estrangement from his domain. The family's financial condition worsened after Tokuhira's death in 1872, which left Saku to care for then five-year-old Isokichi and his two older sisters, Sue and Mon. The young Yoshida did not attend his local school but worked various odd jobs. At the age of nine, he left Ashiya to work at a tobacco store in nearby Hakata, but ended up running away to return to his hometown where he peddled eggs, vegetables, and fish for most of his early teenage years. Then, at the age of 16, Yoshida became a boatman in the coal shipping port of Wakamatsu. He was an indebted boatman to a boss for several years until he became an independent boatman with money provided by his eldest sister, Sue, who was managing a prosperous brothel.[79]

Yoshida began to frequent a world created and inhabited by yakuza in his twenties, after working as a boatman for approximately six years and returning to Wakamatsu after taking a trip to Pusan. Having borrowed more money from Sue, Yoshida gambled. The gamblers with whom he came to associate were usually professional *bakuto* through whom Yoshida was introduced to various bosses. These connections often took him outside Wakamatsu to, for example, Nagasaki where on one occasion he gambled at a high-class restaurant turned gambling hall with bosses from the Kansai region. In addition to being a gambler, Yoshida became a local businessman in 1899 when he opened a small restaurant called Gengintei as a way to support his new wife, Inada Iwa, and their son, Keitarō.

Yoshida's prominence in both the yakuza and business communities paved his path to becoming a yakuza boss. In the same year he opened his restaurant, Yoshida was approached by Wakamatsu's town elders and local business owners who asked him to help stabilize the local yakuza territories. He agreed and began to recruit henchmen such as Nakayama Toyokichi and Okabe Teizō (a future politician himself).[80] Yoshida's arrival as a true *bakuto* boss was marked by his successful suppression of the rival Ezaki-gumi (or Ezaki "family") in February 1900. The story of the event as told by freelance writer Ino Kenji reads like myth: Yoshida, with his henchmen Nakayama and Okabe and only seven or eight other men, was challenged to a fight by Ezaki Mankichi and his 70 to 80 henchmen. Though outnumbered, Yoshida miraculously defeated the seemingly stronger foe. With this victory, however exaggerated in its recounting, Yoshida seems to have maintained or even gained some prominence in the community. By 1909, he was serving as part of a firefighting group and, in the fall of that year, he garnered widespread recognition for mediating a conflict between yakuza in Osaka and Tokyo over which of the cities would gain the affiliation of a highly ranked sumo wrestler.[81]

Yoshida's involvement in politics reached a national level in 1915 when he ran for a Diet seat in the House of Representatives.[82] Although what prompted

Yoshida to run for national office is not clear, it does seem that he was motivated at least in some small part by a dislike of the Seiyūkai. Yoshida allegedly viewed the Seiyūkai as behaving impudently, and while sympathetic with Ōkuma Shigenobu's anti-Seiyūkai efforts, he was concerned about the vitality of the 77-year-old and thus sought to assume the role of injecting youth and energy into the anti-Seiyūkai movement. Yoshida's anti-Seiyūkai stance could have been shaped too by pragmatic calculations. It is possible that he sensed, and hoped to ride to political office, the rising tide of anti-Seiyūkai sentiment and the so-called "Ōkuma boom"; in the 1915 election, the Seiyūkai lost its absolute majority and Yoshida won his Diet seat.[83]

Perhaps more important, Yoshida had a genuine concern for northern Kyūshū and its business interests in particular. The Chikuhō region, which Yoshida represented, was well known for iron and steel production and part of the Kita Kyūshū industrial zone whose rapid growth in the early decades of the twentieth century was fueled by the Chikuhō coalfield. From his contact with the mining industry during his teenage years and owning a small business, Yoshida was likely sympathetic to the needs of the new commercial and industrial class. From this population of the Chikuhō region, including farmers' groups as well as coal miners, he drew his political backers. At one public meeting in Wakamatsu, an audience of 6,000 such supporters gathered, saying, "Let's listen to the boss's (*oyabun no*) speech!"[84] Indeed, in his 1920 bid for a Diet seat, Yoshida ran as a candidate for the Kenseikai, the party that drew most of its support from the new commercial and industrial class.

Once elected to the Diet, Yoshida was willing to act violently. The *Chūgai shōgyō shinpō* article discussed above may have described Yoshida as sitting in the Diet like a dignified and silent "golden buddha," but there were times when he participated in scuffles on the Diet floor. Shortly after he was first elected in 1915, an incident was sparked when Prime Minister Ōkuma Shigenobu stood before a special session of the Diet to express harsh criticism of the Seiyūkai. His words angered a Seiyūkai member named Mutō Kaneyoshi, who stormed toward Ōkuma, seized one of the prime minister's arms, and tried to pull him off the platform. In an attempt to free Ōkuma, Yoshida grabbed Mutō. Several of Yoshida's colleagues then tried to hold him back, resulting in a pile up of politicians on the Diet floor.[85] A similar incident occurred in the spring of 1927, when Vice Chairman Koizumi suggested that no motions be made until the bills in question were discussed. Some Seiyūkai members were upset by this and rushed the vice chairman, at which point Yoshida ran up to Koizumi's seat and pushed several men off the dais.[86]

Yoshida also brought his *bakuto* into the political fold. That Yoshida's henchmen occupied the same violent political space as *ingaidan sōshi* was illustrated

3.1. Yoshida Isokichi at the age of 42 or 43. In Yoshida Isokichi-ō Denki Kankōkai, ed., *Yoshida Isokichi-ō den* (Tokyo: Yoshida Isokichi-ō Denki Kankōkai, 1941).

in 1924, when a brawl in the Diet extended beyond the chamber's walls. The ordeal began as a fight on the Diet floor, which an angered Yoshida wanted to join. He was, however, held back by fellow Kenseikai politician Machida Chūji (future executive of the Minseitō), who jumped on Yoshida's neck to prevent him from exacerbating the situation. Although the disorder inside the Diet eventually died down, it created tension outside the building where approximately ten of Yoshida's henchmen had gathered upon hearing a rumor that their boss had been kicked during the melee. A showdown developed as Yoshida's henchmen faced off against the Seiyūkai *ingaidan*. An outright battle was averted in this instance, however, when Yoshida invited the Seiyūkai *ingaidan* to a banquet at a high-class restaurant in Tsukiji in a gesture of reconciliation.[87] There is much that seems to be omitted from the recounting of this particular incident. It is not clear why Yoshida ultimately decided to smooth over his relationship with the Seiyūkai *ingaidan*. And while this anecdote was intended to demonstrate how Yoshida avoided fights and upheld justice, it is striking that he wanted to join the Diet scuffle in the first place and that Machida stopped him out of concern for problems that would have arisen if Yoshida had entered the fray. Most evident is that Yoshida's henchmen served the same violent and protective function as the Seiyūkai *ingaidan*.

On at least one occasion, the violence of Yoshida's henchmen went beyond ruffianism to murder. On September 27, 1919, Shinagawa Nobuyasu, president of the *Wakamatsu jitsugyō shinbun* and a man sympathetic to the Seiyūkai, was walking home around 9:15 in the evening when he was fatally stabbed in the heart. Shinagawa was known to have supported a Seiyūkai candidate named Ishizaki and to have said critical words about Yoshida. Shinagawa's murderer, Nakanishi Naganosuke, was a henchman of Yoshida Isokichi.[88]

Yoshida's reputation for violence made him a player in one of the major confrontations between the Seiyūkai and Kenseikai. Both parties had long jockeyed for close relationships with industry, and their wealthy *zaibatsu* backers, in an effort to fill party coffers. The particular company at the heart of this conflict was Nippon Yūsen Kabushikigaisha (Japan Mail Steamship Company, hereafter N.Y.K.), the first modern maritime shipping company in Japan. The early Taisho years were particularly profitable for N.Y.K. because of returns on purchases of large ships as well as the establishment of an around-the-world route through the Panama Canal in 1916. Due in large part to the prosperity of the years during and immediately after World War I, the company held several tens of millions of yen in reserves.[89] Political parties vied for these assets, not only because of the money itself, but also because a connection with N.Y.K. would serve as a link to the influential Mitsubishi *zaibatsu*.

The conflict flared in May 1921, when anti-Seiyūkai politicians came to believe that the Seiyūkai was planning to gain control over N.Y.K.'s reserves by forcing the retirement of the company's president and installing someone sympathetic to its interests. This was not the first time the Seiyūkai sought a closer relationship with N.Y.K. In 1914, there had been talk of appointing Okazaki Kunisuke, an influential Seiyūkai member and friend of party president Hara Kei, to the vice presidency of the company. This time, the Seiyūkai's strategy was to disturb a general meeting of stockholders, scheduled for May 30 at the Youth Hall in the Kanda area of Tokyo, by eliciting the help of *sōshi* rumored to belong to a well-known Kantō area nationalist group. Some of the *sōshi* would buy stock in the company to pose as shareholders, while others would be prepared to disrupt the meeting with force as necessary, likely in the hopes of bringing about the president's resignation.[90] This strategy was lifted from *sōkaiya*, so-called "professional stockholders" who were paid by companies to protect their interests by breaking up shareholders' meetings or squaring off against the *sōkaiya* of other companies; in short, they were the financial world's equivalent of *sōshi*, and so it is not surprising that some ruffians were active in both spheres.

The Seiyūkai's attempt to gain influence over N.Y.K. was severely criticized by anti-Seiyūkai politicians. One member of the Kenseikai viewed the Seiyūkai's interest in N.Y.K. as part of the party's plan to extend its reach into all areas of the economy for the sake of profit. Two men who were certain of a Seiyūkai "plot" to gain money and influence were Yamagata Aritomo, former prime minister and elder statesman, and Sugiyama Shigemaru, a politician whose first enterprise had facilitated the development of the Kita Kyūshū region represented by Yoshida. Nefarious plot or not, these men were clearly threatened by the Seiyūkai's strategy to bolster its political position by gaining the money and allegiance of N.Y.K. and the Mitsubishi *zaibatsu*, not out of a sense of moral outrage but out of a desire to curb the power of their main opposition party. Acting on their concern, Yamagata and Sugiyama called on Yoshida's assistance. Yoshida responded by contacting his henchman Okabe Teizō and instructing him to gather men from Kyūshū before the general stockholders' meeting. Hundreds of Yoshida's men eventually made the trip to Tokyo; reports of the specific number ranged from 200 to 500, the larger figure given by Yoshida himself. Of those who arrived in Tokyo, 70 bought stock in N.Y.K. so as to represent the Kenseikai at the meeting, where 160 Seiyūkai-affiliated *sōshi* would be present. Arrangements were also made to guard the outside of the Youth Hall, and Yoshida reserved hospital rooms in the Kanda and Tsukiji areas of Tokyo for potential casualties. Many of the henchmen from Kyūshū gathered at Yoshida's home in the Kōjimachi area of Tokyo, where they prepared pistols and swords. The prevalence of weapons in the house led to the death of one of Yoshida's men, Makita Sadakichi, who was hit by a bullet mistakenly fired by a fellow Yoshida supporter.[91]

Escalating tension between the Seiyūkai and the Kenseikai over N.Y.K. ultimately dissipated. With the increasing journalistic and police attention given to the mobilization of *sōshi* and yakuza in the city, both sides decided to stand down and the Seiyūkai agreed not to disturb the shareholders' meeting. An initial resolution was reached on the grounds of Yasukuni Shrine in Tokyo, and the final settlement meeting, held in Tsukiji, was attended by Yoshida and four of his henchmen. In statements to journalists, Yoshida criticized the Seiyūkai's turn to violent tactics and explained his own actions as a necessary countermeasure to the opposing party's show of force. On the afternoon of May 29, Yoshida spoke to reporters at his Kōjimachi home: "I neither like nor dislike Yūsen [N.Y.K.], but I cannot stand idly by, having heard about [the Seiyūkai's plan] to use violence to realize unjust ambitions. This problem is not just one company's problem, but will create the foundation for an ever more dangerous country." The only reason he turned to force, Yoshida claimed, was because of the Seiyūkai's buildup of *sōshi*.[92] The hypocrisy of Yoshida's denunciation of Seiyūkai violence is particularly poignant when considering that he only had a role in this conflict because he had violent henchmen at his disposal and a reputation for unleashing their physical skills on political enemies.

Yoshida leveraged his violent reputation in a number of other incidents, usually resolving labor disputes in management's favor. Yoshida or his henchmen served as "mediators" at various strikes, such as those involving Asahi Glass Company in 1921, Mitsui Bussan in 1926, the Iriyama Coal Mine in 1927, and the Hayashikane Fishery in 1930.[93] In all of these instances, Yoshida resolved the disputes at minimal cost to management in order to ensure the productivity and smooth operation of industry in his region.

All of this should not suggest that Yoshida was only viewed as a supplier of physical force by fellow politicians. He was fully able to meet with key figures regarding issues of concern to him, one of which was nomination to the House of Peers for those with records of distinguished service. Yoshida forwarded his proposal to several premiers including Katō Kōmei, whom he met at the prime minister's private residence to discuss the difficulties of life as a Diet member. Shortly thereafter, favorable nominations were made to the House of Peers. Yoshida also paid a round of visits to key figures in the ministries of finance, commerce and industry, and home affairs when helping to pass a measure, particularly important for Fukuoka Prefecture, by which half the revenue from mining taxes would go to mining regions instead of the country as a whole.

Even after Yoshida left the Diet in 1932, he continued to be involved in local politics through the later years of his life. In the general election of 1934, Yoshida urged Minseitō candidate Kawanami Arajirō to run for the House of Representatives and rallied for him the support of Diet member Maeda Kōsaku. In return for Maeda's assistance, Yoshida stood behind his proposal for a reduction in the price of electricity and won the backing of the Minseitō; the proposal passed, was approved in Tokyo, and was eventually implemented in April 1937.[94]

Yoshida's death in January 1936 marked the end of a political career fueled by loyalty to regional business interests, physical strength, and a body of violent henchmen. Yoshida may have been notable in these regards, but he was by no means exceptional—not marginalized in a shadowy "underworld," he embodied the qualities and abilities valued by many of his fellow politicians.

Two years before Yoshida left the Diet, Hora Sennosuke assumed a seat in the House of Representatives as a Seiyūkai politician representing Yamaguchi Prefecture in southern Honshū, just across the Shimonoseki Strait from Yoshida's native northern Kyūshū. Like Yoshida, Hora was involved with yakuza early in his life and became a prominent local figure before entering national politics in which he too used violence. But Hora seems more the consummate yakuza boss: he had his own "family" with whom his primary allegiance seemed to lie, he interacted with fellow politicians as one would with "brothers" in a yakuza group, and he was less involved in the pressing political issues of his time. This impression may be due to the tone of his autobiography, in which he sounds proud of his various exploits, but it is also telling that there are few if any mentions of Hora in other contemporary sources. Accordingly, the reasons why he stayed in political office, and why people might have voted for him, are murkier. In his case, intimidation of opponents more than local support may explain his political career. And yet he was still accepted into the ranks of the Seiyūkai.

Hora spent most of his formative years in Kobe, having moved to the city with his family from his birthplace of Wakayama after an intermediate stay in Osaka. His neighborhood was tough; women were seen gambling outside and the young Hora often got into fights. He did enroll in elementary school when he was eight years old and would leave the house every morning with lunch box in hand, but he would head toward the theaters to watch plays instead of going to school. After completing four years of elementary education, he quit school and spent time wandering about. By the age of 14, he was familiar with the red-light district, where he had visited a brothel and had forged a close friendship with a certain Ōshima Hideyoshi who would go on to become a big yakuza boss in Kobe. The young Hora was full of antics, such as getting stark naked at a festival, and at least one of his early adventures involved an encounter with yakuza. At the Aioiza Theater, Hora was watching a play in which popular *sōshi* actor Araki Kiyoshi was to appear when a yakuza in a nearby seat began to make noise. One of the theater's youth told the yakuza to be quiet and the situation exploded soon thereafter as the one yakuza turned out to belong to a group of 30, who ganged up on the youth. Hora responded by picking up a tatami square by the corner and throwing it at one of the yakuza, who started bleeding from its impact. By this point, everyone was standing and the play had been interrupted, so Hora slipped out of the theater.[95]

Hora himself became a yakuza around the age of 14 or 15 through his association with a big yakuza boss named Nanba no Fuku, a famous figure in the Kansai
area who had his base in Osaka. Hora recalled that his eldest sister's husband, the
manager of a construction company in Osaka, always hung a bulletin board with
the name of Nanba's organization (the Nanpuku-gumi) where he was contracting
labor so as to scare away troublesome characters. When Nanba met Hora, the
boss allegedly foresaw a great career for the teenager as a yakuza boss and officially accepted Hora into the family with the *sakazuki* ceremony.[96] Hora became
a young boss of the Nanpuku-gumi by the time he was 18 years old and spent his
time gambling and traveling around Manchuria with a theater company. He also
cavorted with a big yakuza boss from Kobe named Sakai Tatsuzō (called Ōshin)
who had gone to Qingdao with 40 to 50 geisha to open a restaurant.[97]

After these rambunctious teenage years, Hora allegedly decided to cut his ties
with the yakuza world. Reflecting in his autobiography, he endowed his younger
self with wisdom as one can only do in hindsight, claiming that he grew tired
of life as a yakuza which meant having to gamble and having to fight, killing or
getting killed, committing crimes or meeting an early death. Hora recounts that
boss Nanba no Fuku understood his motivations and amicably overturned their
sakazuki and cut their connection. Regardless of the veracity of this story, Hora
continued to act very much like a yakuza. He might have seen his official break
from Nanba as a transition from being a rough-and-tumble yakuza to assuming
the more dignified and mature air of a *kyōkaku,* but his alleged "life of chivalry"
was a euphemism for continued yakuza-like behavior—frequenting red-light
districts, enlarging his tattoo, and brawling in yakuza fights.[98]

After a stint in the army during the Russo-Japanese War, Hora ended up in
Shimonoseki where he expanded his family's business in bamboo baskets used
to transport fish. There, he seems to have maintained a role as a yakuza boss in
practice if not in name. He claimed he was different from yakuza because he had
everyone call him "taishō" (chief) instead of "oyabun," did honest work and lived
an honest life, and always told his henchmen to hold proper jobs and not be gamblers. Among his henchmen, he explained, were members of city and prefectural
assemblies, those involved in construction, and presidents of fish wholesalers
and dockyards. Not only were these industries to which yakuza were typically
drawn, but, more concretely, Hora was also the head of the Kagotora-gumi, a
name formed by the character for basket and the first character of his father
Torakichi's name. And in his autobiography, he compared his 28 henchmen to
the 28 henchmen of legendary Tokugawa-era yakuza Shimizu no Jirōchō. A brief
description of some of his henchmen also makes it quite clear that they were
yakuza: Heikichi liked gambling and was married to a prostitute who worked in
Shimonoseki's red-light district; "The Demon" Kamekichi (Oni no Kamekichi)

was very strong; Haruta no Gonbei was courageous and had once fought with the president of a nationalist organization (the Kokusuikai, to be discussed in the following chapter) at a horse-racing track; Jinbei sold confectioneries but was also fairly well known among yakuza in the Kantō and Kansai regions as well as Kyūshū, Manchuria, and Korea; and Aoki Masakichi was sent to prison for stabbing to death a member of the Communist Party.[99]

Hora also imprinted his body with the mark of a yakuza, a full-body tattoo, but claimed that his restraint in not showing it off demonstrated that he was not a yakuza. He originally had the image of the tragic child hero Umewaka Maru riding a dragon tattooed on his back and both arms when he was around 16 years old but was not able to do his stomach. After he moved to Shimonoseki, Hora decided to complete the design and had an artist come from Kobe to mark his whole body and to give tattoos to ten of his henchmen who did not yet sport the colorful images.[100]

In addition to bearing a tattoo, Hora interacted with the yakuza in Shimonoseki. In recounting one seemingly chance encounter with yakuza, Hora sought to impress upon his readers the extent of his reputation as a powerful figure, comparing himself to Banzuiin Chōbei. But his very mention of Banzuiin as well as the telling of the story itself inadvertently illustrated how connected he was to the world of yakuza that he had allegedly left behind. The incident occurred on a night when Hora had taken some workers from his sawmill to a new red-light district in Shimonoseki where he became angered at how the women at a certain brothel treated his men like country bumpkins. Hora called for the proprietress, who ascended to their second-floor room and promptly incensed him by not apologizing for the behavior of the women. A drunken Hora then said loudly, "Well, it's you then, huh?" which prompted the proprietress and the women to exit the room. Hora and his men were preparing to leave when they looked down from the second floor and noticed that more than 20 *bakuto* who had been called by the proprietress were blocking the entrance to the brothel. He sent his men out the back door and awaited the *bakuto,* who were led by Higuchi no Jinbei and Imamura Takejirō (who was also an amateur sumo wrestler). The man who eventually appeared in front of Hora was one Nakajima, association leader of the red-light district and a friend, who had apparently gotten wind of the incident and scolded Higuchi and Imamura for troubling Hora. Hora claimed that he accepted apologies from the two men, who became his henchmen, and became known in Shimonoseki through this incident.[101]

Clashes with yakuza were not infrequent for Hora, who developed his own strategy to fight against these rivals who interfered with his business. He would use as weapons branding irons in the shape of the characters "Hora-gumi." Hearing of an impending attack, he would start up three or four bellows and place in the fire 20 to 30 irons, then wield these heated rods against the relatively shorter swords and daggers of his yakuza opponents. He found the irons to be strategically effective and legally prudent as well, for he could claim that any action using the irons, as opposed to a more conventional weapon, was justifiable self-defense.[102]

Between incidents, Hora continued to expand his business, becoming a notable local entrepreneur. He often went to Korea where he had workers making wooden boxes, and also recruited Koreans into his Kagotora-gumi. In addition, Hora eventually established 20 sawmills in places such as Yamaguchi, Tottori, and Kumamoto Prefectures; formed construction and ice manufacturing companies; and built the Sanyō Department Store in front of Shimonoseki station. He was also chair of the Shimonoseki Kyūnankai (Shimonoseki Relief Association) and was involved in the entertainment industry, owning dozens of theaters in Hyōgo, Sannomiya, Hiroshima, and Osaka.[103]

Hora's entrance into political life might be explained by all of these community ventures, but the circumstances surrounding his election to the Shimonoseki city assembly in 1929 seem quite strange, indeed unbelievable, in his retelling. According to Hora, he did not even run, much less campaign, for office. At the time, he was consumed with performing in amateur plays and was proud of having landed the leading role in the play and movie *Kunisada Chūji* about the famed Tokugawa-era *bakuto*. He was taken aback when notified by telegram of his victory. Considering that the 1929 election was the first local contest in Shimonoseki under universal manhood suffrage and the number of eligible voters had swelled considerably, it is possible that there was popular support for Hora's "candidacy."[104] Yet the election of Hora without any organized effort, or the existence of such a campaign unbeknownst to Hora, is far-fetched. Regardless of why and how he was elected, Hora allegedly accepted this political role grudgingly and only with the encouragement of his wife Matsu. One of the stated reasons for Hora's hesitation at assuming office was the cost involved in being a politician. A member of the House of Representatives at the time was paid ¥250 a month which was, according to Hora, an adequate sum for one or two terms but insufficient come the third term, when property would have to be sold to meet the expenses of being a politician. Hora mused that during this period, politicians either lost their wealth or were assassinated. Nonetheless, Hora assumed his office in the city assembly, served as vice chair for a short two months, and formed the Shōwakai (Showa Association) out of the neutral faction to which he belonged.[105]

Hora seemed disinterested in party politics, which he glosses as a noble attempt to transcend political parties and do something for his country, and his eventual allegiance to the Seiyūkai was due mostly to his association with Tanaka Giichi, party president and former army minister. Hora first met Tanaka in Hagi, where he went as a city assembly representative to welcome the prominent politician. Hora and his henchmen then hosted Tanaka in Shimonoseki. During his time there, Tanaka allegedly suggested to Hora that they become "brothers" and Hora refused, saying that he should be Tanaka's henchman, a subordinate. Tanaka insisted, however, and the two were apparently joined as "brothers" with the *sakazuki* ceremony. Tanaka supposedly told Hora national secrets, including some regarding the failure of dispatching troops to Shandong and the 1928 assassination of Zhang Zuolin, then encouraged Hora to recruit the 17 members of the neutral faction in the city assembly into the Seiyūkai, which would bring the total number of party assemblymen to 24. Hora agreed, gathered several hundred of his henchmen to see Tanaka off, then ended up accompanying Tanaka to Kobe, where a crowd of people including big yakuza bosses had gathered to support the Seiyūkai president. When Tanaka and Hora parted ways, Hora headed back to Shimonoseki and began trying to recruit the members of the Shōwakai into the Seiyūkai as asked. Eventually, 16 assemblymen in the Shōwakai including Hora joined the party. In September 1929, when Tanaka died suddenly in Shinagawa, Hora went to Tokyo along with 30 to 40 young men who allegedly wore *happi* coats dyed with the characters for "Kagotora-gumi" and helped carry the former prime minister's coffin.[106]

In 1930, Hora ran in the general election for the House of Representatives alongside fellow Seiyūkai candidates from other districts in Yamaguchi Prefecture: Kuhara Fusanosuke, former communications minister in the Tanaka cabinet and former head of Kuhara Kōgyō (Kuhara Mining Company) that eventually became Nippon Sangyō (Nissan); and Matsuoka Yōsuke, a prominent diplomat who would become foreign minister in Konoe Fumimaro's second cabinet. Hora, who ran in the first district of Yamaguchi Prefecture, was criticized by opposition party candidates for his lack of education and skills, but had the support of former justice minister Makino Ryōzō and a comic actor with the first name Gokurō. Gokurō had come to idolize Shimizu no Jirōchō through personal interactions with the legendary yakuza figure. He spoke at Hora's public meetings in front of crowds of coal miners about how Hora might be a boss but did not fight and did not push to have his own way. If Shimizu no Jirōchō was the greatest boss along the Tōkaidō, then Hora was the greatest boss in Japan, said Gokurō, and he must be elected for the sake of the country. Gokurō's need to disavow physical force reflects a trend toward criticizing political party violence in the late 1920s, but this message was likely hollow or even irrelevant to a crowd that was more moved by a general sense of nationalism and romanticization of yakuza as patriotic figures. Hora was elected from Yamaguchi Prefecture into the seventeenth House of Representatives.

In April 1930, when Hora was serving as a freshman Diet member, the main issue of concern was the London Naval Conference at which the Japanese government negotiated with the Americans and the British to scale back limitations on Japan's naval capacity. In this context, Hora did not assume any meaningful political role but was involved in a number of scuffles. Hora's retelling of one such incident, of dubious veracity, was intended to paint him as strong and noble. On this occasion, Seiyūkai politician Ozaki Yukio gave a speech criticizing the stance of the government, which was headed at the time by Hamaguchi Osachi of the rival Minseitō. Ozaki soon paid for these comments—when the representatives retreated to the cafeteria during a break, Ozaki was surrounded by 20 Minseitō Diet members. Hora claims that he barged into the circle around Ozaki, pushed one person aside, and protected Ozaki while making a speech about how the politician should not be treated in this manner. Someone then asked Hora who he was, and he explained that his hundreds and thousands of henchmen were more distinguished than the assembled representatives. This particular skirmish ended with a verbal exchange, with the Minseitō representatives mocking Hora for being such a presumptuous new Diet member especially given his rural roots, and Hora responding with empty verbal retorts. There were apparently times, however, when confrontation escalated to violence. During the early 1931 dis-cussions of the budget, Hora was rushed by 50 Minseitō *ingaidan* members who, according to Hora, were musclemen good at judo or sumo. This attack on Hora resulted in the severe wounding of his guard, his eldest son Toranosuke, who had to be taken to the hospital.[107]

Hora seems to have been embraced by fellow politicians despite, or because of, the incidents above and his reputation as a boss. He belonged to the Shōgokai (Showa 5 [1930] Association), a society of Seiyūkai Diet members who were elected in that year. The association included an impressive roster of politicians: Ōno Banboku, Hayashi Jōji, Matsuoka Yōsuke, Funada Ataru, Nakajima Chi-kuhei, Ōta Masataka, and Inukai Takeru. Hora served as chair of this group that would meet once or twice each month at a high-class restaurant in Shinbashi or Akasaka, but the cost of ¥200–¥300 per meeting for the chair allegedly proved to be too much for Hora who asked Nakajima to assume his duties. Of the members of the Shōgokai, Hora got along particularly well with Ōno Banboku, who by this time had advanced several steps up the political ladder from his time in the Seiyūkai *ingaidan*. Hora respected Ōno, who struck him as a *kyōkaku*-type figure, and supported Ōno's successful 1931 re-election bid by sending five or six of his henchmen to public meetings in Gifu. Ōno was less expressive about his feelings for Hora, but did pen the preface to Hora's autobiography.

Hora ran unopposed in his second election campaign for the House of Rep-resentatives, largely because he discouraged potential candidates from running. He allegedly explained to them that elections were costly, that it would be better if each political faction ran a chosen candidate, and that he would use the money otherwise spent on the election to buy an airplane for the country. He dared

skeptics to run against him, but not surprisingly, none did. Despite the suspi-
ciously smooth path to re-election, Hora eventually decided to leave politics, citing a changing of generations whereby those without education could no longer
represent the people. He spent his post-Diet life pursuing a career in the theater.[108]
Hora's eldest son, Toranosuke, continued the Kagotora-gumi and was elected
to the Shimonoseki city assembly in 1942, becoming chairman of the body in
1945.[109] In the postwar period, Hora was investigated for war crimes because the
Kagotora-gumi was on the list of organizations banned by the Allied occupation,
but he managed to evade the charges.[110]

The phenomenon of mafiosi holding political office was not unique to Japan.
In post–World War II Sicily, Pino Trapani sat on the Palermo town council and
was a member, perhaps also *consigliere* (adviser), of a mafia family. Onorevole
Calogero Volpe, a member of parliament, was known as a "man of honor," and
Giuseppe of the Di Girolamo mafia family was a deputy for the Monarchist or
Liberal Party. In the postwar Italian context, the election of these men suggests
the sheer power and prevalence of mafiosi especially in Sicilian politics, and their
ability to deliver the vote for certain candidates or political parties.[111]

In prewar Japan, the political careers of Yoshida Isokichi and Hora Sennosuke were not indicative of a pervasive mafia presence in politics comparable to
postwar Sicily. Rather, they were a testament to a political culture in which their
strong-arm tactics made them political assets. That they could make the transition from yakuza life to politics so seamlessly reflects how violence operated similarly in both worlds, as an accepted tool for protecting and acquiring a desired
financial or political good.

The fluidity between the ruffianism of the streets and politics at the highest of
levels suggests there was little, if any, stigma or political cost to becoming, or as-
sociating with, a violence specialist. Yakuza bosses such as Yoshida Isokichi and
Hora Sennosuke could be elected to the Diet, *sōshi* organizers such as Murano
Tsuneemon could be visible politicians who rose to positions of prominence,
and *ingaidan* members could go on to become powerful politicians. Ōno Banboku, for example, used the *ingaidan* as a stepping-stone for a lifelong political
career—after his time in the Tesshinkai, he was elected to the Tokyo municipal assembly and the Diet's House of Representatives. In the post–World War II
years, he would help establish the Nihon Jiyūtō (Japan Liberal Party) of which he
would become secretary-general, and would serve as speaker of the house and
vice president of the Jiyū Minshutō (Liberal Democratic Party).[112]

The ability of *sōshi* and yakuza to skirt the line of respectability helps explain
why violence became more deeply institutionalized into party politics in Japan
than in other places, such as England during the mid-nineteenth century or the

United States during the late nineteenth and early twentieth centuries. More than the "toughs" and even the "rent-a-mobs" in England, or the street gangs in the United States, *sōshi* and *ingaidan* were seen as legitimate enough to survive as a political phenomenon. *Sōshi* were not just vagrant and unemployed toughs, but could be farmers or students. And yakuza continued to enjoy an ambiguous status in society because they were, after all, providers of services like gambling and prostitution that were in demand. As long as they did not prey on ordinary citizens, they were not vilified in the public eye. In short, *sōshi* and *bakuto* were less vulnerable to marginalization and criminalization than the gypsies and manual laborers of England or the U.S. street gangs. As such, an *ingaidan* could produce a prominent political leader like Ōno Banboku whereas gangs in the United States were more likely to yield an infamous mafia boss like Al Capone.[113]

The consequences of the institutionalization of violence specialists as well as the violence wielded by *ingaidan* and politicians themselves were not unambiguous. By its very nature, the ruffianism inside and outside the Diet was intended to intimidate, coerce, and shut down discussion. *Ingaidan sōshi* could also exacerbate unevenness between parties, with wealthier parties able to support more ruffians. And *ingaidan* violence became less popular in character as the political parties themselves became "established parties" rather than liberal voices of the people. Yet, on the other hand, the *ingaidan* could serve as a check on the *hanbatsu*, the military, and the bureaucracy. And its violence occasionally overlapped with, even mobilized, popular movements for democratic ends such as protecting constitutional government or enacting universal manhood suffrage.

The very existence of ruffianism and the culture of political violence that surrounded it were thus not themselves fatal to democracy. The danger was that the tacit acceptance of ruffianism helped legitimize the political violence of groups that did not even purport to have democratic intentions or aims. It was the rise of violent fascist movements in the 1920s, the subject of the next chapter, that complicates our assessment of this culture of political violence and its ramifications for prewar Japanese democracy.

4

Fascist Violence

Ideology and Power in Prewar Japan

In his 1943 book *Government by Assassination*, retired Japan correspondent Hugh Byas observed of prewar nationalist groups:

> In Japan…professional patriotism and professional crime drew together and blended in a way that made patriotism a stink in the nostrils. The big patriotic societies were only the one third of the iceberg that shows above water; below, in the depths, a whole underworld of criminals hunted their prey under a mask of patriotism just as Dick Turpin robbed the highways wearing a mask of crepe.[1]

The nationalist organizations that Byas so evocatively described were a rapidly growing phenomenon in Japan during the 1920s and 1930s. These groups wore a variety of political stripes, espousing any one or a combination of ideas including national socialism, reverence for the emperor, military rule, aggressive imperialism, and the preservation of "traditional Japanese values." What most of them shared was a reactionary desire to contain or even crush the unprecedented flourishing of leftist ideologies inspired by the Russian Revolution. Beginning in the late 1910s and 1920s, they felt especially besieged by the intellectuals, workers, students, and other activists who embraced or deepened their commitment to various and sometimes competing strands of leftist thought, from anarchosyndicalism to Marxism and socialism. Radical students spearheaded a left-wing movement, tenant unionism and militancy increased, leftists created and shaped minority organizations such as the Suiheisha (The Levelers), and socialist women were becoming active in labor strikes and political movements. Most worrisome to the nationalist organizations was the expansion of the labor movement, as the major union federation (Nihon Rōdō Sōdōmei, or Japan Federation of Labor) gained members, the number of labor unions quadrupled between 1918 and 1923, and strikes increased in length, size, and level of violence.[2] Many rightist groups were deeply worried about maintaining stability and uninterrupted capitalist production in the face of this leftist activism.

Byas's colorful portrayal of the connection between these nationalist organizations and those he disparaged as criminals may have been overstated, but it was not unfounded. The two groups on which this chapter focuses—the Dai Nihon Kokusuikai (Greater Japan National Essence Association, hereafter Kokusuikai) and the Dai Nihon Seigidan (Greater Japan Justice Organization, hereafter Seigidan)—unquestionably consisted of yakuza.[3] Where Byas's comment is misleading is in its characterization of the criminal element as hidden in the shadows of a murky underworld. In fact, the yakuza were very visible. Particularly in the cases of the Kokusuikai and the Seigidan, the Dick Turpin analogy is not particularly illustrative, for the yakuza were not mere bandits and highwaymen but leaders of these organizations. And the groups themselves were not politically peripheral, but central and powerful players in a movement that had a profound influence in shaping the ideological landscape of prewar Japan. That the Special Higher Police was concerned about these two particular organizations speaks to a fear of their influence.[4] And intellectuals, political commentators, and labor movement organizers also singled them out as notable nationalist groups.

What brought attention to the Kokusuikai and Seigidan was their violence. In Home Ministry parlance, they were "bōryokudan"—literally, violence group(s). The Home Ministry classified bōryokudan into one of four categories by whether their membership consisted of political ruffians or thugs (sōshi or seiji goro), delinquent students (furyō gakusei), pettifogging lawyers (sanbyakumin), or yakuza.[5] Used widely by a number of newspapers as well as labor unionists, the derisive appellation "bōryokudan" highlighted the physical coercion wielded by all of these groups as their most unique, identifiable, and threatening characteristic, and sought to criminalize their violence.

The violence of the Kokusuikai and Seigidan is considered here in the context of the nationalist nexus they created, which wove together party politicians, military men, leaders of big business, and yakuza. This nexus, I argue, should be considered part of a fascist movement whose centripetal pull derived not only from a common desire to neutralize the left and extend Japan's reach on the continent, but also from the conviction that violence should be wielded to achieve these ends. The fascist violence of these groups had a significant impact on the place and future of political parties in prewar politics—ultimately, it helped the state's violent arms assume the reins of government, with disastrous consequences for Japan's democracy.

Fascist Ideologies

There has long been a debate about whether prewar Japan can be considered fascist. Among historians in Japan, it is almost a convention to use the fascist label, and Maruyama Masao's classic conception of a Japanese "fascism from above" continues to hold some currency.[6] Especially for the generation of Japanese scholars who lived through the war, the term "fascism" captures the nightmarish experience of the late 1930s and early 1940s and is a self-flagellating reminder that intellectuals did not do enough to prevent militarism and war. Japan specialists in the United States, on the other hand, do not carry this burden. This explains, in part, why they tend to shy away from the idea of a fascist Japan, though there are notable exceptions.[7] Those who are ready to declare the concept a "failure" point to the ambiguities of the term, the dismal fate of a handful of self-identified fascists, and the inability of fascist intellectuals to translate their ideas into practice.[8] It is, admittedly, not particularly meaningful to discuss whether prewar Japan as some kind of whole was fascist ("fascist Japan"), somewhat unconvincing to refer to the prewar regime as fascist, and debatable to speak of a fascist political system. Yet to throw out the concept because it is not easily defined is to abandon an avenue for comparative analysis, potentially lean toward conclusions that overemphasize Japanese uniqueness, and forgo the possibility of approaching and understanding prewar Japan in new ways. As historian Robert Paxton has pointed out, all broad concepts—liberalism, democracy, capitalism, communism, modernity—can be vague, and slippery when compared across contexts, yet we do not often think of abandoning them.[9]

The preoccupation with a broadly conceived fascist Japan and fascist regimes has sidelined consideration of fascist movements in Japan, and this is especially unfortunate when it comes to the Kokusuikai and Seigidan because they shared much with violent groups in other fascist movements: the *squadrismo* (more commonly known as the Blackshirts) of Italy, and the Sturmabteilung or SA of the Nationalsozialistische Deutsche Arbeiterpartei (National Socialist German Workers' Party or Nazi Party, hereafter NSDAP) in Germany. All of these bodies were forged in the cradle of nationalism, the embrace of the modern nation-state, struggles to carve out a niche on the world stage, ongoing experiments with democracy, and, more specifically, leftist activism and the economic dislocation of the Great Depression. And their ideologies and violence, like the tensions that spawned them, transcended national boundaries.

The Kokusuikai was created by a cooperative effort between Seiyūkai Home Minister Tokonami Takejirō and yakuza bosses. On October 9, 1919, more than

30 bosses dressed in frock coats and crested, pleated pants gathered at 1:00 P.M. in the Tokyo Station Hotel. The bosses had traveled to the capital from the Kansai region (namely Osaka, Kyoto, Nagoya, Kobe, Kure, Yamato, Izumi, and Kokura) expecting to meet with Tokonami. This was not a secretive rendezvous, for the development was covered in major newspapers, many of which printed the names of the yakuza bosses. There was, apparently, some public controversy over who had called for this meeting. Several newspapers reported that Home Minister Tokonami had taken the initiative and they described how a majority of the bosses believed they had been invited to Tokyo by both the home minister and prime minister. Tokonami vehemently denied the newspaper reports, arguing that he had never extended a hand to the yakuza bosses; at least one boss corroborated the home minister's statement, stating that it was the bosses who had suggested the meeting.[10] Nonetheless, Tokonami went ahead with the meeting as planned—the initiation of an alliance with the yakuza, not the working relationship itself, may have been the source of his embarrassment. Thus, around 5:00 P.M. on the ninth, the bosses piled into cars and proceeded to the Home Ministry where they met with Tokonami and other high-ranking officials in the upstairs minister's room.

This meeting laid the groundwork for the founding of the Kokusuikai, which drew its membership primarily from construction contractors and yakuza bosses.[11] What united them, especially considering that many yakuza bosses were also construction contractors, was concern over the negative effects of recent labor union strikes. Four days after the meeting in Tokyo, the bosses gathered to speak of the need to "wave a clenched fist" against such disturbances and to forge an alliance between fellow bosses in the Kansai, Kyūshū, and Kantō regions. Discouraging labor disputes was also portrayed as a greater patriotic duty; one boss explained that he and others had gone to Tokyo because "we thought that even we could be of use to the country."[12] The desire to contain labor unrest was shared by the home minister, who was not only concerned about the destabilizing power of the unions but was also worried that yakuza henchmen would be seduced into joining forces with striking laborers. So central were labor issues that one of the initial proposed names for the association was the Dobokugyō Gikai (Construction Industry Council).[13] This prosaic name was replaced with the more pugnacious Dai Nihon Kokusuikai by the end of October. And in mid-November, Kokusuikai representatives from Kansai together with Kantō yakuza participated in a *sakazuki* ceremony, a ritual traditionally performed by yakuza (but not just yakuza) to initiate members and mark the creation of ties. Conducted with the almost 50 people who filled the hall, the ceremony was part of an evening of rituals and festivities from formal greetings to a banquet, but the gathering of such a large number of bosses from different regions was apparently not without its tensions or awkwardness—there were extended moments when the entire hall fell silent. Nonetheless, the evening solidified the relationship between the Kansai and Kantō bosses of the Kokusuikai. The next morning, a pilot scattered 10,000 handbills from the skies over Tokyo that read: "The nationwide yakuza organizations (kyōkakudan) that live their lives with chivalry are dedicated to imperialism for the sake of the country and here from the air announce to all citizens the establishment of the Dai Nihon Kokusuikai."[14]

The Kokusuikai was not a small, marginal organization; its web of influence extended far beyond its general headquarters in Tokyo through a network of subsidiary bodies from Hokkaidō to Kyūshū, consisting of around 90 branches in the early 1930s. With a handful of exceptions, these local organizations had at least 30 members, with the largest, such as those in Okayama, Osaka, Nagano, Tokushima, and Kyoto, listing more than 2,000. And total membership was estimated to be around 200,000.[15] The initiative for the establishment of branches, at least in some instances, came from general headquarters. In January 1921, for example, the chief director of the Kokusuikai approached a "kyōkaku" named Morioka Tōkichi from Kasagi, in Kyoto, and urged him to found and head a branch of the organization there. Similarly, in Wakayama Prefecture, various people were handpicked to start regional Kokusuikai chapters.[16]

The Kokusuikai and its branches extolled ideas of chivalry, veneration of the imperial house, and "the way of the warrior" (bushidō) to combat "the corruption of national morals and beautiful customs" and to "promote harmony between labor and capital."[17] Central to the Kokusuikai's ideology was its own version of Japanese history—a nationalist remaking of the past that highlighted its purity and authenticity. Celebrated were the 3,000 proud and unblemished years since the country's founding during which time it overcame numerous national crises and courageously stood up to foreign enemies. The foreign was portrayed as a contagion from which the country was protected only through the Yamato, or Japanese, spirit.

Through its explanation of the Yamato spirit, the Kokusuikai legitimized its violence by constructing the use of physical force as historically valued and necessary for the defense of the country. Japan was only able to carry on, it was said, because the samurai who upheld "the way of the warrior" banded together with the people out of their Yamato spirit. Other explanations of the Yamato spirit posited that it was possessed naturally by all of Japan's people but took the particular form of "the way of the warrior" for samurai.[18] In either interpretation, the warrior held a special position separate from, and arguably above, the common person.

The Kokusuikai artfully wove the history of yakuza together with this justification of samurai violence, spinning a tale of how yakuza were embodiments of the Yamato spirit who adopted "the way of the warrior." They referred to themselves not as yakuza, but as *kyōkaku,* chivalrous figures who were not ruffians or thugs but honorable men who were part of an honorable past. Article 1 of the association's rules underscored this theme, stating: "Our association is founded with spirit and is a group of those characterized by chivalry."[19] According to the association's retelling of history, during the Tokugawa period "the way of the warrior" was adopted by certain non-samurai (*minkan*), fearless people who rose from the weak to stand tall with their fellow men. These characters became known as *kyōkaku*—men who chivalrously (out of duty, not desire for money) helped the weak and defeated the strong. The allegedly important role of *kyōkaku* in modern politics was also addressed, with mentions of their ties to nationalist groups founded in the Meiji era such as the Fukuoka Gen'yōsha (Fukuoka Dark Ocean Society), to the development of constitutional and parliamentary government, and to the establishment of party cabinets. It was argued that these politically active *kyōkaku,* though often seen by others as rioters (*bōto*) or extremists, in fact possessed a spirit that continued to be based on "the way of the warrior."

Much like the *kyōkaku* of the Tokugawa period, the Kokusuikai of present-day Japan was to protect the people from a foreign threat—Westernization, and especially the influx of leftist thought. The organization explained that the Meiji period started the humiliating trend of Europeanization, epitomized by the evening parties at the Rokumeikan, the Western-style brick pavilion where men and women dressed in "strange" clothes would dance long into the night. Western ideas were similarly unnatural, which is why it was believed that communism would never develop in Japan. Those who embraced whatever Western ideology was in vogue, be it Wilsonianism or Leninism, were deemed lost in body, soul, and Japaneseness. In the face of Europeanization, which compromised not only Japan's cultural virtues but its diplomacy as well, it was resolved that Japan must preserve its "national essence" as embodied in the national polity (*kokutai*) and the imperial house. The prescribed bulwark against the corruption of Japan's civilization and national essence was none other than "the way of the warrior." The Kokusuikai's violence was thus placed in the context of a noble and self-sacrificing warrior tradition, nationalism, strength, and manhood—the Kokusuikai was to be an organization of "men among men."[20] Violence was not merely justified but glorified as a manly and patriotic way to purify the nation of foreign contagion.

The Seigidan was founded in January 1922 by a yakuza boss named Sakai Eizō and boasted 106 branches by 1932, a majority of which were in Osaka. Total reported membership figures were 70,000 people affiliated with the headquarters in Tokyo and 35,000 with the headquarters in Osaka.[21]

Even more than the Kokusuikai, the Seigidan highlighted the centrality of *kyōkaku* in Japan's history. Sakai spoke frequently of what he called "Japan's way of the *kyōkaku*" (*Nihon kyōkakudō*), especially in his 1927 book that was a compilation of notes on lectures he had delivered in the preceding two years.[22] In a leaflet he distributed to representatives from over 50 countries at the Sixth International Labor Conference in March 1925, Sakai explained "the way of the *kyōkaku*" and how it formed the basis for the Seigidan. Entitled "An Appeal to the World," the pamphlet began with the story of the legendary Tokugawa-era "kyōkaku" Banzuiin Chōbei who allegedly fought against injustice, helped the weak, and defeated the strong. Sakai wrote of how Banzuiin stood up to a group of direct retainers of the shogun (*hatamoto*), the Shiratsuka-gumi, that tormented and bullied the townspeople of Edo. The second character discussed by Sakai was his own predecessor and former boss, Kobayashi Sahei, a Meiji-era "kyōkaku" who was described as someone who took in and guided delinquent youth, helped orphans and the elderly, and sacrificed his life out of duty and for society. Sakai then portrayed himself as part of a new generation, adapting to the changes of the Taisho period as a successor to Kobayashi Sahei and thus forming the Seigidan as a "*kyōkaku* group" (*kyōkakudan*) whose members were willing to risk their lives for country and duty.[23]

Sakai's explanation of the Seigidan's connection to the past was more complex than the Kokusuikai's desire to simply relive the past in the present—he envisioned an organization that upheld the ideals but not the behaviors of previous generations of *kyōkaku*, that demonstrated adherence to time-honored principles through traditional rituals but was modern and timely in purpose. On one hand, Sakai admired the ideals of duty and chivalry exhibited by famous Tokugawa-era "kyōkaku" such as Banzuiin Chōbei, Kunisada Chūji, and Shimizu no Jirōchō. On the other hand, Sakai contradicted himself by arguing that the Seigidan was not an organization of "kyōkaku" in content or in form. He made a point of explaining that members of the Seigidan had honest jobs and were prohibited from gambling, fighting, and drinking heavily. Sakai noted that he himself was active in the business world and that the men of his era had the lofty ideals of shaping public sentiments and reforming national politics. This new generation was not the same as the frightful "kyōkaku" of the past who talked bombastically and lived in a world different from that of the private citizen, as the society of Showa Japan simply would not permit such behavior. This attempt to distance the Seigidan from what might be seen as unsavory aspects of the *kyōkaku*'s past suggests a desire to portray the organization's members as upright citizens, and, by extension, their violence not as criminal but as just, measured, and purposeful.[24]

The stated ideologies of the Kokusuikai and Seigidan resonated with common themes in fascist movements—the creation of a nation's history that stresses the importance of national community as well as ideas of unity and purity, and a self-perception as protectors of the nation against civilizational decay.[25] Violence was not only an acceptable means to protect the nation but was almost beautiful in its nobility, its power to cleanse, and its devotion to the pasts of the samurai and "kyōkaku."[26] By justifying and even glorifying their violence in these ways, the two organizations sought, like the Nazi movement, to portray themselves as both rough and respectable.[27] And the Kokusuikai, especially, demonstrated the *squadrismo* characteristic of "not considering violence a mere instrument but rather a value on which to base the conduct of one's life."[28]

Fascist Violence

The violence of these two organizations may be more revealing of their ideologies than their books and official statements, for their actions were as expressive as their words.[29] On no issue was the contradiction between actions and words more clear than labor-management relations. The Kokusuikai claimed in its writings to "promote harmonious cooperation" between capitalists, laborers, and the government.[30] Sakai Eizō too saw himself and his group as mediators in the struggle between labor and capital and painted himself as evenhanded in his criticisms of both sides.[31] In actuality, labor unions with their tinge of leftist ideologies were viewed as part of the foreign corruption the organizations were attempting to purge, and labor strikes were considered roadblocks to industrial production and thus national progress. Accordingly, "promoting harmonious cooperation" often meant bringing strikers in line with the needs and demands of management. The Kokusuikai and Seigidan regularly stood behind management and functioned primarily as strikebreakers, brought in to intimidate striking laborers. They could bend their stated ideologies to fit practice by constructing management as "the weak" who needed protection from the disruption caused by the laborers, who by striking put themselves in the position of "the strong." It would be just, then, to chivalrously crush the laborers and support management so that industry, and therefore the nation, could grow stronger.

This stance against leftists—not just laborers, but also socialists and communists more broadly—had a parallel in the violence of both the *squadrismo* and the SA. Although Mussolini initially articulated an anticapitalist platform, his later actions were quite the opposite, with his *squadrismo* battling against socialists much like the SA fought communist gangs. Robert Paxton has pointed out that fascist parties that became governing regimes did not carry through their anticapitalist ideology, but instead did away with strikes and independent labor unions.[32] Labor, influenced as it was by leftist ideologies, was a common internal threat and enemy for all of these groups.

In their role as strikebreakers, the Seigidan and Kokusuikai looked and functioned like the paramilitary groups in Italy and Germany. For Sakai Eizō, the similarity was conscious and intentional. Sakai had met with Mussolini on June 13, 1925, and clearly respected the Italian dictator, describing him as a man poor in education and lineage and resources who, with chivalry as his only weapon, raised the banner of justice. To his readers, Sakai characterized the Blackshirts as a "kyōkakudan." Sakai himself was called by some the Mussolini of the East, even though he halfheartedly shrugged off the moniker as he did the fascist label, but that was likely to avoid assuming any negative connotations of the term. It is telling that the Seigidan was called Japan's Blackshirts and that Sakai himself referred to the group as the Kuro Gaitōdan (Black Coats Organization) and had its members wear black shirts.[33]

The uniforms of the Kokusuikai were decidedly like those of state violence specialists, the military and the police. The regulation outfit included a jacket with epaulets, a police hat, a collar, and a belt. All of these pieces displayed the group's emblems, which drew from a body of symbols: the characters for "kokusui," a dove, and a single plum blossom or a branch of plum blossoms likely signifying perseverance. Some epaulets were marked by a plum blossom and a dove; hats carried an emblem of the word "kokusui" framed by branches of plum blossoms; collars had the word "kokusui" over a backdrop of a plum blossom; and belt buckles were emblazoned with "kokusui." Not only did the uniforms clearly mark the organization's members but they also indicated rank. Different patterns on the epaulets and color variations on the emblems indicated whether one was an officer at general headquarters, the leader of a branch, an executive, or a general member. Distinctions could also be marked on the lapel, which was reserved for medals of honor awarded for diligence as well as exceptional and distinguished service.[34]

The Kokusuikai was involved in a number of labor disputes, including the Yahata Ironworks (1920), Singer Sewing Machine Company (1925), and Noda Shōyu (1927–1928) strikes, as well as the Tsurumi Incident (1925).[35] The Seigidan was a part of the Ōsaka Shiden (1924), Noda Shōyu (1927–1928), and Tōyō Muslin (1930) strikes.[36]

So visible was Kokusuikai and Seigidan violence in labor strikes that the Ministry of Justice warned that these organizations must be prevented from following Mussolini's fascist path of using violence to save his country from the spread of communism. And a 1926 law targeting violent acts (Bōryoku Kōi Nado Shobatsu ni Kansuru Hōritsu) not only had provisions related to group coercion, weapons possession, and the disruption of meetings, but in its first article the law

4.1. Sketch of a model Dai Nihon Kokusuikai uniform. In Naimushō Keihokyoku, *Dai Nihon Kokusuikaiin no fukusō ni kansuru ken, Ehime-ken,* June 4, 1935.

also made special mention of crimes committed in the course of mediating labor disputes. Yet the intent of the state's legal arm may have been more to loosely contain, rather than extinguish, the violence of groups such as the Kokusuikai and Seigidan. The state, after all, deeply feared leftist ideologies and had a vested interest in uninterrupted industrial production. This may explain why the 1926 law only called for punishment in the form of seemingly modest fines, from ¥50 to ¥500. Given that the law was relatively toothless, it is not surprising that *bōryokudan* continued to be active in labor strikes through the early 1930s.[37]

The violence of the Kokusuikai and the Seigidan in labor disputes differed from the ruffianism of *sōshi* and *ingaidan* in that it was intended to suppress political activity, not just threaten opponents or disturb gatherings. These nationalist organizations were not attempting to come out ahead of political rivals, but were seeking to snuff out certain ideas and ways of thinking. In this sense, they were much like the *squadrismo* of Italy for whom "political opponents were not adversaries with whom one disagreed, but enemies to eliminate and humiliate by imposing on them a passive obedience."[38] There was, in short, nothing remotely democratic about this violence. And the undemocratic character of the Kokusuikai and Seigidan was underscored in labor disputes by their position of power vis-à-vis union members.

Both the Kokusuikai and a branch of the Seigidan were in league with management in the Noda Shōyu strike of 1927–1928, one of the largest and most expensive strikes in the prewar period. More than 3,500 people directly or indirectly employed by Noda Shōyu were affected by this strike that lasted for over seven months and cost the company and the union over one million yen.[39] Such a prolonged strike touched many of the residents of Noda, the town in Chiba Prefecture where the company based its operations, given that the population of 16,891 included 3,613 employees and their families as well as companies that did business with Noda Shōyu and its workers.[40]

The strike was sparked by a dispute between Noda Shōyu and a subcontractor, Marusan Transportation Company, and was fueled by worker concerns over pay and benefits.[41] The Marusan Transportation Company, a separate joint-stock company created by Noda Shōyu, had been responsible for much of the brewing company's transportation needs for a quarter century. But tensions developed as Marusan employees became members of the local union and refused to deal with the output of Noda Shōyu's Factory Seventeen, the company's largest plant, because it did not have any unionized workers. In response, Noda Shōyu increasingly shifted its business from Marusan to two different subsidiaries, the Noda Transportation Corporation and the Maruhon Transportation Company, causing the earnings of Marusan to decline. On September 15, 1927, the local union stood behind the employees of Marusan and revived demands for wage raises and benefits that it had submitted to Noda Shōyu in April of that year.[42] The strike began the next day, on September 16, and would last for more than 200 days.[43]

Soon after the outbreak of the strike, Noda Shōyu hired violence specialists ostensibly to maintain company security, though this largely meant intimidating workers and strikers. The composition of those hired is difficult to ascertain, since sources (most of which are sympathetic to the laborers) refer to them variously as *bōryokudan,* thugs (*bōkan*), strikebreakers, and Seigidan members.[44] The mention of the Seigidan was probably a reference to the Noda Seigidan, officially established on October 12 and headed by Takanashi Chūhachirō, director of the Shōyū Bank. Although seemingly a local affiliate of the Dai Nihon Seigidan, the extent of the ties between the two branches is unclear. The Noda Seigidan (hereafter Seigidan) did boast a membership of 800–1,000 people, mainly consisting of the town's middle class and small merchants as well as the mayor and town executives.[45] The group's stated mission was to establish peace, promote the town's welfare, uphold an ambiguous concept called "company righteousness" (*kaisha seigi*), and take a position of neutrality in conflicts between labor and capital. The last tenet was questionable at best, considering that the other ideas could be easily manipulated into justifications for suppressing labor unrest, and the platform also used the language of protecting industry and the national polity.[46]

Moreover, the Seigidan took an increasingly promanagement stance in the weeks after its founding.[47] Company management itself thought it "fortunate" that the organization sympathized with its views and policies, as the Seigidan urged strikers to return to work, visited factories in operation, and attempted to unify town opinion against the strikers. On October 29, for example, several Seigidan officers went to Factories Nine and Fifteen, encouraging workers at those operating plants to stay on the job and praising them for not joining their colleagues on the picket line; on November 1 and 2, Seigidan members called on Factories One, Seven, and Twelve.[48] The group also supplied labor and otherwise facilitated the company's operations. And in early November, the Seigidan distributed handbills around town that exhorted strikers to return to work. To the strikers, the Seigidan's support of the company was so clear that the organization was labeled "a group beholden to the company" (*goyō dantai*).[49]

The Seigidan likely recruited yakuza and other strikebreakers, and its members may have acted as *bōryokudan* themselves. The frequency of *bōryokudan* incidents does suggest that at the very least, the distinguished members of the Seigidan, such as the mayor and other town officials, turned a blind eye to violence. After all, physical confrontations could not have gone unnoticed as they spilled beyond the walls of the factory and into the streets of Noda.

Bōryokudan were first reported in Noda in late September, when they were said to be clustered near Factory Fourteen. In response, strikers began to arm—two union organizers and 80 others were arrested for preparing 74 bamboo spears to fight against the *bōryokudan*.[50] By October, at least one newspaper reported an extensive *bōryokudan* presence. The company, it claimed, had hired several hundred *bōryokudan* from Tokyo, stationed them at various plants, and ordered them to carry pistols, daggers, and other weapons as they wandered throughout the town of Noda and clashed with strikers. On October 13, *bōryokudan* led by a company adviser attempted to break up a union meeting.[51] One week later, on the night of October 20, a strike leader and one other person were attacked by 14 or 15 *bōryokudan* affiliated with the Maruhon Transportation Company. The two men were forced into a truck and taken to the Maruhon head office, where a melee erupted between approximately 40 sword-bearing Maruhon supporters and the strikers' guards that had rushed to the scene. Police officers eventually brought an end to the brawl, confiscating weapons and arresting ten strikers and 43 people from the Maruhon side. A leftist newspaper reporting this story took the opportunity to describe the sense of anxiety and sympathy felt by the townspeople for the strikers because of the prevalence of company *bōryokudan*. In addition to these specific incidents, there were reports of how strikers were regularly dragged into cars driven by *bōryokudan*, taken to the company, and forced to work. It was also not unusual for union members to be cut down by traveling groups of *bōryokudan*.[52]

The Kokusuikai's role in the strike was initially more benign and did not elicit the kind of animosity the strikers directed toward the Seigidan. During the early months of the strike, the Kokusuikai attempted to earn a position at the negotiating table as a mediator. Established by Kokusuikai member Gotō Kōjirō, the Noda branch of the organization recruited representatives from headquarters who wanted to be involved in resolving the dispute. On September 23, for example, six executives from the Kantō headquarters of the Kokusuikai went to Noda and visited with both the strikers and the company to offer mediation; they were, however, refused, as were similar overtures by other nationalist leaders and groups. In mid-December, the Kokusuikai again offered to mediate the dispute, but was declined. It is unclear why Noda Shōyu did not accept these offers of help. It could be that the organizations truly intended to mediate an end to the strike, not just act as strikebreakers, in which case the company's cold shoulder could have stemmed from its staunch refusal to negotiate with the strikers.[53]

While the Kokusuikai focused on mediation, tensions continued to escalate between the Seigidan and strikers. Groups of four to five strikers would sneak up to the homes of Takanashi and other Seigidan members and pelt them with excrement. In early November, strikers boycotted stores managed by Seigidan executives to demonstrate their opposition to the behavior of the group and the company. And after a mid-month meeting between Seigidan officers and labor representatives ended without resolution, strikers held a conference and were encouraged to withdraw their savings from the Shōyū Bank because Takanashi was one of its directors.[54]

In addition to the ongoing battle against the Seigidan, strikers also fought with *bōryokudan* that may or may not have included Seigidan members among their ranks. These violent struggles continued through the later months of 1927 and reached a peak in early December, extending beyond Noda to the town of Gyōtoku where Noda Shōyu's Factory Sixteen was located. There, company housing was being used by the strikers as a branch office without the company's authority. When Noda Shōyu threatened to evict the laborers so that the space could be used for company housing as it was intended, they argued that it was their right to remain and refused to yield, raising the company's fears of a widening sense of unrest. A Noda Shōyu executive named Mogi Kunitarō then invited from Tokyo more than 40 *bōryokudan,* who put on headbands, raised a battle cry, and attacked the strikers in Gyōtoku. The strikers, allegedly outfitted with white headbands and singing revolutionary songs, were few in number and eventually defeated.[55]

Strikers using the Noda Theater as a gathering place were also dealt a setback when they were evicted from the premises, this time by the management-backed Kokusuikai with whom Noda Shōyu had apparently decided to cooperate. Upon hearing a rumor that Kuramochi Naokichi was to rally 100 Kokusuikai members to strengthen the company's position, the strikers lit a bonfire at the entrance of the Noda Theater and shops in the town closed their doors early. The company had indeed requested the help of Kokusuikai members who arrived in Noda, although not without mishaps that revealed their choice instruments of violence. One car headed from Tokyo to a Kokusuikai member in Noda was stopped by the police, who confiscated its contents of 12 swords, 18 clubs, 41 cartridges, and two guns. The police also searched the lodgings of four Kokusuikai members where they uncovered one gun, one sword, two daggers, and several dozen iron bars. Although these discoveries led to arrests, the Kokusuikai still managed to evict the strikers. Kuramochi erected a sign over the theater that read "Office of Kuramochi Industries Division" and stationed there over 100 Kokusuikai members. It was clear that at this point, the Kokusuikai had entered the strike on the side of management; the Kokusuikai's Umezu Jinbei held discussions with various company executives and, on December 23, met with the head of the Seigidan.[56]

Bōryokudan violence fanned the flames of the strikers' convictions, encouraging physical clashes and discouraging settlement. The Kokusuikai's takeover of the Noda Theater prompted a retaliatory attack about one month later, in what became the biggest incident of the Noda Shōyu dispute. On the night of January 14, after a public meeting, union members went out into the town of Noda and threw rocks at stores of Seigidan members, breaking 29 storefront windows and displays. The animosity the strikers felt toward their suppressors was also expressed in a handbill that condemned Seigidan members as "bastards" (*yatsura*) and minions of the company. The handbill also venerated those who were fighting courageously against the "capitalist *bōryokudan*."[57] Attempts at mediation in early February consistently failed for a variety of reasons, and the stabbing of four union members by a *bōryokudan* on February 6, the first day of negotiations, certainly did not facilitate reconciliation.[58]

Renewed talks were inspired not by the threat of violence but by a strategic move by the strikers to attract the attention and garner the legitimation of the emperor. The audacity of a direct appeal to the emperor by the vice chair was enough of a shock to bring everyone back to the bargaining table. Company executives, union members, a Seigidan representative, and others negotiated from late March through April and eventually reached a settlement on April 20, 1928. Three hundred people were selected by the company to return to work, and 745 workers resigned.[59] Two days later, in a development that highlighted its main purpose as a strikebreaking body, the Noda Seigidan held a ceremony to mark its dissolution.[60]

The violence of the Seigidan, repressive in its intent, often had the unintended consequence of exacerbating animosities between management and labor. This was seen in the Noda Shōyu strike but was even more stark in the Tōyō Muslin dispute of 1930, in which the Seigidan unequivocally supported the company and physically intimidated workers. The workers, in turn, expressed a bitter and passionate abhorrence of Sakai Eizō and his organization.

The strike was sparked by the company's closure of its cotton-spinning and maintenance divisions and the resulting dismissal of 500 employees. It was announced that the cotton-spinning division would be shut down on September 26 and that all workers staying in the division dormitories would be sent home. Talks were held with labor representatives, company executives, and Sakai, but the union's dissatisfaction with the company's terms encouraged it to stage what was the second demonstration of the year.[61] Of Tōyō Muslin's approximately 2,500 workers, all were members of the Tōyō Muslin branch of the Japan Textile Labor Union (Nihon Bōshoku Rōdō Kumiai Yōmosu Shibu Kyōgikai) and all allegedly participated in the demonstrations; of the workers, over 2,000 were female.[62] In a plea for the support of the townspeople written about a week later, the strikers conveyed their anger with the presence of Sakai at the negotiating table and explained that they discontinued discussions because the company was mobilizing *bōryokudan* in preparation for battle.[63]

On the morning of September 27, Seigidan members arrived by cars at Tōyō Muslin, located outside Tokyo in the town of Kameido, to act as "professional agitators" (*aji puro*) on behalf of the company. At 3:30 that afternoon, workers held a demonstration in the factory, stormed the company office, and managed to seal the Seigidan members into one room. Later in the day, 500 young women who had been forced into their dormitories by police managed to rush past se-curity to stage a demonstration. While these women sang labor songs, those who remained in the dorms broke the screens off their second-floor windows and flew the union flag.[64]

The approximately 200 Seigidan members at the factory seemingly constituted most of the *bōryokudan* in this dispute, battling with the workers on the ground as company-hired security.[65] Compared to the Noda Shōyu strike in which the term "bōryokudan" was used without reference to a specific organization, here the workers clearly considered the Seigidan and *bōryokudan* as one. Ex-plained one laborer to her cohorts, "Girls, the name of these people is Seigidan, but they are really *bōryokudan,* so we can't lose [to them]."[66] Some publications specifically put the name of the Seigidan in parentheses after using the word *bōryokudan.*[67]

The visibility of the Seigidan was so great that the strikers may have labeled some *bōryokudan* as Seigidan even when that may not have been the case. In early October, for example, Tōyō Muslin brought in 16 temporary guards from the Iriyama Coal Mine ostensibly to help the company install machinery and move inventory. The strikers called these guards "*bōryokudan* (Seigidan)" and wrote on a handbill that they must be defeated: "Let's kill all of the Iriyama Coal Mine *bōryokudan!*"[68] The identity of the Iriyama guards is somewhat unclear. There were *bōryokudan* involved in the 1927 Iriyama Coal Mine strike, but Seigi-dan participation seems to have been minimal at best; some sources suggest the *bōryokudan* in the Iriyama strike were yakuza.[69] Regardless, what is notable is the strikers' perception of their opponents as Seigidan *bōryokudan.*

The violence of the *bōryokudan* was sharply criticized and widely publicized by the strikers in numerous union outlets. The Rōnōtō (Labor-Farmer Party), for example, organized a public meeting to oppose violent oppression by the alli-ance among the authorities, capitalists, and *bōryokudan.*[70] Specific incidents were also reported to emphasize the atrocious nature of *bōryokudan* violence and to elicit a desire to fight back against it. Newsletters for strikers carried articles on the injury of 23 factory women by 20 armed company *bōryokudan* under the bold-face headlines: "Company *Bōryokudan* Stab 23 Factory Women with Knives," and "Throw Out the *Bōryokudan.*" In the body of one of these pieces, the *bōryokudan* attacks were condemned as inexcusable.[71] The raiding of dor-mitories by *bōryokudan* also received attention, with one newspaper describing how they went into the rooms of factory girls on the night of October 9 and used straw ropes to bind them.[72] Readers were intended to take from these articles not only the coldhearted nature of the *bōryokudan,* but also the conviction that force would be needed to be victorious over management.[73] Highlighting the violence of the *bōryokudan* was a way the strikers could motivate and justify their own.

The Seigidan eventually receded from the strike, allegedly out of an ambiguous concern that continued participation in an extended dispute with an elusive resolution would arouse suspicions.[74] Whatever the true reasons for retreat, it was clear that Seigidan involvement did not frighten the laborers into passivity or otherwise facilitate settlement of the strike. To the contrary, continued incidents of strikers violently resisting management suggest that the Seigidan presence escalated tensions and solidified the laborers' resolve. The strike was eventually settled on November 21, almost two months after it began.

The Kokusuikai and Seigidan's attempts to suppress the left were not limited to attacks on labor unions and strikers, but extended to others who had a vaguely liberal or leftist tinge. The Kokusuikai, for example, was known for its attempt to prevent the enactment of universal manhood suffrage and for disrupting socialist meetings.[75] And in one of the group's most publicized incidents, it took aim at the Suiheisha, a national organization with a socialist bent that opposed discrimination against the oppressed minority Burakumin. The Kokusuikai squared off against the Suiheisha likely because of fears about an assertively antagonistic Burakumin population, especially worrisome to the Kokusuikai bosses who were construction contractors that hired Burakumin as laborers. Such concerns outweighed the fact that some members of the two groups had friendly relations and that some individuals were connected to both organizations.[76]

What would become known as the Kokusuikai-Suiheisha incident was sparked by an encounter in Nara Prefecture on March 17, 1923, when a Burakumin bride was derided by an elderly man named Morita Kumakichi who held up four fingers (a gesture of insult against Burakumin) as she passed by. Two youths who witnessed Morita's action reported him to the police, and news spread about the incident. The Suiheisha demanded an apology from Morita, who refused and called the Kokusuikai for support.[77] The following morning, there was a skirmish between about 800 Kokusuikai members and approximately 750 Suiheisha activists armed with bamboo sticks and swords, and supporters on both sides continued to assemble from Nara and nearby prefectures. By March 19, two days after the contentious initial incident, the situation escalated and fighting broke out between 1,220 Suiheisha supporters and about 1,200 people from the Kokusuikai, reservist associations, and youth groups.[78] The violence reached such a scale that the governor arranged for backup from the army and from Osaka's police reserves while the local police chief attempted to negotiate an end to the hostilities. At the height of the conflict on March 19, ten assistant police inspectors, 36 police sergeants, and 348 regular policemen had gathered in Nara.[79]

Although the agreement brokered between the Suiheisha and the Kokusuikai on March 20 appeared to favor the Suiheisha because it required an apology from Morita, the subsequent police probe of the incident seems to have been harsher on the Burakumin side. When the police were broken into two investigatory groups, the one assigned to the Suiheisha had 133 police compared to 45 for the Kokusuikai. Similarly, in a separate series of explorations, there were 40 police officers designated to the Suiheisha and 25 to the Kokusuikai. These numbers seem suspicious because the total number of Suiheisha participants was not that much greater than Kokusuikai members (2,940 as opposed to 2,275). Given this disproportionate allocation of police, it was not surprising that there were more Suiheisha than Kokusuikai arrests (35 compared to 12).[80]

In their attack on labor and the left in general, the Kokusuikai and Seigidan were much like the *squadrismo* of Italy and the SA of Germany. All of these groups had a solid grounding in nationalist ideology and considered labor unions and socialists a grave threat to national character and development. One of the primary directives of the *squadrismo* was to fight "bolshevism," especially from around 1920. In the winter of that year, *squadrismo* launched a sustained attack against socialists that lasted well into the spring of 1921. This "systematic campaign of terror" included intrusion into labor conflicts and took aim at trade unions among other socialist institutions.[81] The SA did squabble with the conservative right in a way that the organizations in Japan did not, and both the SA and the *squadrismo* had an initial anticapitalist stage.[82] Yet in practice, all of these bodies fought violently against socialists and labor in an effort to silence, and indeed cleanse, their nations of leftist contamination.

The Nationalist Nexus in the Metropole and Beyond

The fascist violence of the Kokusuikai and Seigidan was all the more oppressive because the two so-called *bōryokudan* were more than just yakuza organizations; they were hubs of a nationalist nexus that drew in politicians, military figures, bureaucrats, and industrialists. These were not low-level men who were affiliates only in name, but prominent figures who assumed leadership roles in these groups. The intimacy of various elite political connections was particularly evident with the Kokusuikai. In February 1926, when the sitting Kokusuikai president died, one politician who reportedly sought the position was Gotō Shinpei. Gotō had enjoyed an illustrious career as the civilian governor of Taiwan, president of the South Manchuria Railway, minister of communications, director general of the colonization bureau, home minister, minister of foreign affairs, and mayor of Tokyo. He was passed over for the Kokusuikai presidency because he was not adequately anticommunist.[83] Three years later, in 1929, a prominent politician did assume leadership of the organization. Suzuki Kisaburō was a former minister of justice and home minister, and he would go on to be president of the Seiyūkai. Standing beside him as chair was politician Takahashi Mitsutake who, among other things, had been chief cabinet secretary under Hara Kei.[84] Military men also featured prominently in the Kokusuikai. In the mid-1930s, the general headquarters' vice president was also a vice admiral in the navy, the chief director a lieutenant general in the army. The directors consisted of four army lieutenant generals, one navy vice admiral, and three navy major generals; the advisers included three navy vice admirals and one army lieutenant general. Also among the Kokusuikai's advisers was seasoned nationalist and Gen'yōsha leader Tōyama Mitsuru.[85]

The nationalist nexus of the Kokusuikai and Seigidan was not only politically significant, but also geographically expansive. Both organizations established bases for operation beyond the boundaries of Japan proper in keeping with a fairly long history of nationalist groups supporting continental expansion. In exporting their violence abroad, members of the Kokusuikai and Seigidan became *tairiku rōnin* (continental adventurers), following in the footsteps of organizations such as the Gen'yōsha. An earlier discussion, in Chapter 2, touched on the Gen'yōsha's violent activities in Korea and Manchuria during the mid-Meiji period that were intended to provoke a more aggressive Japanese foreign policy. The Qingdao branch of the Kokusuikai focused instead on an issue that had preoccupied the organization back at home: labor relations. Here too, at the southern tip of the Shandong peninsula, Kokusuikai members would appear at factories when there were strikes. They were also known to enter conflicts between Japanese and Chinese residents which raised the ire of the Chinese to such an extent that on August 18, 1931, several thousand people physically attacked the Kokusuikai. In addition to widespread hostility, the Qingdao Kokusuikai struggled with internal tensions that were brought to a head when the chief secretary participated in putting down an uprising even after he had been told to restrain his actions. The branch decided to disband on February 20, 1932, despite the wishes of those who wanted to see it endure.[86]

The Kokusuikai in Manchuria was much more vocal in criticizing Japan's foreign policy toward China. When the Mukden branch renamed itself the Kokusuikai Manshū Honbu (Kokusuikai Manchurian Headquarters) in May 1931, it spoke to various concerns about Japan's position in Manchuria. On the evening of May 22, following an afternoon ceremony to induct a new president (a journalist and Tokyo Imperial University graduate), a meeting was held to discuss the current political situation and the future of the organization. The approximately

300 people in attendance heard harsh statements about the weakening of Japan's foreign policy toward China, the lack of thoroughness in dealing with railroad-related issues, and the need for cooperation among the Japanese in Manchuria in light of the difficult situation in foreign relations. The next step was to focus on raising funds, recruiting more members, and selecting leaders who would be dispatched to various zones under the administration of the South Manchuria Railway. An outline of the group's business plans included the construction of a martial arts center (Kokusui Budōkan), but it is not known whether that came to pass.[87] After the Manchurian Incident of mid-September 1931, there was mention of a Manshū Kokusuikai (Manchuria Kokusuikai) founded in October. Whether this was a new body or the renovation of the Kokusuikai's Manchurian Headquarters is unclear. In either case, the organization was said to have about 1,500 members by April 1933.[88]

For the Seigidan, the Manchurian Incident was pivotal in inspiring its decision to expand operations to China. Plans were developed after September 1931 and were put into motion in 1932, when Sakai and several fellow officers took expeditionary trips to Manchuria, first in April then again in June and July. On these scouting missions, they visited various locations, interviewed important government figures as well as military leaders, and managed to win the support of the South Manchuria Railway Company and other financial interests. Present at one meeting in July were representatives from the Mitsui, Sumitomo, Yasuda, and Mitsubishi *zaibatsu*.[89]

The group's vision was to encourage members to emigrate to Manchukuo, as the puppet state in Manchuria was called by the Japanese, and form a "Justice Village" (Seigi-mura). This "village" would serve as a base from which to spread ideas of justice and, more concretely, to secure and police national borders. By July, the Seigidan had already selected 100 members—including 30 from Tokyo, 30 from Kansai, and 20 from Kyūshū—who would be part of the first migration.[90] This group, led by Sakai, arrived in Mukden on August 9, set up an office, and promptly began preparations for the official founding of the Manshū Seigidan.

In the late afternoon of September 8, 1932, an official gathering was held to explain the founding principles of the organization and initiate new members with a *sakazuki* ceremony. Before the 320 Japanese and Chinese in attendance, Sakai spoke about the importance of building a strong Manchukuo that would be a brother to the Japanese. The Manshū Seigidan's charter and rules unveiled on this occasion extolled the virtues of the imperial way, chivalry, and advancement of the peace and welfare of the world's people.[91]

In practice, much of the Seigidan's work revolved around physical force. Members provided policing and security in both Mukden and Xinjing, the sites of the organization's two headquarters, and went on punitive expeditions against insurgents. The head of the Guandong Police Bureau reported that those Seigidan members who immigrated from Japan (as opposed to the drivers, factory hands, and unemployed who joined their ranks in Manchuria) were armed with guns and ammunition and could be seen doing military-style drills and training.[92] Sakai Eizō was referred to in government correspondence as the one responsible for the migration to Manchuria of a majority of the "armed immigrant groups" (busō imindan). Sakai also formed a relationship with local bandits (bazoku); in late September 1932, he allegedly won the allegiance of 1,300 bandits to the state of Manchukuo. The report of this in the Asahi shinbun seems to have holes, but it is worth noting that Sakai was the one who dealt with the bandits, who were a kind of violence specialist. Aside from memos to watch Sakai's movements and those rōnin who associated with him, there seems to have been little legal consequence for the Seigidan's violence.[93]

The Manshū Seigidan, like its nationalist predecessors on the continent, operated with the support of Japanese military figures in China. Just as Tōyama Mitsuru's Gen'yōsha formed alliances with military officers who shared its vision of an expansionist Japan, the Manshū Seigidan forged connections with the military in Manchuria.[94] On the continent as in Japan proper, the Kokusuikai and the Seigidan were both part of a nexus that forwarded aggressive, violent imperialism.

Violence in the Decline of the Political Parties

The intimate ties between politicians and nationalist organizations contributed to the decline of political parties in the 1930s. Although cabinets had long included military men as ministers, in sharing stewardship of the Kokusuikai and Seigidan, politicians had become even more accustomed to sharing political leadership with the military. On a national scale, this idea of joint governance would erode the parties' strength in the 1930s. More important, the Seiyūkai-Kokusuikai relationship in particular contributed to the negative image of the party as distant from the people. Seiyūkai politicians who led or were affiliated with the Kokusuikai became emblematic of how far the political parties had strayed from liberalism, demonstrating that they had indeed become "established parties." Worse still, the Seiyūkai was criticized for not curbing Kokusuikai violence, and political parties as a whole came to be viewed as fundamentally incapable of ensuring order and security.

The connection between the Seiyūkai and Kokusuikai was forged at the Kokusuikai's inception, with Seiyūkai Home Minister Tokonami Takejirō's hand in its establishment. Tokonami continued on as an adviser, but more notable was the assumption of the organization's chairmanship by Murano Tsuneemon. Murano's career trajectory, discussed in Chapter 3, began when he dabbled in violence with the Osaka Incident of 1885. He moved on to become a local *sōshi* organizer, eventually assumed the reins of the Seiyūkai *ingaidan,* and was promoted to Seiyūkai secretary-general. In 1922, Murano became the second chairman in the history of the Kokusuikai. He led the group alongside its president Ōki Enkichi, justice minister from the Hara Kei and Takahashi Korekiyo cabinets. It is difficult to ascertain how much power Murano exercised, but as chairman he had the right to select the president, vice president, and chief director of the Kokusuikai branches. As historian Irokawa Daikichi has commented, Murano's diary included the various Kokusuikai events that he presumably attended. He was certainly not a chairman in name alone.[95]

Murano facilitated some cross-fertilization between the violent elements of the Seiyūkai *ingaidan* and the Kokusuikai, which was further encouraged by fellow party member Mori Kaku. Mori had been recruited into the Seiyūkai *ingaidan* by Hara Kei and subsequently became both a parliamentarian and head of the *ingaidan.* Under his leadership, the *ingaidan* absorbed into its ranks more yakuza, *tairiku rōnin,* and members of nationalist groups—so many that a historian would later describe Mori's group as a "*bōryokudan*-like, *ingaidan*-like organization" (*bōryokudanteki ingaidanteki na soshiki*). And by the latter half of the 1920s, crossover between the Seiyūkai *ingaidan* and nationalist organizations such as the Kokusuikai had become commonplace.[96]

The marriage between the Kokusuikai and the Seiyūkai *ingaidan* was a natural outgrowth of shared ideologies and strategies. Murano had been drawn to the Kokusuikai because of its willingness to contain leftist social movements, and it seems more than coincidental that such cooperation would flourish under the party presidency of Tanaka Giichi, who as prime minister called for the arrest of leftist party members and also backed the expansion of Japanese interests in Manchuria. The style of violence used (organized, purposeful ruffianism) was another common trait.

By this point, the Kokusuikai's relationship to the Seiyūkai was arguably like that of *squadrismo* to the Partito Nazionale Fascista (National Fascist Party, hereafter PNF) in Italy during the early 1920s, or of the SA to the NSDAP in Germany. The PNF carved out a place for *squadrismo* within the party that was so important that, in the words of historian Emilio Gentile, "The link between *squadrismo* and the fascist party was indissoluble."[97] Each section of the party had such an "action squad" that was to promote fascism and defend the nation. In Germany, the SA functioned as a kind of "party militia," a paramilitary organization that served and benefited the interests of a political party. It should be noted that the Kokusuikai had a bit more political autonomy vis-à-vis the Seiyūkai than the

SA had from the NSDAP, and SA violence in elections reached a level that the Kokusuikai's did not. In the 1932 German election, for example, there were over 300 incidents of political violence and 24 deaths as the armed SA clashed with opponents; frustration with the outcome of the election also fueled a "massive terror campaign."[98] Although there were notable differences, all three bodies—the Kokusuikai, *squadrismo*, and SA—played a protective and aggressive role for their respective political parties.

The visibility of Kokusuikai violence made the organization—and the politicians who associated with it—targets of criticism, especially by those on the moderate left. Political violence had become such a routine display that, in 1923, the magazine *Chūō kōron* (The Central Review) ran several series on the phenomenon. In one issue, the critic, philosopher, and historian Miyake Setsurei honed in on the hollowness of the Kokusuikai's ideology, alleging that the Kokusuikai was concerned with neither the "national essence" nor chivalry. The Kokusuikai did not help the weak and crush the strong, as it claimed, but persecuted and menaced the weak. In Miyake's mind, the Kokusuikai was strong and even tyrannical as it wielded political power and financial influence and fought with force. Pacifist Mizuno Hironori echoed this view, emphasizing how the Kokusuikai tormented laborers.[99] Others were particularly offended by the government's active support of, and participation in, the organization's activities. Playwright and writer Kikuchi Kan warned that government complicity in the establishment of violent groups (*bōryoku dantai*) like the Kokusuikai would only promote antagonism between right and left. For him, the Kokusuikai was an ominous harbinger of violent, ideological strife. For socialist and Christian educator Abe Isoo, this strife could already be seen in incidents such as the Kokusuikai-Suiheisha clash of 1923. All these thinkers condemned the government for condoning and even encouraging Kokusuikai violence.[100]

Not only did support of the Kokusuikai taint "the government" writ large, but similarities in the violence of party politics to that of groups like the Kokusuikai also contributed to the delegitimization of political parties. Some lumped *ingaidan* ruffians and the Kokusuikai together by using the same vocabulary to describe them. Watanabe Tetsuzō, a businessman and politician, labeled them both as "shishi." And he made it clear that these "Taisho *shishi*" had no resemblance to their Bakumatsu predecessors. While the *shishi* of the Meiji Restoration discussed issues and propelled Japan onto the world stage, explained Watanabe, the Taisho versions were uneducated, ignorant, cowardly, and so preoccupied with the nation that they did it harm.[101] Others categorized the Kokusuikai and *ingaidan* as slightly different variants of the same violent phenomenon and leveled similar criticisms at both. Like the Kokusuikai, the Seiyūkai was painted as despotic, inflicting its will on a relatively powerless minority. Frequent mention was made of *sōshi* ruffianism, brawls within the Diet, and corruption as evidence of the Seiyūkai's degeneration.[102]

These jabs at the political parties and Diet politics were not intended to be a larger affront on the fundamental idea of parliamentary politics. Indeed, many of these moderate leftists had long supported socialist change through the democratic process. They were intending to take issue not with the political system as a whole, but with the phenomena of violence and violent groups in politics. Their primary concerns related to what the prevalence of violence said about Japan's modernity, civilization, and culture. Miyake lamented how reason and logic were falling victim to force, how Mussolini's rise in Italy and Japan's adulation thereof were illustrative of backwardness, and how the level of Japanese civilization and culture was sinking. The theme of violence as primitive and antithetical to progress, reason, justice, law, and therefore civilized and enlightened politics was taken up by many of Miyake's intellectual colleagues such as Abe, Mizuno, and political theorist Sugimori Kōjirō.[103] Even though they did not intend to open the way for doubt about the legitimacy of parliamentary politics, their discursive construction of violence as a societal and political ill stained the political parties and the Diet. The parties, unlike the Kokusuikai, were governing bodies considered ultimately responsible for the current state of affairs. At a time when violence was seen by some as despotic, uncivilized, and destructive, the persistence of *sōshi* and *ingaidan* violence helped to undermine the parties' legitimacy as rulers.

Not only leftist intellectuals were deeply critical of the Seiyūkai and its violence. In the 1920s, the party became the subject of scathing editorials in mass, mainstream newspapers for its use of violence in the streets and within the halls of the Diet. One incident that served as a lightning rod for such commentary unfolded in March 1926, when parliamentarian Kiyose Ichirō delivered a speech on the floor of the Diet accusing Seiyūkai President Tanaka Giichi of improper spending from a secret army expense account. In response, members of the Seiyūkai stormed onto the dais and beat Kiyose, throwing the parliament into pandemonium. A Seiyūkai politician pulled Kiyose by his shirt from behind, while another Diet member hit him on the head. And in the hallways of the Diet, clashes between *ingaidan* also resulted in injury. A number of those involved in the fray would emerge with bandages, and Kiyose bled from a jab to the neck. One newspaper reported that about 13 "violent parliamentarians" (*bōkō daigishi*) attacked Kiyose, and as many as 16 were eventually indicted in Tokyo Regional Court on the charge of violent assault.[104]

Many newspaper editorials were quick to paint the skirmish as particularly violent. The *Ōsaka mainichi shinbun* noted that there had been many instances when physical force had been used in the Diet but that this case was unique in the number of people who stormed onto the dais itself. Another newspaper

4.2. Published in March 1926, in the aftermath of the attack on parliamentarian Kiyose Ichirō, this cartoon was entitled "An Example of Constitutional Government." In *Kensei o kiki ni michibiku Seiyūkai no bōkō jiken* (Tokyo: Jiyū Bundansha, 1927).

commented on the scale of the violence, observing that no other incident had caused people to fear for their lives. And yet another saw the confusion in the Diet as unusual even for a usually tumultuous body and labeled this violence "the greatest stain on the history of the Diet."[105]

As this comment about the Diet suggests, the incident served as an opportunity to express deep-seated apprehensions about the parliament and political parties. Although the *Tōkyō asahi shinbun* made a plea not to boycott these entities, preferring instead that the violent Diet members not be re-elected, many newspapers gave the sense of an almost existential crisis for both the Diet and the political parties.[106] The *Kyūshū shinbun* observed that the people's confidence in the Diet was decaying and that voices for its repudiation were increasing. An editorial urged the Diet to serve as a model to the people by valuing freedom of speech, and warned that a failure to reform the parliament would invite the indignity of the people—if that were to happen, the Diet would cease to be of any meaning or significance.[107]

Perhaps even more than the Diet, the future of the Seiyūkai was cast into doubt. The *Ōsaka mainichi shinbun* believed that the Seiyūkai politicians had destroyed trust in the party at its root, eroding its prestige and credibility. The Seiyūkai's actions were interpreted by some as violence against the people themselves, violence that denied and contradicted the very foundation of constitutional politics. What was worse, this violence was all the more corrosive because it was wrapped up with other ills such as the tyrannical and despotic oppression of other Diet members' speech and the attempt to discredit opponents (like Kiyose) by labeling them "red."[108] The *Nagasaki nichinichi shinbun* considered criminal not just the use of physical force, but also the party's subsequent efforts to justify its violence and evade responsibility. Similarly, the *Kokumin shinbun* suggested that the Seiyūkai president was indeed involved in some sort of plot. If Tanaka was not guilty, the reasoning went, he would have simply said so instead of resorting to violence. As much as the violence itself, this alleged strategy of obfuscating with physical force was disgraceful. Reflecting on all of these sins, newspapers observed that the Seiyūkai had "dug its own grave."[109]

To formally articulate these various concerns, some 130 journalists and 20 intellectuals (including democracy scholar Yoshino Sakuzō) gathered on April 7 at Hibiya Park to participate in a meeting to denounce and reject Diet violence. Officially named the Convention of Journalists Who Reject Diet Violence (Gikai Bōryoku Haigeki Yūshi Kisha Taikai), the group issued a declaration that formally articulated the stances these journalists had been taking in their editorials: repeated Diet violence was lamentable for constitutional government and a negative influence on the people's thought, the sanctity of the Diet should be respected, and violence should be rejected to protect speech. A resolution was also passed calling for, among other things, self-examination on the part of the political parties and the expulsion of Diet members who were habitually violent. In a somewhat ironic move, the Seiyūkai sent 67 *sōshi* to this meeting disguised as journalists, complete with business cards giving their occupation as newspaper reporters. They made a racket, but in a roll-call vote both the declaration and the resolution passed over the *sōshi*'s objections.[110]

Most insidious of all of these criticisms was a profound doubt about the ability of the Seiyūkai, and political parties in general, to restore order to a violent society. Some of the most vocal intellectuals feared the destabilizing nature of violence would lead to revolution or, as Yoshino Sakuzō foresaw, "anarchistic chaos."[111] Concomitant with the fear of disorder was a desire for order, which encouraged many of these leftist thinkers to turn to the state as a source of stability. There were reminders of the state's duty to maintain social order and calls for the state to be strict in its suppression of violence regardless of its ideological coloring—"Society's vermin that intimidate and extort," exclaimed Mizuno,

"must be exterminated using the sternest of methods."[112] For those who specified, it was the police in particular who were to control violence. As Horie Kiichi
expounded, the police had the responsibility of protecting citizens from danger,
such as "thugs," in various aspects of their daily lives.[113] Most insistent that the
police step up to this task was Abe Isoo, who by August 1923 was calling for the
use of police power against all who were violent and criticizing the police for
not being quicker and more vigorous in executing this task. Abe firmly believed
that police prohibition of violence would gradually lead to a decrease in violent
incidents:

> If the police force took the stand of forbidding all violence, then vio-
> lent incidents would gradually decrease, and so it is undeniable that
> we would have less reason to worry. Of course, it would not be difficult
> for the state's police force to control the degree of violence I have de-
> scribed. If police force is insufficient, military force (*heiryoku*) could
> also be used.[114]

Although he paused a moment on the issue of potential police abuse of state power
and did insist as a caveat that thought and speech must be free, Abe—the Christian pacifist who was a pioneering figure in the Japanese socialist movement—
was not disturbed about the prospect of the state marshalling police and even
military power to crack down on violent individuals. It may have been because of
their moderate ideological stance (unsympathetic with what they considered the
extremes who should be reined in), their adherence to German social democracy
(which was not fundamentally skeptical of the state), or their potent fear of disorder (as well as the perceived lack of alternatives), but none of the thinkers who
advocated greater state control of violence addressed the question of who was to
police the state.

The ease with which these thinkers turned to the enforcement arm of the state,
and not the political parties or parliament, resonated with a general and widespread hesitance about the ability of the party politicians to govern effectively.
Factors that eroded confidence in the political parties included violence as well
as corruption, the devastating economic impact of the Great Depression, and
Minseitō Prime Minister Hamaguchi Osachi's signing of the controversial London Naval Treaty in 1930. But the public displays of violence were powerful symbols of party weakness. And this phenomenon was not unique to prewar Japan;
in Germany too the concern about communist violence and ruffianism in the
streets helped paint the democratic state as inept: "The Nazis sought to portray
themselves as the most vigorous and effective force against the communists—
and, at the same time, to portray the liberal state as incapable of preserving public
security."[115] In Italy, the *squadrismo* railed against the parliament and ineffectual

political parties.[116] The difference in Japan was that the existing political parties were not attacked with one frontal blow from a party or cohesive movement, but by sharp jabs coming from a number of directions thrown by nationalists and militarists of various stripes and from various organizations—some of whom would eventually attain political power and sideline, if not eliminate, party influence.[117] As in Germany and Italy, the idea that some kind of "orderly violence" was needed to control "anarchy" made the ascent of these figures palatable, especially as ruffianism was punctuated not only by assassinations but also by attempted coups d'état.[118]

It is difficult to determine the extent of the connections between the Kokusuikai and the Seigidan, and the militarists and rightists who carried out the assassinations and coups d'état with which we are familiar. But all of them shared a belief in the redemptive power of violence; the young officers' groups of the 1930s, for example, "glorified terrorism and potential martyrdom as purifying acts of sacrifice for the nation."[119] And all of this violence undermined the political parties. The assassinations of financier Yasuda Zenjirō and Hara Kei by rightists in 1921 were worrisome enough on their own, but they were followed by a rapid succession of well-known, high-profile violent incidents in the 1930s: the attack on Prime Minister Hamaguchi Osachi in November 1930; the planned rightist and military coups of March and October 1931; the League of Blood Incident in February and March 1932 that resulted in the deaths of Minseitō leader Inoue Junnosuke and Mitsui director general Dan Takuma; an attempted coup in May 1932 by young naval officers, who assassinated Prime Minister and Seiyūkai President Inukai Tsuyoshi; and the February 26 Incident of 1936, a military rebellion led by junior army officers who murdered Finance Minister Takahashi Korekiyo, Lord Keeper of the Privy Seal Saitō Makoto, and Inspector General of Military Education General Watanabe Jōtarō in their endeavor to carry out a coup d'état. The replacement of Inukai Tsuyoshi by Navy Admiral Saitō Makoto in May 1932 had marked the end of party cabinets, with ten of the 15 ministerial positions going not to party politicians but to bureaucrats and military men. This blow to the parties was the outcome of various high-level machinations, but the conviction that moderate military leaders needed to be placed in political power to contain more radical, violent elements should not be understated.

Concomitant with the decline of the political parties was the fading of the *ingaidan* from the political scene. Their violence had already begun to wane in the late 1920s when the electorate quadrupled with the enactment of universal manhood suffrage. This expanded body of voters first went to the polls for a general election in February 1928, and they were courted more by (nonviolent) speech meetings and groups of campaigning youth than the physical coercion of *sōshi*. The sheer size of the electorate also made it much more prudent for politicians to buy votes rather than violently intimidate voters on this large scale. Then, in the 1930s, the Seiyūkai *ingaidan* was absorbed and replaced by violent nationalist groups like the Kokusuikai.

By the early 1940s, nonstate violence specialists of various sorts seemed to vanish from the political scene. *Ingaidan*-type violence became obsolete when Prime Minister Konoe Fumimaro attempted to create one mass political party in 1940, paving over the political contests and rivalries that had fostered the need for pressure groups. This was also a time when the economic strains of war emptied coffers of funds that would have been needed to hire *sōshi*.[120] The fate of the Kokusuikai and Seigidan is hazy, because there are so few extant sources on the organizations' activities in the late 1930s and early 1940s. Their membership had declined precipitously over the first half of the 1930s—the Kokusuikai's from an alleged 200,000 in 1932 to 25,819 in 1935, the Seigidan's from 105,000 to 19,619. This may have been due to the waning of leftist activism, which took the wind out of the sails of antileftist groups. In any case, by 1942, a government report on nationalist movements did not mention either organization by name.[121] One final point is that many violence specialists, typically male youth, were likely drafted into the armed forces in the early 1940s as extensive wartime military conscription called on the services of young, able-bodied men. *Sōshi* and yakuza thus became providers of physical force not for political parties or nationalist organizations, but for a violent arm of the state.

The violence of the fascist movement as embodied in organizations like the Kokusuikai and Seigidan was powerful—the actualization of an antileftist and expansionist vision that menaced laborers among others and sought to bolster the country's position on the continent. Their violence was such a force because it served the agenda of certain prominent militarists, industrialists, and politicians. It was not the kind of ruffianism wielded between candidates, or factions in a political party, or Diet members of roughly equal footing who wanted to protect themselves and make gains at the level of a personal election victory or parliamentary vote. It was a kind of ruffianism that forwarded an overarching nationalist, capitalist, expansionist ideology bolstered by those in distinct positions of influence.[122]

The ideological weight of their violence made them a political phenomenon much different from, for example, the Pinkerton's National Detective Agency in the United States. Allan Pinkerton, the agency's founder, may have had political convictions of his own, but the Pinkerton detectives who infiltrated labor unions and the Pinkerton Protective Patrol guards who provided security for businesses were not part of a political organization.[123] The Kokusuikai and Seigidan were also distinct from the organized crime groups in the United States that infiltrated unions as labor racketeers. There were some broad similarities: U.S. organized crime groups wielded violence (from assault and battery to murder) against union members and leaders who fought their parasitic influence; generally hurt workers in a host of ways, including theft from union and pension funds; and, especially in the early and mid-twentieth century, were protected from criminal prosecution by politicians who appreciated their support in election campaigns. Nonetheless, they did not seek to subdue or eradicate labor union activity; they certainly did exploit labor unions, but this very exploitation required the continued existence of the unions. Most important, organized crime groups (such as Al Capone's in Chicago) viewed unions as a vehicle for profit or, to use sociologist James Jacob's words, a "cash cow." Their motivations and concerns were largely financial, not ideological.[124]

Not only were the Kokusuikai and Seigidan more than strikebreakers, they were also not just mafias seeking to make money. This is not to say they were unconcerned with profit, but it should not be assumed that financial and political concerns were mutually exclusive. Their activities were unquestionably ideological in their influence, even if varied in their motivations. The political involvement, and perhaps beliefs, of some yakuza force a reconsideration of organized crime as a fundamentally "non-ideological enterprise."[125] The nationalism of these particular yakuza also helps explain why they were part of the fascist movement rather than attacked by it, as the mafia was in Italy. Unlike the Kokusuikai and Seigidan, the Sicilian mafia was a holdout against fascism. In Mussolini's eyes, the mafia challenged his regime by resisting the idea of a unified Italian nation-state and continuing to operate as a state within a state. To destroy the romanticism of these "men of violence" and establish its authority in Sicily, Mussolini criminalized the mafia and made it a target of arrests and trials for much of the 1920s.[126]

It was their nationalist and expansionist ideology that allowed for the prominence of Kokusuikai and Seigidan violence in the prewar Japanese context. Their ideological stand drew in and was buttressed by those in positions of power in the military, industry, and politics. In turn, this nexus justified and gave weight to the organizations' violence. It is always difficult to gauge how widely this use of force was considered legitimate, but it could be speculated that their ideology (if not necessarily their violence) would have resonated with a population in which many enthusiastically embraced nation and empire. And those not involved in labor union or socialist activism may have been fairly apathetic for they were not burdened with the fear of being targets of antileftist violence. All of this made fascist violence distinctly different from that of the left, which not only was short the financial means to work with violence specialists but was also not operating from positions of power or with widespread popular support. The violence of the political parties was on shaky ground, as it lacked the ideological foundation or clothing that it had once had when party *sōshi* had fought against the heavy hand of the government parties, the Meiji oligarchy, or its political descendants. By the 1920s, their ruffianism had begun to look like unpurposeful political infighting. And even those who criticized Kokusuikai violence let the brunt of their condemnation fall on the political parties for failing to maintain order and stability. Ideology, as much as utility, was pivotal in shaping the construction, influence, and fate of the violent.

5

Democracy Reconstructed

Violence Specialists in the Postwar Period

In late May 1946, the *Yomiuri shinbun* ran an editorial that declared violence the enemy of democracy. As part of the effort to build a foundation for a new and peaceful country, the Japanese people were urged to embrace democracy as a force against the remnants of "feudal," violent thinking. Prewar terrorism and military tyranny were evoked as reminders of how violence could run amok, with utterly devastating consequences.[1] The *Yomiuri shinbun* was not alone in its condemnation of violence; the editorial in a mass-circulation daily newspaper was but one expression of a common postwar refrain about the incompatibility of violence and democracy.

This widespread sentiment was a testament to how the experiences of war and occupation fundamentally and profoundly altered Japan's violent democracy. The war exposed the destructive heart of violence at its very worst, extracting a heavy toll from many Japanese who were left in a state of exhaustion and despair.[2] And the atomic bombings of Hiroshima and Nagasaki came to epitomize the catastrophic potential of violence. Writing several years after Japan's surrender, constitutional scholar Suzuki Yasuzō described war as the worst kind of violence in its coercion of others' will and bodies, and the atomic bombing of Hiroshima as the most cruel act of violence in the history of humankind. The bomb, he said, extinguished hope for the future and, if there was another war, would mean the destruction of civilization and the extinction of the human race.[3] Much of the blame for the war, if not the atomic bombings, was placed on the shoulders of militarists and the wartime government. This assignment of responsibility to the country's leaders was encouraged by the Allied occupation authorities, who focused purges and the war crimes trial on those who had been in positions of power. As a result, the military and so-called fascists became associated with the violence of terrorism and war in the minds of many Japanese. So intimate was this connection that it was perfectly natural for the *Yomiuri shinbun* editorial to hold up militarists and fascists as the embodiment of prewar and wartime violence, and for various people to criticize what they saw as excessive or despotic violence in the immediate postwar decades by labeling it militaristic or fascist. The war, and those believed to be responsible for it, became cautionary emblems of what violence could wreak.

Deeply scarred by the war, many Japanese turned to democracy as a bulwark against all that had gone wrong in the preceding decades. As historian John Dower has eloquently illustrated, the occupation authorities orchestrated an ironic democratic revolution from above. Prime among its democratizing reforms was the writing of a new constitution that enshrined the value of pacifism in the famous war renunciation clause of article 9, the conversion of the appointed House of Peers to an elected House of Councillors, and the extension of the vote to women.[4] These institutional changes went hand in hand with the development of a mainstream political culture in which democracy was seen as peaceful and progressive. The desirability of democracy was articulated by many, including Koizumi Shinzō, an economist and former president of Keio University. Koizumi acknowledged that democracy was imperfect but argued that the freedom to criticize and to oppose, to participate in political movements, and to vote constituted a system for societal progress. Democracy was not only preferable to the strongman politics of Mussolini and Hitler and to the absolutism of Soviet Russia, but was also a way to stave off such dictatorships.[5]

As much as the immediate postwar decades witnessed public impatience with violence and a widespread embrace of democracy, they were also a testament to the tenacity of prewar-style politics. Conservative politicians were resurrected out of the ashes of defeat, some still clinging to ideologies rooted in their love of nation and hatred of communism. And they helped spin a conservative web that drew together political fixers, yakuza, big business, and a new ally: the United States. Resemblance to the nationalist nexus of the 1920s and 1930s was not coincidental; many of its players were prewar nationalists and militarists who were given a second life by an occupation force that shared their desire to weaken the socialists and feared communism above all else. It is not surprising, then, that the conservatives came into direct conflict (sometimes violent) with a variegated left, including socialists, labor unionists, and various critics of a strong Japan-U.S. alliance.

These ideological tensions—as well as the friction between those who advocated a new, nonviolent politics and those who continued to believe in the utility and necessity of violent politics—go a long way toward explaining why some violence specialists disappeared while others persisted into the postwar years, why *sōshi* (political ruffians) and *ingaidan* (pressure groups) receded from the political scene while yakuza managed to thrive. They are also the keys to understanding how the nature of political violence changed over the course of the postwar period and why violence gradually lost ground to money as the political tool of choice. The juxtaposition of various transwar continuities and discontinuities is a reminder that postwar politics were reconstructed, not fashioned anew from a completely different cloth. And it once again invites us to reexamine the nature of Japan's perpetually changing violent democracy.

The Decline of *Sōshi* and the Remaking of *Ingaidan* Violence

Broadened participation in politics and a decrease in public tolerance for violence brought an end to the existence of *sōshi* and their institutionalization into political parties. Indeed, the political ruffians so common and visible in party politics from the 1880s through the 1920s did not make much of a reappearance, if any, in the postwar period. Elections, debates, and speech meetings were mostly calm affairs, undisturbed by the intrusions of *sōshi*. And the word "sōshi" itself seemed to drop out of the political vocabulary, even requiring definition on those rare occasions when it was used at all. This waning of a *sōshi* presence was the continuation of a trend that began in the mid-1920s when the enactment of universal manhood suffrage greatly expanded the voting population, making physical intimidation of a large number of voters difficult. Using money to buy votes became a more efficient and cost-effective approach to influencing election outcomes. If the strategy of hiring ruffians to coerce voters lost its appeal with the advent of universal manhood suffrage, it was all the more impractical in the postwar age of universal suffrage. In the April 1946 election, the first in which women went to the polls, roughly half the population was eligible to vote.[6] This was a staggering increase over the one percent of eligible voters in the first general election of 1890.[7]

Sōshi also did not reappear in the violent wings of *ingaidan*, which themselves were a murky phenomenon through the early 1950s. There were infrequent mentions of *ingaidan* in the late 1940s, with the Japan Progressive Party (Nihon Shinpotō)' reported to have had discussions about whether to support such a body.[8] When the Japan Progressive Party merged to create a new party in 1947, the resulting Democratic Party (Minshutō) did form an *ingaidan*. Named the New Life Association (Shinseikai), the group's stated purpose was to expand the scope of the party's extraparliamentary activities. What these operations included, and to what extent they were violent, is unclear. But·the Democratic

Party's *ingaidan* collapsed with the departure of politician Shidehara Kijūrō, even before the party dissolved in 1950.[9]

In 1953, an article in a political journal noted how rare it had become to hear the word "ingaidan." One year later, a commentator explained in a well-known monthly magazine that *ingaidan* of the late 1920s had been known for using violence to disrupt Diet proceedings; he obviously felt this description was necessary for an audience now unfamiliar with the violent function of pressure groups.[10] And in a break from this past, the Reform Party (Kaishintō) claimed it was being progressive by not having such an *ingaidan*. The party argued that the role of the group had been to connect the people with the political parties and suggested that such an intermediary was unnecessary in these more democratic times. This reasoning was questioned by one of the party's rivals, the Liberal Party (Jiyūtō), which speculated that the Reform Party simply lacked the financial resources to have an *ingaidan*.

The Liberal Party officially christened its *ingaidan* in late January 1953, becoming the only party to have a pressure group. Though bearing the *ingaidan* label, the Liberal Party organization was a more staid and less violent version of its prewar counterparts. Previously known during the occupation as the Mutual Exchange Association (Dōkōkai), the renamed Liberal Party *ingaidan* had a total membership of around 375 that was clustered mainly in Tokyo and consisted of party members who did not hold elected office, those who were aspiring candidates, those who had an affinity for politics, and students. The foremost responsibility of the group was to promote party decisions, and to that end the *ingaidan* had stood behind the call for a special election, questioned the director of a special broadcasting bureau about the state of the communist movement, and submitted a resolution about a disturbance in the Tokyo metropolitan assembly. Observers commented on how serious the demeanor of *ingaidan* had become. Gone were the prewar days when it was fun to get a free lunch and some money for being rough and unrefined. Politician and former prewar *ingaidan* member Ōno Banboku recalled fondly how enjoyable it had been to be disorderly and hot-blooded, storm and disturb speech meetings, and tussle with the opposition. Ōno's reminiscence of the roughness and physicality of prewar pressure groups suggested that *sōshi* and the violent wing of *ingaidan* were changed, even unfamiliar, in postwar politics.[11]

The more sober character of *ingaidan* should not be mistaken for a greater sense of political propriety. Party youth, though possibly not formal *ingaidan* members, were hired to hit the campaign trail armed with megaphones and, very likely, money to be doled out as bribes.[12] Moreover, the political parties still retained their potential for violence even though there does not seem to have been an explicitly violent group within *ingaidan*. Included on the list of the Liberal

Party *ingaidan*'s activities, for example, were some that could be interpreted as entailing violence or the possibility of violence: supporting speakers at public meetings, taking "all possible measures" against the attempt of leftist organizations to derail the passage of a bill to prevent destructive activities, and serving as guards of the party president and executives when they campaigned outside Tokyo. In this vein, the men seen walking alongside Prime Minister Yoshida Shigeru were said to be *ingaidan*. It is unclear how often violence was used in the performance of these duties, but starting around the mid-1950s there were occasional mentions of speakers disturbing debates or speech meetings. And one senior *ingaidan* member acceded to calling the *ingaidan* a "wanryokudan" (literally, a force or strength group) because of its charge to protect the party, its members, and its offices in the face of physical assault.[13] In addition to the *ingaidan*, another body within the political parties became known for occasional violence: the *hishodan* (secretarial groups) physically clashed with rival *ingaidan* and party members in scuffles in the Diet building.

What is notable about violence in parliamentary politics of this decade is the absence of violence specialists, or those whose primary responsibility was the wielding of physical force. *Ingaidan, hishodan,* party members, and politicians could and did act violently, but there was no equivalent to the *sōshi* of the prewar era or a designated violent wing within the political parties. This was partly due to the preference for money over violence as an instrument of political influence. But more important was the widespread public intolerance of physical force, which rendered the reemergence of violent groups and violence specialists a risky venture for the political parties. The fear of being disparaged as undemocratic, and how this shaped the form that violence took in parliamentary politics, was especially evident in those physical scuffles that did take place in the mid-1950s.

Violence as a Political and Discursive Weapon in Diet Politics

In the summer of 1954, a political firestorm erupted over a clash between the conservative Liberal Party and the Japan Socialist Party (Nihon Shakaitō, hereafter JSP) on the night of June 3. The incident was sparked by disagreement over a Liberal Party police bill (Keisatsu Hōan) that centralized police forces by doing away with the several hundred existing local autonomous units and merging them with the national rural police to form new prefectural police under the administration of the governor and prefectural public safety commissions. The JSP vehemently opposed the bill because of its concerns about the denial of local autonomy and what it saw as a move back toward a prewar model of a strong, centralized police as an extension of state power. The bill was passed by the House of Representatives on May 15 in a vote of 254 to 127, but became stalled in the House of Councillors.[14] For most of June 3, the Liberal Party had seemed undecided about whether it was going to try to extend the session for the fourth time and slip a vote in under the wire. As the hours passed and the afternoon turned into evening, the JSP worried that its political opponents would attempt to force passage of the bill at the eleventh hour. Indeed, as the JSP had feared, the head of the Representative Steering Committee ended the meeting of that body at some point after 8:00 P.M. and attempted to take the bill to a plenary session of the Diet. In anticipation of this move, the JSP had rallied its *hishodan* to form a picket line between the Diet chairman's office and the main assembly hall so as to barricade him in his office and prevent the convening of a full assembly to extend the session and discuss the bill. And those JSP parliamentarians already in the hall occupied the chairman's seat on the dais. Although the JSP members did not expect to be able to set foot in the chairman's office, an opened rear door allowed them to enter, whereupon they formed a scrum and blockaded the room. Panicked by this intrusion, some Liberal Party members called the police to back up the overwhelmed sergeants-at-arms.[15]

This incident was far less violent than the all-out brawls that had taken place within the Diet building in the prewar period. The JSP's use of bodies to bring about a desired political outcome and the Liberal Party's marshalling of the police could be considered violent, but there was little of the bodily harm or physical damage that was fairly common in prewar skirmishes. And yet, in the context of postwar impatience with violence, there was an outcry against this incident that was broader and louder than any of the 1920s or 1930s. The three mass-circulation dailies were quick to express indignation, issuing a statement on June 11 demanding that the Diet seek to restore the prestige it had lost. Though the brunt of their specific criticisms fell on the JSP, which was urged to think about its use of force to prevent the opening of the Diet, the newspapers beseeched the government, all political parties, and every individual parliamentarian to exercise self-control and to reflect on what had transpired. And they implored all involved to save the situation quickly by putting parliamentary conduct on the right path and behaving in accordance with the majority of popular opinion. The newspapers were concerned that if such a confused condition persisted in the highest organ of state power, the resulting political, economic, and societal anxiety would destroy the foundation of democratic politics.[16] The public was reported to have already been dissatisfied with the ruling Liberal Party and the Yoshida Shigeru cabinet for ignoring the will of the people and making decisions not reflecting public opinion. Now, many were disappointed by the actions of the JSP and harbored antipathy toward parliamentarians in general. Even through the following year, before the general election in February 1955, the public was said to be distrustful of a Diet marred by corruption and violent incidents.[17]

Supporters of the Liberal Party and the JSP used this political malaise, attempting to discredit their political opponents by casting them as violent and undemocratic. Each side of this showdown sought to portray the other as coercive and disruptive of established parliamentary procedure. Two days after the incident, Prime Minister Yoshida spoke at a gathering of Liberal Party parliamentarians and was scathing in his criticism of the JSP. Yoshida accused the party of trampling on freedom of speech, the Diet's liberty, and the spirit of the constitution. The actions of the JSP were described as not only disgraceful but also planned, and part of a larger and secretive plot to destroy the democratic, parliamentary system.[18] Politician Masuda Kaneshichi echoed this characterization of the JSP, arguing that its violent obstruction of parliamentary deliberation was indicative of an ideology that denied and negated the importance of the Diet. To underscore this point, Masuda used language that evoked memories of the prewar period: he painted the JSP as a despotic, feudal, and absolutist minority going against the wishes of the majority political party, not unlike Mussolini. He went so far as to interpret the barricading of the Diet chairman and the occupation of his seat as similar to a coup d'état, suggesting a parallel to the military grabs for power of the 1930s.

Masuda and others also took the opportunity to connect this particular incident with leftist ideology and behavior as a whole, seeking to whip up fear about its violent and destabilizing potential. Masuda contended that the left was resorting to violent and illegal methods to realize the fundamental overturning of society called for by Marxist ideology and claimed the JSP's actions of June 3 exemplified thinking that supported violent revolution.[19] Even more detailed in his explanation of the JSP's wider influence was Tsuda Sōkichi, professor emeritus of Waseda University, who tied both the JSP and the Japan Communist Party (Nihon Kyōsantō) to the violence of labor unions and student movements. The JSP was not simply responsible for one unlawful incident in the Diet, according to Tsuda, but was encouraging the trend of leftist violence that was destroying the country's legal, societal, and moral order.[20]

For its part, the JSP used similar discursive strategies to bring attention to the alleged violence of its rival party. Commentator Katō Hyōji placed the blame for the incident squarely on the Liberal Party's shoulders for its poor administration of Diet affairs and stall tactics, which forced the JSP into a difficult and unfavorable position. At the root of the Liberal Party's misgovernment was, in Katō's view, the coercive nature of Prime Minister Yoshida's politics and cabinet, which aggressively pushed through their agenda. Nishijima Yoshiji of the *Asahi shinbun* concurred, as did Nakamura Akira of Hōsei University, who implied that Yoshida did not think democratically. This was considered especially problematic under the new postwar constitution, which Nakamura interpreted as bestowing the previous powers of the emperor to the prime ministership. Following Yoshida's lead, the Liberal Party majority had adopted an "anything goes" attitude, ignoring people's opinions and making decisions without adequate discussion. Nakamura acknowledged that the JSP had violated the rules of parliamentary politics when it obstructed Diet proceedings, but he firmly believed the incident would not have happened if there had been an open and free dialogue in the Representative Steering Committee. For Katō and Nakamura, it was the Liberal Party's abuse of its position rather than the tactics of the JSP that constituted coercion. Historian Tōyama Shigeki articulated this idea more concisely, speaking of the "violence of the majority" (*tasū no bōryoku*). Tōyama also tapped into fears about repeating prewar mistakes by urging cooperation between progressive political forces to protect peace and stop the "fascismization" (*fashizumuka*) of postwar politics, presumably at the hands of the Liberal Party.[21]

Almost two years after this incident, in May 1956, scuffles broke out again. In this instance, the physical clashes reached such a pitch that the sitting parliament was dubbed "the violent Diet" (*bōryoku kokkai*). There are a number of possible explanations for the escalation of violence. This parliament marked the inauguration of a two-party political system in postwar Japan, which pitted the conservative Liberal Democratic Party (Jiyū Minshutō or Jimintō, hereafter LDP) against the JSP. The LDP was the product of a merger between the Liberal Party and the Japan Democratic Party (Nihon Minshutō) and enjoyed its position as the ruling majority party. In the face of this consolidation of conservative political power, the JSP may have thought that the regular parliamentary process was inadequate to combat what it saw as continued strong-arm tactics of its opposition. There was also a deep ideological division between these two parties, one that resonated with the social strife so rampant beyond the walls of the Diet. The tumult surrounding leftist movements in education and labor were brought into the Diet chamber by the main bill at issue in this outbreak of violence, which affected both the LDP's base of support and an important constituency of the JSP.

The Diet session had opened calmly enough in late 1955, but tensions surfaced when the JSP prevented passage of the LDP's bill (Shōsenkyoku Hōan) to institute a single-seat electoral district system, which would have given the LDP a leg up against the opposition parties.[22] On the coattails of this legislative showdown, in March 1956, the LDP introduced an education bill (Shin Kyōiku Iinkai Hōan) that provoked a head-to-head battle between the two parties. The bill converted publicly elected education committees into bodies appointed by governors and mayors, envisioning these local committees as serving a regulatory role. It was also intended to undercut the Nihon Kyōshokuin Kumiai (Japan Teachers' Union, hereafter Nikkyōsō) that had done well in elections.[23] Needless to say, the bill was opposed by a subset of the JSP that represented the interests of the union, a group with affiliations not just to the leftist political parties but also the Nihon Rōdō Kumiai Sō Hyōgikai (General Council of Trade Unions of Japan, hereafter Sōhyō). Buttressing the LDP's side was a group of municipal leaders and a national association of mayors, constituencies whose support the LDP was courting for the upcoming House of Councillors election.

The disagreement took physical form on May 25, when the 20 or so Nikkyōsō loyalists in the House of Councillors mobilized union members as well as the JSP's *hishodan* and representatives to form picket lines, one of which wrapped around the office of the Education Committee chairman. This continued for four or five days then reached a new level when the LDP decided to force passage of the bill. In response, the JSP dispatched party parliamentarians and the *hishodan* to the chamber, confined the Diet chairman to his office, and blockaded the vice chairman in the LDP anteroom with a picket line. And in a symbolic move reminiscent of the First Movement to Protect Constitutional Government of 1912–1913, the JSP members identified themselves with red carnations, the LDP with white roses.

The violence reached its height in the first several days of June, when the JSP reacted with force to the machinations of the LDP. Around 8:00 P.M. on the first of the month, the Diet chairman called an unscheduled plenary session but closed the doors to the chamber before most of the JSP representatives had arrived. The JSP parliamentarians and *hishodan* then tried to push their way into the chamber, throwing their weight against doors held shut on the other side by sergeants-at-arms. These guards were eventually overwhelmed and were kicked and hit as the JSP members entered the hall. Once inside, the angered JSP representatives beat the vice chairman and attacked the chairman, sending the Diet into chaos. Reports on the number of casualties vary from a dozen to over 30; ambulances arrived on the scene and transported the injured to the hospital.

Up until this point, the Diet chairman had been resistant to police intervention, but after this night, he signed the necessary paperwork. The reserve corps of the Tokyo Metropolitan Police received the request at 2:50 P.M. on June 2, and just a little over half an hour later, 500 police arrived outside the Diet. By 3:45 P.M., they were stationed in the corridor in front of the House of Councillors' chamber and, for a brief time the next morning, they went so far as to enter the hall when the body was in session. For some, this intrusion of state violence into the heart of the parliament at the behest of the LDP was an outrage.[24]

Reactions to this incident built upon those of two years earlier, working from the fundamental idea that coercion and violence were undemocratic. Yet criticisms of violence were more vociferous and strident than they had been in 1954.

This was because of a sense that there was much at stake with the curtain rising on two-party politics, and because of greater awareness of foreign media coverage of Japan's political affairs which fed an embarrassment about the state of the Diet.[25] Most significant was the heightened physical intensity of the clash. This explains not only the impassioned discourse, but also the trend toward excoriating the JSP. What most differentiated the treatment of this from previous incidents was the extent to which the JSP was labeled as the violent and therefore problematic party, even by those who had previously defended its tactics. There was a shared, implied understanding that the JSP's violence had crossed over the line of acceptable political behavior.[26]

The JSP was described not just as undemocratic, as it had been in the past, but criminally so. One commentator accused the party of not understanding and even destroying the fundamental principles and spirit of the new constitution and considered its use of violence a serious crime. The party was also viewed as hypocritical for wielding violence while claiming to protect the peace constitution.[27] A fellow contributor to the same journal cast doubt on the sincerity of the JSP's professions about peace in light of its actions in the Diet, and ostracized the party from genuinely peace-loving people who wanted to prevent a third world war and construct world peace.[28] It should come as no surprise that this author was an LDP parliamentarian, but even JSP sympathizers were more harsh in their judgment of the party than they had been in the past. Nishijima Yoshiji of the *Asahi shinbun,* who had been critical of the Liberal Party and Yoshida Shigeru in 1954, hoped the JSP would leave its violent ways behind. Even though Nishijima agreed with the party's opposition to the bill and was concerned about the LDP's majority position, he essentially called the JSP immature. He urged the party to reflect on its violent actions, embrace parliamentary and democratic politics, and thereby develop into an "adult political party" (*otona no seitō*).[29]

Hand in hand with the biting criticisms of the JSP was a more explicit attempt to portray and defend the LDP as peaceful. Parliamentarian Aoki Kazuo, an unabashed opponent of the JSP, made the dubious claim that the LDP representatives did not offer any resistance to violence and never left their seats in the chamber regardless of what occurred. He went on to declare with confidence that if they did engage in fights, they would surely win because many of their ranks were trained in martial arts. But they refrained from violence because responding with such physical force would be a crime, and the Diet was a place for speech. Aoki also felt it necessary to provide a brief explanation of the LDP's mobilization of the police, minimizing its significance by clarifying that only 15 police (of the 500 present at the Diet) actually entered the chamber and for only several minutes.[30]

There were some objections to the LDP's behavior, along the same lines as those expressed in 1954, but they were relatively muted. The chair of the JSP allegedly repeated the argument that the LDP was undemocratic in the way it set about monopolizing the Diet, and leftist scholars spoke of the despotism of the majority.[31] In one of its editorials, the *Yomiuri shinbun* described the majority's tactic of pushing through its agenda as a kind of violence, but this piece ran before the peak of the violence in early June, after which most attention was focused on the JSP's alleged indiscretions.[32]

Perhaps most relevant to our concern with violence specialists were the kinds of parallels drawn between the JSP and unsavory violent elements of the past. It had already become conventional to denounce the violence of political opponents by likening it to that of prewar militarists and fascists. This discursive strategy was used again with this incident, as when the actions of the subsection of the JSP connected to Nikkyōsō was said to be reminiscent of the imperial militarists at the time of the Manchurian Incident in 1931.[33] The JSP also came to be equated with violent ruffians. In one instance, the JSP was compared to rogues and gangsters (*buraikan*) who understood neither parliamentary politics nor constitutional government.[34] And its methods were said to be the same as those of bandits (*bazoku*) at the time of the Manchurian Incident.[35]

The discourse around this 1956 Diet incident exemplified the widespread intolerance of violence that was a new and distinguishing feature of Japan's postwar democracy. Many who condemned various forms of physical force in politics clearly had their own political agendas and may not have felt as strongly about violence as their words suggested, but it is telling that they chose to hone in on violence as a way to discredit their opponents. At the very least, they assumed that discouragement of violence would resonate with the public. Although there had been outspoken critics of violence in the prewar period, they tended to be in leftist pockets of the political scene, and the antiviolence sentiment was not anywhere near as popular as it was in the immediate postwar decades.

Concerns about the reemergence of political violence or even violence specialists of different kinds, whether militarists or ruffians, created a climate in which it would have been folly for political parties to have *sōshi* or *ingaidan* in the prewar mold. To have openly institutionalized violent figures directly into the political parties would have likely raised the ire of many, and made the political parties a target for vociferous criticism.

The willingness of Diet members and *hishodan* to use their bodies as political weapons did mean there was potential for disagreements to turn physical. But without the presence of *sōshi*, there was no constant reminder or embodiment of violence in parliamentary politics. And without violence specialists hanging

about the halls of the Diet, physical confrontations within the parliament building were less frequent and intense than they had been in the prewar period.

"Bōryokudan" Redux: Yakuza and the Conservative Nexus

Although prewar-style *sōshi* and *ingaidan* were pushed out of postwar politics,
yakuza did not meet the same fate. Instead, they became an integral part of a
conservative nexus that was a reincarnation of the prewar nationalist version
discussed in the previous chapter. That yakuza were a part of this network helps
explain their resilience and continued presence in politics—why the public impatience with the use of physical force did not spell the end of these particular
violence specialists. Conservative political leaders and fixers determined that the
need for, and utility of, yakuza and their violence outweighed the negative effects of any criticism, at least in the initial postwar decades. And, perhaps, it was
hoped that forming loose alliances with yakuza might seem marginally less offensive than institutionalizing *sōshi*-like figures into the political parties; it did, at
least, allow slightly more room for denial and obfuscation.

To understand the postwar emergence of conservative politicians and the
political right, we need to go back to the late 1940s, after the iron curtain was
said to be descending in Europe and the United States had expressed its concern
about Soviet expansion in the Truman Doctrine. Heightened anxieties about
the spread of communism in Japan, the rambunctious character of some labor
unions, and other seemingly unruly popular movements provoked a "reverse
course" in occupation policies whereby anticommunism eclipsed democratization as the Americans' primary concern. Earlier, from 1946 to 1948, the occupation authorities had carried out purges to prevent the resurgence of the prewar
right and help protect the democratizing project. Among those targeted along
with militarists and political leaders were "influential members of ultranational-
istic, terroristic or secret patriotic societies," including the likes of the Gen'yōsha
(Dark Ocean Society). In the initial phase of the occupation, more than 100 organizations were dissolved. At the same time, the occupation had granted labor
the freedom to unionize and had legalized the Japan Communist Party, helping
to spark leftist movements.[36] But in 1949 and 1950, the occupation did an about-
face, removing Japan Communist Party members, unionists, and other leftists
from their positions in the public and private sectors, from heavy industry to
education and communications; this "red purge" cost 21,000 people their jobs.
At the same time, the occupation depurged some prewar militarists and nationalists. Together, the red purge and the depurge facilitated the development of a

conservative hegemony in politics and jump-started the postwar reemergence of right-wing organizations.[37]

Among those given a chance for a new political life was Kishi Nobusuke, who was released from Sugamo Prison in 1948 where he had been held for over three years as a suspected Class A war criminal. Kishi had been a bureaucrat in Manchuria in the late 1930s, where he formed a network of political connections and allegedly filled his own pockets with both legal and illegal profits from the opium trade and the trafficking of capital. From 1941 to 1944, he served as the minister of commerce and industry for Prime Minister Tōjō Hideki and managed the wartime economy. And around that time, Kishi rallied his political allies to form the Kishi New Party (Kishi Shintō), which consisted of Diet members, Japanese businessmen with whom he had worked in China, and nationalists who had been responsible for the attempted coups d'état of 1931. Once released from prison in 1948, Kishi set to work on constructing a conservative political party that could dominate postwar politics. His first attempt, a recreation of both his prewar Kishi New Party and the Association for Defense of the Fatherland (Gokoku Dōshikai), was known as the Japan Reconstruction Federation (Nippon Saiken Renmei); but it failed in its electoral debut. Kishi managed to work his way into the conservative Liberal Party, was elected to the Diet in 1953, was thrown out of the party the next year for trying to undermine it from within, and was taken in by the rival conservative Democratic Party. All the while, Kishi had his eye on the consolidation of conservative power. And in November 1955, he helped orchestrate the merger of the Liberal and Democratic Parties into the LDP, the party that would dominate Japanese politics until the early 1990s. Kishi (brother of future prime minister Satō Eisaku and grandfather of twenty-first-century prime minister Abe Shinzō) became secretary-general of the LDP and served as prime minister from 1957 to 1960.[38] (After 1960, he remained in the Diet until retiring from his seat in 1979.)[39]

What helped the feuding conservatives—and, eventually, the conservative nexus—coalesce was a shared fear of the socialists. The electoral gains enjoyed by some socialist subgroups in the early 1950s and, most immediately, the reunification of the two main factions of the JSP in October 1955 were deeply frightening to the rival conservatives. Along with this antisocialist stance, what held the conservatives together was a dislike of labor union activism, support for business interests, and, for many, the desire for Japan to rearm.

Antipathy toward the left may have brought conservatives together, but what greased the wheels of conservative politics and fueled the construction of LDP hegemony was money. To trace the financing of the LDP and its politicians is to connect many of the nodes of an expansive and powerful conservative web. Some of the contributions to the LDP were technically legal, even if they could be viewed as the buying of influence on party policy. One representative of big business known as the Keizai Dantai Rengōkai (Federation of Economic Organizations, hereafter Keidanren) donated huge sums of money, mainly to conservatives. In January 1955, the federation established a system whereby political contributions from various members would be pooled by an administrative body, the Keizai Saiken Kondankai (Economic Reconstruction Council), and then distributed. The intent behind the creation of this mechanism was to make political financing more transparent by eliminating the many separate transactions that individual corporations and industries had previously been conducting with politicians, political factions, and parties; it was hoped that the attempt to be more open would prevent the public from losing trust in Japanese industry, which had already been tainted by a political bribery scandal the previous year. The money doled out by the council was thus clean, and one of the main administrators of the system, Hanamura Nihachirō, expressed pride that all corporate donations adhered to political finance laws and that the council was scandal free. Nonetheless, the extent of Keidanren's financial power raises questions about the place of big business in democratic politics. It is quite clear that Keidanren played a key role in financing the consolidation of conservative power. In the council's first year, it collected approximately one billion yen, the majority of which went to the two conservative parties. After the establishment of the LDP, which Keidanren had hoped for, Hanamura worked to build the financial foundation of the party, ostensibly to ensure the continued existence of a liberal economic system. In a postwar version of the prewar ties between *zaibatsu* and the major political parties, Keidanren played a crucial role in forming a financial bond between big business and the LDP. From 1955 to 1960, the council distributed ¥2.5 billion; for the election of 1960, it collected ¥800 million, of which ¥770 million was given to the LDP. Keidanren did dole out money to all political parties, except for the communists, but 90 percent of its giving was to the LDP. More telling of Keidanren's influence was the size of its contributions relative to those of other funders—by 1960, the council's donations constituted about 60 percent of all reported political contributions. And as political scientist Richard Samuels has pointed out, this stream of money from the council accounted for only a portion of all financial donations from business to the LDP.[40]

Another strong supporter of the LDP was the U.S. Central Intelligence Agency (CIA), alleged to have provided covert funds to the party and specific conservative politicians. Declassified documents unequivocally reveal that the U.S. government wanted to see a conservative government in Japan. In August 1955, Secretary of State John Foster Dulles spoke of the importance of acting in concert with the conservatives. And several years later, Ambassador to Japan Douglas MacArthur II reported that it was in the best interests of the United States for

Kishi Nobusuke to win what was seen as a crucial election in May 1958.[41] When Kishi proved victorious, the State Department commented that the political climate in Japan was "favorable to the interests of the United States in the Far East" and predicted that "Japan will become an increasingly valuable ally in the Far East."[42] American support for the election of Kishi included financial backing, according to CIA documents and former intelligence officers. And the funding of Kishi in the 1958 election was part of a larger strategy of financing the LDP. According to Alfred C. Ulmer Jr., head of the CIA's Far East operations from 1955 to 1958: "We financed them. We depended on the LDP for information." And Roger Hilsman, who led the State Department's intelligence bureau during the administration of John F. Kennedy, described funding of the LDP and its politicians in the early 1960s as "so established and so routine" that it was accepted as a given and important aspect of U.S. foreign policy toward Japan.[43]

Others in the conservative nexus helped not only with fundraising, but also with organizing support for the LDP. Political fixers, usually acting behind the scenes, leveraged their prewar connections and leadership skills to reinvigorate conservative politics and right-wing groups. It was these men who helped bring yakuza into the conservative fold. One of the most influential political fixers was Sasakawa Ryōichi, who had been imprisoned in 1945 alongside Kishi Nobusuke as a suspected Class A war criminal. In the prewar period, Sasakawa had been a fervent nationalist and supporter of war. He had discontinued his education after completing elementary school (because of family fears that he would turn socialist if he continued his studies, Sasakawa claims), served as a pilot in the Imperial Navy, and then became involved with various nationalistic endeavors. In September 1931, he was installed as president of the Kokusui Taishūtō (National Essence Mass Party), an organization with 23 branches and more than 10,000 members who, following the Italian fascist model, wore black shirts. In 1932, he constructed an air field in Osaka for the purpose of training fighter pilots. The hangar at this facility had space for 70 fighter planes and 20 training planes; ownership of the property eventually passed to the army. From 1935 to 1938, Sasakawa sat in prison, having been arrested for various crimes including extortion and bribery and the planning of violent political crimes, including one against the prime minister—newspapers at the time dubbed him the "don of Japan's violent groups" (*Nihon no bōryokudan no don*). And in 1939, after his release, Sasakawa went to Rome to visit Mussolini.[44]

It was in the 1930s that Sasakawa came to know a fellow nationalist who, like him, would become a postwar political fixer: Kodama Yoshio. Kodama had developed a disdain for leftist ideologies fairly early in his life. Although he had worked as a laborer in various factories and mills and was sympathetic with the difficulties of working life, he vehemently opposed the communist tint of labor unions and the labor movement. In his diary he recalled, "It was difficult for me to understand why the Soviet Union should have to be called our motherland and why Marxism should be forced upon a Japan differing fundamentally in conditions from Russia, in order just to solve the labor-capital dispute."[45] He became enamored with nationalism and in 1929 joined the anticommunist Kenkokukai (National Founding Association) which was led by nationalist leaders Akao Bin and Uesugi Shinkichi. Over the next eight years, Kodama became involved with various nationalist groups and was imprisoned a number of times; he served his longest sentence for planning to assassinate cabinet members.[46] While in prison, Kodama met Fuji Yoshio, a close associate of Sasakawa. Through this connection, Kodama eventually served as East Asia division chief of Sasakawa's Kokusui Taishūtō.

The tie between Sasakawa and Kodama grew stronger in 1941 when Sasakawa was asked by Navy Air Force Headquarters to recommend a colleague who could head up a special purchasing and procurement agency. Sasakawa chose his junior, Kodama, who reluctantly left a part-time arrangement with the army to establish the Kodama Kikan (Kodama Agency) in December 1941. Two years after its founding, Sasakawa's right-hand man, Fuji Yoshio, became vice president of the agency; Sasakawa himself took credit for helping to found the Kodama Kikan and has been described as one of its major supporters. Headquartered in Shanghai, the Kodama Kikan received millions of yen from the navy for its establishment and proceeded to acquire war material for Navy Air Force Headquarters. Kodama's operatives in this endeavor, numbering in the hundreds, were said to consist mainly of "professional criminals, right-wing thugs, and members of the *kenpeitai* (military police)"—making Kodama and his staff a kind of *tairiku rōnin* (continental adventurer).[47] Although Kodama began with the modest duty of providing copper and airplane parts, over time he expanded his reach to include raw material, food, clothing, and vehicles. He also ran mines in China, some of which yielded rare metals such as tungsten and molybdenum. It has also been speculated that Kodama dealt in gold, diamonds, and opium. According to CIA and Army Counterintelligence Corps reports, much of this material was acquired illegally through expropriation and theft or was obtained at costs lower than those reported to the navy so that operatives could pocket greater profits. In addition to illegal revenue, Kodama was paid ¥3.5 billion by the navy between 1941 and 1945, and by the end of the war, he was worth the equivalent of $175 million. In the closing weeks of the war, the property and money of the Kodama Kikan were sent back to Japan; some of this material was allegedly stored in warehouses rented by Sasakawa.[48]

Immediately after the war, Sasakawa and Kodama drew on their financial resources and organizational savvy to back the founding of Hatoyama Ichirō's Liberal Party. It has been suggested by many that money from the sale of some of the

Kodama Kikan's spoils directly funded Hatoyama's efforts. The oft-quoted, but unsubstantiated, figure for this donation is ¥70 million.[49] In addition, Sasakawa and Kodama recruited supporters for the party—including yakuza. When Sasakawa attended the ceremony for the Liberal Party's establishment, he was accompanied by a group of *tekiya* (itinerant merchants and a kind of yakuza). It has also been suggested that Kodama solicited campaign contributions from *tekiya* bosses in the first postwar general election of April 1946.[50] So it seems that neither Kodama nor Sasakawa experienced any kind of postwar apostasy, either in style of politics or ideology. Sasakawa, for one, gave numerous speeches immediately after the war arguing that the West had provoked Japan into war by threatening its survival and that Japan's expansion into Taiwan, Korea, and Manchuria was not an invasion but a blessing for these areas.[51]

The political careers of these two fixers were temporarily put on hold when they were jailed as suspected Class A war criminals. But like Kishi Nobusuke, both were eventually released. It has been assumed that Kodama and Sasakawa were set free in December 1948 because of their anticommunism and perhaps because of promises that they would gather information for either the occupation or the CIA. The latter claim seems questionable. Kodama did approach occupation authorities to offer his intelligence services.[52] But his actual connection to American intelligence was more indirect—Kodama's aid was enlisted by Arisue Seizō, former chief of intelligence at Imperial General Headquarters who, after the war, was recruited by the occupation's intelligence arm (G-2) to establish a clandestine intelligence section within it. Kodama, and his old Kodama Kikan connections on the continent, were involved in a number of Arisue's projects. Although American money was finding its way to Kodama, however indirectly through Arisue, Kodama's attentions were not focused on working for the United States. One of his other pursuits at the time, for example, was blackmailing the Mitsui Corporation out of one billion yen.[53] By 1953, when the CIA had replaced G-2 as the foremost American intelligence organ in Japan, it had become clear that the vaguely shared goal of anticommunism was not always enough to maintain strong alliances. Of Kodama, the CIA determined he was too unreliable to make for a good intelligence operative: "He is a professional liar, gangster, charlatan, and outright thief."[54] Kodama was also described as "a distinct menace, and because of his manipulations of the Japanese underworld, is widely feared and his favor is sought by weak men in high positions."[55]

In the decades that followed, Sasakawa backed right-wing organizations as he had in the prewar period. He served as an adviser to a number of groups and spoke against communism, comparing it to cholera and the plague, and rallied people to put their lives on the line to fight its spread. He also continued to work with Kodama and Kishi to further his next profitable venture: motorboat racing.

Sasakawa used their help to secure Diet passage of a law that gave him a monopoly on the enterprise. And about 15 percent of the revenues from related gambling ventures went to the Zenkoku Mōtābōto Kyōsōkai Rengōkai (Motorboat Racing Association), which Sasakawa founded with seed money from Kodama and the Zaidan Hōjin Nippon Senpaku Shinkōkai (Japan Shipbuilding Industry Foundation), of which Sasakawa assumed the chairmanship in the early 1960s. Included on the staffs of both organizations were former members of his prewar Kokusui Taishūtō. Sasakawa also benefited from the revenues of the Tōkyō-to Mōtābōto Kyōsōkai (Tokyo Motorboat Racing Association), which had Kodama at its helm. At about this point, Sasakawa began to take up philanthropic causes and contributed substantial funds to the United Nations and to the World Health Organization in particular—for his efforts, a bronze statue of Sasakawa stands in the European headquarters of the UN. Sasakawa also made a concerted push to be awarded the Nobel Peace Prize.[56] Although this commendation proved elusive, he did win the Martin Luther King Peace Prize, the UN Peace Prize, and the Linus Pauling Award for Humanitarianism.[57]

Kodama too backed right-wing causes in the postwar period. Though banned from "taking open part" in politics as a condition of his purged status, he was free to pursue political agendas so long as he stayed out of the limelight.[58] So he resumed an active political life after his release from Sugamo Prison and seems to have revived some version of his prewar agency (which U.S. intelligence, at least, continued to call the Kodama Kikan). This network was said to be engaged with the elimination of communist influence from Asia and the construction of Japan as the foundation of an anticommunist league.[59] In keeping with these aims, the agency had a branch in Hokkaidō, for example, from which Kodama allegedly engaged in anti–Japan Communist Party activities. Fund-raising was conducted out of a trading company based in the Marunouchi district of Tokyo.[60] In addition to this particular company, a number of others were considered affiliates of the Kodama Kikan. The agency also garnered the cooperation of various prewar military men and nationalists, such as Ōkawa Shūmei and Miura Giichi.[61] Many of those associated with the Kodama Kikan were rumored to have been part of a larger plan to smuggle supplies to the Chinese Nationalists and to recruit Japanese youth into a volunteer military corps to fight on the anticommunist side. Kodama, however, denied any connection to such efforts.[62]

Over the course of his postwar career, Kodama continued to use and build his various political connections. He and Kishi, for example, seem to have remained collegial even after their years in Sugamo Prison, when they had played the game of *go* together and eaten their meals at the same table. Kishi admits that during his years as prime minister, Kodama would attend meetings at which Kishi was present. And their relationship seems to have been friendly—they would occasionally get together for *go*, Kodama shared whatever he caught when fishing, and they allegedly golfed, once.[63] Kodama also had close ties with Ōno Banboku, discussed in Chapter 3 for his recruitment into the Seiyūkai *ingaidan* in the 1910s. Ōno's political career flourished in the postwar period, despite implication in a major political scandal in 1948. He became speaker of the House of Representatives in 1952, minister of state in 1953, and then served as vice president of the LDP until his death in 1964. Ōno was rumored to have a rough demeanor akin to that of *bakuto* and "kyōkaku." One journalist, in an article with a tabloid-esque quality, chastised him for continuing his fighting ways even after he had become a prominent politician. It was normal for boys to brawl, the reasoning went, but Ōno should not still shake his clenched fist and get into heated scuffles.[64] More to the point, Ōno did not shy away from association with yakuza groups. Even when he was vice president of the LDP, he was photographed at a gathering of big yakuza bosses from the Kansai area, including Honda Nisuke and Hirata Katsuichi—Honda and Hirata were the first and second presidents, respectively, of the yakuza organization Hondakai (Honda Association). The Kobe-based group was originally established in 1938 as the Honda-gumi, changed its name in 1946 to the Hondakai, and had just under 2,000 members in the early 1960s. Included among its enterprises was management of its construction company (Honda Kensetsu Kōgyō).[65]

Kodama himself fostered direct ties with yakuza. At one party that he hosted in September 1956, for example, among the 40 in attendance were about a dozen bosses from various yakuza "families" along with professional wrestlers, officers of a right-wing organization, and Minister of Agriculture and Forestry Kōno Ichirō from the cabinet of Hatoyama Ichirō, another Kodama connection.[66]

Like the postwar resurrection of Kodama and Sasakawa, the rebirth of nationalist organizations is a story of resilience and the strength of old political connections. The right-wing groups of the 1950s most known for their violence were typically hybrids—part yakuza, part political organization—not unlike the Dai Nihon Kokusuikai (Greater Japan National Essence Association) and Dai Nihon Seigidan (Greater Japan Justice Group) of the prewar era. Yakuza, who had been so scarce during the war, managed to rebuild and survive the late 1940s by making money in the black markets that proliferated soon after the end of the war. As early as October 1945, approximately 17,000 such markets had popped up to peddle necessities such as food, toiletries, and clothing, as well as amphetamines. In big cities, yakuza bosses staked out territories in which they managed vendors. In Tokyo, for example, the Matsuda-gumi was in charge of the Shinbashi district, the Shibayama of Asakusa, the Ueda of Ginza, the Sekiguchi of Ikebukuro, and the Ozu and Wada of Shinjuku. And the heads of the yakuza organizations viewed themselves as maintaining order in a rough environment.

One such figure was a Morimoto Mitsuji who took control of the Umeda market in Osaka, extolling the virtues of protecting the weak and defeating the strong while keeping everyone in line, armed with a knife and a pistol. Yet the yakuza presence often did not discourage violence but encouraged it, especially as territorial disputes led to physical clashes. In one incident in June 1946, a gunfight between thousands of yakuza resulted in seven deaths and 34 injuries.

When the economy began to show signs of recovery and black markets became less necessary, yakuza organizations took financial advantage of economic growth by shifting more of their attention to the burgeoning entertainment industry. Gambling, *pachinko* (pinball), bars, restaurants, and prostitution provided opportunities for the extraction of protection money. These revenues were supplemented by supplying labor for the construction and docking industries, a niche that yakuza had occupied in the prewar period and had begun to fill again during the occupation. All of these enterprises brought money into yakuza coffers and funded their development into large organizations and, eventually, powerful mafia syndicates.[67]

When these yakuza organizations took on a political tinge, it was that of the right rather than the left. This remains true to the present day, so much so that the notion of leftist yakuza is laughable. There are some general reasons for this political orientation. It was strategically wise not to upset the ruling conservative hegemony so as to maintain a cordial relationship with the police and others who had the authority to crack down on the yakuza's financial lifelines. Conservatives also tended to stand behind company management in labor disputes. As in the prewar period, it was more lucrative for yakuza to ally with management, who had the funds to pay them for intimidating striking laborers.

At least one yakuza group not only cooperated with right-wing organizations but also became one itself. The Sekine-gumi was a yakuza "family" that managed black markets in the Asakusa, Honjo, and Mukōjima areas of Tokyo. When the head of the Sekine-gumi was arrested by occupation authorities in 1948 on a weapons possession charge, the group was ordered to dissolve. The defunct Sekine-gumi then remade itself into a (legal) political organization, building a reputation as a right-wing group around 1953 and officially establishing itself as the Matsubakai (Pine Needle Association) in September 1959. The Matsubakai platform articulated the organization's desire to prevent the invasion of communist thought into the minds of youth and to bring about the collapse of teachers' unions and other groups that embraced "dangerous ideas." The group also professed views vaguely reminiscent of the prewar period, such as respect for the emperor as a symbol of the nation and hope for the construction of a "Greater Asia" in the future. By 1960, the Matsubakai had six offices in Tokyo and branches in nearby Chiba, Ibaraki, and Gunma Prefectures. The membership of 2,000 to

3,000 people was described by at least one newspaper as consisting mainly of yakuza—*bakuto, tekiya,* and *gurentai* (street gangsters) in particular.[68]

Other right-wing organizations drew heavily on the recent past, making connections with prewar groups and appropriating their ideologies. After the end of the occupation, it seems that former members of the Kantō Kokusuikai, a splinter group of the Dai Nihon Kokusuikai, had maintained or reestablished contact and were planning to convene a "countrywide national essence meeting" (*zenkoku kokusui taikai*) in Tokyo in March 1953.[69] Umezu Jinbei, of the Kantō Kokusuikai, was also approached for advice and help in mobilizing yakuza for the anti-Soviet and anticommunist causes. The man who called on Umezu was politician and lawyer Kimura Tokutarō, who served as minister of justice in two Yoshida Shigeru cabinets. Together, Umezu and Kimura were among those who helped rally *bakuto* and *tekiya* to form the Gokokudan (National Protection Corps) and its subsidiary Gokoku Seinentai (National Protection Youth Corps) in 1954. Also central to the group's founding was Inoue Nisshō who, in the prewar period, had founded the Ketsumeidan (League of Blood) that carried out assassinations in 1932. And among the financial contributors to the Gokokudan were Kodama Yoshio and Sasakawa Ryōichi.[70] Like the Matsubakai, the Gokokudan spoke highly of the emperor but in even stronger terms, describing him as the center of the blood relationship that bound the race together; using ideas from the prewar period, Japan's racial society (*Nihon minzoku shakai*) was also presented as a family.[71]

The prewar legacy was also strong in the case of the Nihon Kokusuikai (Japan National Essence Society, hereafter Kokusuikai), a reorganization of the Dai Nihon Kokusuikai which had dissolved at the end of the war. The Kokusuikai adopted the language and platform of the prewar group, describing itself as an organization of the chivalrous, linking itself not only to the Dai Nihon Kokusuikai but also to an ideal dating back to the yakuza of the Tokugawa period. In addition, it purported to foster love for the fatherland, to absolutely oppose the left, and to protect the "beautiful customs" of Japan's national essence that were a proud part of the country's history and tradition. At the same time, the Kokusuikai adopted language that would be more palatable in a postwar context, claiming not to be rightist and speaking of members' devotion to the eradication of, among other things, "cruel violence" that oppresses the lives of the nation's people. Despite these stated aims, the group did not refrain from using violence and included *bakuto* among its ranks as well as those affiliated with the Gokokudan. Officially established in July 1958, the Kokusuikai was headquartered in Tokyo and had 250 members around 1960.[72]

According to the Metropolitan Police, 28 such organizations claimed to be right-wing political groups but were more like "bōryokudan," to use the police's terminology.[73] Of this number, only a handful—the Matsubakai, Gokokudan, and Kokusuikai prime among them—were repeatedly involved in violent, political incidents. In one such event in October 1958, three men disrupted a meeting of Nikkyōsō at Kudan Hall in Tokyo. The commotion began when one of the intruders set off a smoke bomb then tried to cause panic by holding up a placard that read: "this is dynamite." His accomplices followed suit, igniting two more smoke bombs that darkened the entire room. Two of the three suspects were arrested and found to be members of the Kokusuikai's Seinen Teishintai (Youth Corps). The young man who had set off the first smoke bomb was a 26-year-old leader of the Seinen Teishintai; he was held under suspicion of forceful interference and trespassing.[74] In a similar incident from late March 1959, about 60 members of a dozen right-wing organizations—including the Gokokudan and the Gokoku Seinentai—disrupted a JSP speech meeting by distributing leaflets, heckling speakers, and throwing smoke bombs on the dais.

In the late 1950s, these violent incidents and the seeming consolidation of right-wing organizations worried leftists and others fearful of the resurgence of a violent right wing. The Gokokudan and Kokusuikai were among a dozen or so groups that in March 1959 came together as the Zen Nihon Aikokusha Dantai Kyōgikai (All-Japan Council of Patriotic Organizations), for which Sasakawa and Kodama served as advisers. Not only was the council a federation that included hybrid yakuza and right-wing groups, but many of its other advisers and some of its leaders were connected to violent incidents of the prewar period: Sagōya Tomeo of the Gokokudan had received the death penalty, later reduced to life imprisonment, for his attack on Prime Minister Hamaguchi in November 1930 but was released in 1940; Inoue Nisshō was mentioned above for his connection to the League of Blood and its assassinations of 1932; Miura Giichi was, among other things, involved in the attack on Seiyūkai president Nakajima Chikuhei in 1939; Tachibana Kōzaburō was a key instigator of the May 15 Incident in 1932; Amano Tatsuo had been arrested for the Shinpeitai Incident in 1933 and was implicated in the attack on politician Hiranuma Kiichirō in 1941; and Ōsawa Takesaburō was involved in the failed assassination attempt on former prime minister Wakatsuki Reijirō in 1933.[75] Another right-wing federation that coalesced in 1959 was the Aikokusha Kondankai (Meeting of Patriots), founded on July 11 by 30 heads of 16 right-wing organizations including the Gokokudan and Matsubakai.[76]

As in the prewar period, right-wing organizations were not isolated political entities but part of a more encompassing political nexus—in the immediate postwar decades, there were connections at the highest of levels between violent right-wing groups and politicians. The political ties of the Matsubakai became apparent, for example, through the funeral of the president's wife. The former mayor of Tokyo sent flowers, and many other figures attended, including an ex-superintendent-general of the Metropolitan Police, a previous minister of education, 17 LDP Diet members, and 50 local parliamentarians.[77]

Yakuza thus managed to survive and even thrive, entirely unlike *sōshi*, because of the resurgence of the political right and the mutually beneficial ties they (re)formed with various conservatives. Conservative politicians who were anti-labor and anticommunist could gain from the activities of yakuza groups, who profited financially so long as they were protected by the conservative hegemony. And political fixers like Sasakawa and Kodama were the influential brokers who ensured, and benefited from, the continuation of this arrangement. With a secure place in the conservative nexus, yakuza also operated in an immediate environment that did not fault them, indeed valued them, for their violence—within this part of the political world, prewar-style connections and tactics were still considered assets. And the utility of yakuza was especially beneficial in the political war between the right and the left that was being fought on a number of fronts.

1960: The Apogee of Postwar Violence Specialists

The ideological clashes of the 1950s should not be oversimplified, for both sides had their own internal tensions and were not monolithic; nonetheless, the great schism of the decade was between a conservative right and a progressive left. It was in, and through, these battles that the conservatives were forced to realize that they were operating in a new political environment, that their adherence to prewar ideologies and tactics was bumping up against a substantially changed climate. Indeed, outside the (albeit powerful and expansive) conservative nexus, rightist ideas and political stances did not have the same resonance with the public as nationalism and imperialism did in the prewar period.[78] And progressive movements were more mainstream than they had been in their prewar incarnations. This became plainly visible in 1960, the most politically turbulent year of Japan's postwar history. This moment revealed a fundamental division not just between ideological conservatives and progressives, but between a right that practiced politics as usual and a broad left that did not accept the status quo ante. In this context, when violence specialists were brought into conflicts by those who had traditionally relied on them, they also became the targets of widespread criticism, as pre-existing sentiments about the undemocratic and unprogressive nature of violence were stoked by political and ideological tumult. The year 1960 was a perfect storm of political agitation—the longest labor strike of Japan's history at the Miike Coal Mines in Kyūshū; mass demonstrations in which hundreds of thousands of people protested renewal of the U.S.-Japan Security Treaty; and the very public assassination of JSP chairman Asanuma Inejirō. These were viewed not as discrete incidents, but as part and parcel of the same, larger political struggle.

Tensions at the Mitsui-owned Miike Coal Mines had begun to rise in the autumn of 1959, when company management announced its plan to dismiss about 2,000 workers. The cutback was part of its rationalization strategy, intended to make the mining company more competitive at a time when oil was becoming the energy source of choice. The union balked at this decision and carried out several short strikes. This did not stop the company from letting workers go, many of them union leaders and members, and instituting a lockout in January 1960. In response, the union decided to strike. As part of its efforts, the union formed 24-hour picket lines, and those under the age of 25 were organized into "action corps" (kōdōtai) that were stationed at various company branches and deployed to deal with urgent matters as necessary.

The dispute turned violent in March, with a split in the union and the introduction of violence specialists. The divide in the union was between those who wanted to continue with the strike, and those of a pro-company bent who wanted the strikers to return to work. On March 17, the divorce was made official when the latter group broke off to form a separate, second union (Miike Rōkumi Sasshin Dōmei, or Miike Labor Union Reform Confederation). This second union started off with about 3,000 members and over the next ten days its ranks swelled to around 4,800, or about one-third of the original union, with workers who were uneasy about extending the strike and who were not especially devoted to ideas of class conflict. This second union, backed by management, worked together with company-hired bōryokudan to oppose the strikers. In the name of protective patrol, they were said to parade around town in company sound trucks and motorcycles resembling those of the police, waving Japanese flags and placing bōryokudan on the front lines.

Tensions came to a head in late March, when there were successive violent incidents between the strikers on one side and the second union with bōryokudan support on the other. On March 27, bōryokudan in trucks crashed through the picket line in front of the Nishiyama mine. Those picketers who tried to stop them were attacked with pickaxes and bamboo rods, sprayed with water, and hit with stones. The following afternoon, protesters clashed with bōryokudan and members of the second union at the Mikawa mine. About 1,600 second union faithful, reinforced by bōryokudan, split into three groups and wielded sticks in an attempt to force the 600 strikers back to work. This incident marked the first serious bloodshed of the Miike strike, with 220 reported injured. This showdown spilled over into the next day, when strikers formed a scrum and sang labor

5.1. With clubs and iron bars in hand, company-hired *bōryokudan* assault strikers at the Miike Coal Mines in March 1960. In Jōdai Iwao, Fujimoto Masatomo, and Ikeda Masumi, *1960-nen, Miike* (Tokyo: Dōjidaisha, 2002). Reproduced courtesy of the publisher and the Miike labor union.

songs in anticipation of the arrival of 200 *bōryokudan* in cars and buses. Around 4:00 P.M., a car sped past the checkpoint, pulled up to the south gate, and let off *bōryokudan* who tried to provoke the picketers. Unsuccessful in this attempt, they moved on to the front gate escorted by police. A melee between *bōryokudan* and picketers ensued, during which *bōryokudan* killed protester Kubo Kiyoshi with a sword. When they learned of Kubo's death, the picketers fell silent before they renewed their efforts against the *bōryokudan*. The police then stepped in and took *bōryokudan* to the Arao police station; the next morning, they released everyone but Kubo's suspected murderer. This was a pivotal moment in the Miike strike—the shock of Kubo's death was great enough to thaw the animosity between the two unions, which merged back into one body.[79]

The murder of Kubo brought public attention to the presence of *bōryokudan* in labor disputes and became a lightning rod for criticisms about yakuza excesses as well as the complicity of the police in management-endorsed violence. In the journal of the Japan Communist Party, writer Takagi Takashi commented on how visible right-wing *bōryokudan* had become and noted that they had been involved in a number of strikes in 1959, including those at *Shufu to seikatsu* magazine, Metro Transit, SS Pharmaceuticals, Seikō Electronics, and Yamatake Automotive.[80]

Commentators also made a point of emphasizing that *bōryokudan* were hired professionals, implying that they as specialists were responsible for escalating the violence. Marxist economist Sakisaka Itsurō observed that *bōryokudan* had been loitering about Miike since late 1959. Periodically, they would get drunk and tumble into the union president's office. Sakisaka himself was assaulted with leaflets that read: "Sakisaka is getting a lot of money from the union" and "Red bigwig Sakisaka."[81] Some commentators did not name specific *bōryokudan*, simply calling them "violence organizers" or "tattooed organizers," the tattoos a clear mark of yakuza. These men were described as wearing tattered kimono, using ropes for sashes, and carrying clubs. And it was said that they received around ¥5,000 a day for their services.[82] Others identified the *bōryokudan* involved. The Matsubakai was called out as an organization of *bakuto* known for a pattern of destructive behavior; it was noted that its members' presence at Miike in late March was followed the next month by an attack on the offices of the *Mainichi shinbun,* an act that one writer equated to the prewar assault on the *Asahi shinbun.*[83] Another named *bōryokudan* was the Hi o Tomosu Kai (Association of Burning Light), a front for the right-wing group called the Dai Nihon Seisantō (Greater Japan Production Party). This association was said to have had ties with the company from the very beginning of the dispute. Considering its past actions of running over a union member with a car and destroying property, the group was seen as a dangerous presence. In the Miike dispute, its members took pictures of union protesters, posted them on exhibition boards on the town's main street, and were active participants in the violent incidents of late March, including the one that resulted in the death of Kubo. As the strike intensified, other *bōryokudan,* such as the Yamashiro-gumi and Terauchi-gumi, entered the fray.[84]

The *bōryokudan* presence and the alleged cooperation between these groups and the police were seen as offensive. Writer Takagi placed the blame for the violence of recent labor disputes in part on increased competition between firms but also on police intervention that had become more aggressive since the conflict over the proposed police bill of 1958.[85] Both developments had, in Takagi's view, undercut court mediation in disputes, which had been a more moderate and measured way of resolving disagreements between management and labor. Without an attractive legal avenue for arbitration, companies had turned to both *bōryokudan* and police for assistance. In the *Shufu to seikatsu* strike, the police reportedly stood idly by as company-hired *bōryokudan* threatened union members. Similarly, in the Yamatake Automobile dispute, a patrol vehicle stayed on the sidelines as *bōryokudan* robbed cars and inflicted injuries on strikers. And in the Miike strike, police were described as focusing their attention on union protesters and merely sitting in their bus and watching when *bōryokudan* clashed with union members.[86] In those instances when the police did arrest *bōryokudan,* those caught were all soon released.[87] In the words of the union's Nishiyama branch president, it was clear in the minds of the strikers that the police had themselves become a kind of *bōryokudan*.[88] It is not fair to say, however, that the *bōryokudan* went completely unpunished for their actions. In early April 1960, there was a police crackdown on these groups, the Matsubakai and the Kokusuikai in particular. More than 50 people were arrested, but how long they were held and the severity of their punishment is not known.[89]

The attempt of Miike company management to violently put down the strike with the assistance of *bōryokudan* and the police was seen by union members and their sympathizers as emblematic of a general trend toward the suppression of popular movements. Management, *bōryokudan* violence, the police, and the LDP were consistently characterized as enemies of mass political participation and the will of the people, be it in labor disputes or the protests against renewal of the U.S.-Japan Security Treaty. Especially after the death of Kubo in March and the deadlock in May, more people began to speak of the Miike strike and the treaty protests as being one and the same battle.[90]

The treaty protests were initially sparked by the Kishi government's support for a revised U.S.-Japan Security Treaty, or Anpo. Although somewhat more re-ciprocal than the original 1952 treaty, the latest version maintained the right of the United States to have military bases in Japan. This fundamental provision was offensive to socialists, student organizations, and women's groups, among others, because it was viewed as locking Japan into a subordinate position vis-à-vis a hegemonic United States. There were also fears that the continued U.S. military presence would drag Japan into a war that was not of its own making. Nonethe-less, the Kishi cabinet was satisfied with the revisions and dedicated to coopera-tion with the United States, so the treaty was signed in Washington in January; the hope was to secure Diet ratification by May 20 so that it would become effective before President Dwight Eisenhower's scheduled visit to Tokyo on June 19. In an-ticipation of the approaching May deadline, tens of thousands of people took to the streets in April in a series of protests. By late April, there had been sightings of right-wing groups coming face to face with the agitators. Included among those trying to suppress the demonstrations were the Kokusuikai, Dai Nihon Aikokutō (Greater Japan Patriotic Party), and the Gijintō (Party of Righteous Men), an organization established in 1952 that had a youth corps (Hinomaru Seinentai) and about 500 members.[91]

Kishi and the LDP added fuel to the fire on May 19 when they used coer-cive tactics reminiscent of the 1954 and 1956 Diet incidents to secure ratifica-tion of the treaty. From early in the morning, members of the Matsubakai and the Gijintō, as well as those from the LDP's youth division, occupied the gallery in the Diet chamber as the House of Representatives wrangled over a possible

5.2. Members of the Kokusuikai mobilized to clamp down on the Anpo protests, 1960. In Arahara Bokusui, *Dai uyokushi* (Tokyo: Dai Nihon Kokumintō, 1966).

extension of the Diet session. The LDP sought more time to allow a vote on the treaty, and the JSP filibustered. That afternoon, as machinations around this issue continued, the JSP barricaded the House speaker into his office. And scuffles broke out in the hallways involving JSP and LDP parliamentarians, JSP *hishodan,* LDP *ingaidan,* and yakuza. One JSP secretary alleged that he had been hit in the forehead and kneed in his "vital parts" by a yakuza; two JSP parliamentarians were reportedly beaten by yakuza. Around 6:00 P.M., the speakers of both houses called for the dispatch of approximately 2,000 police to just outside the Diet building. But occasional scuffles and the JSP sit-down continued well into the night; when the bell for the opening of the plenary session rang at 10:25 P.M., the speaker was still stuck in his office. About 20 minutes later, the speaker was still urging the JSP to break apart the picket line that extended from outside his office to the dais in the Diet chamber, but to no avail. The speaker decided to call in 500 police officers to physically dismantle the human barricade by removing the JSP members from the building—the second time in the Diet's history, after 1956, that police entered the Diet chamber. At 11:48 P.M., the speaker was escorted by Diet guards to the dais where he appeared before a chamber in which all who were present were LDP parliamentarians. Not surprisingly, the extension was granted and the treaty ratified.[92]

The ratification of the treaty, and the way it was handled by the LDP, created an uproar that vaulted the protests to new heights. People in the streets were not just opposing the treaty, they were demanding the overthrow of Kishi and the resignation of his cabinet. In early June, protests spread beyond Tokyo and some laborers went on strike as a show of solidarity, halting certain services. To contain this mass popular movement, the LDP turned to *bōryokudan.* It has been widely believed that Prime Minister Kishi himself approached his

5.3. On June 15, 1960, *bōryokudan* attack demonstrators protesting Prime Minister Kishi Nobusuke's renewal of the U.S.-Japan Security Treaty. In Nishii Kazuo, ed., *60-nen anpo, Miike tōsō: 1957–1960* (Tokyo: Mainichi Shinbunsha, 2000). Reproduced courtesy of the *Mainichi shinbun.*

old prison mate Kodama Yoshio and asked him to form a coalition of violent, right-wing groups.[93] Whether Kodama established such an uber organization is unclear, but *bōryokudan* were a visible presence in the June protests. On June 10, both *bōryokudan* and police blocked protesters attempting to present a petition to Eisenhower advanceman James Hagerty when he landed at Haneda Airport. Hagerty's arrival was also noteworthy because he was met by thousands of protesters, some of whom attacked his car while chanting that he return home.

The clash between protesters and *bōryokudan* reached a fevered pitch on June 15, several days before Eisenhower's scheduled visit and the enactment of the treaty. Tens of thousands of protesters marched outside the Diet, mobilized mostly by Sōhyō and Zengakuren (Zen Nihon Gakusei Jichikai Sōrengō, All-Japan Federation of Student Self-Governing Associations).[94] Pitted against them were about 5,000 police and hundreds of *bōryokudan* members, perhaps even close to a thousand, from various groups. These included the Ishin Kōdōtai (Restoration Action Corps), a group established just in advance of this protest, and the Kokusuikai, which was outfitted with armbands and headbands that bore the group's name. Throughout the afternoon there had been scuffles between protesting students and *bōryokudan*. Then just after 5:00 P.M., two Gokoku Seinentai trucks waving flags of the Ishin Kōdōtai drove straight into a group of demonstrators by a House of Councillors gate. Several dozen *bōryokudan* then advanced into the crowd, swinging clubs that had been fitted with nails to inflict greater injury and throwing bottles at those who were trying to escape. Many of those they trampled and threatened to beat to death were ordinary citizens or members of the Shingekidan (Modern Drama Group). As in the Miike strike, protesters were angered by the police who were described as indifferent to, or even complicit with, the violence of the *bōryokudan.* Later in the evening of June 15, altercations between rock-throwing students and club-wielding police resulted in the death of a University of Tokyo student named Kanba Michiko, who became the equivalent of Miike's Kubo Kiyoshi in the eyes of the protesters.[95]

Given the scale of the violence on this day, Kishi announced the next morning that Eisenhower's visit had been cancelled. Then at the stroke of midnight on June 19, the revised U.S.-Japan Security Treaty was enacted. Hundreds of thousands of people gathered outside the Diet on this night to peacefully express their disapproval; by this time, the possibility of blocking the treaty had slipped away, and the violence had passed. And finally, on the morning of June 23, a Kishi broken by the uproar over treaty renewal publicized his decision to resign.

After the furor over treaty renewal and Kishi's strong-arm tactics died down, tens of thousands of anti-treaty protesters redirected their energy to the ongoing Miike dispute, traveling to Kyūshū to join the strikers.[96] Eventually, by the fall of 1960, company management had outlasted the strikers, backed as it was by the police and other mines. In the end, the union members conceded to full implementation of the company's rationalization plan.

With the left and the public at large still reeling from a violent summer, the third and final shock of the year hit in October as the last phase of the Miike dispute was playing itself out. On the afternoon of October 12, JSP Chairman Asanuma Inejirō was giving a televised speech in front of a gathering of more than 1,000 people in Hibiya Hall when he was heckled by members of a right-wing group, who were also scattering anticommunist leaflets from the second floor of the auditorium. Suddenly, a 17-year-old youth named Yamaguchi Otoya stormed onto the stage and fatally stabbed Asanuma with a sword. After being arrested, Yamaguchi explained his motivations for targeting Asanuma: the JSP chairman, in being overly friendly with China and the Soviet Union, was a traitor who had betrayed his own country. Using similar logic, Yamaguchi had planned to kill the Japan Communist Party director as well as the head of Nikkyōsō. On November 2, Yamaguchi executed his own punishment by taking his life.[97]

Upon further investigation, it was found that Yamaguchi had been a member of the Dai Nihon Aikokutō and had a criminal record. The lengthy list of his crimes included, in 1959: disseminating leaflets to anti-treaty protesters (June 25); disrupting a radio broadcast about the treaty revision issue (July 29); breaking

5.4. Under the heading "The Honorable Prime Minister," yakuza and the police are portrayed conspiring to end the Anpo protests, utterly unconcerned with the death of college student Kanba Michiko or the staining of parliamentary politics. The text reads: "We won't yield to extraparliamentary pressure. Demonstrations are our enemy, students are our enemy, women and children are our enemy. Destroy the demonstrators. Beat the Comintern. [Voice switches to that of the cartoonist, Nasu Ryosuke.] When the life of one woman is lost, even though an enemy, can you not express any sympathy?" From *Sekai* 176 (August 1960). Reproduced courtesy of Nasu Miyo, wife of the artist.

through a traffic barricade, throwing smoke bombs, and acting violently toward police at an atomic bomb abolition rally in Hiroshima (August 5); damaging the clothes of a police officer (September 7); trespassing (September 8); handing out leaflets and injuring police (November 16); and yelling from a car through a bullhorn and acting violently toward police officers (December 14). His offenses in 1960 included: disturbing an anti-treaty meeting (March 1); interrupting an anti-treaty demonstration (April 26); wielding violence (May 3); and destroying a signboard marking the location of anti-treaty petitions (May 14). It seems that for many of these offenses, because of his youth, Yamaguchi's punishment was probation.[98]

The assassination of Asanuma was tied to the treaty protests in the minds of many leftists, who considered the JSP chairman an important symbol and leader of the anti-treaty movement. The attack on Asanuma was thus interpreted more broadly as an assault on all citizens who had opposed the treaty. Some commentators took it even further, interpreting the stabbing as a hostile act against those who supported Japan's independence, peace, and democracy.

What connected the assassination with both the anti-treaty movement and the Miike strike was the prominence of right-wing *bōryokudan*, particularly in the view of those with leftist sympathies. By the fall of 1960, there was much discussion about the need to undercut the power of *bōryokudan* as they were "vermin-like" and an evil for peaceful living, and went against the will of citizens. Suggestions on how this was to be done included cracking down on yakuza groups and bringing more attention to their political position, inner workings, and connectedness to the establishment. A professor from the Tokyo University of Education was especially concerned about how violent right-wing organizations were targeting youth for recruitment. This was considered worrisome because this young generation had not experienced the war and, it was implied, could not understand the possible negative ramifications of joining forces with the right wing.[99]

A certain fear about reliving the prewar period informed the way the left framed the political developments of 1960. Vocabulary of the 1930s was resurrected as many were quick to characterize Asanuma's assassination as right-wing "terrorism."[100] There was also a lively debate about whether Japan was witnessing the resurgence of fascism. One thinker and commentator, Kuno Osamu, did not explicitly speak of fascism but did firmly believe the assassination of Asanuma was evidence that the "evil tradition" from the prewar and wartime years, of using violence against a political representative, had not become extinct. As in the prewar period, he argued, the right was using political and ideological murder to create an atmosphere of fear so that it could then pull the country in whatever direction it saw fit. Kuno acknowledged that in the 15 years of the postwar period, people had begun to write about freedom and liberty. But hiding in the shadows, he claimed, was the potential for ideological assassination that only revealed itself with Asanuma's murder. Kuno and others noted how the U.S. press had published articles about recent events in Japan that had to throw into question for U.S. readers the state of Japan's democracy and "civilized society." One commentator agreed that an October 12 article in the *Washington Evening Post*, about how the attack on Asanuma was reminiscent of the militarist assassinations of politicians in the 1920s and 1930s, sparked important questions about whether there was a popular foundation for Japanese fascism.[101]

Others, though worried about right-wing violence, did not think the danger of fascism was terribly serious. The argument on this side was that the spread of a democratic and liberal spirit, as well as the considerable power of citizens, distinguished the current political context from that of the 1920s and 1930s. And one writer noted that Yamaguchi, Asanuma's assassin, could not simply be considered the equivalent of a fascist youth with a Hitler-esque nihilistic psychology because he spoke admiringly of a number of figures, including the emperor, Yoshida Shōin, Saigō Takamori, and Mussolini.[102]

Beyond the political left, the events of 1960 inspired an outpouring of criticism about violence. In some cases, the reproaches were clearly and explicitly directed at a certain political or ideological group, while in other cases, blame was only implied or casually suggested. Most common, however, were blanket condemnations of political violence.[103] The more mainstream newspapers came out with statements against violence. A joint declaration was issued at the height of the treaty protests in mid-June by the *Asahi, Mainichi, Yomiuri, Sankei, Tōkyō, Tōkyō taimusu,* and *Nihon keizai* newspapers calling for the abolition of violence and the protection of parliamentary politics. The statement described the "bloody incidents" on June 15 as regrettable and a source of great anxiety about Japan's future. The use of violence instead of speech was deemed unacceptable, and it was feared that continuation of this trend would destroy democracy and endanger Japan's existence as a nation. Both the ruling and opposition parties were urged to cooperate in order to resolve the situation, respond to the people's hopes for the protection of parliamentary politics, and dispel anxieties.[104]

Similar sentiments were expressed about the Miike dispute. The *Asahi shinbun*, though more critical of the strikers than company management, ended an editorial on the issue by asserting that no good resolution would come from violence and that both parties must find a peaceful method of bringing the disagreement to a close.[105] And Prime Minister Ikeda Hayato, who replaced Kishi in July 1960, criticized collective violence in general (though leftists suspected that "collective violence" was a code word for labor strikes and popular movements). Addressing a plenary session of the House of Representatives on October 21, Ikeda spoke of the need to eliminate all violence, leftist or rightist.[106]

In 1961, various parties introduced bills to the Diet banning violence. In February, the JSP presented a terrorism prevention bill (Tero Bōshi Hōan) that called for severe punishment of political terrorism, defined as murder motivated by political ideology and coercion with weapons where the possibility of murder was very high. In May, the LDP submitted a bill coauthored with the Democratic Socialist Party (Minshu Shakaitō; later Minshatō), a political party founded in January 1960 by a group that had seceded from the JSP. The Political Violence Prevention Bill (Seijiteki Bōryoku Kōi Bōshi Hōan) did not just target murder and bodily injury but elevated misdemeanors such as trespassing to felonies. It also encouraged people to report any suspicion of impending violent acts to the police, and discouraged unlawful and inappropriate behavior by organizations. If a group was deemed to be acting improperly, its members would be prohibited from doing anything for the organization, including publishing organ papers and holding demonstrations or public gatherings, for a maximum of four months. As might be imagined, both bills were criticized. The JSP's proposal was considered by some to be excessive; a similar charge was lobbied against the LDP–Democratic Socialist Party version, which was likened by leftists to the Peace Preservation Law of 1925.[107] With Diet scuffles and demonstrations accompanying these debates, neither bill became law.[108]

Coda: Political Violence after 1960

Viewed in the context of Japan's postwar history, the year 1960 marked a turning point—after the turbulence of the Miike strike, the treaty demonstrations, and the assassination of Asanuma, violence increasingly receded to the political extremes and was forced underground by public intolerance for physical force and greater regulation by the police. This happened gradually; by no means did violence fade overnight or ever disappear. In the early 1960s, for example, a rightist stabbed Kishi six times in the thigh on the afternoon that Ikeda was officially voted his successor, and rightists continued to threaten politicians and even plotted to kill Prime Minister Ikeda.[109] By around the mid-1960s, however, the violent excesses of right-wing groups had provoked crackdowns by the police and politicians, and a distance developed between these organizations and political parties, even the LDP. And in the 1970s, right-wing violence did not grow out of a broad nexus of support but were isolated acts carried out by extremists.[110] On the left, students and workers took to the streets in the late 1960s in mass demonstrations against the education system, perceived Japanese and U.S. imperialism, and the Vietnam War. When some groups threw bombs and used other violent methods, the public turned against the demonstrators and handed the JSP a defeat in the general election of December 1969. As armed struggle waned in the

early 1970s, the left splintered and dispersed, with violence becoming a characteristic of the most extreme groups, like the Sekigunha (Red Army Faction) and
the Higashi Ajia Hannichi Busō Sensen (East Asia Anti-Japanese Armed Front),
which subsequently went underground and were delegitimized.[111]

Violence specialists also became much less visible in political life. Sōshi had
already become virtually extinct in the postwar years, but especially around the
mid-1960s, yakuza distanced themselves from rightist violence (though not from
the right as a whole). It is telling that Kodama Yoshio's confederation of yakuza
groups fell apart in 1965 and that acts of right-wing violence were increasingly
carried out not by hired yakuza but by rightist youth such as Yamaguchi Otoya,
Asanuma's assassin.[112] And the term "bōryokudan" eventually came to refer solely
to organized crime syndicates, not hybrid yakuza-rightist organizations.

Yakuza certainly did not shy away from politics or from the right, but they were
less violence specialists that dealt in physical force and more economic beings
that dealt in corruption. There are a number of reasons for this transformation,
including the growth of yakuza groups into wealthy organized crime syndicates
as well as the public's impatience with political violence. For the yakuza, wielding money was preferable to using violence because financial transactions were
much less visible to the public eye. The need for covertness became all the more
acute in the 1970s, when several high-profile corruption scandals (one of which
involved Kodama Yoshio) soured the public on crooked politicians. Likewise,
politicians needed to keep secret any dealings with political fixers like Kodama or
yakuza, especially as the public became less accepting of mafiosi in the 1980s.[113]
Indeed, the political costs of a revelation of politician-yakuza ties have become
high. Since the early 1990s, public uproar over connections to yakuza have led
to the resignation of Prime Minister Takeshita Noboru and Diet member Kane-
maru Shin and helped precipitate the downfall of Prime Minister Mori Yoshiro.

Japan's early postwar democracy was profoundly affected by a general discomfort with political violence that was expressed by a greatly expanded electorate
and through widespread grassroots participation in politics. Both men and
women could now go to the polls to register their dissatisfaction with what they
deemed to be excessive violence.[114] And protesters could bring about the fall of
a cabinet or force the resignation of politicians. The idea of using the politics
of the street to hold politicians accountable for their actions was not new, for
mass protests had spelled the downfall of cabinets in the prewar period. What
was different was the conception of democracy embraced and forwarded by
these crowds—one that did not allow political leaders and the ruling party to
wield violence, either in domestic politics (inside the Diet, in labor strikes, or
against protesters) or in the international realm (through war or the possession

of nuclear weapons). This demand may have been somewhat hypocritical, especially considering those on the left who wielded violence; nonetheless, the
generally upheld democratic ideal was no longer the imperial democracy of the
prewar years, which had reconciled democracy on one hand with aggressive imperialism on the other.

As a result of these changes in Japan's democracy, money came to outstrip
violence as a tool for political influence over the course of the postwar period.[115]
Conservatives, in particular, discovered that money, a long-time fuel of politics,
could often be more powerful—and discreet—than violence. And so the remaining violence specialists, namely yakuza, came to traffic in funds more than physical force, at least in the political realm. The greater preference for bribery over
violence was a change, but not an evolution, in Japan's democracy. Not only is the
flow of money less visible than physical attacks and thus more difficult to police,
but bribery can also entail more complicity on the part of those involved. Those
voters in prewar elections who were intimidated by *sōshi* at polling places were
acted upon, but those of the postwar period who stopped by the local party office to have some sake on election day or who accepted the money being handed
out on the street were more complicit in corruption. This was especially true in
situations where there was little, if any, implied physical threat. The prevalence of
money politics also meant that those citizens with greater financial means could
have greater political influence; one had to have a certain amount of wealth to
bribe politicians. In some ways, this was true in the prewar period as well, when
it came to hiring *sōshi*. Yet the barriers to entry were lower for *sōshi* in the sense
that any group of youths with some sticks could threaten or intimidate a politician; lack of money would preclude that level of participation in the postwar
period. Corruption and bribery could thus be as insidious, exclusionary, and undemocratic as violence.

All of this is not to say that Japan was no longer a violent democracy. Violence
continued to be a part of popular protests and labor strife during the 1960s even
after yakuza violence faded from the political scene. Even into the 1970s, those
who felt left out of the political system turned to the violence of terrorism and
assassination to help publicize their views, express frustration, and demonstrate
that they were of political consequence. Unresolved questions about how to deal
with the political fringes left open real possibilities for violence. In addition, the
very presence of yakuza, who regularly wielded violence in their other lines of
work, brought a threat of violence to politics.[116] The violence of Japan's democracy may not have been as commonplace, routine, or accepted as it had been in
the prewar period, but democratic politics were laced with a menacing undercurrent of violence that broke through the surface often enough to serve as a
reminder of its presence.

Violence and Democracy

For much of Japan's modern history, violence and democracy have coexisted in an uneasy, complicated, and tense relationship. In Japan, as elsewhere, violence and democracy were drawn into a tenacious embrace that endangered each without destroying the other. Violence did not single-handedly extinguish democratic politics, and democracy was far from being a panacea for violent politics.

Indeed, at the very heart of Japan's violent democracy was a tension: democratic politics attracted the very kind of violence that was often undemocratic in its consequences. In the 1890s, the promulgation of a constitution, the establishment of a parliament, and general elections for a national representative body did not quell the *sōshi* violence of the previous decade but merely encouraged a change in its form, from rebellion and terrorism to ruffianism. The heated political contests and disagreements of democratic politics in the following decades invited *sōshi* ruffianism to be wielded as a tool to influence political outcomes and forward agendas. The antagonism between people's parties and government parties, between candidates for office, and between the main players in a two-party political system all fueled the demand for methods—like violence—to sway, to persuade, and to elicit a desired political behavior. Democratic reforms did not spell the end of violence but transformed it, taking what had been the violence of resistance against, and from outside of, an undemocratic political system and institutionalizing it into the practice of democratic politics.

At the same time that democratic politics perpetuated ruffianism, this ruffianism had various undemocratic ramifications. Its undemocratic character was not always so clear cut, as *ingaidan sōshi* could serve as a check on the power of the *hanbatsu* and occasionally backed party initiatives that expanded political participation and were in line with popular demands. Yet *sōshi* violence was intended to threaten and intimidate, and it disturbed sites of democratic practice such as speech meetings, parliamentary debates, and elections. *Sōshi* could exacerbate unevenness in politics, functioning as an asset to those who had the money to hire them. And their incorporation into the political system helped feed a culture of political violence in which the violent, and those associated with them, viewed their use of physical force as a necessary and acceptable political strategy. By the early 1920s, a two-party political system with party cabinets that was on the road to universal manhood suffrage was intertwined with *ingaidan sōshi* and a culture of political violence.

There were a host of other tensions between violence and democracy. As early as the 1870s and mid-1880s, *bakuto* and *sōshi* who led and participated in the violent incidents of the Freedom and People's Rights Movement embodied the contradiction of using violent means to achieve democratic ends. They unleashed destructive force to construct a different political order, and alienated political enemies to establish a more inclusive political system. In the 1880s and 1890s, assassinations and military expeditions were planned in the name of liberty. *Tairiku rōnin*, who emerged out of the popular and liberal spirit of the Freedom and People's Rights Movement, wielded physical force as part of the violence of imperialism and war. And yakuza bosses like Yoshida Isokichi and Hora Sennosuke were democratically elected to the Diet, at least partly because of their ability to coerce through violence.

Such strains were not, as some historians have claimed, a sign that there was something peculiarly backward about Japanese democracy, that it was plagued by remnants of a feudal past that survived beyond their time.[1] Certain shortcomings of democracy did contribute to the proliferation of violence, the restrictions on suffrage being a prime example. But the very presence of violence was not a political throwback; *bakuto* of the Freedom and People's Rights Movement were part of a grassroots push for democratic reform, *tairiku rōnin* were forwarding continental expansion, *sōshi* were institutionalized into a democratic political system, and organizations such as the Dai Nihon Kokusuikai and Dai Nihon Seigidan were fighting the spread of communism in an attempt to ensure Japan's strength as a capitalist, industrial power. Some of these violence specialists did draw upon ideas and language from the Tokugawa period, portraying themselves and perhaps thinking of themselves as chivalrous "kyōkaku" or the mythologized samurai warrior. But in practice, their political violence was inextricably bound up with the most modern of impulses—the construction of the modern nation-state, parliamentary and constitutional democracy, nationalism, imperialism, and fascism.

The entanglement of violence and democracy, with its varied and ambiguous political consequences, makes it difficult to understand violence and democracy as necessarily and fundamentally at odds. Democracy did not extinguish violence, but could inflame it. And it is not particularly meaningful to frame violence as an obstacle to "democratic consolidation."[2] The *bakuto* and *sōshi* of the Freedom and People's Rights Movement and even the *ingaidan sōshi* illustrate the need to examine the possibility that violence can be wielded in the name of democracy, to forward democratic ends. Put another way, the motivations behind the use of force as well as the underlying causes and ramifications of violence may have just as much to do with "democratization" as violence itself. More generally speaking, to view violence as a hindrance to "democratic consolidation" is to risk embracing the simplistic notion that violence and democracy are inversely proportional, as if declines in violence can be so neatly marked and measured, as if democracy is free of violence. Indeed, the very concept of "democratic consolidation" is of minimal use. The idea that there is a kind of natural, evolutionary march toward a point at which democracy is solid seems misleading in its characterization of a messy process and dangerous in its assumption that democracy is ever secure.

Violence, Fascism, Militarism

In Japan, democracy did buckle, and violence contributed to its dismal fate in the 1930s and early 1940s. That party politicians had a history of working with violence specialists, even some in official uniform, may have made it easier for them to swallow the idea of sharing the responsibility of governing with military men. And the structural embeddedness of political violence bred doubts about the ability of the political parties to maintain order. These concerns born of Japan's violent democracy were exacerbated by fascist groups like the Kokusuikai and Seigidan that elevated the existing culture of political violence beyond accepting or appreciating the use of physical force to celebrating and even glorifying violence as an act of patriotic purification. Buoyed by a sense of self-importance, fascist groups confirmed worries about the impotence of the political parties by flexing their own political muscle. The fascist movement was all the more toxic to democracy because it melded the state (the military and bureaucrats) together with violence specialists (yakuza). The state had had ties to violence specialists before; the Meiji oligarchs stood behind government party *sōshi*, and military personnel on the continent had cooperated with nationalist *tairiku rōnin*. But never had elite state figures and violence specialists been woven together so tightly, as leaders of prominent groups in a political movement. It was, then, both violent democracy and the fascist movement that helped create the context for the attempted military coups d'état of the 1930s.

This is not to say that the institutionalization of ruffianism and a culture of political violence led, inexorably and inevitably, to the rise of military rule in the 1930s. This transition was a complicated one, beyond the main concerns here, shaped among other things by economic dislocation, rural hardship, jingoistic imperialism, high-level machinations, and political corruption. Without these various stresses that precipitated and shaped the breakdown of democratic politics, Japan's violent democracy could have and might have endured indefinitely.

Unlike the ruffianism of *sōshi* and *ingaidan*, there was nothing democratic about the violence of fascist movements and military rule. Indeed, one of the characteristics of fascist violence was the absence of internal frictions and contradictions. There was no tension between violent means and democratic ends, democratic causes and violent consequences, democratic intentions and undemocratic outcomes. The Kokusuikai and Seigidan, for example, were astoundingly straightforward in their use of violence, seeking to suppress those who embraced ideologies with which they did not agree. And the militarist government that assumed Japanese political leadership in the 1930s had no need for *sōshi* or even yakuza because the political heterogeneity that had made such nonstate violence specialists necessary had been obliterated. Instead, they had been replaced by the official violent arms of the state, or state violence specialists: the police and the military. It was when the vitality of political contests had been extinguished, when the tension between democracy and violence had been snuffed out, when the strategies of violence specialists were adopted by the state, that violence took the most frighteningly systematic, dominating, and powerful of forms.[3]

Violence Specialists and History

Violence specialists heightened and embodied the various tensions and ambiguities of Japan's violent democracy. This was in part because of their obvious and defining characteristic: they dealt in violence, which was itself a political tool laden with a multitude of possible meanings depending on who wielded it, how, against whom, and for what ends. Perhaps more pertinent was their ability to blur lines and to complicate any notion of a simple dichotomy between state and society because of their character and position as nonstate actors who served various interests. There were moments when certain violence specialists leveraged their independence from the state to challenge the government and the status quo, as some *sōshi* did in the 1880s and in the era of popular violence. There were other moments when nonstate violence specialists stood behind or with the state, as when *sōshi* worked for government-backed parties in the 1890s, *bōryokudan* stifled labor unrest, and yakuza assumed a place in the postwar conservative nexus. These varied and shifting positions arguably enabled them to endure—violence specialists were something of a moving target for those who sought to condemn them. And their slippery status may have encouraged the state to accept and even support their use of force, as it could attempt to deny any connection to violence specialists if pressed. It may have been more attractive for the state to turn to yakuza, for example, than its own police or the military, because dodging criticisms about possible affiliations with violence specialists was likely easier than responding to charges about the excesses of state violence.

Violence specialists are not just a reflection of, or window into, Japan's political history, be it the fluidity between state and society, the contentious character of democratic politics, or the potency of ideological conflicts. They were also significant as historical actors who shaped the course of politics and political life. At the heart of their influence was their potential and ability to wield violence. Mention has been made at several points of Charles Tilly's compelling argument that the very presence of violence specialists often encourages violent outcomes.[4] These violent outcomes then go on to precipitate different effects, and elicit different responses, than nonviolent possibilities. Even without venturing into the realm of counterfactual history, it can be argued that *bakuto* and *sōshi* helped fuel the violent resistance of the Freedom and People's Rights Movement, which may have nudged the Meiji oligarchs toward democratic reform. As organizers of democratic movements in the first several decades of the twentieth century, *sōshi* and the *ingaidan* to which they belonged animated popular protests, the results of which included the toppling of cabinets. And yakuza collaboration with the Liberal Democratic Party facilitated the consolidation and perpetuation of conservative rule in postwar Japan. In addition to the instrumental value of violence specialists, these figures also shaped the political culture in which they operated. The presence of violence specialists made it more likely that violence would become a regularly wielded political tool rather than one of last resort, and this everydayness served to divorce violence from seriousness of purpose and thoughtful consideration of the consequences of its use. The culture of political violence spun from this mindset contributed to the institutionalization of *sōshi* into party politics and, ultimately, the breakdown of democracy in the 1930s.

Much work still needs to be done on the history of the violent and political violence in Japan. This book has focused on the functions and influence of violence in politics, but we could know more about the process by which the violent of all sorts are created, about what informs, motivates, and shapes people's decisions to swing their fists or take up arms. That would be a project that extends beyond this one and would require the kind of sources (diaries, memoirs, and the like) that are frustratingly scarce when focusing on *sōshi* or yakuza in the street.

Yet if possible, this kind of inquiry would help place the violent in sociological perspective and would underscore an idea implicit in this book—that the violent, including the various violence specialists treated here, were forged by a confluence of factors and were not inherently and inevitably violent.

A Contemporary Perspective on Violent Democracy

Utter defeat in a world war along with postwar occupation by a foreign power transformed Japan's violent democracy into its postwar incarnation. What was most fundamentally altered was the prewar culture of political violence that had been tolerant, even encouraging, of the use of physical force as a political tool. There had been voices of dissent, such as the newspapers in the Meiji period that had attempted to label *bakuto* violence as criminal, and liberal intellectuals and journalists of the 1920s who had painted violence as backward. But in the postwar period, impatience with physical force spread far beyond a handful of critics, and violence was condemned not just as uncivilized, unlawful, destructive, and destabilizing, but also as undemocratic. As violence was increasingly viewed as unacceptable, violence specialists gradually faded from the political scene, were forced deeper underground, or came to wield money more than violence. This should not be taken to mean that the prewar system with its institutionalized ruffianism was purged of the use of physical force; political violence—especially in the form of rightist yakuza and leftist terrorists—continued to pose a threat to Japanese democracy.

Contemporary Japan thus continues to be a violent democracy, though one changed from decades past. Tensions between violence and democracy have eased as violence has become less regular, less ordinary. Politics through physical confrontation is now not an ever-present, very real possibility. Violent politics is neither expected nor routine. And when acts of political violence do occur, they are quickly labeled as undemocratic and typically greeted with public disapproval and shock, precisely because they are not commonplace.[5] But we can still speak of a kind of violent democracy in Japan (as in any other democratic country) because of the enduring threat of, and potential for, violence.[6]

The possibility of violence in Japan's democracy persists in part because yakuza involvement in politics continues. Yakuza may now deal more in money than violence when it comes to politics, but they still embody the threat of physical intimidation and coercion; indeed, yakuza use violence often enough, mainly outside the political world but occasionally within it, to make their threats quite real. Japan is not unique in the continued involvement of violence specialists, organized crime figures and mafiosi in particular, with political life. In Russia, for example, members of organized crime groups have run for political office as independents, representatives of local political associations, and candidates of the Russian Liberal Democratic Party. There have also been discussions since the mid-1990s about the state forging a cooperative relationship with some organized crime groups so as to elicit their help in maintaining order and stability, containing the activities of some of the more brutal of their ilk, and fighting against the Chechen mafia.[7] In Sicily, the mafia can deliver votes to politicians and candidates who curry their favor, as well as threaten and attack those who try to undercut their power and influence.[8] Though in different ways and to different extents, all three of these countries, and others, face the challenge of minimizing the violent potential of organized crime and mafias in democratic politics. And the states themselves are unable or unwilling to deal these groups a serious blow or to fight their extraordinary capacity to adjust and survive.

It is not just places with a significant organized crime and mafia presence that continue to struggle with the embeddedness of violence in democratic politics. Even in countries where nonstate violence specialists do not thrive for various reasons (such as a strong state, effective and enforced laws, and public intolerance), negotiating the relationship between violence and democracy continues to pose a weighty challenge. I would argue that all modern nation-states and all democracies contain within them the potential for violence. The larger issues that have given rise to violence in the history of Japanese democracy—resistance and protest, the presence of unevenness in a political system that espouses equality, competing visions of ideal political and economic systems, reactions of the state and government to perceived threats to its rule, and the question of how to treat political minorities—all remain pertinent to the present day and resonate well beyond Japan. All democracies must also face the issue of the state's own violence specialists to determine when state violence is just and justified, to debate its limits and excesses, and to deliberate a state's attempt to use or misuse the law to legitimize an extension of its violent capacity. State and nonstate violence specialists alike must ultimately be policed by the people, who shoulder the burden of ensuring that the powerful instrumental logic of violence does not drown out profound consideration of its consequences for the practice of democracy.

Glossary

bakuto A gambler and, along with *tekiya,* a kind of yakuza.

bōryokudan In the prewar period, a derisive term that referred to groups known for wielding violence. In the postwar period, a synonym for organized crime syndicates used by their critics. Throughout this book, the term has been adopted to describe violent groups when a more precise identification of their composition is difficult.

hanbatsu The clique of Meiji oligarchs and their protégés who dominated the government from the early Meiji years through the middle of the Taisho period. These men hailed from the domains that spearheaded the Meiji Restoration; after the early 1870s, those from the former domains of Satsuma and Chōshū were predominant.

ikka A yakuza organization, or "family," of fictive kinship ties based on the relationship between a boss and his henchmen.

ingaidan A pressure group within a political party consisting of party members and affiliates who were not elected officials. Included *sōshi,* who were primarily responsible for serving as protectors of the party's politicians and for physically harassing political opponents.

kyōkaku "Men of chivalry," a flattering appellation for yakuza. Describes prominent yakuza bosses, especially those from the latter half of the Tokugawa period. *Kyōkaku* are said to embrace the Robin Hood–like idea of helping the weak and defeating the strong.

mintō People's parties, which were outgrowths or descendants of the Freedom and People's Rights Movement. Describes parties of the mid-Meiji period such as the Jiyūtō (Liberal Party) and the Rikken Kaishintō (Constitutional Reform Party) that opposed the *hanbatsu.*

mushuku An "unregistered," or someone who had neither an official residence nor a place in the status system of the Tokugawa period.

ritō Government parties, which were backed by the *hanbatsu.* Used to describe parties of the mid-Meiji period such as the Taiseikai (Great Achievement Society).

rōnin Various definitions; used here to mean the masterless samurai of the Tokugawa period.

sakazuki ceremony A ritual performed by yakuza (but not just yakuza) involving a *sakazuki* (small sake cup) that solidifies bonds between people or groups. For yakuza, the ceremony typically marks the initiation of members, the forging of a relationship between boss and henchman, the creation of ties between "brothers," or reconciliation between two feuding "families."

shishi Samurai, typically of lower rank, who in the late Tokugawa period took up arms to try to topple the Tokugawa shogunate. These "men of spirit" carried out a campaign of assassination during the late 1850s and early 1860s, directing their attacks at foreigners and those seen to be capitulating to the West.

shizoku Term born of the Meiji period that refers to those of samurai descent, or former samurai.

sōshi Originally young activists of the Freedom and People's Rights Movement who, starting in the late 1880s, became political ruffians who specialized in wielding violence.

tairiku rōnin A broad category of continental adventurers, or those Japanese who traveled to the continent and engaged in activities ranging from political activism and espionage to commercial enterprises. Includes intellectuals, members of nationalist organizations, businessmen, military men, and others, whose motivations for going to the Asian mainland were many and varied.

tekiya An itinerant merchant and, along with *bakuto,* a kind of yakuza. Also known in the Tokugawa period as *yashi.* These merchants often sold shoddy merchandise or used tactics of deception with their customers. Like *bakuto, tekiya* were organized into *ikka* headed by a boss.

yakuza From the Meiji period onward, yakuza can be considered Japanese mafiosi. They provided violence and protection and were involved in industries including prostitution, entertainment, and construction. In the postwar period, they expanded their activities to include corporate blackmail, debt collection, and bankruptcy management. The origins of the yakuza date to the Tokugawa period when they were of two main types: *bakuto* and *tekiya.* This distinction continued to be made into the early post–World War II decades.

Notes

Introduction

1. Jansen argued that the "brighter side" needed to be stressed so as to offset the attention given to Japan's "political inadequacies and spiritual failures" and thereby arrive at a more "balanced estimate" of Japan's modern history. Marius B. Jansen, "On Studying the Modernization of Japan," in *Studies on Modernization of Japan by Western Scholars* (Tokyo: International Christian University, 1962), 11.

2. For two volumes that came out of a series of conferences on the theme of modernization, see Marius B. Jansen, ed., *Changing Japanese Attitudes toward Modernization* (Princeton: Princeton University Press, 1965); R. P. Dore, ed., *Aspects of Social Change in Modern Japan* (Princeton: Princeton University Press, 1967).

3. On the modernization school, see John W. Dower, "E. H. Norman, Japan and the Uses of History," in *Origins of the Modern Japanese State: Selected Writings of E. H. Norman*, ed. John W. Dower (New York: Pantheon, 1975), 55–65; Sheldon Garon, "Rethinking Modernization and Modernity in Japanese History: A Focus on State-Society Relations," *Journal of Asian Studies* 53, no. 2 (May 1994): 346–48; Daniel V. Botsman, *Punishment and Power in the Making of Modern Japan* (Princeton: Princeton University Press, 2005), 6–9. Note Dower's point that E. H. Norman, of an earlier generation, did not attempt to paint Japan positively as his modernization-scholar successors did.

4. Marius B. Jansen, "Ōi Kentarō: Radicalism and Chauvinism," *Far Eastern Quarterly* 11, no. 3 (May 1952): 305–16; Marius B. Jansen, *The Japanese and Sun-Yat Sen* (Cambridge, Mass.: Harvard University Press, 1954).

5. Jansen, "Studying the Modernization of Japan," 1–2. I take issue here with the ways scholars of the modernization school dealt with violence, but I do not eschew the idea that "modernity" and the "modern" are useful categories of analysis or phenomena worthy of study. I therefore feel little discomfort using terms such as "early modern" and "modern" throughout the book.

6. For essays that challenge the idea of Japanese harmony, see Stephen Vlastos, ed., *Mirror of Modernity: Invented Traditions of Modern Japan* (Berkeley: University of California Press, 1998).

7. Robert A. Scalapino, *Democracy and the Party Movement in Prewar Japan* (Berkeley: University of California Press, 1953); George Akita, *Foundations of Constitutional Government in Modern Japan, 1868–1900* (Cambridge, Mass.: Harvard University Press, 1967);

Tetsuo Najita, *Hara Kei in the Politics of Compromise, 1905-1915* (Cambridge, Mass.: Harvard University Press, 1967); Joseph Pittau, *Political Thought in Early Meiji Japan, 1868-1889* (Cambridge, Mass.: Harvard University Press, 1967); Peter Duus, *Party Rivalry and Political Change in Taisho Japan* (Cambridge, Mass.: Harvard University Press, 1968).

8. See Chapter 5 of Shinobu Seizaburō, *Taishō demokurashīshi*, vol. 2 (Tokyo: Kawade Shobō, 1952). For another work written in the 1950s on the "rice riots," see Shōji Kichinosuke, *Kome sōdō no kenkyū* (Tokyo: Miraisha, 1957).

9. For a discussion of Marxist scholars and their treatment of violence, see Suda Tsutomu, "Bōryoku wa dō katararete kita ka," in *Bōryoku no chihei o koete: Rekishigaku kara no chōsen*, ed. Suda Tsutomu, Cho Kyondaru, and Nakajima Hisato (Tokyo: Aoki Shoten, 2004), 14-15.

10. Kinoshita Hanji, *Nihon fashizumushi* (Tokyo: Iwasaki Shoten, 1949); Tanaka Sōgorō, *Nihon fashizumu no genryū: Kita Ikki no shisō to shōgai* (Tokyo: Hakuyōsha, 1949); Maejima Shōzō, *Nihon fashizumu to gikai: Sono shiteki kyūmei* (Kyoto: Hōritsu Bunkasha, 1956). Works that did focus on violence include Kainō Michitaka, *Bōryoku: Nihon shakai no fashizumu kikō* (Tokyo: Nihon Hyōronsha, 1950). Of these four writers, only Tanaka was trained as a historian.

11. English translations of Maruyama's best-known essays on fascism can be found in Maruyama Masao, *Thought and Behaviour in Modern Japanese Politics*, ed. Ivan Morris (Oxford: Oxford University Press, 1963). For a historiographical review essay that includes a discussion of Maruyama's writings on fascism as well as more recent work that has begun to deal with violence, see Katō Yōko, "Fashizumuron," *Nihon rekishi* 700 (September 2006): 143-53.

12. Tanaka Sōgorō, *Nihon kanryō seijishi* (Tokyo: Kawade Shobō, 1954); Rōyama Masamichi, ed., *Nihon no seiji* (Tokyo: Mainichi Shinbunsha, 1955); Suzuki Yasuzō, ed., *Nihon no kokka kōzō* (Tokyo: Keisō Shobō, 1957).

13. On the *minshūshi* scholars, see Carol Gluck, "The People in History: Recent Trends in Japanese Historiography," *Journal of Asian Studies* 38, no. 1 (November 1978): 25-50.

14. Kano Masanao, *Taishō demokurashī* (Tokyo: Shōgakkan, 1976); Yasumaru Yoshio and Fukaya Katsumi, *Minshū undō* (Tokyo: Iwanami Shoten, 1989); Irokawa Daikichi, *Konmintō to Jiyūtō* (Tokyo: Yōransha, 1984). Other works in the 1960s focused on violence: see Murofushi Tetsurō, *Nihon no terorisuto: Ansatsu to kūdetā no rekishi* (Tokyo: Kōbundō, 1962); Morikawa Tetsurō, *Bakumatsu ansatsushi* (Tokyo: San'ichi Shobō, 1967).

15. Roger W. Bowen, *Rebellion and Democracy in Meiji Japan: A Study of Commoners in the Popular Rights Movement* (Berkeley: University of California Press, 1980); Michael Lawrence Lewis, *Rioters and Citizens: Mass Protest in Imperial Japan* (Berkeley: University of California Press, 1990); Andrew Gordon, *Labor and Imperial Democracy in Prewar Japan* (Berkeley: University of California Press, 1991). For a more recent discussion of violence in the context of protest, see David L. Howell, *Geographies of Identity in Nineteenth-Century Japan* (Berkeley: University of California Press, 2005), 89-109.

16. Tetsuo Najita and J. Victor Koschmann, eds., *Conflict in Modern Japanese History: The Neglected Tradition* (Princeton: Princeton University Press, 1982).

17. These issues were taken up recently in a Japanese volume dedicated to examining the place of violence in Japanese history. See Suda Tsutomu, Cho Kyondaru, and Nakajima Hisato, eds., *Bōryoku no chihei o koete: Rekishigaku kara no chōsen* (Tokyo: Aoki Shoten, 2004).

18. Georges Sorel would likely be uncomfortable with my equating force with violence. Sorel draws a clear distinction between force and violence, arguing that force is used by a minority to impose social order whereas violence generally destroys it. Georges Sorel, *Reflections on Violence*, ed. Jeremy Jennings (Cambridge: Cambridge University Press, 1999), 165-66.

19. Someone like Daniel Ross might take issue with my separation of the body from the mind and the literal definition of the body as a corporeal form. His conception of bodies is much more all-encompassing: "Every thing that can be isolated from other things is susceptible to being described as a body." Ross understands violence broadly as an "action forceful enough to produce an effect." Daniel Ross, *Violent Democracy* (Cambridge: Cambridge University Press, 2004), 3–4. While I agree that violence need not be physical, expanding the idea too far runs the danger of equating violence and coercion, confusing useful distinctions. Charles Tilly also warns about using the term "violence" too loosely. Charles Tilly, *The Politics of Collective Violence* (Cambridge: Cambridge University Press, 2003), 4–5.

20. John Keane considers as violence "any uninvited but intentional or half-intentional act of physically violating the body of a person who previously had lived 'in peace.'" John Keane, *Reflections on Violence* (New York: Verso, 1996), 6.

21. Tilly, *Politics of Collective Violence,* 4–5, 35–36. For a similar use of "specialist in violence," see Robert Bates, Avner Greif, and Smita Singh, "Organizing Violence," *Journal of Conflict Resolution* 46, no. 5 (October 2002): 600.

22. Violence specialists such as certain enforcers or even athletes are simply not relevant to Japan's political history so will not be treated. Soldiers and police have been studied elsewhere and could not possibly be done justice in this book; they do make appearances in discussions of their relationships with private violence specialists.

23. Scholars of organized crime and mafias typically understand mafias as a species of the genus organized crime. While all organized crime groups seek a monopoly of an illegal good, the specific commodity of concern for mafias is protection. As explained by Diego Gambetta, who first proposed this definition, "the mafia is a specific economic enterprise, an industry which produces, promotes, and sells private protection." See Diego Gambetta, *The Sicilian Mafia: The Business of Private Protection* (Cambridge, Mass.: Harvard University Press, 1993), 1. Because of their interest in protection, mafias often have more complicated relationships with the state than other organized crime groups.

24. On the reordering purpose of political violence, see David E. Apter, "Political Violence in Analytical Perspective," in *The Legitimization of Violence,* ed. David E. Apter (New York: New York University Press, 1997), 5.

25. On the "antagonistic dimension" of politics and the political, and democratic politics in particular, see Chantal Mouffe, *On the Political* (New York: Routledge, 2005), 2–4.

26. Political theorist John Keane argues unequivocally that violence and democracy are inherently and fundamentally at odds: "violence... is the greatest enemy of democracy as we know it. Violence is anathema to its spirit and substance." John Keane, *Violence and Democracy* (Cambridge: Cambridge University Press, 2004), 1.

27. For a useful historiographical essay on Taisho democracy, see Arima Manabu, "'Taishō demokurashī' ron no genzai: Minshūka, shakaika, kokuminka," *Nihon rekishi* 700 (September 2006): 134–42.

28. Andrew Gordon makes a similar point about the chronologically misleading use of the "Taisho" qualifier; Gordon's concept of "imperial democracy" is a compelling alternative but is not entirely appropriate in this work that focuses on neither emperor nor empire. Gordon, *Labor and Imperial Democracy,* 5–9.

29. Banno Junji, *Meiji demokurashī* (Tokyo: Iwanami Shoten, 2005).

30. Richard J. Samuels, *Machiavelli's Children: Leaders and Their Legacies in Italy and Japan* (Ithaca: Cornell University Press, 2003), 10–15.

31. The historiography on *sōshi* is treated in Chapters 2 and 3, but the dearth of academic research on yakuza needs to be highlighted here. Perhaps the best scholarly work on yakuza in English is Peter B. E. Hill, *The Japanese Mafia: Yakuza, Law, and the State*

(Oxford: Oxford University Press, 2003). There also exists a dissertation by David Harold Stark, "The Yakuza: Japanese Crime Incorporated" (Ph.D. diss., University of Michigan, 1981). A standard text on yakuza was written by two journalists: David E. Kaplan and Alec Dubro, *Yakuza: Japan's Criminal Underworld* (Berkeley: University of California Press, 2003). Sources in Japanese are cited in Chapter 1. Yakuza have long captured popular imaginations, if not the attention of historians. For an interesting article on yakuza films, see Federico Varese, "The Secret History of Japanese Cinema: The Yakuza Movies," *Global Crime* 7, no. 1 (February 2006): 105–24.

1. Patriots and Gamblers

1. The vice commander of the Konmingun, Katō Orihei, testified that there were 1,000 people gathered at the shrine. Tōkyō Izumibashi Keisatsusho, "Dai-ikkai jinmon chōsho: Katō Orihei," November 7, 1884, in *CJSS*, vol. 2, 141. This figure is also cited in Gunma-ken Keisatsushi Hensan Iinkai, ed., *Gunma-ken keisatsushi*, vol. 1 (Maebashi: Gunma-ken Keisatsu Honbu, 1978), 361.

2. *Asahi shinbun*, November 5, 1884, in *CJSS*, vol. 6, 852.

3. Haga Noboru, *Bakumatsu shishi no sekai* (Tokyo: Yūzankaku, 2003), 16–17.

4. On the intellectual history of *sonnō jōi* ideology, see H. D. Harootunian, *Toward Restoration: The Growth of Political Consciousness in Tokugawa Japan* (Berkeley: University of California Press, 1970).

5. W. G. Beasley, *The Meiji Restoration* (Stanford: Stanford University Press, 1972), 147–55, 161, 165; Harootunian, *Toward Restoration*, 41. On distinctions between different kinds of *shishi*, see Beasley, *Meiji Restoration*, 156–59, 162–66; Thomas Huber, "'Men of High Purpose' and the Politics of Direct Action, 1862–1864," in *Conflict in Modern Japanese History*, ed. Tetsuo Najita and J. Victor Koschmann (Princeton: Princeton University Press, 1982), 123–27. Note that while some *shishi* became uncomfortable with certain ways their colleagues used violence, no type of *shishi* was troubled by the very use of violence itself.

6. Many definitions of terrorism emphasize that it is a symbolic act, intended to elicit fear and anxiety (although the centrality of the latter is debated). See Jeff Goodwin, "A Theory of Categorical Terrorism," *Social Forces* 84, no. 4 (June 2006): 2027–32; Grant Wardlaw, *Political Terrorism: Theory, Tactics, and Counter-measures* (Cambridge: Cambridge University Press, 1989), 8–10. If we can define assassination as "an act of killing a prominent person selectively, intentionally, and for political (including religious) purposes," then some assassinations (but not all) could be considered acts of terrorism. This definition of assassination is taken from Asa Kasher and Amos Yadlin, "Assassination and Preventive Killing," *SAIS Review* 25, no. 1 (winter–spring 2005): 44.

7. Marius B. Jansen, *Sakamoto Ryōma and the Meiji Restoration* (Princeton: Princeton University Press, 1961), 103–4, 136; Beasley, *Meiji Restoration*, 173.

8. Haga, *Bakumatsu shishi no sekai*, 94–98. There are some discrepancies between Haga's and Hesselink's versions of the assassination; Hesselink gives the name of the victim as Kumano no Denkichi. Reinier H. Hesselink, "The Assassination of Henry Heusken," *Monumenta Nipponica* 49, no. 3 (autumn 1994): 342.

9. Hesselink, "Assassination of Henry Heusken," 331–37, 344–48.

10. Haga, *Bakumatsu shishi no sekai*, 98–99; Rutherford Alcock, *The Capital of the Tycoon: A Narrative of a Three Years' Residence in Japan*, vol. 2 (New York: Harper & Brothers, 1863), 146–58.

11. Beasley, *Meiji Restoration*, 172.

12. Alcock, *Capital of the Tycoon*, vol. 1, 308–9. Alcock also pointed to at least one case when a British subject was responsible for exacerbating a tense situation by needlessly drawing his gun. Alcock, *Capital of the Tycoon*, vol. 2, 23.

13. Ibid., vol. 1, 216.

14. Ibid., vol. 2, 146. Alcock does not use the term "shishi," but the mention of swords suggests that the assailants were not commoners. *Shishi* normally carried at least one long (*uchigatana*) and one short (*chisagatana*) sword. Haga, *Bakumatsu shishi no sekai*, 29-30.

15. Alcock, *Capital of the Tycoon*, vol. 2, 34; vol. 1, 215-17, 224, 309. Britain was not, of course, free from violent crime, political or otherwise. An article in *The Illustrated London News* from 1862 described "the frequency and the frightful audacity of crimes of violence in the streets of the metropolis." *The Illustrated London News*, December 6, 1862.

16. Huber, "'Men of High Purpose,'" 109.

17. Beasley, *Meiji Restoration*, 161, 188.

18. Quoted in Ian C. Ruxton, ed., *The Diaries and Letters of Sir Ernest Mason Satow (1843-1929), A Scholar-Diplomat in East Asia* (Lewiston: Edwin Mellen Press, 1998), 27.

19. Daniel V. Botsman, *Punishment and Power in the Making of Modern Japan* (Princeton: Princeton University Press, 2005), 135-36.

20. Huber, "'Men of High Purpose,'" 113.

21. Ibid., 112-13; Jansen, *Sakamoto Ryōma*, 131-32. On public displays and official punishment, see Botsman, *Punishment and Power*, 20-28.

22. Beasley, *Meiji Restoration*, 215-18; Botsman, *Punishment and Power*, 136; Jansen, *Sakamoto Ryōma*, 138; Huber, "'Men of High Purpose,'" 116.

23. Marius Jansen makes a similar point in *Sakamoto Ryōma*, 376-77.

24. Richard Maxwell Brown, "Violence and the American Revolution," in *Essays on the American Revolution*, ed. Stephen G. Kurtz and James H. Hutson (Chapel Hill: University of North Carolina Press, 1973), 103-8, 112-15.

25. *Shizoku* did not equate perfectly with those of samurai descent because some who had not been samurai in the Tokugawa period were elevated to *shizoku* status and others who had been samurai (vassals of domainal lords who had supported the shogunate, for example) did not become *shizoku*. Ochiai Hiroki, *Meiji kokka to shizoku* (Tokyo: Yoshikawa Kōbunkan, 2001), 1-3.

26. Stephen Vlastos, "Opposition Movements in Early Meiji, 1868-1885," in *The Cambridge History of Japan*, vol. 5, ed. Marius B. Jansen (Cambridge: Cambridge University Press, 1989), 382-83; Matsumoto Jirō, *Hagi no ran: Maebara Issei to sono ittō* (Tokyo: Taka Shobō, 1972), 131.

27. Kuruhara Keisuke, *Fuun naru kakumeiji: Maebara Issei* (Tokyo: Heibonsha, 1926), 5-6; Matsumoto, *Hagi no ran*, 136-39.

28. John M. Rogers, "Divine Destruction: The Shinpūren Rebellion of 1876," in *New Directions in the Study of Meiji Japan*, ed. Helen Hardacre with Adam L. Kern (New York: Brill, 1997), 408-9, 414, 424, 428-30; Vlastos, "Opposition Movements in Early Meiji," 391-92.

29. Mark Ravina, *The Last Samurai: The Life and Battles of Saigō Takamori* (Hoboken: John Wiley & Sons, 2004), 183-210; Jansen, *Sakamoto Ryōma*, 189; Vlastos, "Opposition Movements in Early Meiji," 398.

30. Ravina, *Last Samurai*, 7-11; Ivan Morris, *The Nobility of Failure: Tragic Heroes in the History of Japan* (New York: Holt, Rinehart and Winston, 1975), 221.

31. Rogers, "Divine Destruction," 438-39.

32. Huber, "'Men of High Purpose,'" 118; Hesselink, "Assassination of Henry Heusken," 350-51.

33. See Gen'yōsha Shashi Hensankai, ed., *Gen'yōsha shashi* (1917; reprint, Fukuoka: Ashi Shobō, 1992); Kuzuu Yoshihisa, *Tōa senkaku shishi kiden*, jō-kan (1933; reprint, Tokyo: Hara Shobō, 1966).

34. Ō Kiryō, "Tairiku rōnin no sakigake oyobi Nisshin sensō e no yakudō," *Kanazawa hōgaku* 36, no. 1-2 (March 1994): 55-56; Watanabe Ryūsaku, *Tairiku rōnin: Meiji romanchishizumu no eikō to zasetsu* (Tokyo: Banchō Shobō, 1967), 71-73; Aida Iichirō,

Shichijūnendai no uyoku: Meiji, Taishō, Shōwa no keifu (Tokyo: Daikōsha, 1970), 82–83; Gen'yōsha Shashi Hensankai, *Gen'yōsha shashi,* 109–13; Tsuzuki Shichirō, *Tōyama Mitsuru: Sono dodekai ningenzō* (Tokyo: Shinjinbutsu Ōraisha, 1974), 43. For a firsthand account of Tōyama's time in prison, see Usuda Zan'un, ed., *Tōyama Mitsuru-ō no majime* (Tokyo: Heibonsha, 1932), 23–24. Ōkubo Toshimichi would not survive beyond 1878, when *shizoku* from Satsuma took his life.

35. Aida, *Shichijūnendai no uyoku,* 84; James H. Buck, "The Satsuma Rebellion of 1877: From Kagoshima through the Siege of Kumamoto Castle," *Monumenta Nipponica* 28, no. 4 (winter 1973): 443.

36. E. Herbert Norman, "The Genyōsha: A Study in the Origins of Japanese Imperialism," *Pacific Affairs* 17, no. 3 (September 1944): 265; Morris, *Nobility of Failure,* 221, 223.

37. For a short summary on the premodern history of gambling, see Yasumaru Yoshio, ed., *"Kangoku" no tanjō,* no. 22 of *Asahi hyakka rekishi o yominaosu* (Tokyo: Asahi Shinbunsha, 1995), 26. For a slightly longer discussion, see Tamura Eitarō, *Yakuza no seikatsu* (Tokyo: Yūzankaku, 1964), 8–16.

38. Tamura Eitarō focuses on temporary laborers and firefighters, while Hoshino Kanehiro suggests that poor peasants, samurai, sumo wrestlers, and craftsmen also became *bakuto.* Tamura, *Yakuza no seikatsu,* 17–19; Hoshino Kanehiro, "Organized Crime and Its Origins in Japan" (unpublished paper), 3. These dens were certainly not the only spaces in which people gambled. Tamura points out that gambling took place on domainal lords' estates (*yashiki*) since they enjoyed extraterritoriality and were thus protected from intrusions of town magistrates (*machi bugyō*) seeking to make arrests. Samurai estates (especially their barracks and storehouses) were also sites for gambling, as they were apparently difficult to enter as well. Tamura, *Yakuza no seikatsu,* 22–23.

Samurai who gambled were troublesome to the Tokugawa shogunate, which in criminalizing gambling meted out stiffer punishments to those of higher status. According to Daniel Botsman, "Under the first set of regulations [of the Kansei Reforms], issued in 1792, foot soldiers [*ashigaru*] and lackeys [*chūgen*] who engaged in any kind of gambling were to be automatically banished from the capital. Although this was not as severe as the punishment stipulated for higher-ranking warriors (they were to be exiled to a distant island), it was undoubtedly a heavier penalty than the fines ordinarily used to punish commoners who gambled. In 1795, moreover, the shogunate supplemented the earlier regulations with a decree stating that all warriors, including foot soldiers and lackeys, would automatically be exiled to a distant island if they were caught gambling within the grounds of their lord's mansion." Botsman, *Punishment and Power,* 72–73.

39. Kanda Yutsuki argues for an intimate connection between the *oyabun-kobun* relationship in *bakuto* organizations and the instructor-disciple, or disciple–sworn brother, relationship in sumo groups. He argues that as sumo wrestlers (a kind of violence specialist in and of themselves) also became *bakuto,* they brought with them their internal structure that helped shaped that of *bakuto* groups. Kanda Yutsuki, *Kinsei no geinō kōgyō to chiiki shakai* (Tokyo: Tōkyō Daigaku Shuppankai, 1999), 247–48.

The *bakuto* in their post–World War II incarnation as large mafia syndicates would remain bound by fictive, not blood, kinship ties. In this aspect, they differed from the Sicilian and Italian American mafias and were more similar to the Russian mafia. See Peter B. E. Hill, *The Japanese Mafia: Yakuza, Law, and the State* (Oxford: Oxford University Press, 2003); Diego Gambetta, *The Sicilian Mafia: The Business of Private Protection* (Cambridge, Mass.: Harvard University Press, 1993); Francis A. J. Ianni, *A Family Business: Kinship and Social Control in Organized Crime* (New York: Russell Sage Foundation, 1972); Federico Varese, *The Russian Mafia: Private Protection in a New Market Economy* (Oxford: Oxford University Press, 2001). For more on *bakuto* organization and ritual as they became increasingly sophisticated after the Tokugawa period, see Tamura, *Yakuza no seikatsu,* 44–45, 94–106; Iwai Hiroaki, *Byōri shūdan no kōzō: Oyabun kobun shūdan kenkyū* (Tokyo: Seishin Shobō, 1963), 128–30, 146–50, 160–61.

40. Masukawa Kōichi, *Tobaku no Nihonshi* (Tokyo: Heibonsha, 1989), 154–55. On the Tokugawa status system and why "mushuku" should not be translated as "homeless," see Botsman, *Punishment and Power,* 59–62. For a classic work in English on the issue of status (also cited by Botsman), see John W. Hall, "Rule by Status in Tokugawa Japan," *Journal of Japanese Studies* 1, no. 1 (autumn 1974): 39–49.

41. On big *bakuto* bosses of this time, see Imagawa Tokuzō, *Kōshō: Bakumatsu kyōkaku den* (Tokyo: Akita Shoten, 1973).

42. Abe Akira, *Edo no autorō: Mushuku to bakuto* (Tokyo: Kōdansha, 1999), 11–16, 20. See also Tamura, *Yakuza no seikatsu,* 179–205; Takahashi Satoshi, *Kunisada Chūji* (Tokyo: Iwanami Shoten, 2000). On the crime of evading a checkpoint, and on the practice of posting "tall signs" (*kōsatsu*), see Botsman, *Punishment and Power,* 19, 46.

43. Ambiguities about the place of *bakuto* in rural communities are reinforced by the lack of detailed information about specific villages and who gained and lost in local interactions. It would be helpful to know the composition of the people who helped the Kantō Regulatory Patrol pursue *bakuto* like Kunisada Chūji, for example, or who in the villages became the targets of extortion, blackmail, and burglary. Ōguchi Yūjirō discusses several crimes from the 1830s in the Tama region, including those with *mushuku* violence, to shed light on how villages dealt with such offenses and what the relationship was like between villages and bodies like the Kantō Regulatory Patrol. Ōguchi Yūjirō, "Mura no hanzai to Kantō torishimari shutsu yaku," in *Kinsei no mura to machi,* ed. Kawamura Masaru-sensei Kanreki Kinenkai (Tokyo: Yoshikawa Kōbunkan, 1988), 79–101.

44. Botsman notes that not all tattoos used to mark criminals were as plain as the lines on the arm preferred by the shogunate: "In Hiroshima Domain, for example, recidivists had the Chinese character for 'dog' tattooed onto the middle of their foreheads. In Kii the character for 'evil' (*aku*) was used." Botsman, *Punishment and Power,* 27–28. For a graphically appealing work on tattoos (also cited by Botsman), see Donald Richie and Ian Buruma, *The Japanese Tattoo* (New York: Weatherhill, 1980). The colorful, elaborate, and decorative tattoos continued to be a marker of yakuza in the post–World War II era.

45. Takie Sugiyama Lebra makes an argument in some ways similar for the postwar period: "Deviancy then can be viewed as a product of cultural strains or as an extreme expression of dominant values, rather than as a contrast to normative culture." Lebra emphasizes that this "extreme" expression is deviant, but for the Tokugawa period *bakuto* (or yakuza) culture was neither extreme nor deviant. Takie Sugiyama Lebra, "Organized Delinquency: *Yakuza* as a Cultural Example," in *Japanese Patterns of Behavior* (Honolulu: University of Hawai'i Press, 1986), 169.

Another example of a *bakuto* (or yakuza) ritual that had its roots in a broader Tokugawa phenomenon was *jingi,* the formalized greeting exchanged between *bakuto* (often between a traveler, or *tabinin,* and the boss of the residence in which he wanted to stay). It was originally performed by traveling artisans (*watari shokunin*) in the Tokugawa period who asked for training and work, and later by traveling laborers to ask for food and lodging from the head of the place where laborers gathered for work (*ninsoku yoseba*). For more on *jingi,* see Iwai, *Byōri shūdan no kōzō,* 262–67; Tamura, *Yakuza no seikatsu,* 59–60; Tamura Eitarō, "Jōshū asobinin fūzoku mondō," in *Ryūmin,* vol. 4 of *Kindai minshū no kiroku,* ed. Hayashi Hideo (Tokyo: Shinjinbutsu Jūraisha, 1971), 218–22. On tattooing methods, see Richie and Buruma, *Japanese Tattoo,* 85–99.

46. Iwai, *Byōri shūdan no kōzō,* 37; George A. De Vos and Keiichi Mizushima, "Organization and Social Function of Japanese Gangs: Historical Development and Modern Parallels," in *Socialization for Achievement: Essays on the Cultural Psychology of the Japanese,* ed. George A. De Vos (Berkeley: University of California Press, 1973), 286–87.

47. Yasumaru, *"Kangoku" no tanjō,* 27–28.

48. James W. White, *Ikki: Social Conflict and Political Protest in Early Modern Japan* (Ithaca: Cornell University Press, 1995), 4–6, 15.

49. Eric Hobsbawm, *Bandits* (New York: Delacorte Press, 1969), 13, 78.

50. Tamura, *Yakuza no seikatsu,* 19, 24. For laws and ordinances that pertained to *kyōkaku,* or "men of chivalry," see Ogata Tsurukichi, *Honpō kyōkaku no kenkyū* (Tokyo: Hakuhōsha, 1933), 309–14.

51. David L. Howell, "Hard Times in the Kantō: Economic Change and Village Life in Late Tokugawa Japan," *Modern Asian Studies* 23, no. 2 (1989): 358.

52. Botsman, *Punishment and Power,* 93–95. For *bakuto,* becoming a *meakashi* could translate into money and higher status. See Abe Yoshio, *Meakashi Kinjūrō no shōgai: Edo jidai shomin seikatsu no jitsuzō* (Tokyo: Chūō Kōronsha, 1981). Many thanks to Amy Stanley for this reference and several others in this chapter.

53. Yasumaru emphasizes this point that with a weak shogunate, a power vacuum was created in which *bakuto* could gain local prominence and challenge established forms of authority. Yasumaru, *"Kangoku" no tanjō,* 28.

54. Hasegawa Noboru, *Bakuto to jiyū minken: Nagoya jiken shimatsuki* (Tokyo: Heibonsha, 1995), 46–47.

55. The Kantō Regulatory Patrol system of 1805 and 1827 consisted of two people each from the four magistrate's offices (*daikansho*), or eight people in total. Under each person from the *daikansho* were two hired foot soldiers (*yatoi ashigaru*), one person of lower status (*komono*), and two guides (*michi annai*). One group consisted of six people, and two groups would join to form one patrol unit. Yasumaru, *"Kangoku" no tanjō,* 27.

56. On the Sicilian mafia's ideas of honor and *omertà* (literally, being a man), see Robert T. Anderson, "From Mafia to Cosa Nostra," *American Journal of Sociology* 71, no. 3 (November 1965): 302; Raimondo Catanzaro, *Men of Respect: A Social History of the Sicilian Mafia,* trans. Raymond Rosenthal (New York: Free Press, 1988), 31; Gaia Servadio, *Mafioso: A History of the Mafia from Its Origins to the Present Day* (New York: Stein and Day, 1976), 27–28. On the "thief-with-a-code-of-honor" (*vor-v-zakone* or *vor-zakonnik*) in Russia, see Varese, *Russian Mafia,* 145–66.

57. The list of artistic productions about Kunisada includes playwright Yukitomo Rifu's *Kunisada Chūji* (1919), Makino Shōzō's film *Kunisada Chūji* (1924), Kinugasa Teinōsuke's film *Wakaki hi no Chūji: Midagahara no satsujin* (1925), novelist Shimozawa Kan's *Kunisada Chūji* (Tokyo: Kaizōsha, 1933), Yamanaka Sadao's film *Kunisada Chūji* (1935), and Taniguchi Senkichi's *Kunisada Chūji* (1960).

58. The connection between gambling and the yakuza can be seen in the origins of that particular term. *Ya-ku-za* stands for eight-nine-three, which was a losing hand in a gambling card game known as *hanafuda* or *hanakaruta.* (Any sum of the cards that ended in zero was the weakest of hands. Since the sum of eight, nine, and three is 20, that particular combination was considered a losing hand.) The word "yakuza" suggests they were regarded as "losers" by some; it is not clear when the term was reappropriated and rid of this negative connotation. See Kata Kōji, *Nihon no yakuza* (Tokyo: Daiwa Shobō, 1993), 17.

59. Diego Gambetta has defined the mafia as "an industry which produces, promotes, and sells private protection." In relation to the attempt to establish a monopoly on protection, "Violence is a means, not an end; a resource, not the final product." Peter B. E. Hill adopts a variation of Gambetta's argument in his treatment of the postwar Japanese mafia. Gambetta, *Sicilian Mafia,* 1–2; Hill, *Japanese Mafia,* 6–35. Gambetta's emphasis on the mafia as an industry differs from those who have defined mafias by their way of life, "a state of mind, a system of thought and action." See Servadio, *Mafioso,* 20, 22.

60. Hasegawa adds that by the beginning of the Taisho period, there were about 14 *bakuto ikka* in Mikawa, of which the Hirai *ikka* was one of the two most important. Hasegawa, *Bakuto to jiyū minken,* 19–22, 29, 70–71.

61. Ibid., 62-63, 68-70, 72-80, 90-91.

62. Ibid., 70-72. For another work on *bakuto* during this period, see Takahashi Satoshi, *Bakuto no Bakumatsu ishin* (Tokyo: Chikuma Shobō, 2004).

63. On the grassroots dimension of the Freedom and People's Rights Movement, see Irokawa Daikichi, *The Culture of the Meiji Period,* trans. and ed. Marius B. Jansen (Princeton: Princeton University Press, 1985), 108-13.

64. Stephen Vlastos and Anne Walthall both argue that peasant protests in the first half of the Tokugawa period, at least, were typically not violent. Walthall notes that even with the destructive protests of *uchikowashi* or smashings, government offices were rarely targets. Stephen Vlastos, *Peasant Protests and Uprisings in Tokugawa Japan* (Berkeley: University of California Press, 1986), 3, 20; Anne Walthall, *Social Protest and Popular Culture in Eighteenth-Century Japan* (Tucson: University of Arizona Press, 1986), 15, 121. Also, James White points out that *bakuto* did not play a prominent role in popular contention before 1868. White, *Ikki,* 185-86.

65. Morinaga Eizaburō, "Gunma jiken: Bakuto to kunda fuhatsu no shibai," *Hōgaku seminā* 20, no. 14 (November 1976): 124; Tamura, "Jōshū asobinin fūzoku mondō," 216; Fukuda Kaoru, *Sanmin sōjōroku: Meiji jūshichinen Gunma jiken* (Tokyo: Seiyun Shobō, 1974), 16.

66. In Usui: the Arai *ikka.* In Takasaki: the Hamagawa, Fukushima, Kaneko, and Ōrui *ikka.* In Tomioka: the Ogushi and Tashima *ikka.* In Fujioka: the Tanaka and Yamayoshiya *ikka.* In Shimo Nita: the Yamatoya *ikka.* Shimizu Yoshiji, *Gunma jiyū minken undō no kenkyū: Jōmō Jiyūtō to gekka jiken* (Takasaki-shi: Asaosha, 1984), 184.

67. The 1878 law capped interest at 20 percent a year for loans less than ¥100, 15 percent for ¥100 to ¥1,000, and 12 percent for more than ¥1,000. The mechanism used (*kirikanekashi*) to get around the law was to take 20 to 30 percent of the principal as an advance on the loan so that, for instance, a lender recorded to have taken out a ¥100 loan would only receive ¥70 or ¥80. If the loan was not repaid in the predesignated amount of time, interest would be assessed, the original loan would be rewritten as a new loan that treated the original principal plus the interest as the new principal, and interest would be charged on the new principal. For example, 5 percent interest would be assessed on a principal of ¥100 (of which only ¥70 or ¥80 was issued) making the new principal ¥105, on which another 20 percent interest would be charged, bringing the total amount owed to ¥126. Tanaka Sen'ya, "Chichibu bōdō zatsuroku," in *Tanaka Sen'ya nikki,* ed. Ōmura Susumu, Kobayashi Takeo, and Koike Shin'ichi (1884; reprint, Urawa: Saitama Shinbunsha Shuppankyoku, 1977), 586-87; Gunma-ken Keisatsushi Hensan Iinkai, *Gunma-ken keisatsushi,* 336-37.

68. The price of one *kin* of raw silk from 1880 to 1885: 1880, ¥6.742; 1881, ¥7.859; 1882, ¥6.936; 1883, ¥5.021; 1884, ¥5.844; 1885, ¥4.983. Gunma-ken Keisatsushi Hensan Iinkai, *Gunma-ken keisatsushi,* 336.

69. Morinaga, "Gunma jiken," 124; Fukuda, *Sanmin sōjōroku,* 16; Hattori Shisō quoted in Shimizu, *Gunma jiyū minken undō,* 187.

70. Gamblers were to be imprisoned for one month to four years and fined ¥5 to ¥200. Gamblers who formed groups, carried weapons, and/or infested neighboring areas were to be imprisoned for one to ten years and fined ¥50 to ¥500. Gambling paraphernalia would be confiscated, and police were permitted to enter any person's home at any time with the equivalent of a warrant. Hagiwara Susumu, "Gunma-ken bakuto torishimari kō," in *Ryūmin,* vol. 4 of *Kindai minshū no kiroku,* ed. Hayashi Hideo (Tokyo: Shinjinbutsu Jūraisha, 1971), 577; Shimizu, *Gunma jiyū minken undō,* 185-86.

71. Fukuda, *Sanmin sōjōroku,* 17; Hagiwara, "Gunma-ken bakuto torishimari kō," 578.

72. The number of people punished in the several years after 1884 were as follows: 1,012 in 1885; 1,002 in 1886; 876 in 1887. Gunma-ken Keisatsushi Hensan Iinkai, *Gunma-ken keisatsushi,* 383. The chart printed in this source skips 1888 but continues through 1892; presumably the data after 1889 are based on punishment under a different

antigambling law, because the Tobaku Han Shobun Kisoku was repealed in 1889. Hagiwara, "Gunma-ken bakuto torishimari kō," 577.

73. To give some examples: Miyabe Noboru of the Yūshinsha had mediated a disagreement between *bakuto* with patience and a light hand, and formed a good relationship with *bakuto* in the region when he served as head of the Maebashi police; *kesshiha* member Arai Kisaburō and Jiyūtō radical Murakami Yasuharu in Chichibu knew *bakuto* boss Iwai Ushigorō; and the Jiyūtō also worked with *bakuto* Iwai Kisaburō, Jōnosuke, and Tamagorō. Tamura, "Jōshū asobinin fūzoku mondō," 215.

74. Fukuda, *Sanmin sōjōroku*, 16–17, 95; Hagiwara Susumu, *Gunma-ken yūminshi* (Tokyo: Kokusho Kankōkai, 1980), 139; Morinaga, "Gunma jiken," 126; see also Sekito Kakuzō, ed., *Tōsui minkenshi* (1903; reprint, Tokyo: Meiji Bunken, 1966).

75. Fukuda, *Sanmin sōjōroku*, 96; Hagiwara, *Gunma-ken yūminshi*, 139.

76. Gunma-ken Keisatsushi Hensan Iinkai, *Gunma-ken keisatsushi*, 337–39; Hagiwara, *Gunma-ken yūminshi*, 137.

77. Uda Tomoi and Wada Saburō, eds., *Jiyūtōshi* (Tokyo: Gosharō, 1910), 206–7.

78. Gunma-ken Keisatsushi Hensan Iinkai, *Gunma-ken keisatsushi*, 339; Hagiwara, *Gunma-ken yūminshi*, 140; Morinaga, "Gunma jiken," 126; Uda and Wada, *Jiyūtōshi*, 207.

79. Fukuda, *Sanmin sōjōroku*, 11, 127, 130–31; Hagiwara, *Gunma-ken yūminshi*, 141; Morinaga, "Gunma jiken," 126.

80. The imprisonment of Seki illustrates the extent to which movement leaders and *bakuto* shared information and protection. There are discrepancies about certain details of this incident, but the general story is as follows. The problem began in January 1884, when Seki illegally opened a gambling establishment that he subsequently learned was being watched by the police. Seki was then approached by Fujita Jōkichi, described by some sources as a detective or agent and an acquaintance of Seki, who suggested that a deal could be brokered: if Seki turned himself in, he would receive only 60 to 70 days of punishment. On Fujita's recommendation, Seki delivered himself to the Matsuida police. But then he received the maximum punishment under the new antigambling law: 10 years of imprisonment with hard labor and a ¥50 fine. Fujita's betrayal of Seki angered Arai *ikka bakuto* Machida Tsurugorō and Jingū Mojūrō, who on April 1 decided to avenge Seki's imprisonment. On the night of April 3, Machida and Jingū bore swords and went to Fujita's home. They waited until a guest departed from the house, then set fire to a door. Fujita came out of the house wielding his sword and attacked a surprised Machida who, not having had time to draw his own weapon, fought back with the club in his hand. Jingū rushed into the fray and fatally injured Fujita, then carried the wounded Machida on his back as they escaped from the scene. Machida did not survive the night, and Fujita died on April 6. The *bakuto* Jingū, who was suffering from injuries to his chest and shoulders, took refuge in the home of people's rights leader Miura Momonosuke who hid him in a storehouse owned by fellow movement organizer Shimizu Eizaburō. Gunma-ken Keisatsushi Hensan Iinkai, *Gunma-ken keisatsushi*, 339–40; Fukuda, *Sanmin sōjōroku*, 97, 100, 110–12; Hagiwara, *Gunma-ken yūminshi*, 140; Morinaga, "Gunma jiken," 126.

81. Estimates for the number of people gathered generally range from 200 to 3,000. Gunma-ken Keisatsushi Hensan Iinkai, *Gunma-ken keisatsushi*, 342; Hagiwara, *Gunma-ken yūminshi*, 141–42; Morinaga, "Gunma jiken," 126.

82. Hagiwara, *Gunma-ken yūminshi*, 142. Some argue that the police station was not actually raided. See Gunma-ken Keisatsushi Hensan Iinkai, *Gunma-ken keisatsushi*, 344; *Shimono shinbun*, May 22, 1884, in *MNJ*, vol. 3, 261.

83. Fukuda, *Sanmin sōjōroku*, 11; Gunma-ken Keisatsushi Hensan Iinkai, *Gunma-ken keisatsushi*, 340, 344; Hagiwara, *Gunma-ken yūminshi*, 142–43; Morinaga, "Gunma jiken," 126–27; *Shimono shinbun*, May 22, 1884, in *MNJ*, vol. 3, 261.

84. Gunma-ken Keisatsushi Hensan Iinkai, *Gunma-ken keisatsushi*, 345; Morinaga, "Gunma jiken," 126–27.

85. In the Meiji Criminal Code of 1880, later known as the Kyū Keihō (Old Criminal Code) to distinguish it from the Criminal Code of 1907, crimes were divided into three categories: grave offenses or felonies (*jūzai*), minor offenses or misdemeanors (*keizai*), and offenses against police regulations (*ikeizai*). "Jūchōeki" and "jūkinko" both translate as "imprisonment with hard labor." *Jūchōeki* was usually a stiffer punishment for grave offenses with a term of nine to 11 years, *jūkinko* generally a punishment for minor offenses with a term of 11 days to five years. *Keichōeki* was also imprisonment with hard labor but for six to eight years. See Articles 1, 22, and 24 of the Meiji Criminal Code in Wagatsuma Sakae, ed., *Kyū hōreishū* (Tokyo: Yūhikaku, 1968), 431.

86. Morinaga, "Gunma jiken," 127; Tamura, "Jōshū asobinin fūzoku mondō," 215.

87. Fukuda argues that Yamada and Seki could not have overtaken the garrison and that the plan laid out for the May 1 attack was a "strategy like a yakuza fight" (*yakuza no kenkateki sakusen*). Fukuda, *Sanmin sōjōroku*, 131–33; Morinaga, "Gunma jiken," 127.

88. Charles Tilly, *The Politics of Collective Violence* (Cambridge: Cambridge University Press, 2003), 4–5.

89. Hagiwara would probably disagree with the political tinge with which I have colored the *bakuto* because he contends the *bakuto* were hired. Someone like Yamada may very well have received money from the leaders, but it seems wrong to see the *bakuto* as mere hired guns. First, it is unclear how the organizers of the incident could have compensated Yamada and Seki adequately for the participation of 2,500 of their henchmen. If money alone were the motivation for the *bakuto*, the sum would presumably have to be substantial. Second, if the *bakuto* were simply hired strongmen, it is unlikely that Yamada and Seki would have been involved in the planning or that such a network would have existed between the *bakuto* and the incident's organizers. See Hagiwara, *Gunma-ken yūminshi*, 142.

90. Hagiwara makes a similar argument, but he sees their parasitic nature as the engine for change in *bakuto* (Hagiwara uses the term "yakuza"). In essence, the yakuza as "social parasites" (*shakaiteki na kiseichū*) adapted to protect themselves and maintain a hold on their new Meiji-era hosts. This line of thinking does not explain why the *bakuto* chose to act in a political realm, much less one that put itself in direct opposition to the Meiji state. If financial well-being was their main concern, they likely would have done just as well to focus on gambling, extortion, prostitution, and the like. Hagiwara, *Gunma-ken yūminshi*, 137–38, 142.

91. Hasegawa, *Bakuto to jiyū minken*, 11, 101–5.

92. The standard length of imprisonment for being caught gambling had been one or two months. Under the new law, it was not uncommon for bosses to serve four years or more and for important henchmen to serve two years or more. Even lower-ranking henchmen might be in prison for a year or so. I draw the parallel to RICO (Racketeer Influenced and Corrupt Organizations Act of 1970), a U.S. federal law, because of the similar targeting of "enterprise crime," which makes it illegal to simply belong to a group or enterprise involved in certain criminal activities.

93. Hasegawa, *Bakuto to jiyū minken*, 126, 140–43, 148–49, 162, 171–76, 183–95, 213–39.

94. Ibid., 203–4, 223–25, 242–45, 251.

95. Kuno and three other Jiyūtō types had been arrested a week earlier for suspected connection with the Iida Incident, an attempt to overthrow the government that was part of the Freedom and People's Rights Movement. It was the December 14 robbery, however, that tied them to the Nagoya Incident. Hasegawa, *Bakuto to jiyū minken*, 251–53.

96. Seven were punished with life imprisonment, some for manslaughter and others for inflicting injury in the commission of a robbery. Eleven would die while imprisoned.

And the basis for the three not-guilty verdicts was insufficient evidence. Hasegawa, *Bakuto to jiyū minken*, 243, 255–58. See also Terasaki Osamu, *Meiji Jiyūtō no kenkyū*, ge-kan (Tokyo: Keiō Tsūshin, 1987), 105–14. Note that Terasaki refers to the Nagoya Incident participants as "shishi."

97. Chishima Hisashi, *Konmintō hōki: Chichibu nōmin sensō to Tashiro Eisuke ron* (Tokyo: Tahata Shobō, 1983), 280, 324; Wagatsuma Sakae et al., eds., *Nihon seiji saiban shiroku: Meiji, go* (Tokyo: Dai-ichi Hōki, 1969), 80.

98. Suda Tsutomu, "'Akutō' no jūkyū seiki: Minshū undō no henshitsu to 'kindai ikōki'" (Tokyo: Aoki Shoten, 2002), 168–72.

99. David Howell points out that many participants in the Chichibu Incident had a millenarian vision. See David Howell, "Visions of the Future in Meiji Japan," in *Historical Perspectives on Contemporary East Asia,* ed. Merle Goldman and Andrew Gordon (Cambridge, Mass.: Harvard University Press, 2000), 107–8. Inada Masahiro makes a similar observation, but he notes that the Chichibu Incident was much more than a "world renewal rebellion" in its direct challenge to the state. Inada Masahiro, *Nihon kindai shakai seiritsuki no minshū undō: Konmintō kenkyū josetsu* (Tokyo: Chikuma Shobō, 1990), 222–23, 226.

100. Ōmiya-gō Keisatsusho, "Dai-ikkai jinmon chōsho: Tashiro Eisuke," November 15, 1884, in *CJS*, 100; *Yūbin hōchi shinbun*, November 6, 1884, in *CJSS*, vol. 6, 381; Takahashi Tetsurō, *Richigi naredo, ninkyōsha: Chichibu Konmintō sōri Tashiro Eisuke* (Tokyo: Gendai Kikakushitsu, 1998), 60; Chishima, *Konmintō hōki*, 45–50, 58.

101. Inada, *Nihon kindai shakai seiritsuki no minshū undō*, 219–20; Azami Yoshio, *Chichibu jikenshi* (Tokyo: Gensōsha, 1990), 60; Takahashi, *Richigi naredo, ninkyōsha*, 60. For more on sericulture in this general region, see Chapter 5 of Kären Wigen, *The Making of a Japanese Periphery, 1750-1920* (Berkeley: University of California Press, 1995). Tashiro's need to borrow money seems to contradict the image of a man with financial means adequate enough to take extrafamilial members into his home(s). It is possible, however, that the figure of 23 people in his household, taken from an 1880 register, was not maintained over the next two to three years. Also, note that some of Tashiro Eisuke's land went to his creditor in the summer of 1885, several months after Tashiro was executed. Hirano Yoshitarō, "Chichibu Konmintō ni ikita hitobito," in *Chichibu Konmintō ni ikita hitobito,* ed. Nakazawa Ichirō (Tokyo: Gendai Shuppankai, 1977), 67.

102. Roger W. Bowen, *Rebellion and Democracy in Meiji Japan: A Study of Commoners in the Popular Rights Movement* (Berkeley: University of California Press, 1980), 53–54; Arai Sajirō, *Chichibu Konmingun kaikeichō: Inoue Denzō* (Tokyo: Shinjinbutsu Ōraisha, 1981), 87; Gunma-ken Keisatsushi Hensan Iinkai, *Gunma-ken keisatsushi*, 347–48.

103. Some historians have pointed to this close relationship between the Konmintō and Jiyūtō in Chichibu as a reason for why feelings of frustration with financial conditions and with the state were forcefully expressed in the form of a popular uprising. Irokawa Daikichi, for example, argues that the overlap between the Konmintō and Jiyūtō in Chichibu led to this violent incident while in the impoverished area of Busō, tensions between the group and the party undermined efforts to stage an effective uprising and, in fact, prompted the Konmintō to attack the banks and financial institutions managed by Jiyūtō members. Irokawa Daikichi, *Konmintō to Jiyūtō* (Tokyo: Yōransha, 1984), 18–19, 23–25; see also Inada, *Nihon kindai shakai seiritsuki no minshū undō*, 24–25, 29–34, 223–24.

104. Takasaki Keisatsusho, "Dai-nikai jinmon chōsho: Kokashiwa Tsunejirō," November 15, 1884, in *CJSS*, vol. 3, 175. There is little, if any, debate about Katō being a *bakuto.* A prosecutor described Katō as someone with influence on *bakuto* society, and Tashiro alluded to Katō's *bakuto* connections in his testimony. Ōmiya-gō Keisatsusho, "Dai-gokai jinmon chōsho: Tashiro Eisuke," November 19, 1884, in *CJS*, 117; Chishima, *Konmintō hōki*, 312.

105. Azami, *Chichibu jikenshi*, 21–22; Bowen, *Rebellion and Democracy*, 277; Chishima, *Konmintō hōki*, 312. For descriptions of Katō as a boss and/or *bakuto*, see also Matsumoto Ken'ichi, "Bōto to eiyū to: Inano Bunjirō oboegaki," *Tenbō* 233 (May 1978): 118; Wagatsuma et al., *Nihon seiji saiban shiroku*, 72.

106. Chishima, *Konmintō hōki*, 115–16; Azami, *Chichibu jikenshi*, 21–22; Takahashi, *Richigi naredo, ninkyōsha*, 27.

107. There is some question as to whether Tashiro ever became an official member of the Jiyūtō. In a police interrogation after the Chichibu Incident, Tashiro stated that he joined the Jiyūtō in late January or early February 1884, but his name was never printed in the *Jiyūtō shinbun* along with other new inductees. Ōmiya-gō Keisatsusho, "Dai-gokai jinmon chōsho: Tashiro Eisuke," 114–15; Chishima, *Konmintō hōki*, 126–28.

108. Ōmiya-gō Keisatsusho, "Dai-gokai jinmon chōsho: Tashiro Eisuke," 116; *Yomiuri shinbun*, November 18, 1884, in Takahashi, *Richigi naredo, ninkyōsha*, 79; Ōmiya-gō Keisatsusho, "Dai-ikkai jinmon chōsho: Tashiro Eisuke," 100; Azami, *Chichibu jikenshi*, 365; Koike Yoshitaka, *Chichibu oroshi: Chichibu jiken to Inoue Denzō* (Tokyo: Gendaishi Shuppankai, 1974), 84; Bowen, *Rebellion and Democracy*, 278; Takahashi, *Richigi naredo, ninkyōsha*, 91–92; Chishima, *Konmintō hōki*, 59; Nakajima Kōzō, *Inoue Denzō: Chichibu jiken to haiku* (Saku: Yūshorin, 2000), 110.

109. Ōmiya-gō Keisatsusho, "Dai-ikkai jinmon chōsho: Tashiro Eisuke," 101; Takahashi, *Richigi naredo, ninkyōsha*, 19–20; Chishima, *Konmintō hōki*, 131.

110. Inoue Mitsusaburō and Shinagawa Eiji, *Shashin de miru Chichibu jiken* (Tokyo: Shinjinbutsu Ōraisha, 1982), 32.

111. Chishima, *Konmintō hōki*, 227–28; Nakajima, *Inoue Denzō*, 6; Azami, *Chichibu jikenshi*, 42; Bowen, *Rebellion and Democracy*, 57; Gunma-ken Keisatsushi Hensan Iinkai, *Gunma-ken keisatsushi*, 349; Irokawa Daikichi, "Minshūshi no naka no Chichibu jiken," *Chichibu* (March 1995): 6.

112. Tashiro's henchman Shibaoka Kumakichi was an asset in the attacks—he participated in two robberies on the night of October 14. He would later serve as treasurer and company commander of the Konmingun. Azami, *Chichibu jikenshi*, 42, 56; Chishima, *Konmintō hōki*, 250; Takahashi, *Richigi naredo, ninkyōsha*, 110–12, 116–19; Gunma-ken Keisatsushi Hensan Iinkai, *Gunma-ken keisatsushi*, 351–52; Wagatsuma et al., *Nihon seiji saiban shiroku*, 75.

113. There are also mentions of specific *bakuto*, such as Aoki Jintarō and his four henchmen, who were all Chichibu rebels. From the *Jiyūtōshi* (1910) in *Jiyū jichi gannen: Chichibu jiken shiryō, ronbun to kaisetsu*, ed. Ide Magoroku (Tokyo: Gendaishi Shuppankai, 1975), 65; Takahashi, *Richigi naredo, ninkyōsha*, 41.

114. Ōmiya-gō Keisatsusho, "Dai-nikai jinmon chōsho: Tashiro Eisuke," November 16, 1884, in *CJS*, 103–4, 106–7; Chishima, *Konmintō hōki*, 279–81. The designation of officers was not unlike that for the *shishi*'s Yamato Rebellion in 1863. Huber, "'Men of High Purpose,'" 117.

115. Ōmiya-gō Keisatsusho, "Dai-nikai jinmon chōsho: Tashiro Eisuke," 107; Chishima, *Konmintō hōki*, 8, 279–81, 315; Takahashi, *Richigi naredo, ninkyōsha*, 149, 153, 234; Bowen, *Rebellion and Democracy*, 60–61; Wagatsuma et al., *Nihon seiji saiban shiroku*, 75.

116. Irokawa, *Konmintō to Jiyūtō*, 25; Gunma-ken Keisatsushi Hensan Iinkai, *Gunma-ken keisatsushi*, 361–62, 371; Chishima, *Konmintō hōki*, 9, 337.

117. Ōmiya-gō Keisatsu Tōbu, "Taiho tsūchi: Tashiro Eisuke," November 15, 1884, in *CJSS*, vol. 1, 31; Chishima, *Konmintō hōki*, 9–10, 316, 337–39; Takahashi, *Richigi naredo, ninkyōsha*, 291–94, 302; Takano, *Chichibu jiken*, 132–33.

118. Bowen, *Rebellion and Democracy*, 64–65; Takahashi, *Richigi naredo, ninkyōsha*, 305; Matsumoto, "Bōto to eiyū to," 117; Wagatsuma et al., *Nihon seiji saiban shiroku*, 76.

119. Sakamoto was likely a henchman of Katō Orihei. Inano Bunjirō was an alleged *bakuto* who in mid-October 1884 had been sentenced to two months of imprisonment with hard labor (*jūkinko*), a ¥4 fine, and six months of surveillance for absconding with money (*kaitai*); he evaded this punishment and joined the Konmintō somewhere around Minano on November 3. Arai had served two months of imprisonment with hard labor (*jūkinko*) and paid a ¥5 fine in September 1883 for a gambling conviction; and Yokota had served 80 days of imprisonment with hard labor (*chōeki*) for his gambling activities. Kobayashi Yūzō was a *bakuto* of the Tamagawa *ikka* who had served two months of imprisonment with hard labor (*jūkinko*) with a ¥5 fine in January 1882, and three months of imprisonment with hard labor (*jūkinko*) with a ¥7 fine for gambling. Kobayashi was originally a spy for the police, but, upon his capture by the Konmingun on November 2, served with the rebel army as far as Nagano Prefecture and killed a policeman from Gunma along the way, a crime for which he was executed the following year in Maebashi. Matsumoto, "Bōto to eiyū to," 117–19, 122–23; Chishima, *Konmintō hōki*, 311, 314; Azami, *Chichibu jikenshi*, 365.

Scholar Arai Sajirō is certainly wrong to say that *bakuto* did not play an important role in the organization of the Chichibu uprising. Arai Sajirō, "Meijiki bakuto to Chichibu jiken: Sono kyojitsu o jimoto shiryō de tadasu," *Shin Nihon bungaku* 34, no. 1 (January 1979): 131.

120. Matsumoto, "Bōto to eiyū to," 125–26; Gunma-ken Keisatsushi Hensan Iinkai, *Gunma-ken keisatsushi*, 373; Bowen, *Rebellion and Democracy*, 65–67; Chishima, *Konmintō hōki*, 11.

121. Tashiro Eisuke was found guilty by Article 138, Section 2, of the Meiji Criminal Code of 1880. Urawa Jūzai Saibansho, "Saiban iiwatashisho: Tashiro Eisuke," February 19, 1885, in *CJSS*, vol. 1, 53–56. Those sentenced to death were: Tashiro Eisuke, Katō Orihei, Arai Shūzaburō, Takagishi Zenkichi, Sakamoto Sōsaku, Kikuchi Kanbei, and Inoue Denzō. Inoue was sentenced even though he successfully evaded capture by escaping to Hokkaidō. Punishments for the leaders of the guerrilla phase of the incident were as follows. Kikuchi Kanbei was sentenced in absentia; his term was reduced to life imprisonment with hard labor (*muki chōeki*) as part of a general amnesty in 1889. Inano was sentenced to 15 years of penal servitude (*tokei*) in Hokkaidō but was released early for an unspecified reason. Kobayashi was sentenced to death for the murder of the policeman. Yokota served eight and Arai served six years of imprisonment with hard labor (*jūchōeki*). Wagatsuma et al., *Nihon seiji saiban shiroku*, 78, 81; Matsumoto, "Bōto to eiyū to," 126–27.

122. See the November 5, 1884, issues of *Asahi shinbun, Meiji nippō,* and *Tōkyō nichinichi shinbun; Meiji nippō,* November 25, 1884; *Tōkyō nichinichi shinbun,* November 15, 1884, in *CJSS*, vol. 6, 852, 965, 951, 627, 506.

123. *Tōkyō nichinichi shinbun,* November 17, 1884, in *CJSS*, vol. 6, 506; Bowen, *Rebellion and Democracy*, 296.

124. Tanaka, "Chichibu bōdō zatsuroku," 586; Bowen, *Rebellion and Democracy*, 259; Chishima, *Konmintō hōki*, 300–301.

125. The quotation is from the English translation of a *Yūbin hōchi shinbun* article that appeared in the *Japan Weekly Mail*, November 8, 1884.

126. *Japan Weekly Mail*, December 13, 1884.

127. *Kaishin shinbun,* November 8, 1884, in *CJSS*, vol. 6, 974.

128. Christopher Duggan, *Fascism and the Mafia* (New Haven: Yale University Press, 1989), 23–27, 85–86.

129. *Chōya shinbun,* November 11, 1884, in Ide, *Jiyū jichi gannen*, 34–35.

130. *Meiji nippō,* November 15, 1884, in *CJSS*, vol. 6, 970. The *Jiji shinpō* also discussed how *bakuto* had infested the villages since the enactment of the gambling law, and the *Yūbin hōchi shinbun* dealt with the gambling law as a possible explanation for why *bakuto*

participated in the incident. *Jiji shinpō*, November 21, 1884; *Yūbin hōchi shinbun*, November 6, 1884, in *CJSS*, vol. 6, 949, 379.

Not unlike the press at the time, Japanese historians too have constructed *bakuto*, and Tashiro Eisuke in particular, in ways that resonate with their interpretation of the larger event—their stand on the issue of Tashiro's identity as a *bakuto* has tended to reveal their underlying framework for understanding the Chichibu Incident. Scholars who argued that Tashiro was not a *bakuto* generally placed the incident squarely in the Freedom and People's Rights Movement or stressed the ideological sophistication of the masses. Inoue Kōji, for example, reduced Tashiro to a mere "figurehead," emphasizing instead the importance of the more politically informed Jiyūtō and Konmintō leaders and the role of the enlightened masses. He generally downplayed the idea of *bakuto* participation in the incident and mentioned that the term "oyabun" could refer to any kind of boss and did not necessarily imply a connection with gambling (a valid point). Chishima Hisashi, who also suggested that the use of "oyabun" to describe Tashiro did not mean that he was a *bakuto* boss, went on to argue that there is no evidence that Tashiro managed a gambling house and that a true *bakuto* boss could have recruited more of his henchmen to participate in the incident. For Chishima, downplaying the criminal element of Tashiro's character was consistent with his overarching interpretation of the incident as centering on the people's desire for justice.

In contrast to Inoue and Chishima, the historians who freely labeled Tashiro a *bakuto* tended to have a positive (even romanticized) view of *bakuto* and were typically not concerned with placing him or the incident in the context of the Freedom and People's Rights Movement. Takahashi Tetsurō only wavered on the question of whether Tashiro was a professional or amateur *bakuto* and focused on the leader's chivalry and sense of justice. Matsumoto Ken'ichi, though only mentioning Tashiro, discussed various other *bakuto* who, he claims, contributed a kind of valor (*eiyū*) to the uprising. Inoue Kōji, *Chichibu jiken: Jiyū minken no nōmin hōki* (Tokyo: Chūō Kōronsha, 1968), 37; Chishima, *Konmintō hōki*, 55, 350–51; Takahashi, *Richigi naredo, ninkyōsha*, 88–90; Matsumoto, "Bōto to eiyū to," 117–28.

Implicit in the desire of Inoue and Chishima to distance *bakuto* from the Chichibu Incident is the assumption that violence and criminality are somehow opposed to democracy. Affirming Tashiro Eisuke's identity as a *bakuto* or acknowledging the extent of *bakuto* participation in this most sustained of the violent incidents in the Freedom and People's Rights Movement would somehow make it seem less democratic, less grassroots, less ideological. Neither Inoue nor Chishima considered the possibility that the incident was both violent and democratic.

For an exceptionally evenhanded and nonromanticized treatment of both Tashiro Eisuke and the Chichibu Incident, see Yasumaru Yoshio, "Konmintō no ishiki katei," *Shisō* 726 (December 1984): 90–95.

131. On the difficulty the Meiji government faced in building up the state's violent arms (the police and the military), see Obinata Sumio, *Nihon kindai kokka no seiritsu to keisatsu* (Tokyo: Azekura Shobō, 1992); D. Eleanor Westney, *Imitation and Innovation: The Transfer of Western Organizational Patterns to Meiji Japan* (Cambridge, Mass.: Harvard University Press, 1987); Tobe Ryōichi, *Gyakusetsu no guntai* (Tokyo: Chūō Kōronsha, 1998); Roger F. Hackett, *Yamagata Aritomo in the Rise of Modern Japan, 1838–1922* (Cambridge, Mass.: Harvard University Press, 1971). Many thanks to Colin Jaundrill for bringing Tobe's book to my attention.

132. Weber's characterization of a state as having a monopoly on the legitimate use of force is problematic not only because the concept of a monopoly is vague, but also because it (wrongly) implies that all state violence is legitimate. See Max Weber, *Economy and Society: An Outline of Interpretive Sociology*, vol. 1, trans. Ephraim Fischoff et al., ed. Guenther Roth and Claus Wittich (Berkeley: University of California Press, 1978), 54.

133. Antonio Gramsci stressed that the political leadership shortchanged political change by not brokering an alliance with the subaltern. He inspired Marxists, who stressed the harshness of government repression. In contrast, Riall focuses on the resistance of local elites to the modern centralizing state. L. J. Riall, "Liberal Policy and the Control of Public Order in Western Sicily 1860–1862," *Historical Journal* 35, no. 2 (June 1992): 345–51, 355, 365–68.

Note that I am using "mafia" with a lowercase "m" here, as opposed to "Mafia" that suggests the existence of a widespread network of mafias, which, as mentioned above, the Italian government claimed was what plagued it in Sicily. On the origins of the mafia in Sicily, see Gambetta, *Sicilian Mafia,* 75–99.

For a classic piece on why the Tokugawa to Meiji transition was relatively smooth, see Thomas C. Smith, "Japan's Aristocratic Revolution," in *Native Sources of Japanese Industrialization* (Berkeley: University of California Press, 1988), 133–47.

134. Brown himself states it well: "The Faustian pact that ordinary citizens made with the so-called forces of order enabled the creation of a modern 'security state' based on administrative surveillance, coercive policing, and the legitimacy that came with restoring and maintaining order." Howard G. Brown, *Ending the French Revolution: Violence, Justice, and Repression from the Terror to Napoleon* (Charlottesville: University of Virginia Press, 2006), 8, 14–16; on "the militarization of repression," 119–233.

2. Violent Democracy

1. Carol Gluck, *Japan's Modern Myths: Ideology in the Late Meiji Period* (Princeton: Princeton University Press, 1985), 42–45; Takashi Fujitani, *Splendid Monarchy: Power and Pageantry in Modern Japan* (Berkeley: University of California Press, 1996), 76–78.

2. George Akita, *Foundations of Constitutional Government in Modern Japan, 1868–1900* (Cambridge, Mass.: Harvard University Press, 1967), 13.

3. Daniel Ross, *Violent Democracy* (Cambridge: Cambridge University Press, 2004), 7–8.

4. Irokawa Daikichi, *The Culture of the Meiji Period,* trans. and ed. Marius B. Jansen (Princeton: Princeton University Press, 1985); Roger W. Bowen, *Rebellion and Democracy in Meiji Japan: A Study of Commoners in the Popular Rights Movement* (Berkeley: University of California Press, 1980); Banno Junji, *Meiji demokurashī* (Tokyo: Iwanami Shoten, 2005).

5. *Jiji shinpō,* April 28, 1882, in *MNJ,* vol. 2, 296; *Yūbin hōchi shinbun,* November 22, 1883, in *MNJ,* vol. 3, 363; Takahashi Hikohiro, "Ingaidan no keisei: Takeuchi Takeshi-shi no kikigaki o chūshin ni," *Shakai rōdō kenkyū* 30, no. 3–4 (March 1984): 106; Ozaki Yukio, *The Autobiography of Ozaki Yukio: The Struggle for Constitutional Government in Japan,* trans. Hara Fujiko (Princeton: Princeton University Press, 2001), 94. Neither Hoshi nor Ozaki seems to have been aware of the Chinese origins of the term "sōshi," which dated back to around 200 B.C. and had connotations of sacrificing oneself for a principle, in particular, opposition to despotic rule. Matenrō Shatō, *Ingaidan shuki: Seitō kaikaku no kyūsho* (Tokyo: Jichōsha, 1935), 57.

6. Tōyama Shigeki et al., eds., "Santama no sōshi," in *Meiji no ninaite,* jō-kan, vol. 11 of *Jinbutsu Nihon no rekishi* (Tokyo: Yomiuri Shinbunsha, 1965), 181.

7. Umeda Matajirō, *Sōshi no honbun* (Tokyo: Hakubundō, 1889), 14. See also Shimizu Ryōzō, *Sōshi undō: Shakai no hana* (Tokyo: Kankōdō, 1887); Uchimura Gijō, *Meiji shakai: Sōshi no undō* (Osaka: Shōundō, 1888). Note that Umeda was attempting to rehabilitate, not maintain, the positive image of *sōshi.* See Kimura Naoe, *"Seinen" no tanjō: Meiji Nihon ni okeru seijiteki jissen no tenkan* (Tokyo: Shin'yōsha, 1998), 276–79.

8. *Kokumin no tomo,* April 3, 1887; *Chōya shinbun,* April 5, 1887.

9. *Chōya shinbun,* September 6, 1887; *Kokumin no tomo,* November 15, 1887.

10. *Chōya shinbun,* February 23, 1888. A Jiyūtō history originally published in 1910 by its founder Itagaki Taisuke also used the terms "sōshi" and "shishi sōshi" to describe those who advocated popular rights. Itagaki Taisuke, *Jiyūtōshi,* ge-kan, ed. Tōyama Shigeki and Satō Shigerō (1910; reprint, Tokyo: Iwanami Shoten, 1958), 279.

11. Irokawa Daikichi argues that these *sōshi* of the first half of the Meiji period, whom he calls "seinen shishi" (youth *shishi*), differed from the ruffians of later decades in their profoundly ideological nature and their clear commitment to the idea of popular rights. Irokawa Daikichi and Murano Ren'ichi, *Murano Tsuneemon den* (Tokyo: Chūō Kōron Jigyō Shuppan, 1969), 142–43.

12. One article listed the incidents in which *sōshi* were involved: the attack on Ōkubo Toshimichi, as well as the Fukushima, Takada, Kabasan, Saitama, Iida, and Shizuoka Incidents. *Kokumin no tomo,* August 15, 1887.

13. Takahashi Tetsuo, *Fuun: Fukushima no minken sōshi* (Tokyo: Rekishi Shunju Shuppan, 2002), 20, 24–25; Wagatsuma Sakae et al., eds., *Nihon seiji saiban shiroku: Meiji, go* (Tokyo: Dai-ichi Hōki, 1969), 43–53; Satō Kōtarō, *Santama no sōshi* (Tokyo: Musashi Shobō, 1973), 10–14. Note that Wagatsuma uses the term "shishi" to describe the Kabasan Incident participants.

14. Wagatsuma et al., eds., *Nihon seiji saiban shiroku,* 53–56; Tezuka Yutaka, *Jiyū minken saiban no kenkyū,* chū-kan (Tokyo: Keiō Tsūshin, 1982), 133. Some were tried for breaking a special law to control explosives, enacted on December 27, 1884, in light of the Kabasan Incident. Tezuka, *Jiyū minken saiban no kenkyū,* 132.

15. *Yūbin hōchi shinbun,* November 22, 1883, in *MNJ,* vol. 3, 363; Anzai Kunio, "Jiyū minkenha sōshi ni miru kokken ishiki to Tōyō ninshiki," in *Ajia rekishi bunka kenkyūjo shinpojiumu hōkokushū: Kindai ikōki no Higashi Ajia, seiji bunka no henyō to keisei* (Tokyo: Waseda Daigaku Ajia Rekishi Bunka Kenkyūjo, 2005), 20; Tōyama et al., "Santama no sōshi," 178, 182; Wagatsuma et al., eds., *Nihon seiji saiban shiroku,* 51; Irokawa Daikichi, ed., *Santama jiyū minken shiryōshū,* vol. 1 (Tokyo: Daiwa Shobō, 1979), 444–49.

16. Manabe Masayuki, "Miyaji Mohei to sōshitachi no gunzō," *Tosa shidan* 211 (August 1999); Tōyama et al., "Santama no sōshi," 166, 190; Takahashi, "Ingaidan no keisei," 89; *Chōya shinbun,* July 28, 1888, in *MNJ,* vol. 4, 5.

17. Historian Anzai Kunio places a great deal of emphasis on 1887 as the year that marked the end of the violent incidents (*gekka jiken*) of the early 1880s and inspired the proliferation of *sōshi.* Anzai Kunio, "Jiyū minken undō ni okeru sōshi no isō: Inoue Keijirō no dōkō ni miru," in *Jiyū minken no saihakken,* ed. Anzai Kunio and Tasaki Kimitsukasa (Tokyo: Nihon Keizai Hyōronsha, 2006), 214–18. Kawanishi Hidemichi makes a similar argument in Kawanishi Hidemichi, "Meiji seinen to nashonarizumu," in *Kindai Nihon shakai to tennōsei: Iwai Tadakuma-sensei taishoku kinen ronbunshū,* ed. Iwai Tadakuma (Tokyo: Kashiwa Shobō, 1988), 139–41.

18. *Chōya shinbun,* November 25, 1887, in *MNJ,* vol. 3, 366.

19. The Public Assembly Ordinance of 1880 required that all political organizations and meetings register with and get approval from local police authorities. Uniformed police could surveil, and break up, such meetings. In addition to prohibiting outdoor meetings, the ordinance forbade connections between different political associations. And servicemen, police, and teachers, as well as students, were not to participate in political activity.

20. Some *undōkai* also included training in military drills, quite literal training of the body in violence. Also note that *undōkai* had been held earlier in the decade, when on at least one occasion, there was a sporting contest (a version of the game capture the flag) that pitted popular rights activists against supporters of the Meiji government. Kimura, *"Seinen" no tanjō,* 64–78.

21. Ozaki, *Autobiography of Ozaki Yukio*, 92.

22. Suzuki Takeshi, *Hoshi Tōru: Hanbatsu seiji o yurugashita otoko* (Tokyo: Chūō Kōronsha, 1988), 77-79; Ozaki, *Autobiography of Ozaki Yukio*, 93-94; Satō, *Santama no sōshi*, 15-16.

23. R. H. P. Mason, "Changing Diet Attitudes to the Peace Preservation Ordinance, 1890-2," in *Japan's Early Parliaments, 1890-1905: Structure, Issues, and Trends*, ed. Andrew Fraser, R. H. P. Mason, and Philip Mitchell (New York: Routledge, 1995), 91-94, 115-17; Ozaki, *Autobiography of Ozaki Yukio*, 95-97; Satō, *Santama no sōshi*, 16. Kimura Naoe convincingly argues that the Peace Preservation Ordinance should be understood as an outcome of *sōshi* posing a political threat to the government. Kimura, *"Seinen" no tanjō*, 108.

24. The Publication Ordinance of 1869, as revised in 1875, stipulated that all publications except newspapers had to be submitted to the Home Ministry for review. The Press Ordinance of 1875 gave the Home Ministry the power to censor newspapers. Both ordinances were used by the Meiji government to control the Freedom and People's Rights Movement.

25. Kimura, *"Seinen" no tanjō*, 108-11.

26. *Tōkyō nichinichi shinbun*, February 17, 1889, in *MNJ*, vol. 4, 651; *Sanyō shinpō*, May 30, 1889, in *MNJ*, vol. 4, 79.

27. *Tōkyō nichinichi shinbun*, December 28, 1888, in *MNJ*, vol. 4, 190; *Yamagata shinpō*, January 15, 1889, in *MNJ*, vol. 4, 6; Kimura, *"Seinen" no tanjō*, 100-101.

28. *Tōkyō nichinichi shinbun*, October 15, 1889, in *MNJ*, vol. 4, 387-88.

29. Kimura, *"Seinen" no tanjō*, 14, 103, 120-21.

30. Jason G. Karlin, "The Gender of Nationalism: Competing Masculinities in Meiji Japan," *Journal of Japanese Studies* 28, no. 1 (winter 2002): 59.

31. Ibid., 41-44, 60. There were some women *sōshi*, though they appear infrequently in sources. For one example, see *Tōkyō nichinichi shinbun*, April 28, 1891, in *MNJ*, vol. 4, 389.

32. Kimura, *"Seinen" no tanjō*, 99, 103, 119-21; Irokawa and Murano, *Murano Tsuneemon den*, 203; *Japan Weekly Mail*, May 28, 1892.

33. Karlin, "Gender of Nationalism," 60.

34. David R. Ambaras, *Bad Youth: Juvenile Delinquency and the Politics of Everyday Life in Modern Japan* (Berkeley: University of California Press, 2006), 69.

35. Ibid., 69-72.

36. Karlin, "Gender of Nationalism," 58; Satō, *Santama no sōshi*, 32.

37. This argument about changes in Santama *sōshi* was made by Irokawa Daikichi, as quoted in Takahashi, "Ingaidan no keisei," 116.

38. *Kokumin no tomo*, August 15, 1887. I was led to this article by Kimura's discussion of the piece in Kimura, *"Seinen" no tanjō*, 43-48.

39. *Chōya shinbun*, September 10, 1887.

40. Ibid., March 31, 1889.

41. Ibid., February 25 and 28, 1890.

42. *Eiri jiyū shinbun*, October 8, 1887.

43. Gen'yōsha Shashi Hensankai, ed., *Gen'yōsha shashi* (1917; reprint, Fukuoka: Ashi Shobō, 1992), 209-11, 223-25; Ishitaki Toyomi, *Gen'yōsha hakkutsu: Mō hitotsu no jiyū minken* (Fukuoka: Nishi Nihon Shinbunsha, 1981), 23.

The last principle was more than an afterthought—Tōyama Mitsuru traveled extensively between Fukuoka, Osaka, and Tokyo promoting people's rights, and fellow Gen'yōsha leaders Hakoda Rokusuke and Shindō Kiheita joined him in the nation's capital to press the Meiji government to establish a parliament. Tsuzuki Shichirō, *Tōyama Mitsuru: Sono dodekai ningenzō* (Tokyo: Shinjinbutsu Ōraisha, 1974), 85; Watanabe Ryūsaku, *Tairiku rōnin: Meiji romanchishizumu no eikō to zasetsu* (Tokyo: Banchō Shobō, 1967), 79-80.

Nakajima Takeshi argues that Tōyama Mitsuru and members of the Gen'yōsha, as well as those of its offshoot the Kokuryūkai, were devoid of ideology. He suggests they cared only about a person's capabilities, spirit, and actions and were more sentimental than intellectual Asianists. Nakajima's point may hold true for pan-Asianists, with which he is primarily interested, but seems to be too dismissive of the nationalist bent of these groups and their leaders. Lack of ideological sophistication does not necessarily mean that ideas such as liberalism or nationalism did not inform or motivate their behavior. Nakajima Takeshi, *Nakamuraya no Bōsu: Indo dokuritsu undō to kindai Nihon no Ajiashugi* (Tokyo: Hakusuisha, 2005), 129.

44. Watanabe Ryūsaku identifies eight categories of *tairiku rōnin*: those who went northward (*hoppō gata*); those who went southward (*nanpō gata*); patriots (*kokushi gata*); political ruffians (*sōshi gata*); the "rear guard" (*kōhō gata*); the vanguard (*senpei gata*); intellectuals (*shisō gata*); and "doers" (*kōdō gata*). Watanabe, *Tairiku rōnin*, 10–11.

45. For a useful historiographical review essay on *tairiku rōnin*, see Zhao Jun, "'Betsudōtai' to 'shishi' no hazama: Kindai rai tairiku rōnin kenkyū no kaiko to tenbō," *Chiba shōdai kiyō* 36, no. 4:123 (March 1999): 105–24. Those who paint *tairiku rōnin* in a romantic hue include Watanabe Ryūsaku (cited above) and Masumi Junnosuke. E. Herbert Norman and Marius Jansen take a harsher view. Masumi Junnosuke, *Nihon seitō shiron*, vol. 3 (Tokyo: Tōkyō Daigaku Shuppankai, 1967); E. Herbert Norman, "The Genyōsha: A Study in the Origins of Japanese Imperialism," *Pacific Affairs* 17, no. 3 (September 1944): 261–84; Marius B. Jansen, *The Japanese and Sun Yat-sen* (Cambridge, Mass.: Harvard University Press, 1954).

46. Ishitaki, *Gen'yōsha hakkutsu*, 134–36; Masumi, *Nihon seitō shiron*, 151; Gen'yōsha Shashi Hensankai, *Gen'yōsha shashi*, 239.

47. Tōyama was taken in by the police in Osaka but along with some other members was released the following day. Gen'yōsha Shashi Hensankai, *Gen'yōsha shashi*, 393–94. Tsuzuki, *Tōyama Mitsuru*, 133–43; Aida Iichirō, *Shichijūnendai no uyoku: Meiji, Taishō, Shōwa no keifu* (Tokyo: Daikōsha, 1970), 93–94; Watanabe, *Tairiku rōnin*, 66–67.

48. Kang Chang-il, "Ten'yūkyō to 'Chōsen mondai': 'Chōsen rōnin' no Tōgaku nōmin sensō e no taiō to kanrenshite," *Shigaku zasshi* 97, no. 8 (August 1988): 16–19, 23–27; Hilary Conroy, *The Japanese Seizure of Korea, 1868–1910: A Study of Realism and Idealism in International Relations* (Philadelphia: University of Pennsylvania Press, 1974), 230–31.

49. There is no conventional English translation of "Ten'yūkyō"—Jun Uchida's is "Heavenly Blessing Heroes," Conroy's is "Saving Chivalry Under Heaven," and Norman's is "Society of Heavenly Salvation for the Oppressed." Jun Uchida, "'Brokers of Empire': Japanese Settler Colonialism in Korea, 1910–1937" (Ph.D. diss., Harvard University, 2005), 42; Conroy, *Japanese Seizure of Korea*, 230–31; Norman, "Genyōsha," 281.

50. Kang, "Ten'yūkyō to 'Chōsen mondai,'" 5–9; Chae Soo Do, "'Ten'yūkyō' ni kansuru ikkōsatsu," *Chūō Daigaku Daigakuin kenkyū nenpō* 30 (February 2001): 442–44.

51. Kuzuu Yoshihisa, *Tōa senkaku shishi kiden*, jō-kan (1933; reprint, Tokyo: Hara Shobō, 1966), 181–94; Nishio Yōtarō, *Tōyama Mitsuru-ō shōden* (Fukuoka: Ashi Shobō, 1981), 215–216; Kang, "Ten'yūkyō to 'Chōsen mondai,'" 15; Ishitaki, *Gen'yōsha hakkutsu*, 174–75.

52. Kuzuu, *Tōa senkaku shishi kiden*, 187–94, 294–95; Kang, "Ten'yūkyō to 'Chōsen mondai,'" 11, 15–16; Ishitaki, *Gen'yōsha hakkutsu*, 175. In its various attempts to acquire arms and ammunition, the Ten'yūkyō technically violated the law that deemed illegal "covert purchase and export of arms for the export of revolution." Members also broke the Japanese government's specific prohibition against selling arms to the Tonghak rebels. Etō Shinkichi and Marius B. Jansen, introduction to *My Thirty-Three Years' Dream: The Autobiography of Miyazaki Tōten*, by Miyazaki Tōten, trans. Etō Shinkichi and Marius B. Jansen (Princeton: Princeton University Press, 1982), xxv; Kang, "Ten'yūkyō to 'Chōsen mondai,'" 10–11.

53. Kang, "Ten'yūkyō to 'Chōsen mondai,'" 13, 15; Kuzuu, *Tōa senkaku shishi kiden*, 295. This was not the first time Gen'yōsha members contributed to military intelligence. In the 1880s, Tōyama Mitsuru sent *tairiku rōnin* to China for intelligence purposes and formed ties with like-minded military men. Norman, "Genyōsha," 278; Ō Kiryō, "Tairiku rōnin no sakigake oyobi Nisshin sensō e no yakudō," *Kanazawa hōgaku* 36, no. 1-2 (1994): 62; Douglas R. Reynolds, "Training Young China Hands: Tōa Dōbun Shoin and Its Precursors, 1886-1945," in *The Japanese Informal Empire in China, 1895-1937*, ed. Peter Duus, Ramon H. Myers, and Mark R. Peattie (Princeton: Princeton University Press, 1989), 212-16.

54. Kang, "Ten'yūkyō to 'Chōsen mondai,'" 28; Ōya Masao, *Ōya Masao jijoden*, ed. Irokawa Daikichi (Tokyo: Daiwa Shobō, 1979), 136-37; Ishitaki, *Gen'yōsha hakkutsu*, 177-179; Uchida, "'Brokers of Empire,'" 44-45; Wagatsuma et al., eds., *Nihon seiji saiban shiroku*, 224-33.

55. Chae Soo Do, "Kokuryūkai no seiritsu: Gen'yōsha to tairiku rōnin no katsudō o chūshin ni," *Hōgaku shinpō* 109, no. 1-2 (April 2002): 163-69, 175-80; Jansen, *Japanese and Sun Yat-sen*, 111.

56. Kuzuu, *Tōa senkaku shishi kiden*, 815-17, 822; Ishitaki, *Gen'yōsha hakkutsu*, 183-85; Nishio, *Tōyama Mitsuru-ō shōden*, 236-37.

57. Ishitaki, *Gen'yōsha hakkutsu*, 185-87; Nishio, *Tōyama Mitsuru-ō shōden*, 235-37; Kuzuu, *Tōa senkaku shishi kiden*, 815; Tōyama Motokazu, *Chikuzen Gen'yōsha* (Fukuoka: Ashi Shobō, 1977), 205-7.

58. *Chōya shinbun*, September 25, 1890.

59. *Japan Weekly Mail*, May 28, 1892.

60. Kimura, *"Seinen" no tanjō*, 113.

61. R. H. P. Mason, *Japan's First General Election, 1890* (Cambridge: Cambridge University Press, 1969), 30-31.

62. Irokawa and Murano, *Murano Tsuneemon den*, 202.

63. Mason, *Japan's First General Election*, 177.

64. Ibid., 52-58, 174-77.

65. Election figure from Akita, *Foundations of Constitutional Government*, 76.

66. Masumi Junnosuke, *Nihon seitō shiron*, vol. 2 (Tokyo: Tōkyō Daigaku Shuppankai, 1966), 163.

67. Mason, *Japan's First General Election*, 193-94.

68. Ueki Emori, *Ueki Emori nikki* (Kōchi: Kōchi Shinbunsha, 1955), 363-64; *Chōya shinbun*, September 16, 1890; Masumi, *Nihon seitō shiron*, vol. 2, 168-69.

69. *Chōya shinbun*, September 13, 1890; *Yomiuri shinbun*, September 14, 1890.

70. Mason, "Changing Diet Attitudes," 98-99; Akita, *Foundations of Constitutional Government*, 77-81.

71. Ueki, *Ueki Emori nikki*, 371-73; *Japan Weekly Mail*, January 10, 1891; *Tōkyō nichinichi shinbun*, January 8, 1891, in *Nyūsu de ou Meiji Nihon hakkutsu: Kenpō happu, Ōtsu jiken, sōshi to kettō no jidai*, ed. Suzuki Kōichi (Tokyo: Kawade Shobō Shinsha, 1994), 161. For an English translation of the *Tōkyō nichinichi shinbun* article, see Mason, "Changing Diet Attitudes," 99-100.

72. Masumi, *Nihon seitō shiron*, vol. 2, 175.

73. Mason, "Changing Diet Attitudes," 101.

74. Masumi, *Nihon seitō shiron*, vol. 2, 176.

75. Mason, "Changing Diet Attitudes," 103-4; *Japan Weekly Mail*, January 17, 1891.

76. The source of this article, and the reason why the numbers are so precise, is unclear so the figures should not be interpreted as terribly reliable. The newspaper provided a breakdown of *sōshi* by party: Jiyūtō, 103; Kokumin Jiyūtō, 42; Kaishintō, 6; Taiseikai, 0.

It also gave figures for specific politicians, such as: Ōi Kentarō, 50; Hoshi Tōru, 30; Endō Hidehirō, 218; Ozaki Yukio, 2. *Chōya shinbun*, February 20, 1891.

77. *Japan Weekly Mail*, February 14, 1891.

78. Ozaki, *Autobiography of Ozaki Yukio*, 130.

79. Ibid.

80. Takahashi Yūsei, *Meiji keisatsushi kenkyū*, vol. 3 (Tokyo: Reibunsha, 1963), 221–23, 225–26, 264–75. Not all members of the Matsukata cabinet supported election interference; Itō Hirobumi, for one, had reservations. See Akita, *Foundations of Constitutional Government*, 99–100.

81. In the years before the 1892 election, Inukai Tsuyoshi spoke of how *mintō* politicians feared being beaten by *sōshi* employed by the government. And a January 7, 1891, article in the *Chōya shinbun* made a distinction between the *mintō sōshi* who wielded sticks and *ritō sōshi* who wielded sabers. (The newspaper could also have been commenting on the ruffianism of saber-wielding police by calling them "sōshi.") Masumi, *Nihon seitō shiron*, vol. 2, 176; *Chōya shinbun*, January 7, 1891.

82. Saga-kenshi Hensan Iinkai, ed., *Saga-kenshi: Kindai hen*, ge-kan (Saga: Saga-ken Shiryō Kankōkai, 1967), 117. According to Ozaki Yukio, the reported number of deaths was 25. Ozaki, *Autobiography of Ozaki Yukio*, 128.

83. *Yomiuri shinbun*, February 13, 15–17, 1892; *Tōkyō nichinichi shinbun*, February 17 and 18, 1892; Kōchi-ken, ed., *Kōchi-kenshi: Kindai hen* (Kōchi: Kōchi-ken, 1970), 231.

84. Deaths were most numerous in Kōchi Prefecture (10), followed by Saga (8), Fukuoka (3), Chiba (2), and Kumamoto (1). Saga had the highest number of wounded (92), with many injured in Kōchi (66), Fukuoka (65), Chiba (40), and Kumamoto (37). Saga-kenshi Hensan Iinkai, *Saga-kenshi*, 117.

85. Shimazu Akira, "Honchō senkyo kanshōshi," *Jinbutsu ōrai* (March 1955): 50. Shimazu does not suggest that the government intentionally focused on these two prefectures.

86. Ozaki, *Autobiography of Ozaki Yukio*, 128.

87. Ishitaki, *Gen'yōsha hakkutsu*, 154–55; Tsuzuki, *Tōyama Mitsuru*, 161; Norman, "Genyōsha," 276.

88. *Yomiuri shinbun*, February 5, 1892.

89. *Tōkyō nichinichi shinbun*, February 17, 1892; *Yomiuri shinbun*, February 17, 1892.

90. *Tōkyō nichinichi shinbun*, February 17, 1892.

91. Ozaki, *Autobiography of Ozaki Yukio*, 127–28.

92. *Yomiuri shinbun*, February 15, 1892.

93. Ibid., February 5, 1892.

94. Ibid., February 12, 1892.

95. *Tōkyō nichinichi shinbun*, February 17, 1892.

96. *Kokumin no tomo*, February 13, 1892.

97. *Yomiuri shinbun*, February 16 and 17, 1892. In another incident in Tachikawa, *mintō sōshi* brought carts loaded with swords and bamboo spears to an election site, and the *ritō sōshi* attempted to "starve" them out by covering up a nearby well to block their access to drinking water. Satō, *Santama no sōshi*, 30–31.

98. *Tōkyō nichinichi shinbun*, February 18, 1892; Irokawa and Murano, *Murano Tsuneemon den*, 203.

99. Ozaki, *Autobiography of Ozaki Yukio*, 128.

100. *Tōkyō nichinichi shinbun*, February 18, 1892.

101. *Yomiuri shinbun*, February 16, 1892.

102. Ibid., February 17, 1892; Shimazu, "Honchō senkyo kanshōshi," 50. Ozaki Yukio only noted postponement in Saga's third electoral district, where two-thirds of the voters abstained when balloting resumed. Ozaki, *Autobiography of Ozaki Yukio*, 128.

103. *Tōkyō nichinichi shinbun*, February 17, 1892; *Yomiuri shinbun*, February 17, 1892.

104. It is not clear if this quote provided by Ozaki was verbatim, and Ozaki was of the political inclination to paint Shinagawa in a negative light. Ozaki, *Autobiography of Ozaki Yukio*, 132–33.

105. For some, a sense of anger toward the Meiji government persisted beyond 1892. One *mintō sōshi*, Shimada Ken'ichirō, called the *ritō sōshi* "toughs" (*gorotsuki*) and was very critical of their attack against the *mintō* (people of justice, in his eyes). Shimada Ken'ichirō, *Ukikusa no hana* (Hamura: Hamura-shi Kyōiku Iinkai, 1993), 314–15; originally written between June 3, 1894, and March 17, 1896.

106. Ozaki, *Autobiography of Ozaki Yukio*, 134.

107. Ibid. For the full text of the resolution, see Jiyūtō Tōhyōkoku, *Senkyo kanshō mondai no tenmatsu* (Tokyo: Jiyūtō Tōhyōkoku, 1892), 86.

108. Ozaki, *Autobiography of Ozaki Yukio*, 132–35; Akita, *Foundations of Constitutional Government*, 98–101; Takahashi, *Meiji keisatsushi kenkyū*, 290–97.

109. Takahashi, *Meiji keisatsushi kenkyū*, 315.

110. There were also some articles in the criminal code that allowed for ambiguity which could be interpreted to the Gen'yōsha's advantage. For example, in the case of a brawl between two or more people, neither side was punishable if the provocateur could not be determined (article 310). The idea of justifiable self-defense could also be marshaled (article 309). Gendai Hōsei Shiryō Hensankai, ed., *Meiji "kyūhō" shū* (Tokyo: Kokusho Kankōkai, 1983), 34, 35, 37, 44.

111. Kimura, *"Seinen" no tanjō*, 112–13. *Sōshi* activity seems to have abated after the 1892 election, but there continued to be scattered reports throughout the rest of the year about *sōshi* violence; examples included a rough election in Kumamoto and an assault on a Diet member. See, for examples, *Chōya shinbun*, August 23, 1892; *Japan Weekly Mail*, September 10, 1892; October 8 and 16, 1892; and November 26, 1892.

112. Takahashi, *Meiji keisatsushi kenkyū*, 322.

113. *Tōkyō nichinichi shinbun*, February 6, 8, 10, 11, 13, 20, 24, 27, and 28, 1894; March 1-3, 1894; *Yomiuri shinbun*, February 16-18 and 27, 1894; March 2 and 3, 1894; *Ōsaka mainichi shinbun*, February 18 and 28, 1894.

114. Ozaki, *Autobiography of Ozaki Yukio*, 147.

115. *Ōsaka mainichi shinbun*, December 16 and 18, 1897.

116. *Yomiuri shinbun*, February 2, 1898.

117. David C. Rapoport and Leonard Weinberg, "Elections and Violence," in *The Democratic Experience and Political Violence*, ed. David C. Rapoport and Leonard Weinberg (London: Frank Cass, 2001), 29.

118. K. Theodore Hoppen, "Grammars of Election Violence in Nineteenth-Century England and Ireland," *English Historical Review* 109, no. 432 (June 1994): 606.

119. Charles Seymour, *Electoral Reform in England and Wales: The Development and Operation of the Parliamentary Franchise, 1832-1885* (1915; reprint, Newton Abbot: David & Charles, 1970), 187.

120. Hoppen, "Grammars of Election Violence," 609.

121. Tyler Anbinder, *Five Points: The 19th-Century New York City Neighborhood That Invented Tap Dance, Stole Elections, and Became the World's Most Notorious Slum* (New York: Free Press, 2001), 27–29, 141–44, 153–58, 277, 321. Street gangs also instigated what have conventionally been called "riots," one of the most famous being the Bowery Boy Riot of 1857. See Anbinder, *Five Points*, 277–96.

122. Richard Franklin Bensel, *The American Ballot Box in the Mid-Nineteenth Century* (Cambridge: Cambridge University Press, 2004), 170.

123. Ibid.

124. Ibid., 171-72.
125. Ibid., 20-21.
126. Rapoport and Weinberg, "Elections and Violence," 29-30.
127. Peter McCaffery, *When Bosses Ruled Philadelphia: The Emergence of the Republican Machine, 1867-1933* (University Park: Pennsylvania State University Press, 1993), 13.
128. Rapoport and Weinberg, "Elections and Violence," 38.
129. Ibid., 19.
130. Ibid., 30.
131. Ibid., 19, 21, 31.
132. On the activities of patrolmen during elections in large U.S. cities, see Robert M. Fogelson, *Big-City Police* (Cambridge, Mass.: Harvard University Press, 1977), 19-20, 34-35.
133. Rapoport and Weinberg, "Elections and Violence," 39.
134. Anbinder, *Five Points,* 326-27.
135. Seymour, *Electoral Reform,* 233; Rapoport and Weinberg, "Elections and Violence," 39.
136. John F. Reynolds, "A Symbiotic Relationship: Vote Fraud and Electoral Reform in the Gilded Age," *Social Science History* 17, no. 2 (summer 1993): 247; Seymour, *Electoral Reform,* 233.
137. On nativism and electoral reform in the United States, see Reynolds, "Symbiotic Relationship," 246; Fogelson, *Big-City Police,* 42.
138. On these electoral laws, see Hayashida Kazuhiro, "Development of Election Law in Japan," *Hōsei kenkyū* 34, no. 1 (July 1967): 98-101. On the 1925 law, see Harold S. Quigley, "The New Japanese Electoral Law," *American Political Science Review* 20, no. 2 (May 1926): 392-95.
139. David E. Apter, "Political Violence in Analytical Perspective," in *The Legitimization of Violence,* ed. David E. Apter (New York: New York University Press, 1997), 3.
140. Victor T. Le Vine, "Violence and the Paradox of Democratic Renewal: A Preliminary Assessment," in *The Democratic Experience and Political Violence,* ed. David C. Rapoport and Leonard Weinberg (London: Frank Cass, 2001), 277-78.

3. Institutionalized Ruffianism and a Culture of Political Violence

1. *Chūgai shōgyō shinpō,* February 17 and 18, 1922. Also named were Nakajima Hōroku who was second rank in judo; Horikiri Zenbei from Fukushima; Yamaguchi Giichi and Saegusa Hikotarō from Osaka; Kasuga Toshifumi who was first rank in judo; Takami Koremichi from Toyama who was quick to fight; Kira Motoo from Ōita; Maida Juzaburō from Aichi; Kogure Sanshirō; and Nakano Seigō.
2. *Chūgai shōgyō shinpō,* February 19, 1922. The article praised Hara Kei for having the foresight to appoint strong people to his cabinet, and also briefly mentioned members of the House of Peers known for their physical strength, such as Higuchi Seikō and Wakatsuki Reijirō.
3. For various takes on the 1920s in particular, see Nihon Gendaishi Kenkyūkai, ed., *1920-nendai no Nihon no seiji* (Tokyo: Ōtsuki Shoten, 1984). For a discussion of the English-language historiography on this topic, see Sheldon Garon, "State and Society in Interwar Japan," in *Historical Perspectives on Contemporary East Asia,* ed. Merle Goldman and Andrew Gordon (Cambridge, Mass.: Harvard University Press, 2000), 155-82.
4. Suzuki Takeshi, *Hoshi Tōru: Hanbatsu seiji o yurugashita otoko* (Tokyo: Chūō Kōronsha, 1988), 25-32, 70-73.

5. Satō Kōtarō, *Santama no sōshi* (Tokyo: Musashi Shobō, 1973), 27–29.

6. Suzuki, *Hoshi Tōru*, 104; Satō, *Santama no sōshi*, 26; Irokawa Daikichi and Murano Ren'ichi, *Murano Tsuneemon den* (Tokyo: Chūō Kōron Jigyō Shuppan, 1969), 198–99; Tōyama Shigeki et al., eds., "Santama no sōshi," in *Meiji no ninaite*, jō-kan, vol. 11 of *Jinbutsu Nihon no rekishi* (Tokyo: Yomiuri Shinbunsha, 1965), 29, 193. See also Hirano Yoshitarō, *Bajō Ōi Kentarō den* (Nagoya: Fūbaisha, 1968), 266–72.

7. Takeuchi Yoshio, *Seitō seiji no kaitakusha: Hoshi Tōru* (Tokyo: Fuyō Shobō, 1984), 88.

8. *Yomiuri shinbun*, February 9 and 13, 1892.

9. Ibid., March 8, 1894.

10. Ozaki Yukio, *The Autobiography of Ozaki Yukio: The Struggle for Constitutional Government in Japan*, trans. Hara Fujiko (Princeton: Princeton University Press, 2001), 101.

11. Ibid., 200. For the original Japanese of "gangster," see Ozaki Yukio, *Gakudō jiden*, vol. 11 of *Ozaki Yukio Gakudō zenshū*, ed. Ozaki Gakudō Zenshū Hensan Iinkai (Tokyo: Kōronsha, 1955), 175.

12. Irokawa and Murano, *Murano Tsuneemon den*, i-ii, 33, 39–40, 202–3; Tōyama et al., "Santama no sōshi," 166, 172; Irokawa Daikichi, *Tama no rekishi sanpo* (Tokyo: Asahi Shinbunsha, 1975), 187–89.

13. Irokawa and Murano, *Murano Tsuneemon den*, 44, 190, 199, 203; Tōyama et al., "Santama no sōshi," 184.

14. Suzuki, *Hoshi Tōru*, 2. For a colorful recounting of Hoshi's refusal to give up the position, see Ozaki, *Autobiography of Ozaki Yukio*, 142–45.

15. Satō, *Santama no sōshi*, 35–37.

16. Inui Teruo, "Gunpu to natta Jiyūtō sōshi: Kanagawa-ken shusshin no 'Tama-gumi' gunpu o chūshin ni," *Chihōshi kenkyū* 32, no. 3 (June 1982): 47–50, 52–54, 56–58. The geographical breakdown of Tama-gumi members: Minami Tama, 108; Tokyo City, 56; Kita Tama, 36; Nishi Tama, 16; Other (within Tokyo), 14; Kanagawa, 36; Chiba, 21; Niigata, 17; Nagano, 14; Toyama, 11; Ibaraki, 11; Ishikawa, 10; Other (outside Tokyo), 82.

17. Peter Duus, *Party Rivalry and Political Change in Taisho Japan* (Cambridge, Mass.: Harvard University Press, 1968), 8–9.

18. Irokawa and Murano, *Murano Tsuneemon den*, 230; Tōyama et al., "Santama no sōshi," 197–98.

19. Suzuki, *Hoshi Tōru*, 139–44; Duus, *Party Rivalry and Political Change*, 10.

20. Irokawa and Murano, *Murano Tsuneemon den*, ii, 234, 236; Satō, *Santama no sōshi*, 46–47.

21. Duus, *Party Rivalry and Political Change*, 3, 10–11.

22. Ōno Banboku-sensei Tsuisōroku Kankōkai Henshū Iinkai, *Ōno Banboku: Shōden to tsuisōki* (Tokyo: Ōno Banboku-sensei Tsuisōroku Kankōkai, 1970), 16; Satō, *Santama no sōshi*, 53.

23. Satō, *Santama no sōshi*, 47–50; Tōyama et al., "Santama no sōshi," 201.

24. Suzuki, *Hoshi Tōru*, 159–71.

25. Takahashi, "Ingaidan no keisei," 95, 109–10, 115; Matenrō Shatō, *Ingaidan shuki: Seitō kaikaku no kyūsho* (Tokyo: Jichōsha, 1935), 60.

26. Ōno Banboku-sensei Tsuisōroku Kankōkai Henshū Iinkai, *Ōno Banboku*, 16.

27. Matenrō, *Ingaidan shuki*, 56–58, 64–70. This source described *ingaidan* as "a group of *rōnin* who like politics" (*seiji aikō no rōnin no ichidan*). Takahashi also acknowledges the nature of the *ingaidan* as violent groups. See Takahashi, "Ingaidan no keisei," 91.

28. Ōno Banboku, *Ōno Banboku kaisōroku* (Tokyo: Kōbundō, 1962), 44–45; Matenrō, *Ingaidan shuki*, 61–63.

29. Ōno, *Ōno Banboku kaisōroku*, 43–44.

30. Tyler Anbinder, *Five Points: The 19th-Century Neighborhood That Invented Tap Dance, Stole Elections, and Became the World's Most Notorious Slum* (New York: Free Press, 2001), 165.

31. Peter McCaffery, *When Bosses Ruled Philadelphia: The Emergence of the Republican Machine, 1867–1933* (University Park: Pennsylvania State University Press, 1993), 11–14.

32. On pressure groups in Britain, see Michael Rush, ed., *Parliament and Pressure Politics* (Oxford: Clarendon Press, 1990).

33. Arnold J. Bornfriend, "Political Parties and Pressure Groups," *Proceedings of the Academy of Political Science* 29, no. 4 (1969): 56. See also Jerome Mushkat, *The Reconstruction of the New York Democracy, 1861–1874* (Rutherford, N.J.: Fairleigh Dickinson University Press, 1981), 144.

34. On an incident of the early 1930s involving charges of bureaucratic and financial corruption, see Richard H. Mitchell, *Justice in Japan: The Notorious Teijin Scandal* (Honolulu: University of Hawai'i Press, 2002).

35. Nagakawa Toshimi took this analogy a bit further, arguing that at some point in time, the boss-henchmen relationships within political parties had been like those between *kyōkaku*, or mentorships of sorts. Nagakawa Toshimi, "Seitō no oyabun, kobun," *Kaizō* (August 1930): 25–33. Watanabe Ikujirō drew a similar parallel, though he was much more critical of the *oyabun-kobun* relationship, especially between politicians. Watanabe Ikujirō, "Seikai, oyabun, kobun," *Seikai ōrai* 12, no. 5 (May 1941): 5–6.

36. Kobayashi Yūgo and Koike Seiichi, eds., *Rikken Seiyūkaishi*, vol. 2 (Tokyo: Rikken Seiyūkaishi Shuppankyoku, 1924), 42.

37. Miyachi Masato, *Nichiro sengo seijishi kenkyū* (Tokyo: Tōkyō Daigaku Shuppankai, 1973), 226–28. Miyachi's phrase "era of popular violence" was given currency in English by Andrew Gordon. See Andrew Gordon, *Labor and Imperial Democracy in Prewar Japan* (Berkeley: University of California Press, 1991), 26–27. On popular violence, see Fujino Yūko, "Sōran suru hitobito e no shisen: Kindai Nihon no toshi sōjō to seiji undō," in *Bōryoku no chihei o koete: Rekishigaku kara no chōsen*, ed. Suda Tsutomu, Cho Kyondaru, and Nakajima Hisato (Tokyo: Aoki Shoten, 2004), 81–110.

38. *Tōkyō nichinichi shinbun*, January 12 and 14, 1913; Yamamoto Shirō, ed., *Rikken Seiyūkaishi*, vol. 3 (1924; reprint, Tokyo: Nihon Tosho Sentā, 1990), 572–73.

39. *Tōkyō nichinichi shinbun*, January 17, 1913; Tsuchikura Sōmei, "Ingaidan tōsōki," *Bungei shunjū* (December 1935): 212.

40. Satō, *Santama no sōshi*, 52–54; Ōno Banboku-sensei Tsuisōroku Kankōkai Henshū Iinkai, *Ōno Banboku*, 12.

41. Ōno, *Ōno Banboku kaisōroku*, 9, 16–22; *Tōkyō nichinichi shinbun*, February 11, 1913. According to Andrew Gordon, 168 people were injured (of whom 110 were police) and 253 people were arrested in the incident. In addition to the attacks on newspaper companies affiliated with or sympathetic to the government, 38 police boxes were smashed. Gordon, *Labor and Imperial Democracy*, 28.

42. Ōno, *Ōno Banboku kaisōroku*, 23–26.

43. Ōno claims that he was arrested under the Peace Preservation Law (Chian Iji Hō), but this could not have been the case because it was not enacted until May 12, 1925. Ōno, *Ōno Banboku kaisōroku*, 30–31. Politician Arima Yoriyasu also mentions the presence of university debate club members in election campaigns. Arima Yoriyasu, *Seikai dōchūki* (Tokyo: Nihon Shuppan Kyōdo, 1951), 16–17.

44. Ōno Banboku-sensei Tsuisōroku Kankōkai Henshū Iinkai, *Ōno Banboku*, 16–17; Ōno, *Ōno Banboku kaisōroku*, 28–34; Takahashi, "Ingaidan no keisei," 98, 100, 106.

45. Takahashi, "Ingaidan no keisei," 104, 107.

46. Ibid., 103, 106–7. Chūō University and Nihon University students allegedly did not have enough time on their hands to participate in *ingaidan*, and Hōsei University was

too small to become a big player in this rivalry. In the early Showa period, when the Meiji University debate club came under new leadership, it switched its allegiances over to the Kenseikai.

47. On Takebe, see Kenneth Szymkowiak, *Sōkaiya: Extortion, Protection, and the Japanese Corporation* (Armonk, N.Y.: M. E. Sharpe, 2002), 37–39.

48. Ōno, *Ōno Banboku kaisōroku,* 43–46.

49. "Ingaidan no shōtai o tsuku," *Seikei jichō* 8, no. 3 (March 1953): 13–14.

50. Carolyn Conley, "The Agreeable Recreation of Fighting," *Journal of Social History* 33, no. 1 (autumn 1999): 57–58.

51. Ōno, *Ōno Banboku kaisōroku,* 43–44.

52. *Yomiuri shinbun,* February 8, 1914.

53. Ozaki, *Autobiography of Ozaki Yukio,* 313. For the original Japanese, see Ozaki, *Gakudō jiden,* 563.

54. Ozaki, *Autobiography of Ozaki Yukio,* 313.

55. In the 1908 election, there were 323 cases of election violations involving 2,826 people. Nagata Hidejirō, "Senkyo no rimen ni hisomu zaiaku," *Nihon hyōron* 2, no. 4 (April 1, 1917): 192. Nagata was the head of the Police Bureau (Keihokyoku) of the Home Ministry. Another source gives lower figures for the 1912 election: 660 cases of election law violations, 78 of which fell into the category of violent intimidation. Yamamoto, *Rikken Seiyūkaishi,* 514. The figures given in a newspaper shortly after the 1915 election were also lower (430 cases, 2,391 people) and broke down by party as follows: Dōshikai, 143 cases, 777 people; Seiyūkai, 142 cases, 915 people; Independents, 84 cases, 512 people; Other, 27 cases, 38 people; Chūseikai (Fair Party), 18 cases, 93 people; Kokumintō, 16 cases, 58 people. *Yomiuri shinbun,* March 26, 1915.

56. Duus, *Party Rivalry and Political Change,* 89–92; Masumi Junnosuke, *Nihon seitō shiron,* vol. 3 (Tokyo: Tōkyō Daigaku Shuppankai, 1967), 280–81; *Jiji shinpō,* April 6, 1915, in Meiji Taishō Shōwa Shinbun Kenkyūkai, ed., *Shinbun shūsei Taishō hennenshi* (Tokyo: Meiji Taishō Shōwa Shinbun Kenkyūkai, 1969), 540.

57. *Yomiuri shinbun,* May 6, 1920. Various Santama *sōshi* organizations were said to have been disbanded around 1915; even if they did not maintain a permanent presence in Tokyo and were less organized, Murano seems to have been able to rally them to his cause when needed. Satō, *Santama no sōshi,* 68.

58. Satō, *Santama no sōshi,* 80–84. Murano was defeated in this election, but maintained a role in politics as a member of the House of Peers to which he was appointed by Hara Kei.

59. Duus, *Party Rivalry and Political Change,* 155–56.

60. Takahashi, "Ingaidan no keisei," 109.

61. *Tōkyō nichinichi shinbun,* January 20, 1924.

62. Tsuchikura, "Ingaidan tōsōki," 216.

63. Satō, *Santama no sōshi,* 92–95.

64. *Asahi shinbun,* June 13, 1927.

65. Thomas R. H. Havens, "Japan's Enigmatic Election of 1928," *Modern Asian Studies* 11, no. 4 (1977): 550; Kenneth Colegrove, "The Japanese General Election of 1928," *American Political Science Review* 22, no. 2 (May 1928): 405. Again, numbers on election violations vary. The *Ōsaka mainichi shinbun* reported that 1,371 people went through the court system for election violations. Of these, 888 were prosecuted. There were far more Minseitō than Seiyūkai supporters prosecuted, 539 as compared to 147. Of those found guilty, only three received any time in prison; the remaining 368 were slapped with fines. *Ōsaka mainichi shinbun,* February 25, 1928.

66. Matsuo Takayoshi, *Futsū senkyo seido seiritsushi no kenkyū* (Tokyo: Iwanami Shoten, 1989), 327.

67. Shūgiin Giin Senkyohō, Hōritsu dai yonjūnana gō (May 5,1925) in Jichishō Senkyobu, ed., *Senkyohō hyakunenshi* (Tokyo: Dai-ichi Hōki, 1990), 185–202. See also Colegrove, "Japanese General Election of 1928," 404. The following year, a law that targeted violent acts (Bōryoku Kōi Nado Shobatsu ni Kansuru Hōritsu) was passed by the Diet. The first article of the law specified a punishment of a maximum of three years of imprisonment with hard labor or a fine of no more than ¥500 for those wielding group violence. Bōryoku Kōi Nado Shobatsu Hōritsu, Hōritsu dai rokujū gō (March 1926). This law was also extended to Korea and Taiwan. Wakatsuki Reijirō (prime minister), "Taishō jūgonen hōritsu dai rokujū gō o Chōsen oyobi Taiwan ni shikō suru no ken," July 19, 1926. At the National Archives of Japan.

68. Matsuo, *Futsū senkyo seido seiritsushi,* 329–30.

69. The new election law did also deal with bribery, but abuses involving violence were presumably more visible and susceptible to punishment than the movement of money.

70. The number of people prosecuted for election disturbances also increased, from 19 to 32. *Yomiuri shinbun,* February 21, 1930.

71. For more on Banzuiin Chōbei, see Tamura Eitarō, *Yakuza no seikatsu* (Tokyo: Yūzankaku, 1964), 170–73.

72. *Chūgai shōgyō shinpō,* February 18, 1922.

73. Matenrō, *Ingaidan shuki,* 60.

74. Arima Yoriyasu, *Shichijūnen no kaisō* (Tokyo: Sōgensha, 1953), 250.

75. Duus, *Party Rivalry and Political Change,* 18–19.

76. Ino Kenji, *Kyōkaku no jōken: Yoshida Isokichi den* (Tokyo: Gendai Shokan, 1994), 7. The appearance of a Yoshida-like character in *Hana to ryū* is also mentioned in Yomiuri Shinbun Seibu Honsha, *Nichiro sensō kara Shōwa e,* vol. 2 of *Fukuoka hyakunen* (Osaka: Naniwasha, 1967), 172–76. Hino Ashihei (real name Tamai Katsunori) was a native of Wakamatsu born to the boss of the Tamai *ikka* ("family") but was sympathetic with leftist causes during his youth. See Hino Ashihei, *Hino Ashihei shū,* vol. 52 of *Nihon bungaku zenshū* (Tokyo: Shinchōsha, 1967), 461–72.

77. Fujita Gorō, *Ninkyō hyakunenshi* (Tokyo: Kasakura Shuppansha, 1980), 195–202; Mizoshita Hideo, "Kore ga 'kawasujimono' no tamashii da!," *Jitsuwa jidai* (October 2001): 38–39.

78. Ino, *Kyōkaku no jōken,* 55–56.

79. Ibid., 16–30. See also Tamai Masao, *Katana to seisho* (Tokyo: Rekishi Toshosha, 1978), 17–18.

80. Okabe Teizō was elected to a municipal assembly in 1921. See Ino, *Kyōkaku no jōken,* 59.

81. Ibid., 30–38, 44–50.

82. Yoshida was apparently the first person from Wakamatsu to be elected to the Diet. See Wakamatsu Kyōdo Kenkyūkai, ed., *Wakamatsu hyakunen nenpyō* (Wakamatsu: Kita Kyūshū Shiritsu Wakamatsu Toshokan, 1969), 42.

83. Yoshida Isokichi-ō Denki Kankōkai, ed., *Yoshida Isokichi-ō den* (Tokyo: Yoshida Isokichi-ō Denki Kankōkai, 1941), 29; Duus, *Party Rivalry and Political Change,* 89.

84. Ino, *Kyōkaku no jōken,* 56–57.

85. Ibid., 61.

86. Yoshida Isokichi-ō Denki Kankōkai, *Yoshida Isokichi-ō den,* 63–64; Ino, *Kyōkaku no jōken,* 86.

87. Arima, *Shichijūnen no kaisō,* 250–51.

88. Yoshida Isokichi-ō Denki Kankōkai, *Yoshida Isokichi-ō den,* 59–62.

89. Ibid., 35. N.Y.K. reserves of ¥6.2 million in 1901 had increased by 37.2 percent between 1906 and 1910, and by 81.0 percent from 1910 to 1914. See William D. Wray, *Mitsubishi and the N.Y.K., 1870–1914: Business Strategy in the Japanese Shipping Industry* (Cambridge, Mass.: Council on East Asian Studies, Harvard University, 1984), 479–81.

90. *Tōkyō nichinichi shinbun*, May 28, 1921, in Yoshida Isokichi-ō Denki Kankōkai, *Yoshida Isokichi-ō den*, 55; Yoshida Isokichi-ō Denki Kankōkai, *Yoshida Isokichi-ō den*, 36; Tamai, *Katana to seisho*, 88–89; Wray, *Mitsubishi and the N.Y.K.*, 474–75.

91. *Tōkyō nichinichi shinbun*, May 27, 28, and 30, 1921; *Tōkyō asahi shinbun*, May 30, 1921, in Yoshida Isokichi-ō Denki Kankōkai, *Yoshida Isokichi-ō den*, 53–57; Yoshida Isokichi-ō Denki Kankōkai, *Yoshida Isokichi-ō den*, 37–39, 45–46. Henchman Okabe Teizō had difficulty leaving Kyūshū and purchasing stock in the company. Okabe, who moved around a great deal, did not have a census register (*koseki tōhon*), which was required documentation for potential shareholders. Even after he managed to borrow someone else's register, he had to maneuver around the local police, who attempted to prevent him from making the trip to Tokyo.

92. *Tōkyō nichinichi shinbun*, May 30, 1921; *Tōkyō asahi shinbun*, May 30, 1921, in Yoshida Isokichi-ō Denki Kankōkai, *Yoshida Isokichi-ō den*, 53, 57. Yoshida Isokichi-ō Denki Kankōkai, *Yoshida Isokichi-ō den*, 50.

93. Ino, *Kyōkaku no jōken*, 71–72; Yoshida Isokichi-ō Denki Kankōkai, *Yoshida Isokichi-ō den*, 117–25. There is some question as to why laborers in this region seem to have supported Yoshida, even though he "mediated" disputes in favor of management. It could be that Yoshida protected laborers' interests more than other mediators might have, or that laborers who voted for him thought that his advocacy of local industry would ultimately serve them well—but this is purely speculation.

94. Yoshida Isokichi-ō Denki Kankōkai, *Yoshida Isokichi-ō den*, 72–75, 135–37.

95. Hora Sennosuke, *Kyōkaroku: Kun'yontō kagotora, Hora Sennosuke den* (Tokyo: Tōen Shobō, 1963), 8–12.

96. The *sakazuki* ceremony made official the relationships within "families," the most important being the one between boss and henchman. The format of the *sakazuki* likely varied; what follows is a description of one, perhaps typical, ceremony. The *sakazuki* was held on an auspicious day in a space that was prepared with the proper adornments and utensils for the ritual. In the altar before which the ceremony was held were hung three scrolls that read from right to left: Hachiman Daibosatsu (deity of archery and war), Amaterasu Ōmikami (Shintō sun deity considered the progenitrix of the imperial line), and Kasuga Daimyōjin (originally the tutelary deity of the Fujiwara house). In front of the altar were sake and thick Japanese paper (*hōshotsuki shinshu*), an offering (*sasagemono*), rice, salt, bonito, and a clipping from a sacred Shintō tree (*sakaki*). Also in the room was a small wooden stand (*sanbō*) with thick Japanese paper (*hōsho*) folded into a triangle, on which was placed a pair of sake bottles, one sake cup, three piles of salt, two fish (arranged with one's back to the other's stomach), and a pair of chopsticks. The central figures of the ceremony were of course the boss and henchman as well as a mediator, and they were observed by members of the *ikka* whose seating arrangement at the event was based on status. The ceremony would begin with the mediator using the chopsticks to rearrange the two fish such that they faced each other. He would then pour three times into the sake cup from the sake bottle on the right, three times again from the sake bottle on the left, then combine the three piles of salt into one, and with the chopsticks would put three pinches into the sake cup. A fish was picked up with the chopsticks and dipped into the sake cup three times, then the cup was filled by one pour from the sake bottle on the right and then from the one on the left. At this point in the ceremony, the mediator placed the sake cup in front of the boss and spoke to the henchman who pledged his loyalty to the boss and the *ikka*. After the henchman and boss both delivered some lines, the boss would drink all of the sake, the mediator would refill the cup, the henchman would drink all of the sake, then the boss and henchman would pour for the mediator. The sake cup would then be wrapped in the paper and given to the henchman by the mediator, signifying that the henchman had officially received the boss's *sakazuki*. The remaining sake in the sake bottles was poured on the fish and the chopsticks,

which would be wrapped in the paper and disposed of in a manner determined by the *ikka*. This *sakazuki* with some modifications was also conducted to solidify the relationship between "brothers." *Sakazuki* were also held as ceremonies of reconciliation between two feuding *ikka*. Iwai Hiroaki, *Byōri shūdan no kōzō: Oyabun kobun shūdan kenkyū* (Tokyo: Seishin Shobō, 1963), 146–50, 160–61; Tamura, *Yakuza no seikatsu*, 98–106.

97. Hora also got married around this time to Matsu, the daughter of a fishmonger with whom Hora's family had a business connection. Hora, *Kyōkaroku*, 13–21.

98. Ibid., 21–22.

99. Ibid., 5, 9, 23–24, 26, 33–35, 38–39, 44, 69–73.

100. Ibid., 48–49.

101. Ibid., 40–44.

102. Ibid., 50–53.

103. Ibid., 67, 76, 78–80; Ino, *Kyōkaku no jōken*, 94–95.

104. In the last restricted Shimonoseki city assembly election, held in 1925, there were 4,942 voters out of a total population of 93,019 (48,591 men, 44,428 women). In 1929, that number was 19,096 out of 104,589 (53,862 men, 50,727 women). See Shimonoseki-shi Shishi Henshū Iinkai, ed., *Shimonoseki-shishi*, vol. 3 (Shimonoseki: Shimonoseki Shiyakusho, 1958), 164–65.

105. Hora, *Kyōkaroku*, 89–92, 102, 104–16. According to Hora, two months after he served as vice chair of the assembly, he became head of the Shimonoseki Chamber of Commerce because of his involvement in a wide range of businesses. He held this office for two months, then assumed the number two position, and eventually quit. Records of the Shimonoseki Chamber of Commerce report that Hora served as vice chair in 1933, and never served as chair. See Shimonoseki Shōkō Kaigisho, *Shimonoseki shōkō kaigisho sōritsu hyakunenshi* (Shimonoseki: Shimonoseki Shōkō Kaigisho, 1981), 10.

106. Hora, *Kyōkaroku*, 117–26. I have not found any mention of the Kagotora-gumi in the mass circulation dailies that covered Tanaka's funeral.

107. Hora, *Kyōkaroku*, 126–42.

108. Ibid., 1–2, 151–58.

109. Nakanishi Teruma, *Shōwa Yamaguchi-ken jinbutsushi* (Yamaguchi-ken: Matsuno Shoten, 1990), 247; Shimonoseki-shi Shishi Henshū Iinkai, *Shimonoseki-shishi*, 174–76.

110. Hora, *Kyōkaroku*, 204–8. Hora claimed that he mentioned his support of Ozaki Yukio to clear him with the Occupation authorities because Ozaki had an American wife, but this explanation is at least somewhat questionable given that Ozaki's wife was English. See Ozaki, *Autobiography of Ozaki Yukio*, 246.

111. Diego Gambetta, *The Sicilian Mafia: The Business of Private Protection* (Cambridge, Mass.: Harvard University Press, 1993), 182–87.

112. Ōno Banboku-sensei Tsuisōroku Kankōkai Henshū Iinkai, *Ōno Banboku*, 46–49, 51–52, 67–68; Takahashi, "Ingaidan no keisei," 97.

113. On Capone, see Laurence Bergreen, *Capone: The Man and the Era* (New York: Simon & Schuster, 1994).

4. Fascist Violence

1. Hugh Byas, *Government by Assassination* (London: George Allen & Unwin, 1943), 226. Although it is conventional to describe many of these organizations as "ultra-nationalist," I prefer "nationalist" as it underscores the idea that most of these groups—and, more specifically, the two on which I focus here—were not on some radical fringe of the political scene. Nor did their willingness to use violence necessarily indicate adherence to a kind of extreme nationalism.

2. See Henry DeWitt Smith II, *Japan's First Student Radicals* (Cambridge, Mass.: Harvard University Press, 1972); Ann Waswo, "The Transformation of Rural Society, 1900–1950," in *The Cambridge History of Japan*, vol. 5, ed. Peter Duus (Cambridge: Cambridge University Press, 1989), 541–605; Ian Neary, *Political Protest and Social Control in Pre-War Japan: The Origins of Buraku Liberation* (Manchester: Manchester University Press, 1989); Vera Mackie, *Creating Socialist Women in Japan: Gender, Labour and Activism, 1900–1937* (Cambridge: Cambridge University Press, 1997); Sheldon Garon, *The State and Labor in Modern Japan* (Berkeley: University of California Press, 1987), 42, 71; Andrew Gordon, *Labor and Imperial Democracy in Prewar Japan* (Berkeley: University of California Press, 1991), 144–48.

3. Most of these yakuza were probably *bakuto* (gamblers) because they were more powerful and had more financial resources than *tekiya* (itinerant merchants). When sources specified the kind of yakuza being discussed, it was almost always *bakuto* and not *tekiya*. But because they were referred to most often as yakuza or *kyōkaku* and not specifically *bakuto*, I have used the term "yakuza" throughout this chapter.

4. The Special Higher Police, specialists in regulating political thought, viewed the Dai Nihon Kokusuikai and Dai Nihon Seigidan as one branch of a three-pronged nationalist movement that also included "pure Japanists" like Kita Ikki and "national socialists" like Ōkawa Shūmei. Keishi Sōkan, "Saikin ni okeru kokkashugi undō jōsei ni kansuru ken," November 5, 1931, in *TKKSS*, vol. 13, 4.

5. Naimushō Keihokyoku, *Bōryokudan zokushutsu bakko no jōkyō* (n.d.), 1–4. The term "bōryokudan" would be resurrected in the postwar period to refer exclusively to organized crime syndicates.

6. See Maruyama Masao, *Thought and Behaviour in Modern Japanese Politics*, ed. Ivan Morris (Oxford: Oxford University Press, 1969).

7. See the discussion of "imperial fascism" in Gordon, *Labor and Imperial Democracy*, 302–30.

8. Peter Duus and Daniel I. Okimoto, "Fascism and the History of Pre-War Japan: The Failure of a Concept," *Journal of Asian Studies* 39, no. 1 (November 1979): 65–68.

9. Robert O. Paxton, *The Anatomy of Fascism* (New York: Alfred A. Knopf, 2004), 21.

10. *Tōkyō asahi shinbun*, October 10 and 14, 1919; *Ōsaka mainichi shinbun*, October 9, 1919, in *TNJ*, 378–79.

11. On association membership, see Moriyasu Satoshi, "Imada Ushimatsu to Suiheisha sōritsusha tachi: Dai Nihon Kokusuikai to Nara-ken Suiheisha," *Suiheisha hakubutsukan kenkyū kiyō* 2 (March 2000): 5.

12. *Tōkyō asahi shinbun*, October 10, 1919, in *TNJ*, 378.

13. *Ōsaka mainichi shinbun*, October 9, 1919, in *TNJ*, 378.

14. *Tōkyō asahi shinbun*, November 15, 1919, in *TNJ*, 379–80. When the organization marked the founding of its Osaka headquarters with a ceremony on December 15, at least 15 yakuza organizations were in attendance. Ōsaka-fu Keisatsushi Henshū Iinkai, *Ōsaka-fu keisatsushi*, vol. 2 (Osaka: Ōsaka-fu Keisatsu Honbu, 1972), 197.

15. A sum of all branch members yields a more modest total membership of 41,000 people. It could be that the figure of 200,000 members includes those who did not belong to a regional branch. Naimushō Keihokyoku Hoanka, *Shakai undō dantai gensei chō*, June 1932, 31. In 1934, the number of branches had decreased slightly from 92 to 87, with the size of the largest local organizations shrinking as well. Total membership also declined to around 36,500. Naimushō Keihokyoku Hoanka, *Shakai undō dantai gensei chō*, June 1934, 39.

The Kantō Kokusuikai, a splinter group of the Dai Nihon Kokusuikai, had ten branches and around 1,300 members in 1932, 16 branches and around 1,900 members in 1934. Naimushō Keihokyoku Hoanka, *Shakai undō dantai gensei chō*, June 1932, 33; Naimushō Keihokyoku Hoanka, *Shakai undō dantai gensei chō*, June 1934, 41.

16. Dai Nihon Kokusuikai Sōhonbu Kaihōkyoku, "Dai Nihon Kokusuikaishi," *Dai Nihon Kokusuikai kaihō*, December 1, 1926, 38–39.

17. See Chinzei Kokusuikai, "Chinzei Kokusuikai kaisoku," in *Kyōchōkai shiryō*, reel 52, 16–18; "Dai Nihon Kokusuikai Ōita-ken honbu kaisoku," in *Kyōchōkai shiryō*, reel 52, 12–13; "Dai Nihon Kokusuikai Ōita-ken honbu setsuritsu shuisho," in *Kyōchōkai shiryō*, reel 52, 14–15; "Dai Nihon Kokusuikai Tanabe shibu sōritsu shuisho," in Naimushō materials at the National Diet Library, 9.5–7, 2334; "Dai Nihon Kokusuikai Yahata shibu kiyaku," in *Kyōchōkai shiryō*, reel 52, 21–22.

18. Dai Nihon Kokusuikai, "Dai Nihon Kokusuikai setsuritsu shuisho," in *Kyōchōkai shiryō*, reel 52 (November 1919), 5; "Wareware no shinjō," *Kokusui* 4 (October 15, 1920). A warrior spirit was also evoked by the *squadrismo* of Italy. See Emilio Gentile, "The Problem of the Party in Italian Fascism," *Journal of Contemporary History* 19 (1984): 256.

19. Dai Nihon Kokusuikai, "Dai Nihon Kokusuikai kari kiyaku," in *Kyōchōkai shiryō*, reel 52 [1919], 9.

20. *Yamato kokusui shinbun*, October 11, 1926; Dai Nihon Kokusuikai, "Dai Nihon Kokusuikai setsuritsu shuisho," 5–7; "Wareware no shinjō"; Dai Nihon Kokusuikai, "Dai Nihon Kokusuikai kari kiyaku," 9; *Ōsaka mainichi shinbun*, November 1, 1919, in *TNJ*, 379; Dai Nihon Kokusuikai, "Dai Nihon Kokusuikai kiyaku setsumei," in *Kyōchōkai shiryō*, reel 52 (November 1919), 7.

21. Again, as with the Kokusuikai, a sum of regional membership only totals about 6,300 people. Naimushō Keihokyoku Hoanka, *Shakai undō dantai gensei chō*, June 1932, 35. In 1934, there were 13 branches with a total membership of around 19,800. Naimushō Keihokyoku Hoanka, *Shakai undō dantai gensei chō*, June 1934, 37.

22. For coverage on one of Sakai's speeches that did touch on "the way of the warrior," see *Tōkyō asahi shinbun*, March 28, 1928. One Kokusuikai member wrote, like Sakai, on *kyōkaku*, though he tended to prefer the vocabulary of "yakuza" and "yakuzadō" (the way of the yakuza). See Umezu Kanbei, *Kyōkaku oyobi kyōkakudō ni tsuite* (Nihon Gaikō Kyōkai, 1941).

23. Sakai Eizō, *Buenryo ni mōshiageru* (Tokyo: Ryūbunkan, 1927), 1–3.

24. Ibid., 35–37, 44, 85–89.

25. The first half of Paxton's definition of fascism: "Fascism may be defined as a form of political behavior marked by obsessive preoccupation with community decline, humiliation, or victimhood and by compensatory cults of unity, energy, and purity." There are parts of the second half of his definition that apply to the case of Japan—although it could not be said that "a mass-based party of committed nationalist militants [were] working in uneasy but effective collaboration with traditional elites," groups like the Kokusuikai and Seigidan did "abandon[] democratic liberties and pursue[] with redemptive violence and without ethical or legal restraints goals of internal cleansing and external expansion." Paxton, *Anatomy of Fascism*, 218.

26. On those who saw beauty in fascist violence, see Ibid., 84–85.

27. Richard Bessel, *Political Violence and the Rise of Nazism: The Storm Troopers in Eastern Germany, 1925–1934* (New Haven: Yale University Press, 1984), 75.

28. Roberta Suzzi Valli, "The Myth of *Squadrismo* in the Fascist Regime," *Journal of Contemporary History* 35, no. 2 (April 2000): 132.

29. Bessel makes a similar point in the German context, arguing that the actions of the SA should themselves be considered Nazi ideology. Bessel, *Political Violence and the Rise of Nazism*, 151–52.

30. Dai Nihon Kokusuikai, "Dai Nihon Kokusuikai setsuritsu shuisho," 7; *Ōsaka mainichi shinbun*, November 1, 1919, in *TNJ*, 379.

31. Sakai, *Buenryo ni mōshiageru*, 62–66.

32. Paxton, *Anatomy of Fascism*, 7, 64, 84.

33. Sakai, *Buenryo ni mōshiageru*, 1, 7, 85, 87; *Yomiuri shinbun*, October 11, 1925; Suzuki Yūko, *Jokō to rōdō sōgi: 1930-nen Yōmosu sōgi*, vol. 1 of *Nihon josei rōdō undō shiron* (Tokyo: Renga Shōbō Shinsha, 1989), 107. The Seigidan uniform was also said to display the character for "north" in homage to Sakai's boss Kobayashi Sahei, also known as "Sahei of the North." *Yomiuri shinbun*, February 18 and 21, 1925.

34. Naimushō Keihokyoku, *Kokusuikaiin no fukusō ni kansuru ken tsūchō, chō fuken*, August 15, 1923; Naimushō Keihokyoku, *Dai Nihon Kokusuikaiin no fukusō ni kansuru ken, Ehime-ken*, June 4, 1935, 13–16.

35. On the Yahata Ironworks strike, see Hirokawa Tadahide, "Yahata seitetsujo ni okeru 1920-nen no sutoraiki," *Jinbun kenkyū* 24, no. 10 (1972): 59–92; *Yahata seitetsujo rōdō undōshi* (Fukuoka: Yahata Seitetsu Kabushikigaisha, Yahata Seitetsujo, 1953). The Tsurumi Incident was a clash between two contractors, each backed by yakuza. See Saitō Hideo, "Keihin kōgyō chitai no keisei to chiiki shakai: Iwayuru 'Tsurumi sōjō jiken' o megutte," *Yokohama shiritsu daigaku ronsō: Jinbun kagaku keiretsu* 40, no. 1 (March 1989): 1–121; Satō Makoto, *Tsurumi sōjō jiken hyakka* (Yokohama: Nisanmaru Kurabu, 1999). On the Singer Sewing Machine strike, see Kamei Nobuyuki, "Shingā mishin gaisha bunten heisa oyobi bunten shunin kaiko mondai ni kansuru ken," in *Kyōchōkai shiryō*, reel 80 (December 17, 1925), 502.

36. On the Osaka Shiden strike, see Watanabe Etsuji, "Rensai intabyū, senzen no rōdō sōgi III: Kōno Takashi-san ni kiku Takanosan e no rōjō senjutsu o amidashita Ōsaka Shiden sōgi," *Gekkan sōhyō* 241 (January 1978): 113.

37. Shihōshō Chōsaka, *Shihō kenkyū* 8 (1928): 509; Ōsaka-fu Keisatsushi Hensan Iinkai, *Ōsaka-fu keisatsushi*, 195–96; *Asahi shinbun*, March 9, 1926, in Tanaka Sōgorō, ed., *Shiryō: Taishō shakai undōshi*, ge-kan (Tokyo: San'ichi Shobō, 1970), 961. In Osaka, the amounts collected from *bōryokudan* for involvement in blackmail and extortion were ¥89,000 in 1931, ¥255,000 in 1935, ¥24,000 in 1936, and ¥27,000 in 1937. Ōsaka-fu Keisatsushi Hensan Iinkai, *Ōsaka-fu keisatsushi*, 201.

38. Gentile, "Problem of the Party in Italian Fascism," 256.

39. Mark W. Fruin, *Kikkoman: Company, Clan, and Community* (Cambridge, Mass.: Harvard University Press, 1983), 183, 200–201.

40. Morinaga Eizaburō, "Noda Shōyu rōdō sōgi jiken: Nihyaku jūnana nichi no chōki, saidai no suto, I," *Hōgaku seminā* 202 (October 1972): 104.

41. Fruin, *Kikkoman*, 183, 195, 201.

42. The six demands submitted to the company on April 10, 1927, were as follows: (1) A ten percent wage increase for men and 20 percent for women; (2) one day more every month to be added in calculating allowances for discharge, retirement, and resignation; (3) apprentice training for coopers in each plant; (4) a minimum year-end bonus to be fixed at one month's pay; (5) promotion to skilled operative status (with certain rights of privilege and permanency in employment) to be fixed at four years; and (6) an extension of full coverage under the Employee Relief Provisions (Kōin Fujo Kitei) to part-time employees. Cited verbatim from Fruin, *Kikkoman*, 201.

43. Ibid., 200; Morinaga, "Noda Shōyu rōdō sōgi jiken, I," 106; Morinaga Eizaburō, "Noda Shōyu rōdō sōgi jiken: Nihyaku jūnana nichi no chōki, saidai no suto, II," *Hōgaku seminā* 203 (November 1972): 88. One of the first actions of the local union was to picket in front of the main gate of Factory Seventeen. It was forced to close temporarily, with production resuming on September 27. See Morinaga, "Noda Shōyu rōdō sōgi jiken, II," 88.

44. Nomura Jōji, "Zen rōdōsha wa kekkishite Kenkokukai o tatakitsubuse!," *Rōdōsha* 13 (February 1928): 41. Because the most common term used in contemporary sources was "bōryokudan," I have adopted it here in cases where a more precise identification of the violent is difficult or impossible.

45. The figure of 800 people was given in Kyōchōkai Rōdōka, ed., *Noda rōdō sōgi no tenmatsu* (Kyōchōkai Rōdōka, 1928), 50. The figure of 1,000 people was provided by Noda Shōyu in Noda Shōyu Kabushikigaisha, ed., *Noda sōgi no tenmatsu* (Chiba: Noda Shōyu, 1928), 30; and *Noda Shōyu Kabushikigaisha nijūnenshi* (Noda-machi, Chiba: Noda Shōyu, 1940), 234.

46. Kyōchōkai Rōdōka, *Noda rōdō sōgi no tenmatsu*, 50-51; Noda Shōyu Kabushikigaisha, *Noda sōgi no tenmatsu*, 32.

47. "Daikyū kōjō sagyō kaishi ni tsuite: Noda Shōyu Kabushikigaisha" (October 1927). At the Ōhara Institute for Social Research, file on Noda Shōyu sōgi 1927.9-1928.4; Kyōchōkai Rōdōka, *Noda rōdō sōgi no tenmatsu*, 27; Machida Tatsujirō (Kyōchōkai councillor), *Rōdō sōgi no kaibō* (Tokyo: Dai-ichi Shuppansha, 1929), 66.

48. Noda Shōyu Kabushikigaisha, *Noda sōgi no tenmatsu*, 30; *Noda Shōyu Kabushikigaisha nijūnenshi*, 234; Noda Shōyu Kabushikigaisha, *Noda sōgi no keika nichiroku*, 38, 44.

49. Nihon Shakai Mondai Kenkyūjo, ed., *Noda kessenki* (Tokyo: Nihon Shakai Mondai Kenkyūjo, 1928), 150, 164; Kyōchōkai Rōdōka, *Noda rōdō sōgi no tenmatsu*, 78.

50. Those arrested were released on September 30. After what became known as the bamboo spear incident, the company sent dismissal notices to union members. See Morinaga, "Noda Shōyu rōdō sōgi jiken, II," 88-89.

51. Morinaga, "Noda Shōyu rōdō sōgi jiken, II," 88-89; [*Shakai minshū shinbun*], in *Kyōchōkai shiryō*, reel 63 (October 23, 1927), 566.

52. [*Shakai minshū shinbun*], 566; Nihon Shakai Mondai Kenkyūjo, *Noda kessenki*, 147-48, 153; Morinaga, "Noda Shōyu rōdō sōgi jiken, II," 90.

53. Kyōchōkai Rōdōka, *Noda rōdō sōgi no tenmatsu*, 59, 70; Machida, *Rōdō sōgi no kaibō*, 64-65; Morinaga, "Noda Shōyu rōdō sōgi jiken, II," 89.

54. Nihon Shakai Mondai Kenkyūjo, *Noda kessenki*, 227; Noda Shōyu Kabushikigaisha, *Noda sōgi no keika nichiroku*, 47; Kyōchōkai Rōdōka, *Noda rōdō sōgi no tenmatsu*, 78-80.

55. Nihon Shakai Mondai Kenkyūjo, *Noda kessenki*, 233-36.

56. Ibid., 238-39, 242-43; *Noda Shōyu Kabushikigaisha rōdō sōgi gaikyō*, in *TKKSS*, vol. 9, 290; Kyōchōkai Rōdōka, *Noda rōdō sōgi no tenmatsu*, 83; Noda Shōyu Kabushikigaisha, *Noda sōgi no keika nichiroku*, 65, 67, 71-72.

57. Rōdō Nōmintō, Tōkyō-fu, Kyōbashi Shibu, "Noda rokusen no kyōdai shokun!!," in *Kyōchōkai shiryō*, reel 63 (January 16, 1928), 568. Eighty people were arrested (including two key union figures), and 34 were prosecuted. Morinaga, "Noda Shōyu rōdō sōgi jiken, II," 90.

58. Kantō Rōdō Dōmeikai, *Noda sōgi no shin'in keika oyobi genjō: Kaisha no kodaiken ni kyokō no senden o kyūsu*, in *Kyōchōkai shiryō*, reel 63 (1928), 498-99; Morinaga, "Noda Shōyu rōdō sōgi jiken, II," 90.

59. Morinaga gives the date of the settlement as April 19, other sources cite April 20. Morinaga, "Noda Shōyu rōdō sōgi jiken, II," 91; Noda Shōyu Kabushikigaisha, *Noda sōgi no keika nichiroku*, 143; Fruin, *Kikkoman*, 205.

60. Kyōchōkai Rōdōka, *Noda rōdō sōgi no tenmatsu*, 51.

61. The workers from the cotton-spinning division to be sent home were to receive travel expenses for three months; each month, they would be paid 26 days of wages equivalent to one-third of standard daily wages. There was a possibility of transfer to the Nerima, Shizuoka, or other factories; if a worker was not called back during a period of three months, a retirement allowance would be issued. Those who opted for immediate retirement would receive 29 days of standard daily wages in addition to the travel expenses and retirement allowance. Workers who commuted instead of living in the dormitory would be given the same payments and choices as stated above except for the travel expenses. For the workers of the maintenance division, there was a possibility of receiving

contract work from the company, in which case they would also be allowed to accept additional work from outside the company. Suzuki, *Jokō to rōdō sōgi,* 49–50; Maruyama Tsurukichi (superintendent-general of the Metropolitan Police) to the Home Ministry, "Yōmosu Kameido kōjō rōdō sōgi ni kansuru ken," in *Kyōchōkai shiryō,* reel 97 (September 30, 1930), 113–14; Shakaikyoku Rōdōbu, ed., *Tōyō Mosurin Kabushikigaisha rōdō sōgi jōkyō* (Shakaikyoku Rōdōbu, 1930), 2.

For a discussion in English of how gender functioned in the strike, see Elyssa Faison, *Managing Women: Disciplining Labor in Modern Japan* (Berkeley: University of California Press, 2007), 93–106.

62. The report by Maruyama Tsurukichi gives the number of laborers as 2,482, while the Shakaikyoku Rōdōbu cites 2,649 laborers, 468 men and 2,181 women. Maruyama Tsurukichi, "Yōmosu Kameido kōjō rōdō sōgi," 113; Shakaikyoku Rōdōbu, *Tōyō Mosurin Kabushikigaisha rōdō sōgi jōkyō,* 1–2.

63. Yōmosu Sōgidan, Zenkoku Rōdō Kumiai Dōmei, Nihon Bōshoku Rōdō Kumiai, "Yōmosu sōgi ni tsuite chōmin shokun ni gekisu," October 2, 1930. At the Ōhara Institute for Social Research, Yōmosu sōgi file 1.

64. Maruyama, "Yōmosu Kameido kōjō rōdō sōgi," 117; Suzuki, *Jokō to rōdō sōgi,* 53; *Tōyō Mosu daisōgi: Reposhū,* September 27, 1930. At the Ōhara Institute for Social Research, Yōmosu sōgi file 1.

65. On one particular night, 300 Seigidan members were to guard the company offices after closing. Maruyama Tsurukichi (superintendent-general of the Metropolitan Police) to the Home Ministry, "Yōmosu Kameido kōjō rōdō sōgi ni kansuru ken," in *Kyōchōkai shiryō,* reel 97 (October 1, 1930), 106.

66. Suzuki, *Jokō to rōdō sōgi,* 52–53.

67. *Zenkoku taishū shinbun,* October 11, 1930; "Geki!!," October 5, 1930. At the Ōhara Institute for Social Research, Yōmosu sōgi file 1.

68. Maruyama Tsurukichi (superintendent-general of the Metropolitan Police) to the Home Ministry, "Yōmosu Kameido kōjō rōdō sōgi ni kansuru ken," in *Kyōchōkai shiryō,* reel 97 (October 10, 1930), 133–34; "Geki!!"

69. Some newspapers reported that some of the "thugs" (*bōto*) in the Iriyama strike were henchmen of a yakuza boss. *Fukushima minpō,* January 21, 1927; *Fukushima minyū,* January 21, 1927, in Murata Sunao, ed., *Yomigaeru chitei no kiroku: Banjaku, Iriyama rōdō sōgi shiryō shūsei,* vol. 1 (Iwaki: Iwaki Shakai Mondai Kenkyūkai, 1984), 190–91. As mentioned in the previous chapter, Yoshida Isokichi also claims to have been a mediator in the Iriyama Coal Mine strike.

70. The party also wanted to overthrow the Hamaguchi Cabinet. Rōnōtō, "Yōmosu sōgi ōen bōatsu hantai, datō Hamaguchi naikaku no enzetsukai ni tsuite," October 3, 1930. At the Ōhara Institute for Social Research, Yōmosu sōgi file 1.

71. *Yōmosu sōgi tōsō nyūsu* 6, October 11, 1930. At the Ōhara Institute for Social Research, Yōmosu sōgi file 2; *Kantō gōdō rōdō kumiai nyūsu* 1, October 11, 1930. At the Ōhara Institute for Social Research, Yōmosu sōgi file 1.

72. *Tōyō Mosu daisōgi,* October 11 and 21, 1930; Tōyō Mosurin Sōgidan Honbu, untitled handbill, October 7, 1930. At the Ōhara Institute for Social Research, Yōmosu sōgi file 1; *Zenkoku taishū shinbun,* October 11, 1930.

73. Nihon Bōshoku Rōdō Kumiai Yōmosu Sōgidan, *Yōmosu sōgi nippō,* October 10 and 15, 1930. At the Ōhara Institute for Social Research, Yōmosu sōgi file 2; Nihon Bōshoku Rōdō Kumiai Kamei, "Yōmosu sōgi wa saigo no kessen da!," 1930. At the Ōhara Institute for Social Research, Yōmosu sōgi file 1.

74. Rōdō Undōshi Kenkyūkai and Rōdōsha Kyōiku Kyōkai, eds., *Nihon rōdō undō no rekishi: Senzen hen* (Tokyo: San'ichi Shobō, 1960), 186.

75. Watanabe Tetsuzō, "Taishō shishi ron," *Chūō kōron* 38, no. 12 (November 1923): 83; Shihōshō Chōsaka, *Shihō kenkyū,* 509–10.

76. Yamamura Masako, "Suiheisha, Kokusuikai tōsō jiken no kentō: Saiban kiroku o chūshin to shite," *Buraku kaihō kenkyū* 27 (September 1981): 161–64. Many thanks to Jeff Bayliss for bringing this article to my attention.

77. Moriyasu, "Imada Ushimatsu to Suiheisha sōritsusha tachi," 2; Neary, *Political Protest and Social Control,* 87; Yamamura, "Suiheisha, Kokusuikai tōsō jiken no kentō," 136, 140.
The head of the Nara Prefecture branch of the Kokusuikai was a man named Imada Ushimatsu. Born in 1854, Imada became addicted to gambling when young, was disowned by his parents at the age of 14, and returned home two years later only to run away and become a laborer. He was sent to Hokkaidō as punishment for a crime he committed, was released in 1907, and was involved in the founding of the Kokusuikai in 1919. Imada arrived on the scene on March 18, but his precise role in the incident is unclear. See Moriyasu, "Imada Ushimatsu to Suiheisha sōritsusha tachi," 2–4, 8.

78. The numbers of Kokusuikai supporters were 800 on March 18; 1,200 on March 19; and 275 on March 20. The figures for the Suiheisha: 750 on March 18; 1,220 on March 19; and 970 on March 20. "Suiheisha tai Kokusuikai sōjō jiken," in *Tanemura-shi keisatsu sankō shiryō* (n.d.), 44–46. At the National Archives of Japan.

79. The numbers of assembled police were 81 on March 18; 394 on March 19; 218 regular forces and 17 special forces on March 20 and 21. "Suiheisha tai Kokusuikai sōjō jiken," 36–38.

80. Ibid., 48–51, 55.

81. Adrian Lyttelton, *The Seizure of Power: Fascism in Italy, 1919–1929* (New York: Routledge, 2004), 38, 53–54.

82. Peter H. Merkl, *The Making of a Stormtrooper* (Princeton: Princeton University Press, 1980), 100, 299; Conan Fischer, *Stormtroopers: A Social, Economic and Ideological Analysis, 1929–35* (London: George Allen & Unwin, 1983), 149, 186.

83. Gotō was also friendly with the Seigidan; he apparently once called upon Sakai Eizō and his organization to help evict all of the tenants on a Gotō family property. Sakai, *Buenryo ni mōshiageru,* 89–94.

84. Arahara Bokusui, *Dai uyokushi* (Tokyo: Dai Nihon Kokumintō, 1966), 53.

85. Naimushō Keihokyoku, *Dai Nihon Kokusuikaiin no fukusō,* [17–18].

86. Kawagoe Shigeru (Japanese consul general in Qingdao) to the foreign minister, "Chintō Kokusuikai kaisan ni kansuru ken," *Gaimushō kiroku,* April 1, 1932, 208–9; *Asahi shinbun,* August 20, 1931.

87. Kantō-chō Keimukyokuchō (head of the Guandong Police Bureau) to the vice minister of overseas affairs, vice minister of foreign affairs et al., "Kokusuikai hoten honbu no kaishō to sono katsudō," *Gaimushō kiroku,* July 1, 1931, 196–205.

88. Oguri Kazuo (governor of Fukuoka Prefecture) to the home minister, foreign minister et al., "Manshū Kokusuikai kanji no gendō ni kansuru ken," *Gaimushō kiroku,* April 5, 1933, 240.

89. This practice of earning at least tacit approval from authorities was a strategy that had been used domestically; one chief director had even held a conference at an inn with a mayor, the head of the city assembly, and important figures from the police, the Home Ministry, and the Ministry of Justice. Chief Director Nakayasu also sent new year's greeting cards to local authorities, including the head of the Kyoto police. Dai Nihon Kokusuikai Sōhonbu Kaihōkyoku, "Dai Nihon Kokusuikaishi," 37, 42.

90. Fujinuma Shōhei (superintendent-general of the Metropolitan Police) to the home minister et al., "Nihon Seigidan no Manshū shinshutsu ni kansuru ken," *Honpō imin kankei zakken: Manshūkokubu, Gaimushō kiroku,* July 28, 1932, 1–2; Naimushō Keihokyoku, ed., *Shakai undō no jōkyō,* vol. 7 (1935; reprint, Tokyo: San'ichi Shobō, 1972), 282.

91. Kantō-chō Keimukyokuchō (head of the Guandong Police Bureau) to the vice minister of foreign affairs et al., "Dai Manshū Seigidan no seihaishiki kyokō," *Gaimushō*

kiroku, September 13, 1932, 313–4; Oguri Kazuo (governor of Fukuoka Prefecture) to the home minister et al., "Manshū Seigidan seihaishiki kyokō no ken," *Gaimushō kiroku,* September 12, 1932, 308; Kantō-chō Keimukyokuchō (head of the Guandong Police Bureau) to the vice minister of overseas affairs, cabinet secretary et al., "Dai Manshū Seigidan danki," *Gaimushō kiroku,* September 25, 1932, 319–21, 325.

92. Kantō-chō Keimukyokuchō, "Dai Manshū Seigidan no seihaishiki kyokō," 315; Ōsaka-fu chiji (governor of Osaka) to the home minister et al., "Shin Manshūkoku ni okeru Seigidan no kōdō, sono hoka ni kansuru ken," *Gaimushō kiroku,* September 15, 1932, 317.

93. Eishima Kazue (Japanese consul general in Tianjin) to the foreign minister, "Manshū kankei rōnin raiō mata katsudō keitōhyō sōfu no ken," *Shina rōnin kankei zakken, Gaimushō kiroku,* March 17, 1933, 416–21; *Asahi shinbun,* September 29, 1932.

In one case, Ikeda Hideo was investigated after "visiting" an electric company in Pusan with several thousand people. His name showed up on the membership rolls for Seigidan branches in Manchuria, but it was believed he was using the Manshū Seigidan name to extort money for his own personal gain. Yoshizawa Seijirō (Japanese consul general in Xinjing) to the foreign minister and envoy in Manchukuo, "Jishō Manshūkoku Seigidan sōmu Ikeda Hideo no dōsei ni kansuru ken," *Shina rōnin kankei zakken, Gaimushō kiroku,* April 25, 1934, 424–25.

94. Fujinuma, "Nihon Seigidan no Manshū shinshutsu ni kansuru ken," 2–3; Oguri, "Manshū Seigidan seihaishiki kyokō no ken," 308.

95. *Tōkyō asahi shinbun,* August 12, 1922; Irokawa Daikichi, *Ruten no minkenka: Murano Tsuneemon den* (Tokyo: Daiwa Shobō, 1980), 342, 345–346.

96. Maejima Shōzō, "Shishiteki pucchi to kokka kenryoku," *Nihonshi kenkyū* 24 (May 1955): 57; Takahashi Hikohiro, "Ingaidan no keisei: Takeuchi Takeshi-shi no kikigaki o chūshin ni," *Shakai rōdō kenkyū* 30, no. 3–4 (March 1984): 107. Like the Kokusuikai, the Taishō Sekishindan (Taisho True Spirit Organization) was another nationalist group that included Seiyūkai executives among its leadership. Irokawa, *Ruten no minkenka,* 340.

97. Gentile, "Problem of the Party in Italian Fascism," 254. Roberta Suzzi Valli might take issue with this characterization of the *squadrismo,* as Valli considers them more of a "militia party" than a "party militia." Valli, "Myth of *Squadrismo* in the Fascist Regime," 133.

98. Thomas Childers and Eugene Weiss, "Voters and Violence: Political Violence and the Limits of National Socialist Mass Mobilization," *German Studies Review* 13, no. 3 (October 1990): 482–83. The difference in scale of fascist violence in Japan and Germany has much to do with variations in the power and popularity of fascism in these countries but also with the aims of these fascist organizations. The Kokusuikai and Seigidan were fascist in many ways, but they did not have a clearly articulated vision of fascist rule, nor was the seizure of political power the overarching goal of their violence. Although the two organizations were tied to the military, they did not seek to catapult it to power in the same way the *squadrismo* did for Mussolini or the SA did for the Nazis. Their violence was thus circumscribed by their focus on quashing the left and waned as the left was contained and suppressed.

99. Miyake Setsurei, "Kokusuikai ni nozomu," *Chūō kōron* 38, no. 1 (January 1923): 213–14; Mizuno Hironori, "Bōryoku mokunin to kokka hinin," *Chūō kōron* 38, no. 1 (January 1923): 206. Both articles were part of a series: "Bōryokuteki dantai no sonzai o mokunin suru tōkyoku no taiman o kyūdan suru."

100. Kikuchi Kan, "Bōryoku ni tayorazushite ote no koto o shorishitashi," *Chūō kōron* 38, no. 9 (August 1923): 95; Abe Isoo, "Kokkateki 'chikara' no hatsugen o kōhei nara shimeyo," *Chūō kōron* 38, no. 9 (August 1923): 74. Both articles were part of the series: "Bōkō, kyōhaku kyōsei nado ni taisuru tōkyoku no torishimari no kantai o katanzu." Abe

Isoo, "Hōchikoku ni bōryoku o yurusu to wa nanigoto ka," *Chūō kōron* 38, no. 1 (January 1923): 220; Abe Isoo, "Bōryoku ni taisuru kokumin no futetteiteki taido," *Kaizō* 6, no. 5 (May 1924): 94; Inoue Kinji, "Gunshū shinri ni tsūgyō seyo," *Chūō kōron* 38, no. 9 (August 1923): 102.

101. Watanabe, "Taishō shishi ron," 84–85.

102. Horie Kiichi, "Bōryokuteki dantai no sonzai o mokunin suru ka," *Chūō kōron* 38, no. 1 (January 1923): 212; Inoue, "Gunshū shinri ni tsūgyō seyo," 102.

103. Miyake Setsurei, "'Chikara' o tanomu no hei," *Chūō kōron* 38, no. 9 (August 1923): 80–83; Sugimori Kōjirō, "Bōryoku to bunka," *Chūō kōron* 36, no. 13 (December 1921): 99; Sugimori Kōjirō, "Bōryoku no ronrisei," *Chūō kōron* 49, no. 6 (June 1934): 41, 43–44; Abe, "Hōchikoku ni bōryoku o yurusu to wa nanigoto ka," 216, 219; Mizuno, "Bōryoku mokunin to kokka hinin," 205, 210.

104. *Nagasaki nichinichi shinbun*, March 26, 1926, in *KKMSBJ*, 36; *Kyūshū shinbun*, March 26, 1926, in *KKMSBJ*, 40; *Jiji shinpō*, March 25, 1926, in *KKMSBJ*, 49; *Ōsaka nichinichi shinbun*, March 31, 1926, in *KKMSBJ*, 47; *Seiji keizai tsūshin*, April 6, 1926, in *KKMSBJ*, 60.

105. "Seiyūkai no bōkō jiken," March 30, 1926, in *KKMSBJ*, 33; *Tokushima mainichi shinbun*, March 27, 1926, in *KKMSBJ*, 45; *Jiji shinpō*, March 26, 1926, in *KKMSBJ*, 23–24.

106. *Tōkyō asahi shinbun*, March 25, 1926, in *KKMSBJ*, 20; *Jiji shinpō*, March 26, 1926, in *KKMSBJ*, 23.

107. *Kyūshū shinbun*, March 26, 1926, in *KKMSBJ*, 40–41.

108. *Ōsaka mainichi shinbun*, March 26, 1926, in *KKMSBJ*, 31; *Kyūshū shinbun*, March 26, 1926, in *KKMSBJ*, 42; *Kokumin shinbun*, March 26, 1926, in *KKMSBJ*, 52; *Chūgai shōgyō shinpō*, March 26, 1926, in *KKMSBJ*, 51.

109. *Nagasaki nichinichi shinbun*, March 26, 1926, in *KKMSBJ*, 39; *Nichiman chōhō*, March 26, 1926, in *KKMSBJ*, 37; *Tokushima mainichi shinbun*, March 27, 1926, in *KKMSBJ*, 43; *Kokumin shinbun*, March 25, 1926, in *KKMSBJ*, 21–22; *Nichiman chōhō*, March 26, 1926, in *KKMSBJ*, 27.

110. *Seiji keizai tsūshin*, April 7, 1926, in *KKMSBJ*, 61–64.

111. Yoshino Sakuzō, "'Kokka' no hoka 'chikara' no shiyō o yurusazu," *Chūō kōron* 38, no. 1 (January 1923): 201; Inoue, "Gunshū shinri ni tsūgyō seyo," 100, 104; Mizuno, "Bōryoku mokunin to kokka hinin," 207–8.

112. Mizuno, "Bōryoku mokunin to kokka hinin," 207; Mizuno Hironori, "Isshi dōjin tare," *Chūō kōron* 38, no. 9 (August 1923): 94–95.

113. Horie, "Bōryokuteki dantai no sonzai o mokunin suru ka," 210.

114. Abe, "Kokkateki 'chikara' no hatsugen o kōhei nara shimeyo," 74, 76–77.

115. Paxton, *Anatomy of Fascism*, 84.

116. Valli, "Myth of *Squadrismo* in the Fascist Regime," 134.

117. On political party influence in the 1930s, see Gordon Mark Berger, *Parties out of Power in Japan, 1931–1941* (Princeton: Princeton University Press, 1977).

118. Michael Mann, *Fascists* (Cambridge: Cambridge University Press, 2004), 175.

119. Gregory J. Kasza, "Fascism from Below? A Comparative Perspective on the Japanese Right, 1931–1936," *Journal of Contemporary History* 19, no. 4 (October 1984): 617.

120. Takahashi, "Ingaidan no keisei," 107–10, 118.

121. Naimushō Keihokyoku, *Shakai undō dantai gensei chō*, June 1932, 31, 35; Naimushō Keihokyoku, *Shakai undō dantai gensei chō*, June 1935, 45–46; Keihokyoku Hoanka, "Senji shita ni okeru kokkashugi undō torishimari no hōshin," July 1942, in *TKKSS*, vol. 14, 234–35.

122. The argument that violence can be viewed as powerful, and as a kind of power, differs from Hannah Arendt's well-known contention that violence is distinct from power because violence "always needs *implements*" (italics in original). But perhaps power, like

violence, is always expressed, exerted, and mediated through "implements," broadly defined. See Hannah Arendt, *On Violence* (New York: Harcourt, Brace & World, 1969), 4.

123. Frank Morn, *"The Eye That Never Sleeps": A History of the Pinkerton National Detective Agency* (Bloomington: Indiana University Press, 1982), 96–99.

124. James B. Jacobs, *Mobsters, Unions, and Feds: The Mafia and the American Labor Movement* (New York: New York University Press, 2006), xi–xii, 1–2, 26, 32–34, 100–101, 107–8. The American example also differs from the Japanese case in that "gangsters" were hired by both sides—unions and management—in violent labor conflicts. Indeed, the union's willingness to solicit this kind of aid facilitated organized crime's entry into labor racketeering. Jacobs, *Mobsters, Unions, and Feds*, 24.

125. Howard Abadinsky, in his textbook definition of organized crime, claimed that such groups were a "non-ideological enterprise" that did not have "political goals" and were "not motivated by ideological concerns." For Abadinsky, the lack of an ideology was an essential, defining characteristic of organized crime. Howard Abadinsky, *Organized Crime* (Chicago: Nelson-Hall, 1985), 5.

126. Christopher Duggan, *Fascism and the Mafia* (New Haven: Yale University Press, 1989), 95–97, 145, 147, 227–37.

5. Democracy Reconstructed

1. *Yomiuri shinbun*, May 22, 1946.

2. On exhaustion and despair in the immediate postwar years, see Chapter 3 of John W. Dower, *Embracing Defeat: Japan in the Wake of World War II* (New York: W. W. Norton, 1999).

3. Suzuki Yasuzō, "Bōryoku: Toku ni minshushugi ni okeru bōryoku ni tsuite," *Riron* 10–11 (November 1949): 24–25.

4. For more on the occupation's democratizing efforts, see Dower, *Embracing Defeat*, especially Part 4.

5. Koizumi Shinzō, "Bōryoku to minshushugi," *Keiei hyōron* 4, no. 9 (September 1949): 4–6.

6. The number of eligible voters for the April 1946 election was 36,878,420. The population figures for this time are fairly unreliable, with estimates in the 70 to 78 million range. The *Asahi nenkan* gives the population within Japan in April 1946 at 73,114,136. Election Department, Local Administration Bureau, Ministry of Internal Affairs and Communications, "Fixed Number, Candidates, Eligible Voters as of Election Day, Voters and Voting Percentages of Elections for the House of Representatives (1890–1993)," http://www.stat.go.jp/english/data/chouki/27.htm; *Asahi nenkan* (Osaka: Asahi Shinbunsha, 1948), 374. On the difficulties of ascertaining accurate population figures for this period, see Allan B. Cole, "Population Changes in Japan," *Far Eastern Survey* 15, no. 10 (May 1946): 149–50.

7. The absence of violence and relative lack of corruption in this election could also be explained by the watchful eye of the occupation authorities who dispatched troops for surveillance during the campaign as well as the relatively empty treasuries of the newly established political parties which were not yet in a financial position to bribe voters or hire ruffians. On election surveillance, see SCAP Government Section, *Political Reorientation of Japan: September 1945 to September 1948*, vol. 1 (Washington: U.S. Government Printing Office, 1949), 316. This is not to say that the early postwar elections were free from irregularities. On violations of the election law, see Richard J. Samuels, *Machiavelli's Children: Leaders and Their Legacies in Italy and Japan* (Ithaca: Cornell University Press, 2003), 227.

8. *Yomiuri shinbun*, September 18, 1946. There were several other articles around this time about *ingaidan*, but few of them even mentioned violence. For two examples, see *Yomiuri shinbun*, September 16 and 21, 1946.

9. Ibid., February 10, 1949; "Ingaidan no shōtai o tsuku," *Seikei jichō* 8, no. 3 (March 1953): 13.

10. Nishijima Yoshiji et al., "Zadankai: Kokkai, bōryoku, minshū," *Sekai* 104 (August 1954): 76–77. The participants in this roundtable were Nishijima Yoshiji, Nakamura Akira, Tōyama Shigeki, and Katō Hyōji. As part of this discussion, Nakamura Akira offered that the Diet building had been more treacherous in the prewar period because anyone was allowed to walk the corridors which were considered "paths of the people." Entrance did not become more restricted, he claimed, until the planned but prohibited general strike of February 1, 1947.

11. "Ingaidan no shōtai," 13–14.

12. Tabata Izuho, "Bōryoku to seitō," *Jinbutsu ōrai* 1, no. 7 (July 1952): 25.

13. "Ingaidan no shōtai," 13–14; *Yomiuri shinbun*, April 20, 1956.

14. Hori Yukio, *Sengo seijishi, 1945–1960* (Tokyo: Nansōsha, 2001), 211–12.

15. Nishijima et al., "Zadankai," 74–76.

16. Yomiuri Shinbunsha, Asahi Shinbunsha, and Mainichi Shinbunsha, "Sumiyaka ni seikyoku o shūshū seyo," June 11, 1954, in *Sekai* 104 (August 1954): 78.

17. *Yomiuri shinbun*, June 5, 1954; February 1, 1955; Nishijima et al., "Zadankai," 79.

18. *Yomiuri shinbun*, June 5, 1954.

19. Masuda Kaneshichi, "Minshū seiji to bōryoku: Danko chōbatsu subeshi," *Keizai jidai* 19, no. 7 (July 1954): 32–35.

20. Tsuda Sōkichi, "Bōryoku seiji e no ikari: Dō naru bai mo bōryoku o haijo seyo," *Bungei shunjū* 32, no. 12 (August 1954): 73–76.

21. Nishijima et al., "Zadankai," 74–77, 79–82.

22. Nishijima Yoshiji, "Kokkai wa are de yoi ka," *Seiji keizai* 9, no. 7 (July 1956): 4; Aoki Kazuo, "Yurusarenu Shakaitō no bōryoku: Muteikō de shūshishita Jimintō," *Keizai jidai* 21, no. 7 (July 1956): 36.

23. Hori, *Sengo seijishi*, 245–48.

24. Yamaguchi Rinzō, "Bōto shita sangiin: Dai nijūyon tsūjō kokkai no makugire," *Seiji keizai* 9, no. 7 (July 1956): 22–23; Nojima Teiichirō, "Bōryoku kokkai to sangiin," *Seiji keizai* 9, no. 7 (July 1956): 24–25.

25. Economist Kitaoka Juitsu opened his article with a section on how the recent "disgraceful affair" had been exposed for everyone to see, both domestically and internationally, through coverage in newspapers, radio, television, and newsreels. Kitaoka Juitsu, "Bōryoku kokkai no hihan to taisaku," *Keizai jidai* 21, no. 7 (July 1956): 29.

26. One poll conducted in June 1956 asked the question: "Where does responsibility for the violence lie?" Forty-two percent of the respondents replied the JSP while only 15.8 percent named the LDP. Another poll question focused specifically on the JSP's violence: "What do you think of [the] resort to force by the minority Socialists as a form of parliamentary tactics?" Only 20.0 percent found it "unavoidable," while 72.4 percent answered "inexcusable." United States Department of State, "Internal Affairs of Japan, 1955–1959," June 12, 1956, U.S. National Archives, Decimal File 794.00/6 1256, C-009, Reel 26.

27. Nojima, "Bōryoku kokkai to sangiin," 24.

28. Miyazawa Taneo, "Hatoyama naikaku o shinninshite: Shakaitō o hihan suru," *Keizai jidai* 21, no. 7 (July 1956): 41.

29. Nishijima, "Kokkai wa are de yoi ka," 4–5. Nishijima was not alone in expressing this sentiment. A commentator was quoted in the *Yomiuri shinbun* suggesting that the Shakaitō could become more "adult." *Yomiuri shinbun*, May 31, 1956.

30. Aoki, "Yurusarenu Shakaitō no bōryoku," 37.

31. Nojima, "Bōryoku kokkai to sangiin," 24.
32. *Yomiuri shinbun*, May 31, 1956.
33. Nojima, "Bōryoku kokkai to sangiin," 24.
34. *Yomiuri shinbun*, May 20, 1956.
35. Aoki, "Yurusarenu Shakaitō no bōryoku," 37.
36. SCAP Government Section, *Political Reorientation of Japan*, 18, 20. The directive for the purge was in keeping with the terms of the Potsdam Declaration, which stated: "There must be eliminated for all time the authority and influence of those who have deceived and misled the people of Japan into embarking on world conquest, for we insist that a new order of peace, security, and justice will be impossible until irresponsible militarism is driven from the world." In the case of nationalist groups, "influential members" were defined as those who had at any time: "1. Been a founder, officer, or director of; or 2. Occupied any post or authority in; or 3. Been an editor of any publication or organ of; or 4. Made substantial voluntary contributions (a sum or property the value of which is large in itself or large in proportion to the means of the individual in question) to any of the [banned] organizations or their branches, subsidiaries, agencies or affiliates." United States Department of State, *Occupation of Japan: Policy and Progress* (Washington: United States Government Printing Office, 1946), 99–100, 106. On the reemergence of a radical left and popular movements, see Dower, *Embracing Defeat*, 254–67.
37. Dower, *Embracing Defeat*, 271–73.
38. Samuels, *Machiavelli's Children*, 148–49, 226–32.
39. CIA Biographical Sketch, "Kishi Nobusuke," July 29, 1980, U.S. National Archives, CIA Name File, Box 66, Folder: Kishi Nobusuke.
40. Tamaki Kazuhiro, *Keidanren to Hanamura Nihachirō no jidai* (Tokyo: Shakai Shisōsha, 1997), 109–13; Hanamura Nihachirō, *Seizaikai paipuyaku hanseiki: Keidanren gaishi* (Tokyo: Tōkyō Shinbun Shuppankyoku, 1990), 3, 13, 19–20, 84–86; Chitoshi Yanaga, *Big Business in Japanese Politics* (New Haven: Yale University Press, 1968), 84–86; Samuels, *Machiavelli's Children*, 233.
41. Haruna Mikio, *Himitsu no fairu: CIA no tai Nichi kōsaku*, vol. 2 (Tokyo: Kyōdō Tsūshinsha, 2000), 146–48, 206–9.
42. United States Department of State, Bureau of Far Eastern Affairs, "The Political Climate in Japan," [1958], U.S. National Archives, Subject Files Relating to Japan, 1954–1959, Lot File 61D68, C-0099, Reel 3.
43. *New York Times*, October 9, 1994. For more on CIA funding of Japanese politicians, see Michael Schaller, *Altered States: The United States and Japan since the Occupation* (Oxford: Oxford University Press, 1997), 125, 136, 153, 165, 195.
44. Iguchi Gō, Shimoyama Masayuki, and Kusano Hiroshi, *Kuromaku kenkyū: Takemura Masayoshi, Sasakawa Ryōichi, Kobari Rekiji* (Tokyo: Shin Kokuminsha, 1977), 199–201, 204, 208–9; Haruna Mikio, *Himitsu no fairu: CIA no tai Nichi kōsaku*, vol. 1 (Tokyo: Kyōdō Tsūshinsha, 2000), 284–85; Samuels, *Machiavelli's Children*, 243; Kaga Kōei, "Sasakawa Ryōichi kuromaku e no michi," *Bungei shunjū* 71, no. 1 (October 1993): 299, 302.
45. Kodama Yoshio, *I Was Defeated* (Japan: R. Booth and T. Fukuda, 1951), 5–13. Originally published in Japanese as *Ware yaburetari* in 1949.
46. Haruna, *Himitsu no fairu*, vol. 1, 259; Hori Yukio, "Sengo seijishi no naka no uyoku: Kodama Yoshio ni miru kuromaku no yakuwari," *Ekonomisuto* 54, no. 12 (March 16, 1976): 22; Hori Yukio, *Uyoku jiten* (Tokyo: Sanryō Shobō, 1991), 240; Iizuka Akio, "Nihon no kuromaku: Kodama Yoshio," *Chūō kōron* 91, no. 4 (April 1976): 153; Kodama, *I Was Defeated*, 16–57.
47. Michael Petersen, "The Intelligence That Wasn't: CIA Name Files, the U.S. Army, and Intelligence Gathering in Occupied Japan," in *Researching Japanese War Crime Records: Introductory Essays* (Washington: National Archives and Records Administration,

Nazi War Crimes and Japanese Imperial Government Records Interagency Working Group, 2006), 208.

48. SCAP Investigation Division, Interrogation of Yoshida Hikotarō, in "Records Pertaining to Rules and Procedures Governing the Conduct of Japanese War Crimes Trials, Atrocities Committed Against Chinese Laborers, and Background Investigation of Major War Criminals," June 4, 1948, reel 15, 3–5; Kodama, *I Was Defeated*, 115, 119, 126; Kaga, "Sasakawa Ryōichi kuromaku," 304–5, 308; Iguchi, *Kuromaku kenkyū*, 196–97, 234–36; Samuels, *Machiavelli's Children*, 243; Petersen, "Intelligence That Wasn't," 208–9.

Kodama's partner Yoshida Hikotarō, who Kodama claimed was merely a "subordinate," reported to occupation authorities that the profits from the agency were divided equally between himself and Kodama after the war, with Yoshida's share of the partnership being ¥20 million in cash and all but two of their mines. Kodama stated that the agency had a cash profit of ¥60 million, two-thirds of which was given to Yoshida, and claimed that his own share was used for "welfare work." Kodama also reported that his real estate and personal property holdings were valued at ¥6.5 million. SCAP Investigation Division, Interrogation of Yoshida Hikotarō, 6; SCAP Investigation Division, Interrogation of Kodama Yoshio, in "Records Pertaining to Rules and Procedures Governing the Conduct of Japanese War Crimes Trials, Atrocities Committed Against Chinese Laborers, and Background Investigation of Major War Criminals," June 14, 1948, reel 15, 4; Haruna, *Himitsu no fairu*, vol. 1, 264–65; Hashimoto Shin, "GHQ himitsu shiryō ga kataru 'kuromaku' no jitsuzō," *Bunka hyōron* 333 (November 1988): 107–9; Hori, "Sengo seijishi no naka no uyoku," 22; Iizuka, "Nihon no kuromaku," 153; Ino Kenji, "Kuromaku o hitsuyō to shita misshitsu seiji: Kodama Yoshio 'akusei, jūsei, ransei,'" *Asahi jānaru* 18, no. 20 (May 21, 1976): 60.

According to one report, Kodama made approximately ten flights from Shanghai to Japan in August 1945 to transport capital back to Japan. General Headquarters, United States Army Forces Pacific, Office of the Chief of Counter Intelligence, October 18, 1945, U.S. National Archives, CIA Name File, Box 67, Folder: Kodama Yoshio, vol. 1.

49. The figure estimated by the U.S. government was a more modest ¥10 million. Security Group, Control and Analysis Branch, C/S Section, October 24, 1956, U.S. National Archives, CIA Name File, Box 67, Folder: Kodama Yoshio, vol. 2.

Kodama was described as "one of the strongest behind-the scene [*sic*] backers of Prime Minister Hatoyama" in the mid-1950s. See CIA Report, December 14, 1956, U.S. National Archives, CIS-2829, CIA Name File, Box 67, Folder: Kodama Yoshio, vol. 2.

50. Ino, "Kuromaku o hitsuyō to shita misshitsu seiji," 60; David E. Kaplan and Alec Dubro, *Yakuza: Japan's Criminal Underworld* (Berkeley: University of California Press, 2003), 63; Samuels, *Machiavelli's Children*, 243–44; Iguchi, *Kuromaku kenkyū*, 225.

51. Iguchi, *Kuromaku kenkyū*, 226–27.

52. According to one report of 1952, "He [Kodama] is reliably reported as wishing to offer his anti-Communist information gathering facilities to Occupation authorities." Counter Intelligence Review, Number Eight, Personalities: Kodama Yoshio, April 15, 1952, U.S. National Archives, CIA Name File, Box 67, Folder: Kodama Yoshio, vol. 1.

53. For more on Kodama's relationship with Mitsui, see CIA Report, January 25, 1951, U.S. National Archives, Report ZJL-540, CIA Name File, Box 67, Folder: Kodama Yoshio, vol. 1.

54. Petersen, "Intelligence That Wasn't," 199–200, 210–11; Haruna, *Himitsu no fairu*, vol. 1, 286–88; Kaga, "Sasakawa Ryōichi kuromaku," 313.

55. CIA Report, April 19, 1951, U.S. National Archives, File 44-5-3-52, Report ZJL-604, CIA Name File, Box 67, Folder: Kodama Yoshio, vol. 1.

56. Iguchi, *Kuromaku kenkyū*, 238–40, 246–47; Samuels, *Machiavelli's Children*, 243–44; Haruna, *Himitsu no fairu*, vol. 1, 288; Kaga, "Sasakawa Ryōichi kuromaku," 308.

57. Also, by the mid-1980s, the estimated worth of Sasakawa's empire was $8.4 billion. CIA Biographical Sketch, "Sasakawa Ryōichi," March 5, 1987, U.S. National Archives, CIA Name File, Box 111, Folder: Sasakawa Ryōichi.

58. Counter Intelligence Review, Number Eight, Personalities: Kodama Yoshio, April 15, 1952, U.S. National Archives, CIA Name File, Box 67, Folder: Kodama Yoshio, vol. 1.

59. CIA Report, December 8, 1949, U.S. National Archives, File 44-7-8-9yl, Report ZJL-236, CIA Name File, Box 67, Folder: Kodama Yoshio, vol. 1.

60. CIA Report, January 5, 1950, U.S. National Archives, File 44-7-8-9y3, Report ZJL-243, CIA Name File, Box 67, Folder: Kodama Yoshio, vol. 1.

61. CIA Report, November 10, 1949, U.S. National Archives, File 44-7-8-8yl, Report ZJL-220, CIA Name File, Box 67, Folder: Kodama Yoshio, vol. 1; CIA Report, November 17, 1949, U.S. National Archives, File 44-7-8-9y, Report ZJL-222, CIA Name File, Box 67, Folder: Kodama Yoshio, vol. 1; CIA Report, April 4, 1952, U.S. National Archives, Report ZJLA-1909, CIA Name File, Box 67, Folder: Kodama Yoshio, vol. 1.

62. CIA Report, "Smuggling (?) or Secret Recruiting (?)," October 31, 1949, U.S. National Archives, CIA Name File, Box 67, Folder: Kodama Yoshio, vol. 1. There were also uncorroborated CIA reports of purgees, including Kodama, plotting a coup d'état. CIA Report, October 31, 1952, U.S. National Archives, File 44-7-15-25, Report ZJJ-239, CIA Name File, Box 67, Folder: Kodama Yoshio, vol. 2.

63. Kishi Nobusuke, *Kishi Nobusuke kaikoroku: Hoshu gōdō to anpo kaitei* (Tokyo: Kōsaidō Shuppan, 1983), 456-57. Kishi also offered a halfhearted defense of Sasakawa Ryōichi, claiming that Sasakawa was not as strange as the general public made him out to be. Hara Yoshihisa, ed., *Kishi Nobusuke shōgen roku* (Tokyo: Mainichi Shinbunsha, 2003), 361.

64. Tomita Nobuo, "Sengo uyoku no kinō to yakuwari: Kodama Yoshio to shin Nikkyō o chūshin ni," *Ekonomisuto* 43, no. 28 (June 1965): 67; Takagi Takeo, "Ōno Banboku to iu otoko," *Seikai ōrai* 18, no. 12 (December 1952): 31-32.

65. "Ninkyō ni tsunagaru hoshu seijika," *Shūkan yomiuri*, August 18, 1963, 12-13.

66. CIA Report, December 14, 1956, U.S. National Archives, CIS-2829, CIA Name File, Box 67, Folder: Kodama Yoshio, vol. 2. It would later be rumored that Kodama supported Kōno Ichirō as a candidate for the prime ministership. CIA Report, December 14, 1962, U.S. National Archives, Report FJT-8890, CIA Name File, Box 67, Folder: Kodama Yoshio, vol. 2.

67. Dower, *Embracing Defeat*, 140-44; Peter B. E. Hill, *The Japanese Mafia: Yakuza, Law, and the State* (Oxford: Oxford University Press, 2003), 42-47.

68. *Asahi shinbun*, April 2, 1960; "Shuyō uyoku dantai ichiranhyō," October 1960, in *"Asanuma jiken" kankei shiryōshū* (1960), 2; Hori, *Uyoku jiten*, 550-51. The membership figure given in a rightist publication that came out in 1966 was approximately 1,000 people. Arahara Bokusui, *Dai uyokushi* (Tokyo: Dai Nihon Kokumintō, 1966), 744-45.

69. *Yomiuri shinbun*, January 22, 1953.

70. It was reported that Kodama Yoshio donated ¥50,000, and Sasakawa ¥10,000, to the Gokokudan. CIA Report, August 5, 1957, U.S. National Archives, XF-3-207416(5b3), CIA Name File, Box 67, Folder: Kodama Yoshio, vol. 2.

71. Ōno Tatsuzō and Takagi Takashi, "Asanuma ansatsu jiken to uyoku bōryokudan: Sengo uyoku bōryokudan no jittai, seijiteki yakuwari, haikei," *Rōdō hōritsu junpō* 395 (October 1960): 21; Hori, *Uyoku jiten*, 235. There is some speculation that Kimura had attempted to organize a large, anticommunist yakuza group as early as 1951. Ino, "Kuromaku o hitsuyō to shita misshitsu seiji," 60; Hori, "Sengo seijishi no naka no uyoku," 22. By the first half of 1960, the Gokokudan had estimated earnings of ¥1,880,000 and expenses of ¥1,800,000. *Asahi nenkan* (Osaka: Asahi Shinbunsha, 1961), 244.

72. Keishichō, "Uyoku shiryō," in *"Asanuma jiken" kankei shiryōshū* (1960), 12-13; "Shūyō uyoku dantai ichiranhyō," 2; Hori, *Uyoku jiten*, 474-75. As with the Matsubakai,

there is an alternate membership figure, this one being 370 people. Arahara, *Dai uyokushi*, 741–44.

73. "Bōryoku no ōkō to seiji," *Sekai* (June 1960): 185.

74. *Yomiuri shinbun*, October 14, 1958.

75. Tomita, "Sengo uyoku no kinō to yakuwari," 66.

76. "Bōryoku no ōkō to seiji," 183–84.

77. Nakamoto Takako, *Watashi no anpo tōsō nikki* (Tokyo: Shin Nihon Shuppansha, 1963), 90–91. For a list of similar public revelations of yakuza-politician ties, as well as a discussion of yakuza and local politics, see *Yomiuri shinbun*, May 16, 1960.

78. This is why I use the term "right-wing" in the postwar political context, whereas the preferred word for the prewar period was "nationalist."

79. Kimura Masataka, "Nikumi bōryoku shūrō to Kubo-san no shi," *Gekkan rōdō mondai* 279 (October 1980): 36–37; Jōdai Iwao, Fujimoto Masatomo, and Ikeda Masumi, *1960-nen, Miike* (Tokyo: Dōjidaisha, 2002), 41, 45, 53; Miike Tankō Rōdō Kumiai, "Tatakau yama no ketsui: Genchi no jijō wa kō da," *Gekkan sōhyō* 34 (April 1960): 36.

80. Takagi Takashi, "Ugokidashita uyoku bōryokudan no haikei," *Zenei* 169 (June 1960): 23.

81. Ōuchi Hyōe and Sakisaka Itsurō, "Miike no tatakai o mitsumete," *Sekai* 174 (June 1960): 26.

82. Kyokutō Jijō Kenkyūkai, ed., *Miike sōgi: Kumiai undō no tenki o shimesu sono jissō to kyōkun* (Tokyo: Kyokutō Shuppansha, 1960), 234.

83. Takagi, "Ugokidashita uyoku bōryokudan," 27. The *Mainichi shinbun* was attacked by the Matsubakai on April 2, just four days after the death of Kubo, because of a story the paper had run on the close relationship between conservative politicians and *bōryokudan*. As part of their attempt to disrupt the office, the culprits set off smoke bombs and damaged presses. Nakamoto, *Watashi no anpo tōsō nikki*, 90.

84. Miike Tankō Rōdō Kumiai, "Tatakau yama no ketsui," 36; Ōuchi and Sakisaka, "Miike no tatakai o mitsumete," 26.

85. The most controversial part of the bill permitted police to take coercive action, including entrance onto private property, in order to prevent a crime that seemed like it would greatly disturb public order. The opposition used many tactics, such as picket lines and barricades, that were the same as those from the 1954 and 1956 controversies. In the face of strong resistance, the bill was dropped. See D. C. S. Sissons, "The Dispute over Japan's Police Law," *Pacific Affairs* 32, no. 1 (March 1959): 34–37.

86. Takagi, "Ugokidashita uyoku bōryokudan," 24–25; Miike Tankō Rōdō Kumiai, "Tatakau yama no ketsui," 36.

87. Ōuchi and Sakisaka, "Miike no tatakai o mitsumete," 26–27.

88. Kimura, "Nikumi bōryoku shūrō to Kubo-san no shi," 37.

89. *Yomiuri shinbun*, April 8 and 12, 1960.

90. Jōdai et al., *1960-nen, Miike*, 81; Kimura, "Nikumi bōryoku shūrō to Kubo-san no shi," 36.

91. *Yomiuri shinbun*, April 26, 1960; "Shuyō uyoku dantai ichiranhyō," 2. The Dai Nihon Aikokutō was established in 1951, headed by Akao Bin, and had about 30 members in 1960. The group's principles included revision of the constitution and remilitarization, strengthening of the U.S.-Japan alliance, forming an anticommunist Asian alliance, and delegitimizing the communist party. Throughout the mid-1950s, group members were imprisoned for committing violent crimes. Kōan Chōsachō, "Uyoku dantai no gensei," October 1960, in *"Asanuma jiken" kankei shiryōshū* (1960), 10–11.

92. Shinobu Seizaburō, *Anpo tōsōshi: Sanjūgonichikan seikyoku shiron* (Tokyo: Sekai Shoin, 1969), 162, 167–68, 171–72, 175; Nishii Kazuo, ed., *60-nen anpo, Miike tōsō: 1957–1960* (Tokyo: Mainichi Shinbunsha, 2000), 125; George R. Packard, *Protest in Tokyo: The Security Treaty Crisis of 1960* (Princeton: Princeton University Press, 1966), 238–41.

93. In an interview, Kishi claimed that he did not call upon right-wing organizations but did mobilize fire brigades and youth groups from outside Tokyo. Hara, *Kishi Nobusuke shōgen roku*, 292.

94. Sōhyō had been formed in 1950 out of a merger of militant labor unions. Sōhyō encouraged aggressive grassroots tactics to win gains on issues of job safety, overtime, and wage increases. Zengakuren was established in 1948 and was initially composed mainly of Japan Communist Party members on college campuses. But by the end of the 1950s, the group was taking up political causes beyond the ivory tower and had become more inclusive in its membership.

95. Nishii, *60-nen anpo, Miike tōsō*, 127–29, 140, 153; Nakamoto, *Watashi no anpo tōsō nikki*, 219, 243–45; Packard, *Protest in Tokyo*, 289–90, 294–96; *Asahi shinbun*, June 16, 1960; Chūō Iinkai Kanbukai, "Seimei," June 15, 1960, in *Anpo tōsō: 60-nen no kyōkun* (Tokyo: Nihon Kyōsantō Chūō Iinkai Shuppankyoku, 1969), 185–86.

96. Jōdai et al., *1960-nen, Miike*, 81.

97. Nishii, *60-nen anpo, Miike tōsō*, 155; Okazaki Masuhide, "Asanuma jiken to uyoku," *Zenei* 176 (December 1960): 185.

98. Keimushō Keijikyoku, "Saikin ni okeru uyoku kankei shuyō keiji jiken no shori jōkyō," October 1960, in *"Asanuma jiken" kankei shiryōshū* (1960), 2–14.

99. Ōno and Takagi, "Asanuma ansatsu jiken to uyoku bōryokudan," 19–20, 23–24; "Bōryoku no ōkō to seiji," 185; Watanabe Yōzō, "Hō to bōryoku," *Shisō* 438 (October 1960): 118; Kinoshita Hanji, Tsurumi Shunsuke, and Hashikawa Bunzō, "Tero, kokkai, kaigi: Asanuma shisatsu jiken no shisōteki haikei to rekishiteki imi," *Shisō no kagaku* 23 (November 1960): 71.

100. Okazaki, "Asanuma jiken to uyoku," 184; Sakisaka Itsurō, "Asanuma-san no shi to kojinteki terorizumu," *Shakaishugi* 110 (November 1960): 2.

101. Kuno Osamu, "Minshushugi no genri e no hangyaku: Asanuma iinchō shisatsu jiken no shisōteki imi," *Shisō* 437 (October 1960): 67–69, 72–73; Takano Minoru, "Asanuma ansatsu o meguru seikyoku," *Rōdō keizai junpō* 14, no. 453 (October 1960): 7.

102. Ōno and Takagi, "Asanuma ansatsu jiken to uyoku bōryokudan," 24; Sakisaka, "Asanuma-san no shi to kojinteki terorizumu," 7; Kinoshita et al., "Tero, kokkai, kaigi," 70–71.

103. Some commentators on the left were suspicious of these blanket condemnations of violence, afraid that concerns about physical force would become a reason for suppressing popular movements, demonstrations, and the right to strike. Sakisaka, "Asanuma-san no shi to kojinteki terorizumu," 6; Kinoshita et al., "Tero, kokkai, kaigi," 77.

104. *Mainichi shinbun*, June 17, 1960.

105. *Asahi shinbun*, July 8, 1960, in *Miike sōgi: Shiryō*, ed. Mitsui Kōzan Kabushikigaisha (Tokyo: Nihon Keieisha Dantai Renmei Kōhōbu, 1963), 954–55.

106. *Yomiuri shinbun*, October 21, 1960.

107. "Seiji tero to shūdan kōdō," *Sekai* 187 (July 1961): 190–92; Nishio Masayoshi, "Bōryoku to shakaishugi," *Shakai shisō kenkyū* 13, no. 7 (July 1961): 11.

108. For a critical take on this violence by a foreign press, see "Mobocracy Again," *Time Magazine* (June 16, 1961).

109. Packard, *Protest in Tokyo*, 304–5.

110. Peter J. Katzenstein and Yutaka Tsujinaka, *Defending the Japanese State: Structures, Norms and the Political Responses to Terrorism and Violent Social Protest in the 1970s and 1980s* (Ithaca: Cornell University Press, 1991), 30–33.

111. Ibid., 14, 20, 24–25; Peter J. Katzenstein, *Left-wing Violence and State Response: United States, Germany, Italy and Japan, 1960s–1990s* (Ithaca: Cornell University Press, 1998), 2–4.

112. The Matsubakai also dissolved in 1965. Hori, *Uyoku jiten,* 550.

113. Public tolerance of yakuza decreased because of incidents in which intergang conflict led to the death of innocent civilians and because of the increasingly predatory nature of yakuza activities. See Hill, *Japanese Mafia,* 138–46.

114. Such was the case in the early 1950s, for example, when voters punished the Japan Communist Party for its extreme tactics by handing it a blow at the polls; in the 1952 election, the party lost all of its seats in the House of Representatives.

115. This is not to say that corruption and bribery were absent from prewar politics. See Chapters 2 and 3 of Richard H. Mitchell, *Political Bribery in Japan* (Honolulu: University of Hawai'i Press, 1996). On political corruption in the postwar period, see Chapter 9 of Samuels, *Machiavelli's Children,* and Jacob M. Schlesinger, *Shadow Shoguns: The Rise and Fall of Japan's Postwar Political Machine* (Stanford: Stanford University Press, 1999).

116. The violent potential of yakuza was considered valuable even by the Korean Central Intelligence Agency, which had planned to enlist yakuza to kidnap (future president) Kim Dae Jung from Tokyo in 1973. The idea was aborted for fear that the Japanese police would uncover the plot. *Daily Yomiuri,* October 14, 2007.

Afterword

1. Maruyama Masao makes this kind of argument about "feudal remnants" in his treatment of the Dai Nihon Kokusuikai and Dai Nihon Seigidan. See Maruyama Masao, *Thought and Behavior in Modern Japanese Politics,* ed. Ivan Morris (Oxford: Oxford University Press, 1969), 27–28.

2. On violence and "democratic consolidation," see Mark Ungar, Sally Avery Bermanzohn, and Kenton Worcester, "Introduction: Violence and Politics," in *Violence and Politics: Globalization's Paradox,* ed. Kenton Worcester, Sally Avery Bermanzohn, and Mark Ungar (New York: Routledge, 2002), 3–4.

3. Violence of the militarist state is beyond the scope of this book, but it does reinforce an idea that was mentioned briefly in Chapter 1: state violence is not necessarily legitimate; like all forms of violence it must be debated and justified. The idea that state violence is legitimate is perpetuated by Max Weber's oft-repeated definition of a state as having a monopoly on the legitimate use of physical force. Although a viable state does need to have the strength to put down violent resistance to its rule, the problematic implication of this characterization is that the violence monopolized by the state is legitimate. Weber does not discuss who is to determine the legitimacy of the state's violence. See Max Weber, *Economy and Society: An Outline of Interpretive Sociology,* vol. 1, trans. Ephraim Fischoff et al., ed. Guenther Roth and Claus Wittich (Berkeley: University of California Press, 1978).

4. Charles Tilly, *The Politics of Collective Violence* (Cambridge: Cambridge University Press, 2003), 4–5.

5. Both the August 2006 arson of the home of the mother of Liberal Democratic Party politician Katō Kōichi by a member of a right-wing organization and the April 2007 murder of Nagasaki Mayor Itō Itchō by a yakuza were framed and publicly condemned as assaults on democracy. The issue of assigning responsibility for acts of violence was, however, not so straightforward. On Prime Minister Koizumi Jun'ichirō's response to the attack on Katō, see Gavan McCormack, *Client State: Japan in America's Embrace* (New York: Verso, 2007), 26–28.

6. Daniel Ross would likely disagree with the distinction I draw between the potential for, and actual acts of, violence. His conception of "violent democracy" is predicated

solely on the violent potential of democracy. See the introduction in Daniel Ross, *Violent Democracy* (Cambridge: Cambridge University Press, 2004).

7. Federico Varese, *The Russian Mafia: Private Protection in a New Market Economy* (Oxford: Oxford University Press, 2001), 180–84.

8. Diego Gambetta, *The Sicilian Mafia: The Business of Private Protection* (Cambridge, Mass.: Harvard University Press, 1993), 182–87.

Bibliography

Abbreviations

CJS   Saitama Shinbunsha, ed. *Chichibu jiken shiryō*. Vol. 1. Tokyo: Saitama Shinbunsha Shuppanbu, 1971.

CJSS   Inoue Kōji, Irokawa Daikichi, and Yamada Shōji, eds. *Chichibu jiken shiryō shūsei*. Vols. 1, 2, 3, 6. Tokyo: Nigensha, 1984–89.

KKMSBJ *Kensei o kiki ni michibiku Seiyūkai no bōkō jiken*. Tokyo: Jiyū Bundansha, 1927.

MNJ   Edamatsu Shigeyuki et al., eds. *Meiji nyūsu jiten*. Vols. 3, 4. Tokyo: Mainichi Komyunikēshonzu, 1986.

TKKSS   Ogino Fujio, ed. *Tokkō keisatsu kankei shiryō shūsei*. Vols. 9, 13, 14. Tokyo: Fuji Shuppan, 1991–92.

TNJ   Edamatsu Shigeyuki et al., eds. *Taishō nyūsu jiten*. Vol. 4. Tokyo: Mainichi Komyunikēshonzu, 1987.

Works Cited

Abadinsky, Howard. *Organized Crime*. Chicago: Nelson-Hall, 1985.

Abe Akira. *Edo no autorō: Mushuku to bakuto*. Tokyo: Kōdansha, 1999.

Abe Isoo. "Bōryoku ni taisuru kokumin no futetteiteki taido." *Kaizō* 6, no. 5 (May 1924): 88–95.

———. "Hōchikoku ni bōryoku o yurusu to wa nanigoto ka." *Chūō kōron* 38, no.1 (January 1923): 216–21.

———. "Kokkateki 'chikara' no hatsugen o kōhei nara shimeyo." *Chūō kōron* 38, no. 9 (August 1923): 74–79.

Abe Yoshio. *Meakashi Kinjūrō no shōgai: Edo jidai shomin seikatsu no jitsuzō*. Tokyo: Chūō Kōronsha, 1981.

Aida Iichirō. *Shichijūnendai no uyoku: Meiji, Taishō, Shōwa no keifu*. Tokyo: Daikōsha, 1970.

Akita, George. *Foundations of Constitutional Government in Modern Japan, 1868-1900*. Cambridge, Mass.: Harvard University Press, 1967.

Alcock, Rutherford. *The Capital of the Tycoon: A Narrative of a Three Years' Residence in Japan*. 2 vols. New York: Harper & Brothers, 1863.

Ambaras, David R. *Bad Youth: Juvenile Delinquency and the Politics of Everyday Life in Modern Japan*. Berkeley: University of California Press, 2006.

Anbinder, Tyler. *Five Points: The 19th-Century New York City Neighborhood That Invented Tap Dance, Stole Elections, and Became the World's Most Notorious Slum*. New York: Free Press, 2001.

Anderson, Robert T. "From Mafia to Cosa Nostra." *American Journal of Sociology* 71, no. 3 (November 1965): 302–10.

Anzai Kunio. "Jiyū minkenha sōshi ni miru kokken ishiki to Tōyō ninshiki." In *Ajia rekishi bunka kenkyūjo shinpojiumu hōkokushū: Kindai ikōki no Higashi Ajia, seiji bunka no henyō to keisei*. Tokyo: Waseda Daigaku Ajia Rekishi Bunka Kenkyūjo, 2005.

———. "Jiyū minken undō ni okeru sōshi no isō: Inoue Keijirō no dōkō ni miru." In *Jiyū minken no saihakken*, ed. Anzai Kunio and Tasaki Kimitsukasa. Tokyo: Nihon Keizai Hyōronsha, 2006.

Aoki Kazuo. "Yurusarenu Shakaitō no bōryoku: Muteikō de shūshishita Jimintō." *Keizai jidai* 21, no. 7 (July 1956): 36–37.

Apter, David E. "Political Violence in Analytical Perspective." In *The Legitimization of Violence*, ed. David E. Apter. New York: New York University Press, 1997.

Arahara Bokusui. *Dai uyokushi*. Tokyo: Dai Nihon Kokumintō, 1966.

Arai Sajirō. *Chichibu Konmingun kaikeichō: Inoue Denzō*. Tokyo: Shinjinbutsu Ōraisha, 1981.

———. "Meijiki bakuto to Chichibu jiken: Sono kyojitsu o jimoto shiryō de tadasu." *Shin Nihon bungaku* 34, no. 1 (January 1979): 126–31.

Arendt, Hannah. *On Violence*. New York: Harcourt, Brace & World, 1969.

Arima Manabu. "'Taishō demokurashī' ron no genzai: Minshūka, shakaika, kokuminka." *Nihon rekishi* 700 (September 2006): 134–42.

Arima Yoriyasu. *Seikai dōchūki*. Tokyo: Nihon Shuppan Kyōdo, 1951.

———. *Shichijūnen no kaisō*. Tokyo: Sōgensha, 1953.

Asahi nenkan. Osaka: Asahi Shinbunsha, 1948 and 1961.

Asahi shinbun.

Azami Yoshio. *Chichibu jikenshi*. Tokyo: Gensōsha, 1990.

Banno Junji. *Meiji demokurashī*. Tokyo: Iwanami Shoten, 2005.

Bates, Robert, Avner Greif, and Smita Singh. "Organizing Violence." *Journal of Conflict Resolution* 46, no. 5 (October 2002): 599–628.

Beasley, W. G. *The Meiji Restoration*. Stanford: Stanford University Press, 1972.

Bensel, Richard Franklin. *The American Ballot Box in the Mid-Nineteenth Century*. Cambridge: Cambridge University Press, 2004.

Berger, Gordon Mark. *Parties out of Power in Japan, 1931–1941*. Princeton: Princeton University Press, 1977.

Bergreen, Laurence. *Capone: The Man and the Era*. New York: Simon & Schuster, 1994.

Bessel, Richard. *Political Violence and the Rise of Nazism: The Storm Troopers in Eastern Germany, 1925–1934*. New Haven: Yale University Press, 1984.

Bornfriend, Arnold J. "Political Parties and Pressure Groups." *Proceedings of the Academy of Political Science* 29, no. 4 (1969): 55–67.

Bōryoku kōi nado shobatsu hōritsu. Hōritsu dai rokujū gō. March 1926. At the National Archives of Japan.

"Bōryoku no ōkō to seiji." *Sekai* (June 1960): 183–87.

Botsman, Daniel V. *Punishment and Power in the Making of Modern Japan*. Princeton: Princeton University Press, 2005.

Bowen, Roger W. *Rebellion and Democracy in Meiji Japan: A Study of Commoners in the Popular Rights Movement*. Berkeley: University of California Press, 1980.

Brown, Howard G. *Ending the French Revolution: Violence, Justice, and Repression from the Terror to Napoleon*. Charlottesville: University of Virginia Press, 2006.

Brown, Richard Maxwell. "Violence and the American Revolution." In *Essays on the American Revolution*, ed. Stephen G. Kurtz and James H. Hutson. Chapel Hill: University of North Carolina Press, 1973.

Buck, James H. "The Satsuma Rebellion of 1877: From Kagoshima through the Siege of Kumamoto Castle." *Monumenta Nipponica* 28, no.4 (winter 1973): 427–46.

Byas, Hugh. *Government by Assassination*. London: George Allen & Unwin, 1943.

Catanzaro, Raimondo. *Men of Respect: A Social History of the Sicilian Mafia*. Trans. Raymond Rosenthal. New York: Free Press, 1988.

Chae Soo Do. "Kokuryūkai no seiritsu: Gen'yōsha to tairiku rōnin no katsudō o chūshin ni." *Hōgaku shinpō* 109, no. 1–2 (April 2002): 161–84.

———. "'Ten'yūkyō' ni kansuru ikkōsatsu." *Chūō Daigaku Daigakuin kenkyū nenpō* 30 (February 2001): 439–50.

Childers, Thomas, and Eugene Weiss. "Voters and Violence: Political Violence and the Limits of National Socialist Mass Mobilization." *German Studies Review* 13, no. 3 (October 1990): 481–98.

Chinzei Kokusuikai. "Chinzei Kokusuikai kaisoku." In *Kyōchōkai shiryō*. Reel 52.

Chishima Hisashi. *Konmintō hōki: Chichibu nōmin sensō to Tashiro Eisuke ron*. Tokyo: Tahata Shobō, 1983.

Chōya shinbun.

Chūgai shōgyō shinpō.

Chūō Iinkai Kanbukai. "Seimei." June 15, 1960. In *Anpo tōsō: 60-nen no kyōkun*. Tokyo: Nihon Kyōsantō Chūō Iinkai Shuppankyoku, 1969.

CIA Biographical Sketch. "Kishi Nobusuke." July 29, 1980. U.S. National Archives. CIA Name File. Box 66. Folder: Kishi Nobusuke.

———. "Sasakawa Ryōichi." March 5, 1987. U.S. National Archives. CIA Name File. Box 111. Folder: Sasakawa Ryōichi.

CIA Report. November 10, 1949. U.S. National Archives. File 44-7-8-8yl. Report ZJL-220. CIA Name File. Box 67. Folder: Kodama Yoshio. Vol. 1.

———. November 17, 1949. U.S. National Archives. File 44-7-8-9y. Report ZJL-222. CIA Name File. Box 67. Folder: Kodama Yoshio. Vol. 1.

———. December 8, 1949. U.S. National Archives. File 44-7-8-9yl. Report ZJL-236. CIA Name File. Box 67. Folder: Kodama Yoshio. Vol. 1.

———. January 5, 1950. U.S. National Archives. File 44-7-8-9y3. Report ZJL-243. CIA Name File. Box 67. Folder: Kodama Yoshio. Vol. 1.

———. January 25, 1951. U.S. National Archives. Report ZJL-540. CIA Name File. Box 67. Folder: Kodama Yoshio. Vol. 1.

———. April 19, 1951. U.S. National Archives. File 44-5-3-52. Report ZJL-604. CIA Name File. Box 67. Folder: Kodama Yoshio. Vol. 1.

———. April 4, 1952. U.S. National Archives. Report ZJLA-1909. CIA Name File. Box 67. Folder: Kodama Yoshio. Vol. 1.

———. October 31, 1952. U.S. National Archives. File 44-7-15-25. Report ZJJ-239. CIA Name File. Box 67. Folder: Kodama Yoshio. Vol. 2.

———. December 14, 1956. U.S. National Archives. CIS-2829. CIA Name File. Box 67. Folder: Kodama Yoshio. Vol. 2.

———. August 5, 1957. U.S. National Archives. XF-3-207416(5b3). CIA Name File. Box 67. Folder: Kodama Yoshio. Vol. 2.

———. December 14, 1962. U.S. National Archives. Report FJT-8890. CIA Name File. Box 67. Folder: Kodama Yoshio. Vol. 2.

———. "Smuggling (?) or Secret Recruiting (?)." October 31, 1949. U.S. National Archives. CIA Name File. Box 67. Folder: Kodama Yoshio. Vol. 1.

Cole, Allan B. "Population Changes in Japan." *Far Eastern Survey* 15, no. 10 (May 1946): 149–50.

Colegrove, Kenneth. "The Japanese General Election of 1928." *American Political Science Review* 22, no. 2 (May 1928): 401–7.

Conley, Carolyn. "The Agreeable Recreation of Fighting." *Journal of Social History* 33, no. 1 (autumn 1999): 57–72.

Conroy, Hilary. *The Japanese Seizure of Korea, 1868–1910: A Study of Realism and Idealism in International Relations.* Philadelphia: University of Pennsylvania Press, 1974.

Counter Intelligence Review. Number Eight. Personalities: Kodama Yoshio. April 15, 1952. U.S. National Archives. CIA Name File. Box 67. Folder: Kodama Yoshio. Vol. 1.

"Daikyū kōjō sagyō kaishi ni tsuite: Noda Shōyu Kabushikigaisha" (October 1927). At the Ōhara Institute for Social Research. File on Noda Shōyu sōgi 1927.9–1928.4.

Daily Yomiuri.

Dai Nihon Kokusuikai. "Dai Nihon Kokusuikai kari kiyaku." In *Kyōchōkai shiryō.* Reel 52. 1919.

———. "Dai Nihon Kokusuikai kiyaku setsumei." In *Kyōchōkai shiryō.* Reel 52. November 1919.

Dai Nihon Kokusuikai. "Dai Nihon Kokusuikai setsuritsu shuisho." In *Kyōchōkai shiryō.* Reel 52. November 1919.

"Dai Nihon Kokusuikai Ōita-ken honbu kaisoku." In *Kyōchōkai shiryō.* Reel 52.

"Dai Nihon Kokusuikai Ōita-ken honbu setsuritsu shuisho." In *Kyōchōkai shiryō.* Reel 52.

Dai Nihon Kokusuikai Sōhonbu Kaihōkyoku. "Dai Nihon Kokusuikaishi." *Dai Nihon Kokusuikai kaihō.* December 1, 1926, 34–43.

"Dai Nihon Kokusuikai Tanabe shibu sōritsu shuisho." At the National Diet Library, in the Naimushō materials. 9.5–7.

"Dai Nihon Kokusuikai Yahata shibu kiyaku." In *Kyōchōkai shiryō.* Reel 52.

De Vos, George A., and Keiichi Mizushima. "Organization and Social Function of Japanese Gangs: Historical Development and Modern Parallels." In *Socialization for Achievement: Essays on the Cultural Psychology of the Japanese,* ed. George A. De Vos. Berkeley: University of California Press, 1973.

Dore, R. P., ed. *Aspects of Social Change in Modern Japan.* Princeton: Princeton University Press, 1967.

Dower, John W. "E. H. Norman, Japan and the Uses of History." In *Origins of the Modern Japanese State: Selected Writings of E. H. Norman,* ed. John W. Dower. New York: Pantheon, 1975.

———. *Embracing Defeat: Japan in the Wake of World War II.* New York: W. W. Norton & Company, 1999.

Duggan, Christopher. *Fascism and the Mafia.* New Haven: Yale University Press, 1989.

Duus, Peter. *Party Rivalry and Political Change in Taisho Japan.* Cambridge, Mass.: Harvard University Press, 1968.

Duus, Peter, and Daniel I. Okimoto. "Fascism and the History of Pre-War Japan: The Failure of a Concept." *Journal of Asian Studies* 39, no. 1 (November 1979): 65–76.

Eiri jiyū shinbun.

Eishima Kazue (Japanese consul general in Tianjin) to the foreign minister. "Manshū kankei rōnin raiō mata katsudō keitōhyō sōfu no ken." *Shina rōnin kankei zakken, Gaimushō kiroku.* March 17, 1933.

Election Department, Local Administration Bureau, Ministry of Internal Affairs and Communications. "Fixed Number, Candidates, Eligible Voters as of Election Day, Voters and Voting Percentages of Elections for the House of Representatives (1890–1993)." http://www.stat.go.jp/english/data/chouki/27.htm.

Etō Shinkichi and Marius B. Jansen. Introduction to *My Thirty-Three Years' Dream: The Autobiography of Miyazaki Tōten,* by Miyazaki Tōten. Trans. Etō Shinkichi and Marius B. Jansen. Princeton: Princeton University Press, 1982.

Faison, Elyssa. *Managing Women: Disciplining Labor in Modern Japan.* Berkeley: University of California Press, 2007.

Fischer, Conan. *Stormtroopers: A Social, Economic and Ideological Analysis, 1929–35.* London: George Allen & Unwin, 1983.

Fogelson, Robert M. *Big-City Police.* Cambridge, Mass.: Harvard University Press, 1977.

Fruin, Mark W. *Kikkoman: Company, Clan, and Community.* Cambridge, Mass.: Harvard University Press, 1983.

Fujino Yūko. "Sōran suru hitobito e no shisen: Kindai Nihon no toshi sōjō to seiji undō." In *Bōryoku no chihei o koete: Rekishigaku kara no chōsen,* ed. Suda Tsutomu, Cho Kyondaru, and Nakajima Hisato. Tokyo: Aoki Shoten, 2004.

Fujinuma Shōhei (superintendent-general of the Metropolitan Police) to the home minister et al. "Nihon Seigidan no Manshū shinshutsu ni kansuru ken." *Honpō imin kankei zakken: Manshūkokubu, Gaimushō kiroku.* July 28, 1932.

Fujita Gorō. *Ninkyō hyakunenshi.* Tokyo: Kasakura Shuppansha, 1980.

Fujitani Takashi. *Splendid Monarchy: Power and Pageantry in Modern Japan.* Berkeley: University of California Press, 1996.

Fukuda Kaoru. *Sanmin sōjōroku: Meiji jūshichinen Gunma jiken.* Tokyo: Seiyun Shobō, 1974.

Fukushima minpō.

Fukushima minyū.

Gambetta, Diego. *The Sicilian Mafia: The Business of Private Protection.* Cambridge, Mass.: Harvard University Press, 1993.

Garon, Sheldon. "Rethinking Modernization and Modernity in Japanese History: A Focus on State-Society Relations." *Journal of Asian Studies* 53, no. 2 (May 1994): 346–66.

———. *The State and Labor in Modern Japan.* Berkeley: University of California Press, 1987.

———. "State and Society in Interwar Japan." In *Historical Perspectives on Contemporary East Asia,* ed. Merle Goldman and Andrew Gordon. Cambridge, Mass.: Harvard University Press, 2000.

"Geki!!" October 5, 1930. At the Ōhara Institute for Social Research. Yōmosu sōgi file 1.

Gendai Hōsei Shiryō Hensankai, ed. *Meiji "kyūhō" shū.* Tokyo: Kokusho Kankōkai, 1983.

General Headquarters, United States Army Forces Pacific, Office of the Chief of Counter Intelligence. October 18, 1945. U.S. National Archives. CIA Name File. Box 67. Folder: Kodama Yoshio. Vol. 1.

Gentile, Emilio. "The Problem of the Party in Italian Fascism." *Journal of Contemporary History* 19 (1984): 251–74.

Gen'yōsha Shashi Hensankai, ed. *Gen'yōsha shashi.* 1917. Reprint, Fukuoka: Ashi Shobō, 1992.

Gluck, Carol. *Japan's Modern Myths: Ideology in the Late Meiji Period.* Princeton: Princeton University Press, 1985.

———. "The People in History: Recent Trends in Japanese Historiography." *Journal of Asian Studies* 38, no. 1 (November 1978): 25–50.

Goodwin, Jeff. "A Theory of Categorical Terrorism." *Social Forces* 84, no. 4 (June 2006): 2027–46.

Gordon, Andrew. *Labor and Imperial Democracy in Prewar Japan.* Berkeley: University of California Press, 1991.

Gunma-ken Keisatsushi Hensan Iinkai, ed. *Gunma-ken keisatsushi.* Vol. 1. Maebashi: Gunma-ken Keisatsu Honbu, 1978.

Hackett, Roger F. *Yamagata Aritomo in the Rise of Modern Japan, 1838–1922.* Cambridge, Mass.: Harvard University Press, 1971.

Haga Noboru. *Bakumatsu shishi no sekai.* Tokyo: Yūzankaku, 2003.

Hagiwara Susumu. "Gunma-ken bakuto torishimari kō." In *Ryūmin*. Vol. 4 of *Kindai minshū no kiroku*, ed. Hayashi Hideo. Tokyo: Shinjinbutsu Jūraisha, 1971.
———. *Gunma-ken yūminshi*. Tokyo: Kokusho Kankōkai, 1980.
Hall, John W. "Rule by Status in Tokugawa Japan." *Journal of Japanese Studies* 1, no. 1 (autumn 1974): 39–49.
Hanamura Nihachirō. *Seizaikai paipuyaku hanseiki: Keidanren gaishi*. Tokyo: Tōkyō Shinbun Shuppankyoku, 1990.
Hara Yoshihisa, ed. *Kishi Nobusuke shōgen roku*. Tokyo: Mainichi Shinbunsha, 2003.
Harootunian, H. D. *Toward Restoration: The Growth of Political Consciousness in Tokugawa Japan*. Berkeley: University of California Press, 1970.
Haruna Mikio. *Himitsu no fairu: CIA no tai Nichi kōsaku*. Vols. 1, 2. Tokyo: Kyōdō Tsūshinsha, 2000.
Hasegawa Noboru. *Bakuto to jiyū minken: Nagoya jiken shimatsuki*. Tokyo: Heibonsha, 1995.
Hashimoto Shin. "GHQ himitsu shiryō ga kataru 'kuromaku' no jitsuzō." *Bunka hyōron* 333 (November 1988): 100–10.
Havens, Thomas R. H. "Japan's Enigmatic Election of 1928." *Modern Asian Studies* 11, no. 4 (1977): 543–55.
Hayashida Kazuhiro. "Development of Election Law in Japan." *Hōsei kenkyū* 34, no. 1 (July 1967): 51–104.
Hesselink, Reinier H. "The Assassination of Henry Heusken." *Monumenta Nipponica* 49, no. 3 (autumn 1994): 331–51.
Hill, Peter B. E. *The Japanese Mafia: Yakuza, Law, and the State*. Oxford: Oxford University Press, 2003.
Hino Ashihei. *Hino Ashihei shū*. Vol. 52 of *Nihon bungaku zenshū*. Tokyo: Shinchōsha, 1967.
Hirano Yoshitarō. *Bajō Ōi Kentarō den*. Nagoya: Fūbaisha, 1968.
———. "Chichibu Konmintō ni ikita hitobito." In *Chichibu Konmintō ni ikita hitobito*, ed. Nakazawa Ichirō. Tokyo: Gendai Shuppankai, 1977.
Hirokawa Tadahide. "Yahata seitetsujo ni okeru 1920-nen no sutoraiki." *Jinbun kenkyū* 24, no. 10 (1972): 59–92.
Hobsbawm, Eric. *Bandits*. New York: Delacorte Press, 1969.
Hoppen, K. Theodore. "Grammars of Electoral Violence in Nineteenth-Century England and Ireland." *English Historical Review* 109, no. 432 (June 1994): 597–620.
Hora Sennosuke. *Kyōkaroku: Kun'yontō kagotora, Hora Sennosuke den*. Tokyo: Tōen Shobō, 1963.
Hori Yukio. *Sengo seijishi, 1945–1960*. Tokyo: Nansōsha, 2001.
———. "Sengo seijishi no naka no uyoku: Kodama Yoshio ni miru kuromaku no yakuwari." *Ekonomisuto* 54, no. 12 (March 16, 1976): 21–24.
———. *Uyoku jiten*. Tokyo: Sanryō Shobō, 1991.
Horie Kiichi. "Bōryokuteki dantai no sonzai o mokunin suru ka." *Chūō kōron* 38, no. 1 (January 1923): 210–13.
Hoshino Kanehiro. "Organized Crime and Its Origins in Japan." Unpublished paper.
Howell, David L. *Geographies of Identity in Nineteenth-Century Japan*. Berkeley: University of California Press, 2005.
———. "Hard Times in the Kantō: Economic Change and Village Life in Late Tokugawa Japan." *Modern Asian Studies* 23, no. 2 (1989): 349–71.
———. "Visions of the Future in Meiji Japan." In *Historical Perspectives on Contemporary East Asia*, ed. Merle Goldman and Andrew Gordon. Cambridge, Mass.: Harvard University Press, 2000.
Huber, Thomas. "'Men of High Purpose' and the Politics of Direct Action, 1862–1864." In *Conflict in Modern Japanese History*, ed. Tetsuo Najita and J. Victor Koschmann. Princeton: Princeton University Press, 1982.

Ianni, Francis A. J. *A Family Business: Kinship and Social Control in Organized Crime.* New York: Russell Sage Foundation, 1972.

Ide Magoroku, ed. *Jiyū jichi gannen: Chichibu jiken shiryō, ronbun to kaisetsu.* Tokyo: Gendaishi Shuppankai, 1975.

Iguchi Gō, Shimoyama Masayuki, and Kusano Hiroshi. *Kuromaku kenkyū: Takemura Masayoshi, Sasakawa Ryōichi, Kobari Rekiji.* Tokyo: Shin Kokuminsha, 1977.

Iizuka Akio. "Nihon no kuromaku: Kodama Yoshio." *Chūō kōron* 91, no. 4 (April 1976): 152–60.

The Illustrated London News.

Imagawa Tokuzō. *Kōshō: Bakumatsu kyōkaku den.* Tokyo: Akita Shoten, 1973.

Inada Masahiro. *Nihon kindai shakai seiritsuki no minshū undō: Konmintō kenkyū josetsu.* Tokyo: Chikuma Shobō, 1990.

"Ingaidan no shōtai o tsuku." *Seikei jichō* 8, no. 3 (March 1953): 13–14.

Ino Kenji. "Kuromaku o hitsuyō to shita misshitsu seiji: Kodama Yoshio 'akusei, jūsei, ransei.'" *Asahi jānaru* 18, no. 20 (May 21, 1976): 59–61.

———. *Kyōkaku no jōken: Yoshida Isokichi den.* Tokyo: Gendai Shokan, 1994.

Inoue Kinji. "Gunshū shinri ni tsūgyō seyo." *Chūō kōron* 38, no. 9 (August 1923): 99–104.

Inoue Kōji. *Chichibu jiken: Jiyū minken no nōmin hōki.* Tokyo: Chūō Kōronsha, 1968.

Inoue Mitsusaburō and Shinagawa Eiji. *Shashin de miru Chichibu jiken.* Tokyo: Shinjinbutsu Ōraisha, 1982.

Inui Teruo. "Gunpu to natta Jiyūtō sōshi: Kanagawa-ken shusshin no 'Tama-gumi' gunpu o chūshin ni." *Chihōshi kenkyū* 32, no. 3 (June 1982): 45–64.

Irokawa Daikichi. *The Culture of the Meiji Period.* Trans. and ed. Marius B. Jansen. Princeton: Princeton University Press, 1985.

———. *Konmintō to Jiyūtō.* Tokyo: Yōransha, 1984.

———. "Minshūshi no naka no Chichibu jiken." *Chichibu* (March 1995): 6–8.

———. *Ruten no minkenka: Murano Tsuneemon den.* Tokyo: Daiwa Shobō, 1980.

———, ed. *Santama jiyū minken shiryōshū.* Vol. 1. Tokyo: Daiwa Shobō, 1979.

———. *Tama no rekishi sanpo.* Tokyo: Asahi Shinbunsha, 1975.

Irokawa Daikichi and Murano Ren'ichi. *Murano Tsuneemon den.* Tokyo: Chūō Kōron Jigyō Shuppan, 1969.

Ishitaki Toyomi. *Gen'yōsha hakkutsu: Mō hitotsu no jiyū minken.* Fukuoka: Nishi Nihon Shinbunsha, 1981.

Itagaki Taisuke. *Jiyūtōshi.* Ge-kan. Ed. Tōyama Shigeki and Satō Shigerō. 1910. Reprint, Tokyo: Iwanami Shoten, 1958.

Iwai Hiroaki. *Byōri shūdan no kōzō: Oyabun kobun shūdan kenkyū.* Tokyo: Seishin Shobō, 1963.

Jacobs, James B. *Mobsters, Unions, and Feds: The Mafia and the American Labor Movement.* New York: New York University Press, 2006.

Jansen, Marius B., ed. *Changing Japanese Attitudes toward Modernization.* Princeton: Princeton University Press, 1965.

———. *The Japanese and Sun Yat-sen.* Cambridge, Mass.: Harvard University Press, 1954.

———. "Ōi Kentarō: Radicalism and Chauvinism." *Far Eastern Quarterly* 11, no. 3 (May 1952): 305–16.

———. "On Studying the Modernization of Japan." In *Studies on Modernization of Japan by Western Scholars.* Tokyo: International Christian University, 1962.

———. *Sakamoto Ryōma and the Meiji Restoration.* Princeton: Princeton University Press, 1961.

Japan Weekly Mail.

Jichishō Senkyobu, ed. *Senkyohō hyakunenshi.* Tokyo: Dai-ichi Hōki, 1990.

Jiji shinpō.

Jiyūtō Tōhyōkoku. *Senkyo kanshō mondai no tenmatsu.* Tokyo: Jiyūtō Tōhyōkoku, 1892.

Jōdai Iwao, Fujimoto Masatomo, and Ikeda Masumi. *1960-nen, Miike.* Tokyo: Dōjidaisha, 2002.

Kaga Kōei. "Sasakawa Ryōichi kuromaku e no michi." *Bungei shunjū* 71, no. 1 (October 1993): 298–314.

Kainō Michitaka. *Bōryoku: Nihon shakai no fashizumu kikō.* Tokyo: Nihon Hyōronsha, 1950.

Kaishin shinbun.

Kamei Nobuyuki. "Shingā mishin gaisha bunten heisa oyobi bunten shunin kaiko mondai ni kansuru ken." In *Kyōchōkai shiryō.* Reel 80. December 17, 1925.

Kanda Yutsuki. *Kinsei no geinō kōgyō to chiiki shakai.* Tokyo: Tōkyō Daigaku Shuppankai, 1999.

Kang Chang-il. "Ten'yūkyō to 'Chōsen mondai': 'Chōsen rōnin' no Tōgaku nōmin sensō e no taiō to kanrenshite." *Shigaku zasshi* 97, no. 8 (August 1988): 1–37.

Kano Masanao. *Taishō demokurashī.* Tokyo: Shōgakkan, 1976.

Kantō-chō Keimukyokuchō (head of the Guandong Police Bureau) to the vice minister of foreign affairs et al. "Dai Manshū Seigidan no seihaishiki kyokō." *Gaimushō kiroku.* September 13, 1932.

Kantō-chō Keimukyokuchō (head of the Guandong Police Bureau) to the vice minister of overseas affairs, cabinet secretary et al. "Dai Manshū Seigidan danki." *Gaimushō kiroku.* September 25, 1932.

Kantō-chō Keimukyokuchō (head of the Guandong Police Bureau) to the vice minister of overseas affairs, vice minister of foreign affairs et al. "Kokusuikai hoten honbu no kaishō to sono katsudō." *Gaimushō kiroku.* July 1, 1931.

Kantō gōdō rōdō kumiai nyūsu 1. October 11, 1930. At the Ōhara Institute for Social Research. Yōmosu sōgi file 1.

Kantō Rōdō Dōmeikai. *Noda sōgi no shin'in keika oyobi genjō: Kaisha no kodaiken ni kyokō no senden o kyūsu.* In *Kyōchōkai shiryō.* Reel 63. 1928.

Kaplan, David E., and Alec Dubro. *Yakuza: Japan's Criminal Underworld.* Berkeley: University of California Press, 2003.

Karlin, Jason G. "The Gender of Nationalism: Competing Masculinities in Meiji Japan." *Journal of Japanese Studies* 28, no. 1 (winter 2002): 41–77.

Kasher, Asa, and Amos Yadlin. "Assassination and Preventive Killing." *SAIS Review* 25, no. 1 (winter-spring 2005): 41–57.

Kasza, Gregory J. "Fascism from Below? A Comparative Perspective on the Japanese Right, 1931–1936." *Journal of Contemporary History* 19, no. 4 (October 1984): 607–29.

Kata Kōji. *Nihon no yakuza.* Tokyo: Daiwa Shobō, 1993.

Katō Yōko. "Fashizumuron." *Nihon rekishi* 700 (September 2006): 143–53.

Katzenstein, Peter J. *Left-wing Violence and State Response: United States, Germany, Italy and Japan, 1960s–1990s.* Ithaca: Cornell University Press, 1998.

Katzenstein, Peter J., and Yutaka Tsujinaka. *Defending the Japanese State: Structures, Norms and the Political Responses to Terrorism and Violent Social Protest in the 1970s and 1980s.* Ithaca: Cornell University Press, 1991.

Kawagoe Shigeru (Japanese consul general in Qingdao) to the foreign minister. "Chintō Kokusuikai kaisan ni kansuru ken." *Gaimushō kiroku.* April 1, 1932.

Kawanishi Hidemichi. "Meiji seinen to nashonarizumu." In *Kindai Nihon shakai to tennōsei: Iwai Tadakuma-sensei taishoku kinen ronbunshū,* ed. Iwai Tadakuma. Tokyo: Kashiwa Shobō, 1988.

Keane, John. *Reflections on Violence.* New York: Verso, 1996.

———. *Violence and Democracy.* Cambridge: Cambridge University Press, 2004.

Keihokyoku Hoanka. "Senji shita ni okeru kokkashugi undō torishimari no hōshin." July 1942. In *Tokkō keisatsu kankei shiryō shūsei*, ed Ogino Fujio. Vol. 14. Tokyo: Fuji Shuppan, 1992.

Keimushō Keijikyoku. "Saikin ni okeru uyoku kankei shuyō keiji jiken no shori jōkyō." October 1960. In *"Asanuma jiken" kankei shiryōshū*. 1960.

Keishichō. "Uyoku shiryō." In *"Asanuma jiken" kankei shiryōshū*. 1960.

Keishi Sōkan. "Saikin ni okeru kokkashugi undō jōsei ni kansuru ken." November 5, 1931. In *Tokkō keisatsu kankei shiryō shūsei*, ed. Ogino Fujio. Vol. 13. Tokyo: Fuji Shuppan, 1992.

Kikuchi Kan. "Bōryoku ni tayorazushite oote no koto o shorishitashi." *Chūō kōron* 38, no. 9 (August 1923): 95–96.

Kimura Masataka. "Nikumi bōryoku shūrō to Kubo-san no shi." *Gekkan rōdō mondai* 279 (October 1980): 36–37.

Kimura Naoe. *"Seinen" no tanjō: Meiji Nihon ni okeru seijiteki jissen no tenkan*. Tokyo: Shinyōsha, 1998.

Kinoshita Hanji. *Nihon fashizumushi*. Tokyo: Iwasaki Shoten, 1949.

Kinoshita Hanji, Tsurumi Shunsuke, and Hashikawa Bunzō. "Tero, kokkai, kaigi: Asanuma shisatsu jiken no shisōteki haikei to rekishiteki imi." *Shisō no kagaku* 23 (November 1960): 70–79.

Kishi Nobusuke. *Kishi Nobusuke kaikoroku: Hoshu gōdō to anpo kaitei*. Tokyo: Kōsaidō Shuppan, 1983.

Kitaoka Juitsu. "Bōryoku kokkai no hihan to taisaku." *Keizei jidai* 21, no. 7 (July 1956): 29–31.

Kōan Chōsachō. "Uyoku dantai no gensei." October 1960. In *"Asanuma jiken" kankei shiryōshū*. 1960.

Kobayashi Yūgo and Koike Seiichi, eds. *Rikken Seiyūkaishi*. Vol. 2. Tokyo: Rikken Seiyūkaishi Shuppankyoku, 1924.

Kōchi-ken, ed. *Kōchi-kenshi: Kindai hen*. Kōchi: Kōchi-ken, 1970.

Kodama Yoshio. *I Was Defeated*. Japan: R. Booth and T. Fukuda, 1951.

Koike Yoshitaka. *Chichibu oroshi: Chichibu jiken to Inoue Denzō*. Tokyo: Gendaishi Shuppankai, 1974.

Koizumi Shinzō. "Bōryoku to minshushugi." *Keiei hyōron* 4, no. 9 (September 1949): 4–6.

Kokumin no tomo.

Kokumin shinbun.

Kunisada Chūji. Directed by Makino Shōzō. 1924.

Kunisada Chūji. Directed by Taniguchi Senkichi. 1960.

Kunisada Chūji. Directed by Yamanaka Sadao. 1935.

Kuno Osamu. "Minshushugi no genri e no hangyaku: Asanuma iinchō shisatsu jiken no shisōteki imi." *Shisō* 437 (October 1960): 67–74.

Kuruhara Keisuke. *Fuun naru kakumeiji: Maebara Issei*. Tokyo: Heibonsha, 1926.

Kuzuu Yoshihisa. *Tōa senkaku shishi kiden*. Jō-kan. 1933. Reprint, Tokyo: Hara Shobō, 1966.

Kyōchōkai Rōdōka, ed. *Noda rōdō sōgi no tenmatsu*. Kyōchōkai Rōdōka, 1928.

Kyokutō Jijō Kenkyūkai, ed. *Miike sōgi: Kumiai undō no tenki o shimesu sono jissō to kyōkun*. Tokyo: Kyokutō Shuppansha, 1960.

Kyūshū shinbun.

Lebra, Takie Sugiyama. "Organized Delinquency: Yakuza as a Cultural Example." In *Japanese Patterns of Behavior*. Honolulu: University of Hawai'i Press, 1986.

Le Vine, Victor T. "Violence and the Paradox of Democratic Renewal: A Preliminary Assessment." In *The Democratic Experience and Political Violence*, ed. David C. Rapoport and Leonard Weinberg. London: Frank Cass, 2001.

Lewis, Michael Lawrence. *Rioters and Citizens: Mass Protest in Imperial Japan*. Berkeley: University of California Press, 1990.

Lyttelton, Adrian. *The Seizure of Power: Fascism in Italy, 1919–1929*. New York: Routledge, 2004.

Machida Tatsujirō (Kyōchōkai councillor). *Rōdō sōgi no kaibō*. Tokyo: Dai-ichi Shuppan-sha, 1929.

Mackie, Vera. *Creating Socialist Women in Japan: Gender, Labour and Activism, 1900–1937*. Berkeley: University of California Press, 1997.

Maejima Shōzō. *Nihon fashizumu to gikai: Sono shiteki kyūmei*. Kyoto: Hōritsu Bunkasha, 1956.

———. "Shishiteki pucchi to kokka kenryoku." *Nihonshi kenkyū* 24 (May 1955): 55–63.

Manabe Masayuki. "Miyaji Mohei to sōshitachi no gunzō." *Tosa shidan* 211 (August 1999).

Mann, Michael. *Fascists*. Cambridge: Cambridge University Press, 2004.

Maruyama Masao. *Thought and Behaviour in Modern Japanese Politics*. Ed. Ivan Morris. Oxford: Oxford University Press, 1969.

Maruyama Tsurukichi (superintendent-general of the Metropolitan Police) to the Home Ministry. "Yōmosu Kameido kōjō rōdō sōgi ni kansuru ken." In *Kyōchōkai shiryō*. Reel 97. September 30, October 1, and October 10, 1930.

Mason, R. H. P. "Changing Diet Attitudes to the Peace Preservation Ordinance, 1890–2." In *Japan's Early Parliaments, 1890–1905: Structure, Issues and Trends*, ed. Andrew Fraser, R. H. P. Mason, and Philip Mitchell. New York: Routledge, 1995.

———. *Japan's First General Election, 1890*. Cambridge: Cambridge University Press, 1969.

Masuda Kaneshichi. "Minshu seiji to bōryoku: Danko chōbatsu subeshi." *Keizai jidai* 19, no. 7 (July 1954): 32–35.

Masukawa Kōichi. *Tobaku no Nihonshi*. Tokyo: Heibonsha, 1989.

Masumi Junnosuke. *Nihon seitō shiron*. Vols. 2, 3. Tokyo: Tokyo Daigaku Shuppankai, 1966–67.

Matenrō Shatō. *Ingaidan shuki: Seitō kaikaku no kyūsho*. Tokyo: Jichōsha, 1935.

Matsumoto Jirō. *Hagi no ran: Maebara Issei to sono ittō*. Tokyo: Taka Shobō, 1972.

Matsumoto Ken'ichi. "Bōto to eiyū to: Inano Bunjirō oboegaki." *Tenbō* 233 (May 1978): 117–28.

Matsuo Takayoshi. *Futsū senkyo seido seiritsushi no kenkyū*. Tokyo: Iwanami Shoten, 1989.

McCaffery, Peter. *When Bosses Ruled Philadelphia: The Emergence of the Republican Machine, 1867–1933*. University Park: Pennsylvania State University Press, 1993.

McCormack, Gavan. *Client State: Japan in America's Embrace*. New York: Verso, 2007.

Meiji nippō.

Meiji Taishō Shōwa Shinbun Kenkyūkai, ed. *Shinbun shūsei Taishō hennenshi*. Tokyo: Meiji Taishō Shōwa Shinbun Kenkyūkai, 1969.

Merkl, Peter H. *The Making of a Stormtrooper*. Princeton: Princeton University Press, 1980.

Miike Tankō Rōdō Kumiai. "Tatakau yama no ketsui: Genchi no jijō wa kō da." *Gekkan sōhyō* 34 (April 1960): 31–42.

Mitchell, Richard H. *Justice in Japan: The Notorious Teijin Scandal*. Honolulu: University of Hawai'i Press, 2002.

———. *Political Bribery in Japan*. Honolulu: University of Hawai'i Press, 1996.

Mitsui Kōzan Kabushikigaisha, ed. *Miike sōgi: Shiryō*. Tokyo: Nihon Keieisha Dantai Ren-mei Kōhōbu, 1963.

Miyachi Masato. *Nichiro sengo seijishi kenkyū*. Tokyo: Tōkyō Daigaku Shuppankai, 1973.

Miyake Setsurei. "'Chikara' o tanomu no hei." *Chūō kōron* 38, no. 9 (August 1923): 80–83.

———. "Kokusuikai ni nozomu." *Chūō kōron* 38, no. 1 (January 1923): 213–16.

Miyazawa Taneo. "Hatoyama naikaku o shinninshite: Shakaitō o hihan suru." *Keizai jidai* 21, no. 7 (July 1956): 38–41.

Mizoshita Hideo. "Kore ga 'kawasujimono' no tamashii da!" *Jitsuwa jidai* (October 2001): 34–39.

Mizuno Hironori. "Bōryoku mokunin to kokka hinin." *Chūō kōron* 38, no. 1 (January 1923): 204–10.

——. "Isshi dōjin tare." *Chūō kōron* 38, no. 9 (August 1923): 93–95.

"Mobocracy Again." *Time Magazine* (June 16, 1961).

Morikawa Tetsurō. *Bakumatsu ansatsushi*. Tokyo: San'ichi Shobō, 1967.

Morinaga Eizaburō. "Gunma jiken: Bakuto to kunda fuhatsu no shibai." *Hōgaku seminā* 20, no. 14 (November 1976): 124–27.

——. "Noda Shōyu rōdō sōgi jiken: Nihyaku jūnana nichi no chōki, saidai no suto, I." *Hōgaku seminā* 202 (October 1972): 104–6.

——. "Noda Shōyu rōdō sōgi jiken: Nihyaku jūnana nichi no chōki, saidai no suto, II." *Hōgaku seminā* 203 (November 1972): 88–91.

Moriyasu Satoshi. "Imada Ushimatsu to Suiheisha sōritsusha tachi: Dai Nihon Kokusui-kai to Nara-ken Suiheisha." *Suiheisha hakubutsukan kenkyū kiyō* 2 (March 2000): 1–29.

Morn, Frank. *"The Eye That Never Sleeps": A History of the Pinkerton National Detective Agency*. Bloomington: Indiana University Press, 1982.

Morris, Ivan. *The Nobility of Failure: Tragic Heroes in the History of Japan*. New York: Holt, Rinehart and Winston, 1975.

Mouffe, Chantal. *On the Political*. New York: Routledge, 2005.

Murata Sunao, ed. *Yomigaeru chitei no kiroku: Banjaku, Iriyama rōdō sōgi shiryō shūsei*. Vol. 1. Iwaki: Iwaki Shakai Mondai Kenkyūkai, 1984.

Murofushi Tetsurō. *Nihon no terorisuto: Ansatsu to kūdetā no rekishi*. Tokyo: Kōbundō, 1962.

Mushkat, Jerome. *The Reconstruction of the New York Democracy, 1861–1874*. Rutherford, N.J.: Fairleigh Dickinson University Press, 1981.

Nagakawa Toshimi. "Seitō no oyabun, kobun." *Kaizō* (August 1930): 25–33.

Nagasaki nichinichi shinbun.

Nagata Hidejirō. "Senkyo no rimen ni hisomu zaiaku." *Nihon hyōron* 2, no. 4 (April 1, 1917): 192–93.

Naimushō Keihokyoku. *Bōryokudan zokushutsu bakko no jōkyō*. N.d.

——. *Dai Nihon Kokusuikaiin no fukusō ni kansuru ken, Ehime-ken*. June 4, 1935.

——. *Kokusuikaiin no fukusō ni kansuru ken tsūchō, chō fuken*. August 15, 1923.

——, ed. *Shakai undō no jōkyō*. Vol. 7. 1935. Reprint, Tokyo: San'ichi Shobō, 1972.

Naimushō Keihokyoku Hoanka. *Shakai undō dantai gensei chō*. June 1932, June 1934, and June 1935.

Najita, Tetsuo. *Hara Kei in the Politics of Compromise, 1905–1915*. Cambridge, Mass.: Harvard University Press, 1967.

Najita, Tetsuo, and J. Victor Koschmann, eds. *Conflict in Modern Japanese History: The Neglected Tradition*. Princeton: Princeton University Press, 1982.

Nakajima Kōzō. *Inoue Denzō: Chichibu jiken to haiku*. Saku: Yūshorin, 2000.

Nakajima Takeshi. *Nakamuraya no Bōsu: Indo dokuritsu undō to kindai Nihon no Aji-ashugi*. Tokyo: Hakusuisha, 2005.

Nakamoto Takako. *Watashi no anpo tōsō nikki*. Tokyo: Shin Nihon Shuppansha, 1963.

Nakanishi Teruma. *Shōwa Yamaguchi-ken jinbutsushi*. Yamaguchi-ken: Matsuno Sho-ten, 1990.

Neary, Ian. *Political Protest and Social Control in Pre-War Japan: The Origins of Buraku Liberation*. Manchester: Manchester University Press, 1989.

New York Times.

Nichiman chōhō.

Nihon Bōshoku Rōdō Kumiai Kamei. "Yōmosu sōgi wa saigo no kessen da!" 1930. At the Ōhara Institute for Social Research. Yōmosu sōgi file 1.

Nihon Bōshoku Rōdō Kumiai Yōmosu Sōgidan. *Yōmosu sōgi nippō.* October 10 and 15, 1930. At the Ōhara Institute for Social Research. Yōmosu sōgi file 2.

Nihon Gendaishi Kenkyūkai, ed. *1920-nendai no Nihon no seiji.* Tokyo: Ōtsuki Shoten, 1984.

Nihon Shakai Mondai Kenkyūjo, ed. *Noda kessenki.* Tokyo: Nihon Shakai Mondai Kenkyūjo, 1928.

"Ninkyō ni tsunagaru hoshu seijika." *Shūkan yomiuri* (August 18, 1963): 12–17.

Nishii Kazuo, ed. *60-nen anpo, Miike tōsō: 1957–1960.* Tokyo: Mainichi Shinbunsha, 2000.

Nishijima Yoshiji. "Kokkai wa are de yoi ka." *Seiji keizai* 9, no. 7 (July 1956): 4–5.

Nishijima Yoshiji et al. "Zadankai: Kokkai, bōryoku, minshū." *Sekai* 104 (August 1954): 73–93.

Nishio Masayoshi. "Bōryoku to shakaishugi." *Shakai shisō kenkyū* 13, no. 7 (July 1961): 11–13.

Nishio Yōtarō. *Tōyama Mitsuru-ō shōden.* Fukuoka: Ashi Shobō, 1981.

Noda Shōyu Kabushikigaisha, ed. *Noda sōgi no tenmatsu.* Chiba: Noda Shōyu, 1928.

Noda Shōyu Kabushikigaisha nijūnenshi. Noda-machi, Chiba: Noda Shōyu, 1940.

Noda Shōyu Kabushikigaisha rōdō sōgi gaikyō. In *Tokkō keisatsu kankei shiryō shūsei,* ed. Ogino Fujio. Vol. 9. Tokyo: Fuji Shuppan, 1991.

Nojima Teiichirō. "Bōryoku kokkai to sangiin." *Seiji keizai* 9, no. 7 (July 1956): 24–26.

Nomura Jōji. "Zen rōdōsha wa kekkishite Kenkokukai o tatakitsubuse!" *Rōdōsha* 13 (February 1928): 41–48.

Norman, E. Herbert. "The Genyōsha: A Study in the Origins of Japanese Imperialism." *Pacific Affairs* 17, no. 3 (September 1944): 261–84.

Ō Kiryō. "Tairiku rōnin no sakigake oyobi Nisshin sensō e no yakudō." *Kanazawa hōgaku* 36, no. 1–2 (March 1994): 55–77.

Obinata Sumio. *Nihon kindai kokka no seiritsu to keisatsu.* Tokyo: Azekura Shobō, 1992.

Ochiai Hiroki. *Meiji kokka to shizoku.* Tokyo: Yoshikawa Kōbunkan, 2001.

Ogata Tsurukichi. *Honpō kyōkaku no kenkyū.* Tokyo: Hakuhōsha, 1933.

Ōguchi Yūjirō. "Mura no hanzai to Kantō torishimari shutsu yaku." In *Kinsei no mura to machi,* ed. Kawamura Masaru-sensei Kanreki Kinenkai. Tokyo: Yoshikawa Kōbunkan, 1988.

Oguri Kazuo (governor of Fukuoka Prefecture) to the home minister et al. "Manshū Seigidan seihaishiki kyokō no ken." *Gaimushō kiroku.* September 12, 1932.

Oguri Kazuo (governor of Fukuoka Prefecture) to the home minister, foreign minister et al. "Manshū Kokusuikai kanji no gendō ni kansuru ken." *Gaimushō kiroku.* April 5, 1933.

Okazaki Masuhide. "Asanuma jiken to uyoku." *Zenei* 176 (December 1960): 184–92.

Ōmiya-gō Keisatsusho. "Dai-gokai jinmon chōsho: Tashiro Eisuke." November 19, 1884. In *Chichibu jiken shiryō,* ed. Saitama Shinbunsha. Vol. 1. Tokyo: Saitama Shinbunsha Shuppanbu, 1971.

———. "Dai-ikkai jinmon chōsho: Tashiro Eisuke." November 15, 1884. In *Chichibu jiken shiryō,* ed. Saitama Shinbunsha. Vol. 1. Tokyo: Saitama Shinbunsha Shuppanbu, 1971.

———. "Dai-nikai jinmon chōsho: Tashiro Eisuke." November 16, 1884. In *Chichibu jiken shiryō,* ed. Saitama Shinbunsha. Vol. 1. Tokyo: Saitama Shinbunsha Shuppanbu, 1971.

Ōmiya-gō Keisatsu Tōbu. "Taiho tsūchi: Tashiro Eisuke." November 15, 1884. In *Chichibu jiken shiryō shūsei,* ed. Inoue Kōji, Irokawa Daikichi, and Yamada Shōji. Vol. 1. Tokyo: Nigensha, 1984.

Ōno Banboku. *Ōno Banboku kaisōroku.* Tokyo: Kōbundō, 1962.
Ōno Banboku-sensei Tsuisōroku Kankōkai Henshū Iinkai. *Ōno Banboku: Shōden to tsuisōki.* Tokyo: Ōno Banboku-sensei Tsuisōroku Kankōkai, 1970.
Ōno Tatsuzō and Takagi Takashi. "Asanuma ansatsu jiken to uyoku bōryokudan: Sengo uyoku bōryokudan no jittai, seijiteki yakuwari, haikei." *Rōdō hōritsu junpō* 395 (October 1960): 19–24.
Ōsaka-fu chiji (governor of Osaka) to the home minister et al. "Shin Manshūkoku ni okeru Seigidan no kōdō, sono hoka ni kansuru ken." *Gaimushō kiroku.* September 15, 1932.
Ōsaka-fu Keisatsushi Henshū Iinkai. *Ōsaka-fu keisatsushi.* Vol. 2. Osaka: Ōsaka-fu Keisatsu Honbu, 1972.
Ōsaka mainichi shinbun.
Ōsaka nichinichi shinbun.
Ōuchi Hyōe and Sakisaka Itsurō. "Miike no tatakai o mitsumete." *Sekai* 174 (June 1960): 11–27.
Ōya Masao. *Ōya Masao jijoden.* Ed. Irokawa Daikichi. Tokyo: Daiwa Shobō, 1979.
Ozaki Yukio. *The Autobiography of Ozaki Yukio: The Struggle for Constitutional Government in Japan.* Trans. Hara Fujiko. Princeton: Princeton University Press, 2001.
———. *Gakudō jiden.* In *Ozaki Yukio Gakudō zenshū,* ed. Ozaki Gakudō Zenshū Hensan Iinkai. Vol. 11. Tokyo: Kōronsha, 1955.
Packard, George R. *Protest in Tokyo: The Security Treaty Crisis of 1960.* Princeton: Princeton University Press, 1966.
Paxton, Robert O. *The Anatomy of Fascism.* New York: Alfred A. Knopf, 2004.
Petersen, Michael. "The Intelligence That Wasn't: CIA Name Files, the U.S. Army, and Intelligence Gathering in Occupied Japan." In *Researching Japanese War Crime Records: Introductory Essays.* Washington: National Archives and Records Administration, Nazi War Crimes and Japanese Imperial Government Records Interagency Working Group, 2006.
Pittau, Joseph. *Political Thought in Early Meiji Japan, 1868–1889.* Cambridge, Mass.: Harvard University Press, 1967.
Quigley, Harold S. "The New Japanese Electoral Law." *American Political Science Review* 20, no. 2 (May 1926): 392–95.
Rapoport, David C., and Leonard Weinberg. "Elections and Violence." In *The Democratic Experience and Political Violence,* ed. David C. Rapoport and Leonard Weinberg. London: Frank Cass, 2001.
Ravina, Mark. *The Last Samurai: The Life and Battles of Saigō Takamori.* Hoboken: John Wiley & Sons, 2004.
Reynolds, Douglas R. "Training Young China Hands: Tōa Dōbun Shoin and Its Precursors, 1886–1945." In *The Japanese Informal Empire in China, 1895–1937,* ed. Peter Duus, Ramon H. Myers, and Mark R. Peattie. Princeton: Princeton University Press, 1989.
Reynolds, John F. "A Symbiotic Relationship: Vote Fraud and Electoral Reform in the Gilded Age." *Social Science History* 17, no. 2 (summer 1993): 227–51.
Riall, L. J. "Liberal Policy and the Control of Public Order in Western Sicily 1860–1862." *Historical Journal* 35, no. 2 (June 1992): 345–68.
Richie, Donald, and Ian Buruma. *The Japanese Tattoo.* New York: Weatherhill, 1980.
Rōdō Nōmintō, Tōkyō-fu, Kyōbashi Shibu. "Noda rokusen no kyōdai shokun!!" In *Kyōchōkai shiryō.* Reel 63. January 16, 1928.
Rōdō Undōshi Kenkyūkai and Rōdōsha Kyōiku Kyōkai, eds. *Nihon rōdō undō no rekishi: Senzen hen.* Tokyo: San'ichi Shobō, 1960.
Rogers, John M. "Divine Destruction: The Shinpūren Rebellion of 1876." In *New Directions in the Study of Meiji Japan,* ed. Helen Hardacre with Adam L. Kern. New York: Brill, 1997.

Rōnōtō. "Yōmosu sōgi ōen bōatsu hantai, datō Hamaguchi naikaku no enzetsukai ni tsuite." October 3, 1930. At the Ōhara Institute for Social Research. Yōmosu sōgi file 1.

Ross, Daniel. *Violent Democracy.* Cambridge: Cambridge University Press, 2004.

Rōyama Masamichi, ed. *Nihon no seiji.* Tokyo: Mainichi Shinbunsha, 1955.

Rush, Michael, ed. *Parliament and Pressure Politics.* Oxford: Clarendon Press, 1990.

Ruxton, Ian C., ed. *The Diaries and Letters of Sir Ernest Mason Satow (1843–1929), A Scholar-Diplomat in East Asia.* Lewiston: Edwin Mellen Press, 1998.

Saga-kenshi Hensan Iinkai, ed. *Saga-kenshi: Kindai hen.* Ge-kan. Saga: Saga-ken Shiryō Kankōkai, 1967.

Saitō Hideo. "Keihin kōgyō chitai no keisei to chiiki shakai: Iwayuru 'Tsurumi sōjō jiken' o megutte." *Yokohama Shiritsu Daigaku ronsō: Jinbun kagaku keiretsu* 40, no. 1 (March 1989): 1–121.

Sakai Eizō. *Buenryo ni mōshiageru.* Tokyo: Ryūbunkan, 1927.

Sakisaka Itsurō. "Asanuma-san no shi to kojinteki terorizumu." *Shakaishugi* 110 (November 1960): 2–7.

Samuels, Richard J. *Machiavelli's Children: Leaders and Their Legacies in Italy and Japan.* Ithaca: Cornell University Press, 2003.

Sanyō shinpō.

Satō Kōtarō. *Santama no sōshi.* Tokyo: Musashi Shobō, 1973.

Satō Makoto. *Tsurumi sōjō jiken hyakka.* Yokohama: Nisanmaru Kurabu, 1999.

Scalapino, Robert A. *Democracy and the Party Movement in Prewar Japan.* Berkeley: University of California Press, 1953.

SCAP Government Section. *Political Reorientation of Japan: September 1945 to September 1948.* Vol. 1. Washington: U.S. Government Printing Office, 1949.

SCAP Investigation Division. Interrogation of Kodama Yoshio. In "Records Pertaining to Rules and Procedures Governing the Conduct of Japanese War Crimes Trials, Atrocities Committed Against Chinese Laborers, and Background Investigation of Major War Criminals." June 14, 1948. Reel 15.

SCAP Investigation Division. Interrogation of Yoshida Hikotarō. In "Records Pertaining to Rules and Procedures Governing the Conduct of Japanese War Crimes Trials, Atrocities Committed Against Chinese Laborers, and Background Investigation of Major War Criminals." June 4, 1948. Reel 15.

Schaller, Michael. *Altered States: The United States and Japan since the Occupation.* Oxford: Oxford University Press, 1997.

Schlesinger, Jacob M. *Shadow Shoguns: The Rise and Fall of Japan's Postwar Political Machine.* Stanford: Stanford University Press, 1999.

Security Group, Control and Analysis Branch, C/S Section. October 24, 1956. U.S. National Archives. CIA Name File. Box 67. Folder: Kodama Yoshio. Vol. 2.

Seiji keizai tsūshin.

"Seiji tero to shūdan kōdō." *Sekai* 187 (July 1961): 190–92.

"Seiyūkai no bōkō jiken." March 30, 1926. In *Kensei o kiki ni michibiku Seiyūkai no bōkō jiken.* Tokyo: Jiyū Bundansha, 1927.

Sekito Kakuzō, ed. *Tōsui minkenshi.* 1903. Reprint, Tokyo: Meiji Bunken, 1966.

Servadio, Gaia. *Mafioso: A History of the Mafia from Its Origins to the Present Day.* New York: Stein and Day, 1976.

Seymour, Charles. *Electoral Reform in England and Wales: The Development and Operation of the Parliamentary Franchise, 1832–1885.* 1915. Reprint, Newton Abbot: David & Charles, 1970.

Shakaikyoku Rōdōbu, ed. *Tōyō Mosurin Kabushikigaisha rōdō sōgi jōkyō.* Shakaikyoku Rōdōbu, 1930.

[*Shakai minshū shinbun*]. In *Kyōchōkai shiryō.* Reel 63. October 23, 1927.

Shihōshō Chōsaka. *Shihō kenkyū* 8 (1928).

Shimada Ken'ichirō. *Ukikusa no hana.* Hamura: Hamura-shi Kyōiku Iinkai, 1993.

Shimazu Akira. "Honchō senkyo kanshōshi." *Jinbutsu ōrai* (March 1955): 48–52.

Shimizu Ryōzō. *Sōshi undō: Shakai no hana.* Tokyo: Kankōdō, 1887.

Shimizu Yoshiji. *Gunma jiyū minken undō no kenkyū: Jōmō Jiyūtō to gekka jiken.* Takasaki-shi: Asaosha, 1984.

Shimonoseki-shi Shishi Henshū Iinkai, ed. *Shimonoseki-shishi.* Vol. 3. Shimonoseki: Shimonoseki Shiyakusho, 1958.

Shimonoseki Shōkō Kaigisho. *Shimonoseki shōkō kaigisho sōritsu hyakunenshi.* Shimonoseki: Shimonoseki Shōkō Kaigisho, 1981.

Shimono shinbun.

Shimozawa Kan. *Kunisada Chūji.* Tokyo: Kaizōsha, 1933.

Shinobu Seizaburō. *Anpo tōsōshi: Sanjūgonichikan seikyoku shiron.* Tokyo: Sekai Shoin, 1969.

———. *Taishō demokurashīshi.* Vol. 2. Tokyo: Kawade Shobō, 1952.

Shōji Kichinosuke. *Kome sōdō no kenkyū.* Tokyo: Miraisha, 1957.

"Shuyō uyoku dantai ichiranhyō." October 1960. In *"Asanuma jiken" kankei shiryōshū.* 1960.

Sissons, D. C. S. "The Dispute over Japan's Police Law." *Pacific Affairs* 32, no. 1 (March 1959): 34–45.

Smith, Henry DeWitt II. *Japan's First Student Radicals.* Cambridge, Mass.: Harvard University Press, 1972.

Smith, Thomas C. "Japan's Aristocratic Revolution." In *Native Sources of Japanese Industrialization.* Berkeley: University of California Press, 1988.

Sorel, Georges. *Reflections on Violence.* Ed. Jeremy Jennings. Cambridge: Cambridge University Press, 1999.

Stark, David Harold. "The Yakuza: Japanese Crime Incorporated." Ph.D. diss., University of Michigan, 1981.

Suda Tsutomu. *"Akutō" no jūkyū seiki: Minshū undō no henshitsu to "kindai ikōki".* Tokyo: Aoki Shoten, 2002.

———. "Bōryoku wa dō katararete kita ka." In *Bōryoku no chihei o koete: Rekishigaku kara no chōsen,* ed. Suda Tsutomu, Cho Kyondaru, and Nakajima Hisato. Tokyo: Aoki Shoten, 2004.

Suda Tsutomu, Cho Kyondaru, and Nakajima Hisato, eds. *Bōryoku no chihei o koete: Rekishigaku kara no chōsen.* Tokyo: Aoki Shoten, 2004.

Sugimori Kōjirō. "Bōryoku no ronrisei." *Chūō kōron* 49, no. 6 (June 1934): 37–44.

———. "Bōryoku to bunka." *Chūō kōron* 36, no. 13 (December 1921): 97–99.

"Suiheisha tai Kokusuikai sōjō jiken." In *Tanemura-shi keisatsu sankō shiryō.* N.d. At the National Archives of Japan.

Suzuki Kōichi, ed. *Nyūsu de ou Meiji Nihon hakkutsu: Kenpō happu, Ōtsu jiken, sōshi to kettō no jidai.* Tokyo: Kawade Shobō Shinsha, 1994.

Suzuki Takeshi. *Hoshi Tōru: Hanbatsu seiji o yurugashita otoko.* Tokyo: Chūō Kōronsha, 1988.

Suzuki Yasuzō. "Bōryoku: Toku ni minshushugi ni okeru bōryoku ni tsuite." *Riron* 10–11 (November 1949): 24–59.

———, ed. *Nihon no kokka kōzō.* Tokyo: Keisō Shobō, 1957.

Suzuki Yūko. *Jokō to rōdō sōgi: 1930-nen Yōmosu sōgi.* Vol. 1 of *Nihon josei rōdō undō shiron.* Tokyo: Renga Shōbō Shinsha, 1989.

Szymkowiak, Kenneth. *Sōkaiya: Extortion, Protection, and the Japanese Corporation.* Armonk, N.Y.: M. E. Sharpe, 2002.

Tabata Izuho. "Bōryoku to seitō." *Jinbutsu ōrai* 1, no. 7 (July 1952): 22–26.

Takagi Takashi. "Ugokidashita uyoku bōryokudan no haikei." *Zenei* 169 (June 1960): 23–32.

Takagi Takeo. "Ōno Banboku to iu otoko." *Seikai ōrai* 18, no. 12 (December 1952): 30–32.

Takahashi Hikohiro. "Ingaidan no keisei: Takeuchi Takeshi-shi no kikigaki o chūshin ni." *Shakai rōdō kenkyū* 30, no. 3–4 (March 1984): 91–118.

Takahashi Satoshi. *Bakuto no Bakumatsu ishin.* Tokyo: Chikuma Shobō, 2004.

———. *Kunisada Chūji.* Tokyo: Iwanami Shoten, 2000.

Takahashi Tetsuo. *Fuun: Fukushima no minken sōshi.* Tokyo: Rekishi Shunjū Shuppan, 2002.

Takahashi Tetsurō. *Richigi naredo, ninkyōsha: Chichibu Konmintō sōri Tashiro Eisuke.* Tokyo: Gendai Kikakushitsu, 1998.

Takahashi Yūsei. *Meiji keisatsushi kenkyū.* Vol. 3. Tokyo: Reibunsha, 1963.

Takano Minoru. "Asanuma ansatsu o meguru seikyoku." *Rōdō keizai junpō* 14, no. 453 (October 1960): 3–7.

Takasaki Keisatsusho. "Dai-nikai jinmon chōsho: Kokashiwa Tsunejirō." November 15, 1884. In *Chichibu jiken shiryō shūsei,* ed. Inoue Kōji, Irokawa Daikichi, and Yamada Shōji. Vol. 3. Tokyo: Nigensha, 1984.

Takeuchi Yoshio. *Seitō seiji no kaitakusha: Hoshi Tōru.* Tokyo: Fuyō Shobō, 1984.

Tamai Masao. *Katana to seisho.* Tokyo: Rekishi Toshosha, 1978.

Tamaki Kazuhiro. *Keidanren to Hanamura Nihachirō no jidai.* Tokyo: Shakai Shisōsha, 1997.

Tamura Eitarō. "Jōshū asobinin fūzoku mondō." In *Ryūmin.* Vol. 4 of *Kindai minshū no kiroku,* ed. Hayashi Hideo. Tokyo: Shinjinbutsu Jūraisha, 1971. Originally published as Tamura Eitarō. "Jōshū asobinin fūzoku mondō." *Nihon no fūzoku* 2, no. 4 (April 1939): 8–29.

———. *Yakuza no seikatsu.* Tokyo: Yūzankaku, 1964.

Tanaka Sen'ya. "Chichibu bōdō zatsuroku." In *Tanaka Sen'ya nikki,* ed. Ōmura Susumu, Kobayashi Takeo, and Koike Shin'ichi. 1884. Reprint, Urawa: Saitama Shinbunsha Shuppankyoku, 1977.

Tanaka Sōgorō. *Nihon fashizumu no genryū: Kita Ikki no shisō to shōgai.* Tokyo: Hakuyōsha,1949.

———. *Nihon kanryō seijishi.* Tokyo: Kawade Shobō, 1954.

———, ed. *Shiryō: Taishō shakai undōshi.* Ge-kan. Tokyo: San'ichi Shobō, 1970.

Terasaki Osamu. *Meiji Jiyūtō no kenkyū.* Ge-kan. Tokyo: Keiō Tsūshin, 1987.

Tezuka Yutaka. *Jiyū minken saiban no kenkyū.* Chū-kan. Tokyo: Keiō Tsūshin, 1982.

Tilly, Charles. *The Politics of Collective Violence.* Cambridge: Cambridge University Press, 2003.

Tobe Ryōichi. *Gyakusetsu no guntai.* Tokyo: Chūō Kōronsha, 1998.

Tokushima mainichi shinbun.

Tōkyō asahi shinbun.

Tōkyō Izumibashi Keisatsusho. "Dai-ikkai jinmon chōsho: Katō Orihei." November 7, 1884. In *Chichibu jiken shiryō shūsei,* ed. Inoue Kōji, Irokawa Daikichi, and Yamada Shōji. Vol. 2. Tokyo: Nigensha, 1984.

Tōkyō nichinichi shinbun.

Tomita Nobuo. "Sengo uyoku no kinō to yakuwari: Kodama Yoshio to shin Nikkyō o chūshin ni." *Ekonomisuto* 43, no. 28 (June 1965): 65–69.

Tōyama Motokazu. *Chikuzen Gen'yōsha.* Fukuoka: Ashi Shobō, 1977.

Tōyama Shigeki et al., eds. "Santama no sōshi." In *Meiji no ninaite.* Jō-kan. Vol. 11 of *Jinbutsu Nihon no rekishi.* Tokyo: Yomiuri Shinbunsha, 1965.

Tōyō Mosu daisōgi: Reposhū. September 27, 1930; October 11 and 21, 1930. At the Ōhara Institute for Social Research. Yōmosu sōgi file 1.

Tōyō Mosurin Sōgidan Honbu. Untitled handbill. October 7, 1930. At the Ōhara Institute for Social Research. Yōmosu sōgi file 1.

Tsuchikura Sōmei. "Ingaidan tōsōki." *Bungei shunjū* (December 1935): 210–17.

Tsuda Sōkichi. "Bōryoku seiji e no ikari: Dō naru bai mo bōryoku o haijo seyo." *Bungei shunjū* 32, no. 12 (August 1954): 72–79.

Tsuzuki Shichirō. *Tōyama Mitsuru: Sono dodekai ningenzō.* Tokyo: Shinjinbutsu Ōraisha, 1974.

Uchida, Jun. "'Brokers of Empire': Japanese Settler Colonialism in Korea, 1910–1937." Ph.D. diss., Harvard University, 2005.

Uchimura Gijō. *Meiji shakai: Sōshi no undō.* Osaka: Shōundō, 1888.

Uda Tomoi and Waga Saburō, eds. *Jiyūtōshi.* Tokyo: Gosharō, 1910.

Ueki Emori. *Ueki Emori nikki.* Kōchi: Kōchi Shinbunsha, 1955.

Umeda Matajirō. *Sōshi no honbun.* Tokyo: Hakubundō, 1889.

Umezu Kanbei. *Kyōkaku oyobi kyōkakudō ni tsuite.* Nihon Gaikō Kyōkai, 1941.

Ungar, Mark, Sally Avery Bermanzohn, and Kenton Worcester. "Introduction: Violence and Politics." In *Violence and Politics: Globalization's Paradox,* ed. Kenton Worcester, Sally Avery Bermanzohn, and Mark Ungar. New York: Routledge, 2002.

United States Department of State. *Occupation of Japan: Policy and Progress.* Washington: U.S. Government Printing Office, 1946.

———. "Internal Affairs of Japan, 1955–1959." June 12, 1956. U.S. National Archives. Decimal File 794.00/6 1256. C-009. Reel 26.

United States Department of State, Bureau of Far Eastern Affairs. "The Political Climate in Japan." [1958]. U.S. National Archives. Subject Files Relating to Japan, 1954–1959. Lot File 61D68. C-0099. Reel 3.

Urawa Jūzai Saibansho. "Saiban iiwatashisho: Tashiro Eisuke." February 19, 1885. In *Chichibu jiken shiryō shūsei,* ed. Inoue Kōji, Irokawa Daikichi, and Yamada Shōji. Vol. 1. Tokyo: Nigensha, 1984.

Usuda Zan'un, ed. *Tōyama Mitsuru-ō no majime.* Tokyo: Heibonsha, 1932.

Valli, Roberta Suzzi. "The Myth of *Squadrismo* in the Fascist Regime." *Journal of Contemporary History* 35, no. 2 (April 2000): 131–50.

Varese, Federico. *The Russian Mafia: Private Protection in a New Market Economy.* Oxford: Oxford University Press, 2001.

———. "The Secret History of Japanese Cinema: The Yakuza Movies." *Global Crime* 7, no. 1 (February 2006): 105–24.

Vlastos, Stephen, ed. *Mirror of Modernity: Invented Traditions of Modern Japan.* Berkeley: University of California Press, 1998.

———. "Opposition Movements in Early Meiji, 1868–1885." In *The Cambridge History of Japan.* Vol. 5. Ed. Marius B. Jansen. Cambridge: Cambridge University Press, 1989.

———. *Peasant Protests and Uprisings in Tokugawa Japan.* Berkeley: University of California Press, 1986.

Wagatsuma Sakae, ed. *Kyū hōreishū.* Tokyo: Yūhikaku, 1968.

Wagatsuma Sakae et al., eds. *Nihon seiji saiban shiroku: Meiji, go.* Tokyo: Dai-ichi Hōki, 1969.

Wakaki hi no Chūji: Midagahara no satsujin. Directed by Kinugasa Teinōsuke. 1925.

Wakamatsu Kyōdō Kenkyūkai, ed. *Wakamatsu hyakunen nenpyō.* Wakamatsu: Kita Kyūshū Shiritsu Wakamatsu Toshokan, 1969.

Wakatsuki Reijirō (prime minister). "Taishō jūgonen hōritsu dai rokujū gō o Chōsen oyobi Taiwan ni shikō suru no ken." July 19, 1926. At the National Archives of Japan.

Walthall, Anne. *Social Protest and Popular Culture in Eighteenth-Century Japan.* Tucson: University of Arizona Press, 1986.

Wardlaw, Grant. *Political Terrorism: Theory, Tactics, and Counter-measures.* Cambridge: Cambridge University Press, 1989.

"Wareware no shinjō." *Kokusui* 4 (October 15, 1920).

Waswo, Ann. "The Transformation of Rural Society, 1900–1950." In *The Cambridge History of Japan*. Vol. 6. Ed. Peter Duus. Cambridge: Cambridge University Press, 1989.

Watanabe Etsuji. "Rensai intabyū, senzen no rōdō sōgi III: Kōno Takashi-san ni kiku Takanosan e no rōjō senjutsu o amidashita Ōsaka Shiden sōgi." *Gekkan sōhyō* 241 (January 1978): 108–14.

Watanabe Ikujirō. "Seikai, oyabun, kobun." *Seikai ōrai* 12, no. 5 (May 1941): 5–6.

Watanabe Ryūsaku. *Tairiku rōnin: Meiji romanchishizumu no eikō to zasetsu.* Tokyo: Banchō Shobō, 1967.

Watanabe Tetsuzō. "Taishō shishi ron." *Chūō kōron* 38, no. 12 (November 1923): 83–85.

Watanabe Yōzō. "Hō to bōryoku." *Shisō* 438 (October 1960): 108–20.

Weber, Max. *Economy and Society: An Outline of Interpretive Sociology.* Vol. 1. Trans. Ephraim Fischoff et al. Ed. Guenther Roth and Claus Wittich. Berkeley: University of California Press, 1978.

Westney, D. Eleanor. *Imitation and Innovation: The Transfer of Western Organizational Patterns to Meiji Japan.* Cambridge, Mass.: Harvard University Press, 1987.

White, James W. *Ikki: Social Conflict and Political Protest in Early Modern Japan.* Ithaca: Cornell University Press, 1995.

Wigen, Kären. *The Making of a Japanese Periphery, 1750–1920.* Berkeley: University of California Press, 1995.

Wray, William D. *Mitsubishi and the N.Y.K., 1870–1914: Business Strategy in the Japanese Shipping Industry.* Cambridge, Mass.: Council on East Asian Studies, Harvard University, 1984.

Yahata seitetsujo rōdō undōshi. Fukuoka: Yahata Seitetsu Kabushikigaisha, Yahata Seitetsujo, 1953.

Yamagata shinpō.

Yamaguchi Rinzō. "Bōto shita sangiin: Dai nijūyon tsūjō kokkai no makugire." *Seiji keizai* 9, no. 7 (July 1956): 22–23.

Yamamoto Shirō, ed. *Rikken Seiyūkaishi.* Vol. 3. 1924. Reprint, Tokyo: Nihon Tosho Sentā, 1990.

Yamamura Masako. "Suiheisha, Kokusuikai tōsō jiken no kentō: Saiban kiroku o chūshin to shite." *Buraku kaihō kenkyū* 27 (September 1981): 136–76.

Yamato kokusui shinbun. At the Freedom and People's Rights Movement Archive.

Yanaga Chitoshi. *Big Business in Japanese Politics.* New Haven: Yale University Press, 1968.

Yasumaru Yoshio, ed. *"Kangoku" no tanjō.* No. 22 of *Asahi hyakka rekishi o yominaosu.* Tokyo: Asahi Shinbunsha, 1995.

———. "Konmintō no ishiki katei." *Shisō* 726 (December 1984): 78–97.

Yasumaru Yoshio and Fukaya Katsumi. *Minshū undō.* Tokyo: Iwanami Shoten, 1989.

Yomiuri shinbun.

Yomiuri Shinbun Seibu Honsha. *Nichiro sensō kara Shōwa e.* Vol. 2 of *Fukuoka hyakunen.* Osaka: Naniwasha, 1967.

Yomiuri Shinbunsha, Asahi Shinbunsha, and Mainichi Shinbunsha. "Sumiyaka ni seikyoku o shūshū seyo." June 11, 1954. In *Sekai* 104 (August 1954): 78.

Yōmosu Sōgidan, Zenkoku Rōdō Kumiai Dōmei, Nihon Bōshoku Rōdō Kumiai. "Yōmosu sōgi ni tsuite chōmin shokun ni gekisu." October 2, 1930. At the Ōhara Institute for Social Research. Yōmosu sōgi file 1.

Yōmosu sōgi tōsō nyūsu 6. October 11, 1930. At the Ōhara Institute for Social Research. Yōmosu sōgi file 2.

Yoshida Isokichi-ō Denki Kankōkai, ed. *Yoshida Isokichi-ō den.* Tokyo: Yoshida Isokichi-ō Denki Kankōkai, 1941.

Yoshino Sakuzō. "'Kokka' no hoka 'chikara' no shiyō o yurusazu." *Chūō kōron* 38, no. 1 (January 1923): 201–4.

Yoshizawa Seijirō (Japanese consul general in Xinjing) to the foreign minister and envoy in Manchukuo. "Jishō Manshūkoku Seigidan sōmu Ikeda Hideo no dōsei ni kansuru ken." *Shina rōnin kankei zakken, Gaimushō kiroku.* April 25, 1934.

Yūbin hōchi shinbun.

Yukitomo Rifu. *Kunisada Chūji.* 1919.

Za gurafikku.

Zenkoku taishū shinbun.

Zhao Jun. "'Betsudōtai' to 'shishi' no hazama: Kindai rai tairiku rōnin kenkyū no kaiko to tenbō." *Chiba shōdai kiyo* 36, no. 4 (March 1999): 105–24.

Index

Fukushima Incident (1882), 44, 201n12
Funada Ataru, 105
Futsū Senkyo Hō (Universal Manhood
 Suffrage Law; 1925), 90–91

Gambetta, Diego, 187n23, 192n59
gambling, 20; criminalization of,
 190n38; popularity of, 22, 27; sites for,
 190n38; yakuza and, 192n58. *See also*
 antigambling regulations; *bakuto*
"gangster," vs. yakuza, 5–6
Gendōkan, 18
General Council of Trade Unions of Japan.
 See Nihon Rōdō Kumiai Sō Hyōgikai
Gentile, Emilio, 129
Gen'yōsha (Dark Ocean Society): electoral
 interference by, 65; expansionist foreign
 policy promoted by, 55–57, 65, 126;
 ideology of, 202–3n43; Kokusuikai and,
 126; Kōyōsha renamed, 53; *kyōkaku*
 and, 113; military alliances of, 55–57,
 128, 204n53; nationalist organizations
 and, 126; police leniency with, 68;
 post-WWII purging of, 150; *shishi*
 identity appropriated by, 19–20; *sōshi*
 membership of, 53; *tairiku rōnin* of,
 53–57, 204n53; violence of, 54–56
Germany, Nazi: democratic state portrayed
 as inept in, 134; fascist ideology in, 115,
 125, 215n29; fascist organizations in, 110,
 115, 116, 125, 129–30; fascist violence in,
 220n98. *See also* Nationalsozialistische
 Deutsche Arbeiterpartei; SA
Gifu, 69
Gijintō (Party of Righteous Men), 165–66
Go-Daigo (emperor), 16
Gokokudan (National Protection Corps),
 159, 160, 226nn70–71
Gokoku Seinentai (National Protection
 Youth Corps), 159, 160, 167–68
Gokurō (comic actor), 104
Gordon, Andrew, 4, 187n28, 209n41
Gotō Kōjirō, 120
Gotō Shinpei, 125–26, 219n83
Gotō Shōjiro, 48, 49, 67
Government by Assassination (Byas), 108
Gramsci, Antonio, 200n133
Great Britain: election fraud punished
 in, 72; Namamugi Incident and, 15,
 16; political violence in, 10, 70, 106–7;
 violent crime in, 189n15
Great Depression, 110, 134
Greater Japan Justice Organization. *See*
 Seigidan

Greater Japan National Essence Association.
 See Kokusuikai (Greater Japan National
 Essence Association (pre-WWII group))
Greater Japan Patriotic Party. *See* Dai Nihon
 Aikokutō
Greater Japan Production Party (Dai Nihon
 Seisantō), 164
Grote, George, 70
Gualtiero, Filippo, 38
Guangdong (China) Police Bureau, 128
guerillas, 37, 57
Gunma Incident (1884), 27–30
Gunma Prefecture, 33, 69, 158
gunpudan, 78–79
Gyōtoku (Chiba Pref.), 121

Hagerty, James, 167
Hagi Rebellion (1876), 18
Hagiwara Susumu, 195nn89–90
hakama sōshi, 50, 50 fig. 2.1
Hakoda Rokusuke, 19, 53, 202n43
Hamaguchi Osachi, 134, 135, 160, 218n70
Hanamura Nihachirō, 152
Hana to ryū (Hino), 93, 211n76
hanbatsu (ruling clique), 60; democratic
 reforms of, 42, 179, 202n43; election
 interference by, 64–70, 72, 88; *ingaidan*
 as check on influence of, 83–84, 107,
 175; *mintō* compromise with, 79–80,
 83; *mintō* electoral victories as threat
 to, 60, 68; *mintō* opposition to, 79,
 206n105; party cabinets as subversion
 of, 79; popular activism against, 1, 26,
 53, 179; *ritō* backed by, 57; ruffianism
 encouraged by, 58–59; *sōshi* as threat
 to, 202n23; *sōshi* electoral violence and,
 59–60; *sōshi* ties to, 177; state violence
 initiated by, 42; *tairiku rōnin* and, 53–54,
 57; transcendental cabinets controlled
 by, 61, 89
Hara Kei, 98; assassination of, 135; cabinet
 of, 75, 89, 126, 129, 207n2; as first party
 prime minister, 75; Murano and, 210n58;
 Seiyūkai *ingaidan* and, 129
harmony, supposed Japanese cultural
 affinity with, 3, 4
Haruta no Gonbei, 102
Hasegawa Noboru, 25, 31, 192n60
Hata District (Kōchi Pref.), 65, 66
Hatoyama Ichirō, 154–55, 157, 225n48
Hayashi Jōji, 105
Hayashikane Fishery, 99
Hayashi Yūzō, 62
Hayes, Rutherford B., 71

Lightning Source UK Ltd.
Milton Keynes UK
UKHW020814030920
369273UK00008B/933/J